QUEER DIASPORAS

Edited by
Michèle Aina Barale,
Jonathan Goldberg,
Michael Moon, and
Eve Kosofsky Sedgwick

EDITED BY

Cindy Patton

AND

Benigno Sánchez-Eppler

QUEER DIASPORAS

DUKE UNIVERSITY PRESS

DURHAM AND LONDON

2000

© 2000 Duke University Press
"Of Queens and Castanets:
Hispanidad, Orientalism, and Sexual
Difference" © 1999 Sylvia Molloy
All rights reserved
Printed in the United States of
America on acid-free paper ∞
Typeset in Minion by Tseng
Information Systems, Inc.
Library of Congress Cataloging-in-
Publication Data appear on the last
printed page of this book.

CONTENTS

ACKNOWLEDGMENTS

This project has taken us nearly six years to complete. Thus, we first thank all of the authors for their patience and cheerfulness. We hope that the final product was worth the wait. We would also like to thank several people who were instrumental in getting the manuscript processed: Calinda Lee, Lynell Thomas, Mary Stuart Petty, and Karen Sánchez-Eppler.

BENIGNO SÁNCHEZ-EPPLER *and* CINDY PATTON

Introduction: With a Passport Out of Eden

At first glance, most naturalizations of heterosexuality, with their attendant un/naturalization of homosexuality, seem to presume an Eden where the essential man and the essential woman were all alone. After a period of time that is generally regarded as short, the human pair sinned. The Fall that ensued from those little bites of apple caused every misery and sin, and left us with the tragicomic, propagating heterosexual couple as the ostensible center of desire.

A closer examination of the foundational Western narrative suggests another reading: that male God and male Adam had a homosocial thing going until female Eve was created and the compulsory, bi-gender couple was formed. That most intimate pairing of male creature and male creator was disrupted by the introduction of a supernumerary Other body, as much as by the sexual union of these differently sexed humans. The introduction of a gender difference that catalyzed human desire — carnal knowledge — installed an ungodly ambivalence on day six of the world's creation. God may have created Eve, but this gift to his buddy had an unintended consequence: the transferral of divine human homophilia into a human-centered heterosexuality left God in the lurch. On this reading, compulsory heterosexual coupling is less a stroke of creativity (or a coup d'état that installs human agency as sexual desire), than it is a morphological intrusion that genders and then jeopardizes the exclusivity of the (same-sex) bond between God and Man.

This tangled story of buddy-love lost has all the sophistication of a John Hughes teen flick where geeky guy meets his best friend's girl. The fundamental, homoerotic, masculine love finds its conduit in a feminine form, and bears all the ambivalence of motive and incoherence of narrative described by Eve Sedgwick in *Between Men*. But the narrators of Genesis, with their emphasis on expulsion, on territorial detail, suggest more; although this is not in any obvious way a "gay" displacement, the simultaneity of the expulsion from Eden and the installation of heterosexuality suggest that Western sexual and diasporal discourses are fundamentally, if anxiously, related. The central project of this volume is to ask how a variety of bodies involved in the gyrations of postmodernity have borne the weight of this connection, and to what effect.

Resident Identities and Transient Names

The debate over identity's essence or lack of essence has been well-rehearsed both in gender and in lesbian and gay studies. Similarly, the significance of translocation is taken as a presupposition among scholars of ethnic diaspora and within postcolonial studies. The conjunction of these exciting, against-the-grain bodies of work produces a line of inquiry as intent on deconstructing universalizing ideas about sexuality as it is insistent on catching the lilt of each local articulation of desire. Now, identity is viewed as strategic, rather than essential, contingent on, reproduced, decaying, co-opted, in relation to material and discursive factors that, especially in the context of sexualities, are always a complex lamination of local onto global onto local. Sexuality is intimately and immediately felt, but publicly and internationally described and mediated. Sexuality is not only not essence, not timeless, it is also not fixed in place; sexuality is on the move. With this new clarity, we are in a better position to analyze the valences of body-in-place and consider the transformations in sexualities that move between — indeed, may have been produced at — the interstices of specific geopolitical territories. Translocation itself, movement itself, now enter the picture as theoretically significant factors in the discussion of sexuality. We revisit Eden with new sentiments: not expulsion and shame, but questions about how ideas of origin and return are inflected by ideas of sexual propriety—Derrida reminds us of the combination of proper and property—and sexual alterity. Attending to the mobility of sexuality across the globe and body, as a materiality and a discourse (but we'd rather not have separated what must now insistently be joined with a copula), brings new insights into the individual and collective paths of queer escape and reconstitution.

Against the current poles of discussion about sexuality, which primarily rely on theories of individual development or of social group formation, examination of specific modes and effects of incremental displacement—bodily, discursive, and/or territorial—*on* or *as* sexuality, reveals an extraordinarily complex picture of the frictional relation between geopolitics and embodied desires. Ego psychology, and even psychoanalysis, and the various forms of social construction theory, ultimately assume that what the body and psyche have are either essentially transportable or are entirely socially located, fixed and found in situ. But the essays here show that "being" gay, homosexual, lesbian, joto, internacional, tortillera, like that, battyman, bakla, katoi, butch, et cetera, entails answering or not answering to those terms and the desires they purport to index, in a given place, for a given duration. When a practitioner of "homosexual acts," or a body that carries any of many queering marks moves between officially designated spaces—nation, region, metropole, neighborhood, or even culture, gender, religion, disease—intricate realignments of identity, politics, and desire take place.

However, the effects of movement, of tectonic shifts between differently produced and carried identities and differentially textured places are far from uniform. Resulting alterations have repercussions for the mobile body, in the former "home," as the vacuum left, but also as intermittent mail, bodily homecomings, and even as monumentalized remembrances of the queer and the dead that continue after transmogrification. Describing such queer peregrinations and considering their incomplete local and global effects requires that we move beyond the now-banal recognition that sexual identities are constructed, are formed as denials, as loss. The focus of attention is no longer on whether identity is ever not constructed, on whether official territorial marks can ever be coextensive with bodies' identifications, but instead on how to make sense of the always poignant and sometimes hilarious labors of re-invention and renegotiation in new places, or in reimagined old ones.

The essays here take a somewhat different position than those recent defenders of identity who argue that apparently essentialist claims are moments of strategic assertion, not psychically delusional or politically disabling counternarratives, as alleged by some antiessentialist critics. In fact, delineating the particular claims to "self" adopted or enacted in migration/dispersion/trans-/dislocation does highlight the utility of identities, but we do not want to replace the focal position of "secured identity" with an equally static idea of place, as if identity were malleable and strategic on top of mute, fixed place. An identity is not merely a succession of strategic moves but a highly mobile cluster of claims to self that appear and transmogrify in and of place. But place is also a mobile imaginary, a form of desire. Place is acted upon by identifiers—by identifications—that occur, as events, on/in "it." The question of the political effectiveness of strategic essentialism is, therefore, misdirected. What must be interrogated, and harnessed?: the intersection, the collision, the slippage between body-places; the partial transformation of those places; the face installed by dissimulation in place.

Treating place in this way requires some theoretical pliability not found in most work that objectifies (rather than morphs) materiality. It is useful to consider the distinction de Certeau (1988) draws between strategy and tactic:

> ... strategies pin their hopes on the resistance that the *establishment of a place* offers to the erosion of time. (38)
>
> A tactic insinuates itself into the other's place, fragmentarily, without taking it over in its entirety, without being able to keep it at a distance. (xix)
>
> Tactics [depend] on a clever utilization of time, of the opportunities it presents and also of the play that it introduces into the foundations of power. (38–39)

If we follow de Certeau, we see that strategy implies a considered and double investment—in a particular identity and in the space that has proven useful to identity's durable materialization. The appearance of a fleeting vision of self-sameness suggests a tactical use of identity, a kind of projection over a terrain that it does not hope to make its own. This difference is important: for de Certeau, strategy is possible only when an actor can make herself appear to be a single thing against a stable grid of possibilities rendered more or less stable. This entails not only the strategic assertion of identity, but a strategic and collaborative assertion of proper, or fixed, place. This double gesture of

identity necessarily occurs with the assistance of an equally strategically prof-
fered opposition: tenant/landlord; worker/boss; gay/homophobe. Together,
these pairs, though possessing different degrees of "power over," establish a
domain of struggle, which necessarily reinvests in the very terms that need
upending. Rather than transforming the fundamental conditions of the oppressed, such "propriety" results in what Nietzsche called a slave morality, a
sort of resentful attack on the Master, but within the moral universe the Master prescribes. Influenced by Foucault (and of course, Foucault's Nietzsche!),
de Certeau suggests we consider the ways in which tactics erode the terms
of the "proper" space. But we need better tools to appreciate the nuanced
materiality and corrosive power of this kind of dissident performance. We
still see these as largely cultural politics, thought to be at some distance from
the realpolitik of class struggle. But this division of politics into strategic-
material and tactical-discursive forms is founded on claims that the important politics concern the antagonism between identifiable pairs that face off
in a mute place of maximal engagement. As Manalansan and Buckley suggest
here, there is a surplus of materiality over the proper, of sexuality over sexual
identity. For Manalansan, the transmigratory divas of the New York-Filipino
religious ritual are always neither here nor there, but somehow, through play,
in both. Buckley's Japanese kitchens are the scene, but not the location, of
gender production: the beautiful display of trash from the kitchen as well as
the consumption of handsome lunches produced there suggest that gender
circulates through, and reconfigures, rather than settles in, the kitchen.

A cursory reading of these perversions could easily collapse into nostalgia for the ordinary, for politics free of compromise. But Manalansan and
Buckley point away from the trivialization of the quotidian. By examining
the precise forms and the specific assaults made by practices of everyday life
they recompose the most fundamental places—of resistance. By shifting the
focus away from the question of the subaltern's visibility within, or identity in
the face of, official and public spaces, de Certeau doesn't valorize their everyday defacements of the "system" they inhabit. By taking tactics seriously, he
sought to redefine, or at least expand the scope of, the politics of the oppressed: "Thus a North African living in Paris or Roubaix (France) insinuates
into the system imposed on him by the construction of low-income housing
development or of the French language the ways of 'dwelling' (in a house or a
language) peculiar to his native Kabylia. He superimposes them and, by that

combination, creates for himself a space in which he can find ways of using the constraining order of the place or of the language. Without leaving the place where he has no choice but to live and which lays down its law for him, he establishes within it a degree of plurality and creativity" (Certeau 1988, 30).

De Certeau suggests that we reconsider the role and efficacy of tactics, which in their very enactment, deny the utility of permanently taking place as identity. Instead, tactics emphasize timing that destabilizes the static place produced as a collaborative strategy between representatives of the oppressed (in democracies) and those oppressors who benefit from their specific enumeration. De Certeau admits, following the military theories of von Clausewitz, from whom these insights are drawn, that tactics are the mode of the weaker party. But, extending Foucault's analysis of mechanisms of power, de Certeau sees tactics not as contesting power over something, but as regulating the timing of power as flow. Combining de Certeau's tactic/strategy distinction with an emphasis on movement—at a minimum, perpetual "in/out"—helps pinpoint how queer migrants take or find a location and transform it from a marginal trench in a census tract to a gay municipality, from a beleaguered gay ghetto to a vital gay neighborhood, or, into an event of solidarity within the fluidity of translocation. We no longer need a developmental model to chart the complex, transiently formed and reformed sexual definitions that would not otherwise etch a formal record. They no longer sit in time, as prepolitical, or presexual, but they exist as timing, desire sparked as real bodies rub the proper the wrong way.

Rerouting de Certeau's reading of Foucault back through Foucault's sentinel area of interest, sexuality, we can now easily see why it is absurd to insist that preconscious homosexual desire will, given the right conditions, inevitably develop into gay identity and gay community. When observed against the muted backdrop of the proper, it is difficult to draw a clear line between a "strategic" identity and one that is taken up and dropped, played out, but not believed in. However, if we reintroduce malleable, tropic space, if we try to look at sexualities on the move, we can begin to glimpse the political and life-saving differences between strategic and tactical propositions of self. Sánchez-Eppler's account of Reinaldo Arenas's autobiographical refashionings, Cobham's account of Claude McKay's homosocial relations with his white patron and mentor, Walter Jekyll, and Manalansan's diasporic divas, demonstrate the extent to which strategic identities become imbricated in their collaboratively hypostatized place and then have trouble remaining the same, that is, have trouble being an identity during migration.

Rhonda Cobham studies the textual mechanisms through which Claude McKay transforms his homosocial relations to provide the basis for the fictional male-female mentoring engagement in his only novel set in Jamaica. Although McKay always defended his island patron from the charges of cultural and sexual exploitation, Cobham's reading of *Banana Bottom* suggests that the Jekyll-McKay liaison may share in the queer affectivity extensively described in relation to the patronage system of the Harlem Renaissance. Writing as a diasporic subject, with the Harlem Renaissance orientalized as the site of queerness, McKay reinvents his native land as the fictional space of unspoken heterosexual tensions. Their genesis, however, seems to be in his own relations with Jekyll: McKay's identification as "straight," and his desire to work out in fiction the complex erotics of patronage across colonial borders, cannot rest in an autobiographically "true" identificatory space. His sentiments migrate, but the personification of them must mesh with the "proper" of the place to which he goes.

Benigno Sánchez-Eppler tracks another author's successive displacement from rural Cuba to Havana to gay underground and prison, and finally to U.S. outness — via the infamous Mariel boatlift — where he opens up an anti-Castro gay front inside the Reagan coalition. Due to the impossibly disjunct political articulations, Arenas cannot find a singular voice with sufficient range to narrate his life as a "whole." Rather than force a chronology, with its pretense of unifying perspective, on the multiplying folds of his life, Arenas opts to continually rewrite his autobiography from his different emplacements. Sánchez-Eppler turns to Arenas's final autobiography to examine how practices of self-invention and self-authentication simultaneously give life and produce death. Sealed with a suicide note, Arenas closes his "complete works" as a monument that stands awaiting the moment in Cuban history when the queer dead can be repatriated. Arenas remains imperturbably queer and Cuban, even as his own displacement forces him to reread each through the other. His impending death preempts his hope for a Cuba–U.S. border permeable enough for him to pass as an openly gay man. Arenas is not trapped between two irreconcilable identities — gay and Cuban — which he must either adopt or drop. Nor is he isolated against alternating backdrops — Cuban homophobia or American anticommunism. Rather, we see him continuously and tactically reworking the dramatis personae and physical spaces of his world: United States against Cuba; latinized versus anglicized homoeroticisms; disease solutions—Cuban quarantine and American exile; formats of self-narration—autobiography and suicide note.

In these two essays, we see that moving about takes away the certainty of strategy's gain in place. These subjects go into circulation, into time, into a flux where survival of self-definition, and inducement to mutual aid, accrue through timing. As we have each, no doubt, discovered for ourselves, whatever we may be (or have been), even when we hardly move at all, there are places and times in which we simply are not, or are not quite, primarily that. Asserting strategy, emplacing essence, in the form of some recent identities' rhetoric, we are bound to look at displacements as experiences in which we move from place to place secure in, or fated to, the presumed imperturbability of what we are; we cling to that "core" that should remain reliably itself—our selves—despite the whirls of the world around us. If we move attached to such certainty but experience relocation troubles, we frantically search the apparently parallel structures of our race, ethnicity, nationality, gender, and sexuality to resecure what suddenly feel like mismatched and struggling essences. But if frantic realignment is all we do, we risk ignoring the full effect of moving on the elemental swirl of identity. We risk underutilizing the power of tactical maneuvers, of queer timings, to alter territory, to leave burn marks as our trace, to get a face from defacement.

Martin Manalansan's record of the recent transformation of a religious pageant by a group of gay Filipinos in New York offers a more hopeful story of going with the flow. The Santacruzan, an evolving Filipino syncretization of the Catholicism brought by colonizing Spain, is a flexible religious form with an open stock of characters that actually invite queer restaging. Manalansan makes a good case for the term "transmigration" over exile or immigration—indicating the crossing and recrossing of spaces, a movement and re-symbolization process that stitches the real to the imaginary, de-emphasizing extrusion and loss. Preparing for and enacting Santacruzan creates a public space for a double mischief: gay can be Filipino in ways prevented by homophobia back home, and Filipino can be gay despite the racism in mainstream gay spaces. An informant glories in the authenticity of his costume made by a dressmaker in the Philippines specifically for his queenly appearance in the Santacruzan performed in New York. Another describes the joy experienced in this connective performance as "playing with the world." His informants' uncertainty about whether to be "gay" in any mainstream movement sense helps us better estimate the loss of tactical mobility that comes with the gains of strategically defensible places. That hegemonic homophobia has been forced to yield control of gay-claimed territories provides new targets in times of backlash; sustaining sexuality in and through the labile and migratory Santacruzan allows for subterfuge and, perhaps, survival.

We want to be cautious, however, about any inherited overemphasis on place as ethnically or politically defined "area," as in the multidisciplinary academic endeavors already existing under various rubrics of "areas studies." Accepting this form of naturalized place may occlude the transnational/transregional differences in modes for constituting sexualities and make it difficult to track, for example, use of ideas about movement in policy debates. Patton reveals the ways that two different medical frames for mapping AIDS produces quite different "epidemics" among rather differently conceived bodies, with ominously divergent solutions. "Americans" may arrive at an "isolated" place only to confront the very American discourse that now, grafted into local discourses, has beaten them there. Using examples from the AIDS epidemic, she suggests that the narrative mobility of science itself constructs people and places. The intersecting movement of two scientific thought-styles—epidemiology and tropical medicine—imagine and reimagine global health through terms like "Asia," "Southeast Asia," "Asia and the Pacific Rim," and "Pattern Three," each of which imagines different causes of and solutions to pathology. There is not, finally, a nameable place underneath, which could serve as the referent for a new, more sensitive cartographic nomenclature. Literal place-names reestablish European geography as the arbiter of whose health matters, while scientific concepts like "risk group" cede real people to sciences that are as interested in the history of the germ as they are in the health of our bodies.

Robertson finds a tactical use of gender peering out from an earlier discursive collusion between East and West. She examines early-twentieth-century Japanese newspaper accounts of lesbian double suicide alongside Japanese anthropological and medical applications of Western terms. For those Japanese men of science, the imported terms *homosexual* and *heterosexual* provided an explanation for a historical phenomenon and made sense of something new: the "modern girl." Here, the academic discourses about "others" (in the West) travel to a place where they are used to name local practices. But there is both a surplus and a lack to the external label. In this mismatch, there is a negotiation of meaning in which the local practice may stretch to meet the label, and the label gets infused with the particularity of the local practice. In Robertson's example, the expected homophobic alignment between suicide and queerness is occluded by the very Japaneseness of suicide, even when enacted by a Westernized, mannish, female cross-dresser and her femme "review girl."

These two essays raise questions about Benedict Anderson's enduringly influential *Imagined Communities* (1983). Anderson shows how the dispersion of ideas of place and nation-ness are fundamentally related to what he calls print capitalism. But he by no means intends to suggest that "it's all discourse." Indeed, one of the major concerns of recent activist research has been to deconstruct regional and national rubrics, while trying to pay attention to the "real people" who might also inhabit the discursively fantasized space. A focus on the drift of discourse, especially in the form of national and international media, policy, and the academic writings that border on them, rather than on the bodies who may convey, relay, delay, or contest such flows, extends and problematizes Anderson's formulation. By examining the results of dispersion of "internal" discourses of sexuality across national borders, Patton and Robertson augment Anderson by suggesting that trans-, extra-, and intratextually global policy, research, and media destabilize the nation by demanding that they accommodate *meta* sexualities: scientific propositions about "human sexuality" that are discursively mobile because they are not specific to a national place. But how does this recognition of alterity install queerness? Why does it place so much stress on the "identity" variables that must be organized by the nation?

Bodies do not rest stably in a place until a discourse overtakes, agitates, and names their desires. Rather, bodies pack and carry tropes and logics from their homelands; they seek out an "imagined community" of intrinsic queerness, which they read about between the lines of international media and policy. But traveling the paths of international policy, global media, academic disciplines, and nationalist ideologies, discourses themselves may travel even faster. Dislocated bodies may refind their native discourses when they get "there," as if they have "discovered" that the Other elsewhere is "naturally" the same. By the same token, the intrusive discourses may construct as unnatural a queerness that had always lain in want of a recategorizing discourse. Science, as Patton's and Robertson's essays show, provides an especially powerful metafoundation for insisting on sexualities' sameness, naturalness, and distribution across politically naturalized borders.

Daniel Boyarin adds further evidence to this claim that migrating academic thinking—as well as the imaginary spaces they inhabit and produce—prove especially critical in establishing the terms of twentieth-century identity. But here, there is a twist: whereas the Japanese researchers and the AIDS policy makers sought a univocal discourse—"science"—to ground their actions, the politics of alterity actually adopts a bivocal grounding discourse. Boyarin's reading Freud's *Moses and Monotheism* opens new vistas for understanding Jewish identity as it traumatically lost its place in early-twentieth-century Europe and was re-placed in a Promised Land. He notes that Herzl's formulation of modern Zionism emerges in the same historical moment as Freudian psychoanalysis, and that both are in tension with the contemporaneous emergence of the terms *homosexuality* and *heterosexuality*. The concepts of muscular Christianity and evolutionary superiority suffused the European national norms with whiteness and heterosexuality, leaving the Jew and the homosexual, if not explicitly equated, then uncomfortably aligned as degenerate. Boyarin recognizes that Freud's struggle with his own homoerotic feelings may have colored Freud's Moses white and chiseled him virile. With one foot firmly planted in the new consolidated space of queer/Jewish knowledge, Freud moves between his dreams and memories of city-names that figure the shifting relation between queer and Jew. Boyarin argues that the alterity of these two ways of experiencing the rise of the modern nation in the twentieth century disavowed and combined with each other to produce modern, Western Otherness as a symptom of the incompleteness of the Enlightenment project. Possessed of intimate access to—knowledge of—the text of these two Others, Freud, as the bitextual cartographer, travels across disjunct spaces that sign the incapacity of modern identity to be stable.

All of these essays perform necessary therapeutics for any thinking that occludes bodies and places. But how to move on? How to read with the feinting and yawing of our desiring subjects as they move? Sylvia Molloy provides another framework for reconsidering the constitution of subaltern identities. Molloy rejects the idea that only Eurocentrism orientalizes. She introduces the concept of *errancia*—wandering—to discuss the payoff of a "fiction of displacement." She examines the work of Chilean author, D'Halmar (a concoted name, which Molloy argues is the author's first production of errancy), whose exotic reading, much more than any actual travels, provide the impetus to orientalize the metropole of Spain. Unlike the classic formulation, in which the Eurocentric subject orientalizes the colony, D'Halmar recuperates the Orient in Spain, and especially in Al-Andulusian Seville, rather than in hyper-Western Chile, as the site of diversity and hybridity that includes the queerness that had to remain unspoken in his Chilean home.

Marcie Frank offers another way to apprehend the successive transmutations of the actual bodily sites of desire. She focuses on two ultrapostmodern 'zines from the sexually perverse and linguistically queered Quebec, where *plotte* means both "cunt" and "map." Frank shifts the analytic lens from movement of bodies over territories, to focus on the transmigration of nationalism and sexuality across different bodily organs. Not yet independent of Anglo-Canada, but nevertheless not a colony to be reabsorbed into France, Quebec is never a proper or even singular place. The explicitly postnationalist, postgender 'zines represent a penis that is not a probe but a hollow tube or purse whose head unscrews to carry its owner's belongings. The anus, the least gender-determinate and most queer organ, becomes the center of pleasure and desire, the place where the body will not know whether it is going or coming.

The distance between queer Santacruzan performances or postmodern Montreal and the pre-Stonewall mass-marketed lesbian pulp fiction of Ann Bannon suggests that much about urban gay life changed between the 1950s and 1990s. However, suggests Michèle Aina Barale, public gay-identity fighting for civil rights and queer politicos who work hard at refusing and upending any mark of sexual identity may have only changed the surface of queer geography without altering the magnetic pull of perverse orienteering. The vicissitudes of finding queer space expressed in Bannon's Beebo Brinker novels, "low art" of a very modern sort, reveal a concern with toponymy that seems way ahead of its time. Bannon and her pulp publisher Fawcett needed to invent an audience of loyal lesbian and gay readers from a market of unreliable and promiscuous seekers of unconventional sleaze. Their solution is a book cover that signs its own sign-twisting ability to be, improbably enough, the ground zero of a brave new world. Barale recognizes that the cover is itself a queer space, and doubly so: a fictional rendering of "real" city traffic signs that already mark an "actual" queer space. This reading-over-reading underscores the obvious presence of queer location that remains, nevertheless, unreadable for those who refuse to see. But once seen by willing eyes, the read-over signs etch themselves on the landscape that corresponds not only to an official map, but materializes queerness here-and-now.

Sandra Buckley employs a similar strategy of reading-over-reading novels, films, official waste disposal mandates, and advertising campaigns for "new" traditional, extended family dwellings to describe the cultural flows of post-modernity, food production, and waste. These are the frenetic elements of cultural flow. In a hyperpostmodern Japan, the kitchen—the space through which these cultural flows must inevitably pass—becomes a space of both national identity and queerness. Rice and its manipulation into beautiful food-objects is the pinnacle of national femininity. The consumption of these tasty treats at school, displays both the mother's Japaneseness and the son's masculinity as the object of excruciating care. Even the proper assemblage and disposal of garbage simultaneously display the civic duty and feminine accomplishment of the person who disposes of it. In *Kitchen,* the displacement of the mother through death—becoming waste—invites the father to take the woman's place as a transsexual—waste becoming. If he knows how to make rice, the homosexual man, can re-place himself in the kitchen, performing the femininity that would, elsewhere, reflect his own masculinity.

On the heels of these disintegrations, and in order to reinforce the implosive force of mobile sexuality as a speaking subject, we close the volume with an interview, edited into a monologue. Amir Sumaka'i Fink and Jacob Press found Walid at the territorial hub of the West's preeminent site of fatefully linked diasporas. Walid is a young Arab growing up gay in the State of Israel, passing as a Jew in his homosexual encounters, openly gay on the Internet, terrified and excited by his perpetual liaison with "occupying" soldiers, exacting his own secret reversal of the phrase hurled at him almost daily on his university campus—"Fuck the Arabs!"

Anxiously poised in the space between an "as told to" autobiography and an ethnography, Walid's symptomatic engagement with several kinds of promised lands is simultaneously academically disreputable and proof positive that the fragmented bodies treated so lovingly through several disciplines have their own new micrologics of expression. No doubt, Fink and Press's questions and edits have shaped the Walid we know here, and, in choosing this among the many such testimonials Fink and Press have collected, our own assault on identity is only less obvious for having occluded what was left out. But the present disciplinary anxiety about the modes and extent of our re- and misrepresentation of what we purport to know is only a sign that the neopositivist urges that most of us would disavow still haunt our postfoundationalist lives. And so, our final curtain is queerly diasporic, the return of the true fabulation—Santacruzan performer R.E., Walid, Arenas, D'Halmar—to a central place in our considerations. The young queer Arab whose parcel of self-deceptions, longings, and hard-learned lessons were, in 1964, novelized/translated by Paul Bowles as *A Life Full of Holes,* is back in full force. Walid jabs at our sentimentality with his matter-of-fact account of a life comprised of fragments, lacking conjunctions, receding at each turn from the impossible connections that we might try to make. Here at the envelope's edge, we toy with retrieving the body underneath the discourse, with snatching him from the infelicities of his settlement in a restrictive place. Walid eludes us: he is, or stands for, the bodies we can treat only as ballistic units in an imploding-reterritorializing quagmire.

In Walid we see in relief a "practice of everyday life" (Certeau 1988), a flatly narrated story of homosexuality in motion, that uses tactical queerness to cruise places occupied by normative straightness, anti-Arab violence, and homophobia. Walid's candid discussion of his life reveals the ambiguous structure of the closet as a space that simultaneously contains homosexuality and spreads it. Listening carefully to his fabulations made possible in and through the dispersion of discourse and the disintegration of boundaries saves "the Author," but not as someone who can give us our truth. *Fabuleurs* are, at last, not our mirrors, but the framers of tactics, who confront us with the limits of our own possibly freeing, possibly nihilistic clutching to the identity we each know best.

CINDY PATTON

Migratory Vices

For both visitors and the host country, tourism becomes a risky business when tours and sex are sold together. In some cases, as in Thailand, a country's tourist industry is heavily based on the packaged sex holiday, catering for those who go abroad to do things they would probably never do at home. (Panos Institute 1989, 88)

Q: How can the sexual spread of AIDS be prevented while travelling?
Do not have sex with prostitutes (male or female) or casual acquaintances, even in countries claiming that they have no AIDS problem. . . . If having sex with someone who may be infected, men should use a condom each time from start to finish, and women should make sure that their partner uses one. . . . Finally, remember that the fewer sexual partners you have, the lower your risk of exposure to the virus that causes AIDS. (Global Programme on AIDS 1989, 35)

Sex Tourism

By the late 1980s, policymakers and pamphleteers were offering reeling, if disjunct, advice on global travel and AIDS. Some argued that the globaliza- tion of sexualities was inherently dangerous, while others merely tried to con- vince travelers to apply abroad the practices they had been admonished to take up at home. But in both extremes, the confusion about who might infect whom—and *where*—displaced the issue of who is responsible for ensuring that sex is conducted safely. In the first example, the attempt to hold more powerful nations responsible for the transformation of overt colonial relations into covert tourist relations leads the avowedly critical Panos Institute to almost beg for some extranational body to step in and protect developing countries afflicted with sex trade. In this reasoning, HIV rests primarily in the bodies of only barely disguised Western perverts who "do things they would probably never do at home." In the second example, the traveling body needs to protect itself from the unquestioned duplicity of countries that, like the apocryphal lover, lie about their infection. Here, HIV is banished to an "elsewhere" in relation to an unstated but unmistakable United States or Europe "here." These two international policy organizations' incapacity to decide where AIDS *is*—in bodies or in places—and how it *moves*—vectorially from the First World or in the bodies returning to it—is not coincidental. The neat story that we tell about AIDS does indeed have two versions that construct and reconstruct bodies, places, and movement, though not necessarily in regular or predictable ways.

These two styles of narration are not so much opposite as composite; authors are required to work around the logical inconsistencies that telling a story in two ways at the same time creates. Even the official story, which might easily have restricted itself to one model or the other, opened out onto two kinds of story: "Researchers believe that the virus was present in isolated population groups years before the epidemic began. Then the situation changed: people moved more often and traveled more; they settled in big cities; and lifestyles changed, including patterns of sexual behavior. It became easier for HIV to spread, through sexual intercourse and contaminated blood. As the virus spread, the isolated disease already existing became a new epidemic" (Global Programme on AIDS 1989, 6).

Although this account has become commonplace, closer examination reveals complex, at some points incompatible ideas about disease and its translocation. Crisscrossing temporal and geographic tropes, the account vacillates between the *story* of a virus and a *description* of bodies who might disperse it. "The virus" is first described as lodged in a timeless and immobile *place:* grounded in an "isolated population" until modernity stepped in to inscribe time and a mania for travel. "Now," people move and change, carrying with them the dangerous combination of their new sexual practices and their contaminated blood. Miraculously (inevitably?), an epidemic ensued. Modernity catapulted the virus, which had once lived peacefully among unnamed "population groups," into an epidemic of history-changing proportions.

The sketchy official account is the narrative template that allows for a plethora of more detailed versions of the story. The central role of the migratory body is anonymous, allowing reporters and international health policy analysts to enliven their accounts with "real people," to "put a face on AIDS." Almost *anyone* can be implicated as the problematic mobile body. A Canadian airline steward or jet-set gay tourist, an African truck driver or the rural woman who now sells him sex on the edges of the city, a male migrant laborer who crosses national borders to feed his family, the soldier who defends his country or invades another: these are the vivid characters alleged to have brought HIV from Africa, from Haiti, from anywhere but "here."

The official story completely naturalizes the idea that it was denationalized bodies and not corporate and state blood-banking practices that first dispersed HIV. Once available as a narrative model, the travelogue version allows officials to refuse the knowledge they have of their own small corner of the pandemic. The Taiwanese account to which I'll turn in a moment is typical in failing to register what it knows about its own epidemic. A "transiting" American homosexual is forever cited as the first known case of AIDS (in 1984), even though officials soon realized that infected blood products had beaten him there. True, in 1984, the then-new antibody test was not widely in use, and no one could have known that hemophiliacs throughout the island had already been infected with HIV. But once the "Pattern Three" nations (the official Global Program on AIDS designator for the countries of Asia and a few other places where "AIDS arrived late") registered their epidemics in the bodies who most nearly matched the image of the epidemic they believed they would avoid—homosexual foreigners with AIDS who appeared in their midst—they were loathe to change their story of AIDS's local genesis. Written as an analog to the existing stories about travelers (such as Patient Zero or Angolan mercenaries) dispersing HIV, the official travelogue account converts the emergency debarkation of the American in Taiwan into the possible origin of the local epidemic. Even though he was so sick he had to be rushed from the airport to the hospital, and, thus, was unlikely to have conducted a frenzied crusade to infect locals, the transiting American is the synecdoche for healthier, and therefore invisible, homosexuals who might have been physically capable of sex on the road. Imagining this penetration of the national border was far easier than recognizing that blood banks had wittingly and intentionally foisted poorly screened blood on poor countries who continued reluctantly to accept potentially infected products.

But despite the common tactic of placing infection in the body of an Other, the U.S. media and international policy discourse each define the geography of disease differently and rely on structurally different concepts of how disease moves. At the risk of oversimplifying the historical development of two disjunct models of disease, I want to suggest that these differences have a great deal in common with the thought-styles of epidemiology and of tropical medicine, which, in turn, propose different solutions to pathology: epidemiology dreams of eradicating disease, while tropical medicine holds out hope for immunity. As formal disciplines, epidemiology and tropical medicine are much more historically related than my use of their thought-styles suggests: they fold into each other, bicker over their explanatory power, recruit bodies and disease to legitimate their complex temporalizing and spatializing systems. What interests me here is not the degree to which policy or media enterprises officially use these subdisciplines by citing or alluding to apparently established truths about disease, but the ways in which writers unconsciously imitate the tropes of either or both in hopes of adding a veneer of scientific authority to their narrative productions.[1] These imitative technologies enable and promote different, conflicting, and multiple institutional strategies of control, which, finally, have enormous if unpredictable consequences for those subject to their regimes.

The science of AIDS, as it trickles through policy and media, substantially informs popular interpretations of the epidemic, shaping the experience of those directly affected and forming the moral logic that makes policing, in fact or through resource distribution, not only popularly acceptable, but apparently humane. The narratives of scientific progress that emphasize the coherence and additive nature of scientific research, help rationalize discriminatory policy and continued pursuit of unwarrantedly narrow research questions. What I am suggesting, then, is that the two different ways of telling the story of AIDS, or better yet, the multiple permutations of them, can be used to justify different policies and plans for managing the epidemic. In relating specific documents to larger, abstract medical logics and suggesting that neither research paradigms nor the various levels of policy and representation are logically coherent, I hope to indicate the operation of power that is occluded by apparently scientific or objective stories of AIDS.

This essay is one of a series in which I have contemplated the incoherences among three registers of discourse about the HIV pandemic:

(1) the national U.S. discourse about its own epidemic, as observed in the U.S. media, a national discourse about AIDS that is the apotheosis of what Foucault (1973) described in his account of the rise of modernist knowledge. His "empirico-transcendental doublet" takes itself as both the object of inquiry and the subject of knowledge,[2] much as the Centers for Disease Control studies the public it both represents and protects (1995).

(2) the denationalized discourse about the pandemic as a global phenomenon, present in documents from the World Health Organization (WHO) and other transnational, nongovernment organizations (NGOs), which relies on a kinder, gentler form of knowledge. Territorially divested but anxious not to offend member states, the postcolonial positivist science the WHO practices through NGO projects extracts local knowledge and translates it into "scientific knowledge" on which can be based the "cooperative" policies and programs that retranslate people's knowledge back into their local vernacular as safe-sex advice or care programs — as if the intruders have been culturally sensitive.

(3) the imperialist Euro-American discourse about the AIDS epidemic in so-called developing countries, evident in the U.S. media and in the general outline of international research projects. Imperialist discourses acknowledge places outside the First World authorial center, but project them as a screen or laboratory for performing ideological or real (vaccine trials?) procedures that promise to solve the master countries' internal epidemic or to absolve their responsibility for the devastation they have wrought *outside* their borders. The United States displaces its global responsibility by blaming AIDS on Africans, meanwhile conducting vaccine trials in Africa that would be unethical at home, in hopes of developing a product that would find its first users in the United States (1990; 1992).

The two pieces of advice that began this essay represent variants within the second category. The WHO description of the epidemic that followed, though generated from within a transnational space, now stands as the ur-narrative to which all registers of discourse must attend, if they are to make sense.³ I want to elaborate the two, central, logical motifs that govern this elaborate interlacing of stories about AIDS.

Tropical Medicine and Epidemiology: Competing Colonialisms

Many of the concepts in Western tropical medicine and epidemiology developed in relation to nineteenth- and early-twentieth-century colonial expansion. Tropical medicine, obviously, from its very name, dealt with the problems Euro-Americans encountered in their local occupations, merging empirical science with the fantasy of the colony. As Bruno Latour (1988) has suggested, the displacement of the scientific laboratory from the academy to the field was crucial to the "discovery" of etiologic agents. Not only did displacement literally produce the isolated research conditions necessary for finally establishing germ theory, but it provided the colonial imaginary with a series of metonymically linked spaces: the colony of scientists in the client state colony studying the colony of germs on the surface of the agar plate. This cemented a homological turn of mind that could justify colonial power as an extension of the emerging modern will-to-control through positive science.

Tropical medicine wedded imperial notions of health and geography to the bourgeois notion of the domestic as a space within a space (the public). Colonial movement is bidirectional along a single axis of domesticity; movement into the constructed domestic space of the colony is always accompanied by nostalgia for "going home." Tropical medicine relies on a diasporal imagining of displacement and return that presumes that local diseases do not affect indigenous people in the same way that they affect the Euro-American occupier. A tropical disease is always proper to a place, to *there*, but only operates *as disease* when it afflicts people from *here*. Pathogens in a locale enter into the history of medicine only when consolidated as disease in the colonist's body. The colonist's ailing body is heroic, not the victim of his or her dislocation, but the most intimate site for domesticating the tropics. Tropical disease is contained by virtue of already being *there*, in the "tropics": even if he (*sic*) could not always get well, the colonist could always go home.

Critically, the very idea of tropical medicine rests on the ability to reliably separate an indigenous population perceived to be physically hearty but biologically inferior from a colonizing population believed to be biologically superior but nevertheless subject to tropical illnesses. Sustaining this medical paradox requires perpetually refilling the category, "exotic ailment." Tropical medicine grows out of and supports the idea that the First World body is the proper gauge of health: the Third World is the location of disease, even while its occupants are not the subjects of tropical medicine. Tropical medicine, then, *points* to an existing map and a hierarchy of bodies.

Epidemiology, on the other hand, is performative. By sharply demarking pathogen and body, epidemiology created the scientific means to declare that some, but not all, conjunctures of body/pathogen are "disease," even "epidemic." Less concerned than tropical medicine to detail the diseases that may befall the Euro-American body in a place, epidemiology visualizes the place of the body in the temporal sequence called "epidemic." The story's hero is no longer the body fighting disease, but epidemiology, the "disease detective," which alone has the power to visualize and disrupt the "natural history" of germs' vectorial movement.

An "epidemic" is more cases than expected, a deceptively simple definition that hides the messy truth that declaring an epidemic depends on cultural perceptions about who is likely to be sick and to what degree. In the tropics, every Euro-American might get sick: it is expected. Epidemiology reverses tropical medicine's concern with who may fall ill by removing disease from the natural environment and placing it in the body. Instead of viewing tropical inhabitants as more or less immune to the diseases that surround them, *indigene* are now themselves the location of disease — reservoirs, carriers. Epidemiology defines the boundaries of a disease by constituting a category of subject ("risk group"), an imagined community produced through vectors that epidemiology simulates as though they were discovered.[4] Bodies are at once subject to and perpetrators of pathology, both "sick" and reservoirs or carriers in the larger network of disease.

An "epidemic" is vectorial; migratory sites of pathology can at any time be linked. Each new locale becomes a new center capable of projecting its vectorial links with yet more periphery, which in turn become new centers. Links are multidirectional; it makes no sense to speak of diaspora or return, but of movement ever outward from the center.

If in theory anyone could be a vector, epidemiology's statistical procedures "discovered" that some bodies were more likely than others to carry (transport/harbor) disease. Bereft of a stable *place* of pathology, epidemiology must constantly construct and correlate populations and subpopulations in order to make epidemics visible, hence the interest in technologies of "surveillance" and of "sentinel studies."

These two schemes envision different maps of world health, which, in turn, have two effects in the current management of the HIV pandemic, one quite literal and the other representational. The administration of global health funding occurs largely through a model related to the tropical image of the world, while HIV and related disease surveillance literally employs epidemiology, produced and administered through an aberrant WHO branch called the Global Programme on AIDS (GPA). Thus, the GPA generates scientific data and proposes policy based in one concept of disease, while the WHO attempts to effect and fund AIDS policy and programs through another. Predictably enough, participant countries are often hostile to the programs designed by the GPA and some of the most powerful funding countries refuse to adopt GPA policy guidelines — for example, the United States has not taken up the call to decriminalize homosexuality and prostitution proposed by the very project it so heavily funds and promotes.

The second level of effect concerns popular representation of the epidemic: accounts of AIDS in newspapers, pamphlets, and books aimed at general readers vacillate between the accounts that the two different stories make possible. Thus, a wide and contradictory set of stereotyped ideas about the epidemic and those it affects can gain credibility through invoking either or both medical thought-styles. The tropes and logics characteristic of each thought-style secure, almost as a scientific citation, more wildly fictional accounts: any cultural stereotype or political idea that can be recirculated or challenged through this association with science has far greater power than a stereotype that stands on its own.

Mapping AIDS: From Regions to Patterns

A deeply spatial imagining of disease like that of tropical medicine echoes in the World Health Organization's division of the world into six administrative regions. This simultaneously naturalizes the units and cedes influence within them. Since funds come from developed countries and go to—with the most delicate of strings—countries that the West is interested in developing, the WHO is in a tricky position: it must take care neither to offend the donor countries, nor to make policies that are unpalatable to the client states. This role has become increasingly daunting as feelings about national identity have changed: transnational capital has made the identities of industrialized nations an impediment to their global economic survival (think of the North American Free Trade Agreement [NAFTA] or the European Economic Community), even while the increasing conflation of religious or ethnic and national identity in developing countries has given patriotism an apocalyptic meaning. National identities only seem to matter to those who have no other form of capital.

Established in the midst of Euro-American colonial forays, the WHO regions reflect the unconscious of a particular historical epoch and the moral vision of the world that the declining colonial powers hoped to effect. Perhaps not surprisingly, the entire Western hemisphere is a single unit — the Pan American Health Organization (PAHO) — with its head offices in Washington, D.C. The nineteenth- and twentieth-century hemispheric isolationism, which at once insured U.S. domination over the Latin American countries and prevented Europeans from commenting much on it, is reproduced in the kinds of policies and programs PAHO engaged in prior to the HIV pandemic: disease lay in the *south*.

Europe and the British Isles are a second unit, although there is usually little participation from the United Kingdom. In a sort of repression-castration, Britain (though home to colonial subjects) has withdrawn from the circumglobal empire it once created. Although U.K.-based nongovernment organizations have been active in Third World health projects, their enthusiastic volunteerism doesn't quite overcome the national responsibility Britain bears for many of its former colonies' deplorable economic state.

Britain also refuses to participate with its European neighbors, themselves reconfigured several times in the twentieth century. Europe has now banded together to produce a *collective* relation to the vast colonial territories of Africa, which several nations once differentially administered and which still have the names — or at least the borders — that intra-European competition produced as trophies. In the context of the AIDS epidemic, and corresponding in time to the move toward an economically united Europe, the European group has been the most effective region in the world at developing HIV-related antidiscrimination policy. Using the emerging European Community governing bodies, which partially map the space WHO defines as a health region, countries have brought pressure to bear on one another to promote more humanitarian care, to support local organizing, and to develop cooperative projects in the Third World, especially African countries. In the face of a disease that so poignantly defies nationality, European countries' invocation of human rights enable them to relinquish some control over national health policy, muting the political effects of national borders without challenging formal national sovereignty. Nevertheless, their *collective* relation to their former client states in Africa has reinscribed a more general Eurocentrism in the face of an Other more different than the differences among themselves.

Asia and the Pacific are divided into two regions: much of Asia and Australia and most of the Pacific Rim islands comprise the Western Pacific region, while Mongolia, the subcontinent, and some of the South East Asian islands comprise the South East Asia region.

With the spectacular exception of research on Thailand's vast sex trade, there was little WHO regional or national effort to deal with AIDS in the South East Asia region in the 1980s. The shift to addressing AIDS in the 1990s has occurred in the context of resurgent nationalism and religious fundamentalism. If the rubric of region afforded European countries a means to blur national distinctions in order to embrace the exigencies of a global pandemic, subsuming nation to region in Asia produced an oppositional stance in relation to the West. Asserting the resistive rhetoric of Asian values on the global stage capitalized on and reversed the orientalist compaction of the extra-Euro-American, non-African space under the figure "Asia." Asian values demanded that Westerners make good on their promises of cultural sensitivity, as if all, or any, of the effective global actors could be bound, by a logic of anti-imperialism, to "human rights," to reading the "values" of the Orient as, once again, inscrutable, illegible to Western values. Under this mantle of disidentificatory rhetoric at the highest level of cultural value, once disparate cultures could now unite, if only in the moment when they chafed against non-"Asian" (and non-African?) ideas, which underwrote open border and antidiscrimination policies, and the concept of individual autonomy implicit in safe-sex education and proposals to decriminalize homosexuality and prostitution.

To some extent, health officials from the nations of these two regions perceive AIDS and AIDS-prevention advice to be intrinsically connected to sexualities that have emerged as an effect of the colonial legacy.[5] Sex tourism, the proliferation of sexual discussion, and the representations that seem necessary to promoting safe sex are each seen as resting on Euro-American concepts of sexuality. While colonial management had enormous effects on local sexualities, postcolonial recuperation of idealized lost pasts often produces moralities closer to the maligned Victorianism that a "return to" Asian values ought to reject. Implicitly setting up an opposition between a rich, traditional sexuality and an Americanized or Europeanized one devoid of meaning, condoms — the global emblem of safe sex — are understood as a cultural imperialist tool.[6] An Indian campaign, which mobilized the then-current nationalist tendency to reconstruct a precolonial classicism as the true national culture, associated condoms with an alien culture in which sexual pluralism requires promiscuity. The lushly illustrated campaign proposed the kama sutra as safe sex: the practices that Westerners view as the ultimate form of sexual experimentation, become a new kind of monogamy, more exciting than the possibilities for partner change that condoms seem to afford: "many positions with one, better than one position with many" (Global Programme on AIDS 1993, 4).

The Western Pacific region deserves additional comment, since the next section of this essay will consider the failure to pursue HIV prevention there. The insidious Eurocentrism of the WHO map is nowhere clearer than in this region, which lumps together *developing* nations with Japan and the largely Anglo (though multicultural) Australia.[7] Past WHO programs in this region mimicked the Europe-Africa structure, confounding colonial relations and races: (white) Australia inherited responsibility for the British Empire — it had, in fact, once been a labor colony — but Japan, as racial Other to the West, was excused for its long-standing imperialist ambitions. Like the South East Asia region, neither individual countries nor WHO took much interest in the possibility that AIDS might finally arrive in the region's developing countries.

Japan and Australia, however, came to occupy strange roles in the epidemic: as a *nation,* Japan, by reputation perverse and hyperindustrialized, would appear to need exhaustive HIV education along the lines of its competitor, the United States. But since prevention education had, by the mid-1980s, boiled down to condom use, and since Japan's couples are already ranked first among nations as measured by condom use, it was difficult to imagine how to make the need for condoms seem like bad news.[8] As the universal signifier of safe sex, condoms arrived *too soon* to symbolize the negative side-effect of promiscuity and AIDS. But, as a result, the highly aesthetic Japanese condoms posed a serious challenge to the American product, even though the culture of male acceptance that insured high levels of condom use in Japan remained an embargoed cultural product in the United States. Australia, too, now lists its rough-and-tough Ansell condoms as its most popular export.

In the 1980s, Japan emerged as the economic and to some extent cultural competitor for the United States, while Australia withdrew from its Anglo heritage as its leaders attempted to identify with its regional neighbors. Ironically, Australia's model responsiveness to the epidemic—whose epidemiologic profile is virtually identical to that of the United States and Britain—only further widened the political gap between itself and the fetishized Asia, the constituent nations of which were not so enthusiastic to be the composite object of Australian national identification. Their mutual past as British colonies notwithstanding, Australia had difficulty writing itself into a postcolonial Asia, which, however grave the national differences, was, at the most abstract level of global identificatory discourse, fashioning for itself a history of *continuous* cultural solidarity. The form of unity imagined underneath "Asian values" was a *return,* precisely the opposite of the *Afhebung* of cultural difference implicit in the humanist multiculturalism of the Australian state, which, in turn, views itself as the zenith of liberal pluralism and social welfare. The ambivalent cultural and economic relationship between Australia and its regional siblings was encapsulated in a late-1980s campaign: apparently directed toward Anglo-Australian travelers, the ad featured a Qantas jet sporting a condom, and it was unclear whether such prophylaxis would contain the advanced epidemic in Australia, or prevent tourists from bringing more back from elsewhere.

The fifth and sixth regions are Africa (in fact, sub-Saharan Africa) and the Eastern Mediterranean, which includes some of North Africa. Here, geography belies religious history: a closer look reveals that the Eastern Mediterranean area encompasses the nations that are the strongholds of Islam.[9] These latter nations were insistent, until the early 1990s, that the austerity their religious commitments demanded served as a virtual barrier against HIV.

The idea of regions insists on a correspondence to features of natural geography, encompassed in ideas like hemispheres or continents. But while PAHO, Europe, and Africa—"the West"—are each comprised of roughly contiguous countries, South East Asia, the Eastern Mediterranean, and the Western Pacific each have marooned segments — a map of the South East Asia region looks more like territorial islands than island territories.

The human sociopolitical patterns that reinforce the apparent naturalness of "regions" lent an air of destiny to the colonial structure, which remains as a shadow in the names sublated in favor of its regional designations. The idea of regions has been slow to change, and WHO continues to be simultaneously a disinvested global administrator and a covert stabilizer of historico-political relations that seem natural only because "region" seems to harken back to a toponomy prior to colonial mappings. Like the veritable geology that produces this naturalized geography, changes in national territories have never forced the remapping of WHO regions. Rarely have countries been reassigned, nor have the regions been reconceptualized in order to address changes in the health status or needs of countries' citizenry. If similarities exist in the health and disease that occurs within a region, this is a result of collisions between a germ's ambitions to extend its locale and the accidents of geopolitics that place and displace bodies; health continues to be administered on a regional basis.

Enter the Global Programme on AIDS: *The Mann Era*

The strange cartography wrought by compromises in an economically variable political context did not serve the needs of the American public health officials who first joined the World Health Organization with the hope of globalizing America's hard-won lessons about AIDS. Under the direction of an epidemiologically oriented American (the late Jonathan Mann) with experience within the U.S. public health system, the highly autonomous Global Programme on AIDS adopted a different mapping of the world, one importantly, but not completely coherently, underwritten by epidemiologic understandings of the disease writ large.

Displacing the deeply inscribed geography of the regional system, the GPA proposed a *disease-specific* nomenclature, broadly dividing the world into spatially contiguous but, more importantly, temporally conceived "patterns," which were numbered, not coincidentally, in roughly the order in which epidemiologists first identified the global "emergence" of densities of cases circa 1984–85. The shift from a complicated system defined by geopolitical regions and nations to a flatter, simpler map related to incidence probability obscured the fact that each *pattern* was actually defined using different criteria. Though cast in the general temporal sequence secured by emphasizing epidemiologic reasoning, each pattern continues to tautologically reconstitute the criterion that originally defined it. Pattern One, commonly called "AIDS," refers not to the basic transmission category of intercourse, but to the gender-exclusive category, intercourse between men. Pattern Two, or what is now usually called "African AIDS," refers to places where intercourse between people of "opposite" genders appears to account for most cases of transmission. Pattern Three, "where AIDS arrived late," was defined through absence of cases, primarily, the initially blank space of Asia.

The linguistic shift from regions to patterns echoed the more subtle shift away from a conceptualization of the *place* of disease, from one which naturalized geography, to one that simulated statistical distribution. The regional and pattern schemes coexist: the larger *administrative* map, used to allocate resources, is related to colonial notions of geography, while the GPA's predictive map refers to spaces supposedly defined by transmission routes. This mismatch between surveillance and resource allocation proved devastating for the two Asian regions, now collapsed into the noble "Pattern Three." Worse yet, since both geography and the concepts that are part of the ideas about transmission are already gender coded, women would bear the brunt of the missed opportunity for prevention and for the medical malfeasance of ill-developed health care delivery systems. If epidemiology to some extent helped normalize homosexuality in the nations whose hazy trace was still visible (as "the West") in Pattern One, and the colonialist guilt of tropical thinking promoted at least some aid for the more cooperative nations in Pattern Two, both the epidemiological tendencies of the GPA and tropical distribution values would desert the one place where either — through prevention or primary care delivery — might have been able to do something worthwhile *before* AIDS finally arrived.

Queering "Asian Homosexuality"

Virtually all of the professional and popular accounts of the HIV pandemic notice the initial conflation of AIDS with supposedly deviant sexual practices, but this linkage was more critical to the definition of the new syndrome than is usually recognized. Even the emergence of substantial numbers of AIDS cases among heterosexuals did not diminish the association of AIDS with sexual deviancy. Instead, heterosexuals who happened to contract HIV were assumed to be practicing some bizarre form of sex. The epidemiological accident that many of the people diagnosed with HIV in Africa claimed to be heterosexual, according to Western researchers' odd and even prurient definitions, only made it easier for the U.S. media and scientists themselves to believe that only perverse bodies were subject to HIV: African heterosexuality was persistently described as perverse, precultural, primitive.

Ironically, the initial *lack* of HIV, constitutive of Pattern Three, contributed to the association of HIV with another kind of sexual perversion. Because they had conflated a pattern (devised by a supragovernmental agency) and a people ("Asians"), researchers and policymakers continued in their strange practice of invoking racist stereotypes as epidemiology: they interpreted the low relative incidence of HIV among Asian nations' citizens and among non-gay Asian Americans as an indicator of sexual conservatism, even asexuality, on the part of "Asians." Many of the first AIDS cases diagnosed in Pattern Three occurred among hemophiliac men or were attributed to male-male sex with Western homosexuals: this could either have been interpreted as the late arrival of the epidemic or as evidence that "Asia" was otherwise an invulnerable space. In general, officials from the nations that still defined their national perimeters—despite having been de-bordered through the GPA designation—diminished the difference between infected individuals and their local cohorts who did not use blood products or have homosexual sex. HIV was constructed as an import that struck locals independently of one another; the social patterns that were apparently necessary for conversion of isolated cases into an epidemic were argued to be absent. A remarkable version of this negotiation of the epidemic occurred in Taiwan.

Writing less than two years after the end of nearly four decades of martial law, in a nation trying desperately to be readmitted to the official union of nations, the Director-General of the Department of Health of the Taiwan Provincial Government tried to split the difference between the epidemiological and tropical narratives, as he described the line HIV traced on its way to his tiny country: "AIDS has been identified only within the past ten years in central Africa; from there it quickly spread to Haiti and then to the U.S. and to Europe. It came very late to Taiwan: in December 1984 an American transiting [*sic*] Taiwan was found to have full-blown AIDS. This triggered our first major concern over the fatal disease. However a rapid increase in the number of AIDS patients locally, the spread of the disease to other parts of Taiwan, development of AIDS among HIV carriers in hemophiliacs, the diversification of risk groups — all have followed the same pattern seen in Western countries and throughout the world" (C.-J. Lee 1989). Two crucial elements leave open Taiwanese officials' future options for retelling the arrival of AIDS and, thus, shifting the country's location in the epidemic: the relativity of time and the exceptionality of Africa (and heterosexual transmission). First, though the period for viewing the epidemic is short—"ten years"—the American transitting in 1984 is described as "very late."

It is, of course, a simple fact that when the Western countries were overwhelmed by case numbers, Asian countries' HIV counts were low. But epidemiology and tropical medicine interpret this in different ways, which have enormously different implications for how to respond. From the standpoint of epidemiology, early incidence could only be considered low *in comparison to the realization in the West of how high numbers could go*. New York once had low numbers, as did Boston, Pittsburgh, Wichita, Dubuque, and Tiny Town, U.S.A. Early incidence in *any* epidemic will always, at least in retrospect, be low: that is the definition of epidemic. What is important to realize is that by 1989 (indeed, probably earlier) statistical simulation of administratively defined patterns had superseded the regional/geopolitical map to such an extent that the figure of the epidemic curve was naturalized as the universal *and* local history of AIDS. But the temporal grounding could still give in to the spatializing concepts of tropical thinking once policymakers considered the conditions for local spread: instead of viewing Asian nationals as a series of potentially connected bodies — indeed, connected across national borders — in which the chain of a future series of transmissions could be interrupted, the GPA and the Taiwanese health minister (and most of his peers) invoked tropical logic to conceive Asia as a place in which HIV would naturally and necessarily *not spread*.

The shift from an implicit time frame to a geography is redoubled when, invoking the now-standard account discussed earlier, the Taiwanese health minister explicitly situates Africa as the epidemic's origin: (homosexual) AIDS/Pattern One/"Western countries" constitute the relevant epicenter, the paradigm for dispersion in Pattern Three. This turn toward the West means that if the health minister can deny the possibility of major homosexual transmission, he can deny that Taiwan will see many "Taiwanese" cases. Though officially designated Patterns Two and Three by the crypto-American GPA of the 1980s, Africa and Asia came to figure two extremes, two different visions of the West's epidemiological future. Each pattern held out a lesson: if you don't use condoms, you'll turn into Africa; if you don't have sex, you can be Asia. Africa is always infectious, Asia always infectable. Both invoking and displacing the obvious gendering of the regions, epidemiologists could refuse to explore how men in African countries got infected, or how, in Asian countries, heterosexual women and men, and male homosexuals who had no contact with Westerners, might become infected or begin to infect each other.

In equating Taiwan's epidemic with that in the West, the director-general must tacitly accept the presence of native homosexuals. His colleagues provide considerable detail about the now-admitted, but tabooed, indigenous homosexuality in order to show that local homosexuals do not engage in the dangerous practices that have proliferated HIV among their equivalents in the licentious West. "According to the statements on the questionnaires, kissing was the most common sexual practice but, after extensive interviewing, male homosexuals often admitted anal intercourse as well. . . . None described practices of 'fisting.' . . . Low prevalence of HIV-1 was detected in several high risk groups. If the results of the questionnaire and interview are accepted as reliable, homosexual behavior in Taiwan appears to be much less promiscuous than in the western world" (H.-C. Lee 1989). These reports figure Taiwan's resistance to the epidemic as primordial, a vague, almost feminine incapacity to become infected except by outsiders. Though more willing to admit to its own homosexuals than many of its neighbors, Taiwan is not unusual in its quick switch from the employment of supranational epidemiology to the postcolonialist reenvisioning of an "Asian" difference. Unfortunately, this meant that they embraced the same temporal logic that asserted intervention in Africa as "too late," without regarding their own country as a place where AIDS "arrived late," and therefore, as an ideal candidate for aggressive prevention campaigns. Sadly, it was risk-reduction programs and not HIV that truly arrived late.

Feminizing "Asian AIDS*"*

Initially, Western discussions about HIV in Asia came through supposed exposés of Australian and American sex tourism. This collision of orientalism and Victorian sexual attitudes produced a frenzy of pseudoconcern over Asian women and children, who were supposedly being swept up into imported Western perversions. Regrettably, this moral panic served less to educate, aid, or protect women, children, or sex-hustling men than it did to police the Western deviant, whose culpability for infection was never, in any event, epidemiologically established.

This representation of passive Asian victims of sex tourism did not unlink Asians from their long-standing role as a Western figure of drug and sexual deviance: women and children so exotic they lure Western men to their beds and Asian men too drugged on opium to care. This complex of media representations and the tropical medical idea of AIDS they invoked, doubly feminized Asia in the context of global AIDS policy: Asia was both passive ("AIDS *arrives* late") and, like the popular Anglo trope of the prematurely developed pubescent girl, Asia was alluring beyond her own comprehension, *attracting* the fatal attention. In the context of already-indicted Asian perversion, the description of "sex tourists" seeking sexual outlets for practices that were stigmatized "at home," suggested that such men were Westerners. In fact, Western reports long neglected to mention that the bulk of the "Asian" sex-tourism market was wealthy "Asians" from industrial centers like Japan, who were merely seeking cheaper services than the ones they paid dearly for at home. The media coverage served to intensify the long-standing stereotype of the homosexual sex tourist. Inverting the growing belief in the West that a positive gay identity increased an individual's likelihood of sustaining a safe-sex practice, homosexual sex tourists, now presumed to be both closeted at home and unconcerned about their partners abroad, were cast as the most likely conduits for HIV.

While transnational sex work is of concern to health-system planners and those concerned with workers' rights, the West's admission to *this* form of colonial intercourse *rationalizes* the more organized state and corporate forms of domination. By representing Asia as feminized, as victimized in the one domain of global regulation (sexuality) within which the West still feels confident of its moral benevolence, the West can ignore the global flows of capital that offer women jobs just as deadly or dead-end as their participation in the transnational sex trade. By focusing on the active culpabilities of individual (if phantasmatic) sex tourists, Western health officials avoided acknowledging that their neglect of Asian countries on their own terms was responsible for the late development of HIV-prevention programs. Because "Asia" was treated largely as an object of tourists' fantasies, the GPA waited to act until HIV was well enough established in Asia to produce an epidemic. Only in the early 1990s did WHO develop policy—largely dealing with prostitution—to manage the burgeoning HIV epidemic, which the WHO's late involvement helped create.

Even this concern about HIV in Asia, and especially in Thailand, was not inevitable; indeed, given that it occurred on the heels of scientists' announcement of their interest in conducting vaccine trials there, the belated international interest in Asian bodies is suspicious. Some years ago I suggested that the ways in which "Africa" and "Africans" were described—Africans won't use condoms; Africa is a disaster; in Africa, AIDS is a disease of poverty (rather than of individual acts)—would enable researchers to conduct HIV vaccine trials there, trials that would not pass ethical muster elsewhere (Patton 1991). Some of those trials continue, but the temporal logic that once promoted Africa as the original locale of "AIDS" is now used to suggest that Africa is already lost, allowing research attention to refocus on a more cooperative land that science proposes to save. Thus, Asia, "where AIDS arrived late," now meets the conditions necessary to conduct the highly controversial HIV vaccine trials.

The poignant claim that education is our only vaccine has backfired: if scientists can convince us that education cannot work, then vaccine trials, whatever their ethical status, are the only hope, a humanitarian effort to avert an imminent disaster that cannot be stopped through behavioral change (i.e., safe sex and improved blood screening). The media pitched in on this ideological campaign, tropicalizing the bodies epidemiologists were tallying for vaccine research. Media reports suggested that uncontrollable elements propel the Asian sex trade: "foreign" men's sex drive and the culture of poverty that drives men and women to sell their bodies to "foreigners," indeed, to queers. Place, or rather, location in an alterity, is so fundamental to this discourse that many ethicists accept the argument that placebo control vaccine studies in Asia are ethical. "Saving Asia," the final chapter in the larger temporal narrative proposed by epidemiology, closes the book on the no-longer-blank-space. "Saving Asia" justifies the very stereotypes about sexuality that dismissed the possibility that *Asia,* as a place, might ever be annexed by the AIDS epidemic. Imagined as the direct or indirect victims of Western perverts' incursions, the bodies that occupy the space, Asia, are effectively treated as the property of the Western science that cannot, finally, save them.

Science or the People

The discursive aspects of the AIDS epidemic are a particularly spectacular example of the switching, drifting, *bricoleur* use of supposedly disinvested descriptive frames, a tragic lesson in the extent to which medical knowledge is mediated in radically different ways, with compounding ill effects. The peregrination of narrative tropes, which I have tried to identify here, and their instantiation as and through the structure of the WHO and GPA, defy science's view of itself as coherent and belie policy and media writers' beliefs that they can "apply" objective knowledge. Put bluntly, scientists and policymakers *can't* keep their story straight.

But these slips and slides in the ways transnational and national bodies talk about AIDS have profound consequences for the policies and practices that are more immediately palpable to us in our local worlds. The point is, of course, that AIDS is not a fixed thing, not a natural phenomenon that necessarily engenders one response or another, one representation or another. The disease hits people in particular locations, but the concepts and responses that aggregate as "AIDS" inextricably frame those local experiences. Activism, too, only fully takes on meaning in context, and for AIDS activism, a key part of that context is medical thought. Work on AIDS interacts in complex ways with historically changing systems of medical knowledge and government power. The nexus of these two—the global organizations that fund and direct policy, and the media that represent the global epidemic to countries and the world—forms a crucial context for how the epidemic will be handled in the years to come. If activism is to retain its critical edge, its various capacities to touch individual lives and change global policy, we must understand how the thought-styles available through medicine pull activism in one direction, deflect it into another.

I have always argued that biomedical discourse and practices are key dimensions of global and local policies, though not in regular and straightforward ways. I've suggested here that representation and policy are most importantly circumscribed by two medical thought-styles of long duration. Both the traditional left and the minoritizing approaches to resistance, which work primarily on the ideology and practices of the state, view the distribution of care and the conduct of science as principally an extension of the state. These forms of analysis, while useful, are partial: they will always underestimate the power of biomedicine to set the terms through which bodies become visible as the location of an epidemic. It is not as simple as determining which is more powerful, science or the state, but instead describing how the state, science, and public media overlap, detach, and collide, and with what effects on the bodies we are trying to protect. Without a doubt, the United States has set important global trends, but equally, the international and transnational responses have shaped the way the United States represents its place in the epidemic to itself. The analysis here has tried to ground the shifting global representations of AIDS not in a single nation's policy or even in international organizations, but in the medical thought-styles that encourage the narration of AIDS in different ways for different purposes.

Notes

1   I treat policy documents and media accounts as "stories" that work together, though imperfectly. The media may lay out a framework that policymakers prefer, because it makes sense of the choices they pose and enact. But the media also criticize, or simply get wrong, the various policies that emanate from professional circles. Thus, the two as often create problems of narration for each other as they work in concert to shore up the fictive versions of scientific concepts, themselves already entangled in the subgenres of policy and media. Science sometimes rejects or corrects both, but, most obviously in the tropical model, it relies on existing colonial policies and travelogue formats to define the field of interest and produce its findings for a public. Epidemiology only seems less dependent on fiction because it deals in statistical concepts, which few are willing to see as themselves a kind of hyperfiction. Indeed, with the advent of global capital media, we are at ease figuring ourselves into the simulacrum world of epidemiology, measuring our distance from an epicenter in miles and lifestyles culled from the numbers and the hyperbolic definition of risk groups.

2   "Man, in the analytic of finitude, is a strange empirico-transcendental doublet,

since he is a being such that knowledge will be attained in him of what renders all knowledge possible. . . . For the threshold of our modernity is situated not by the attempt to apply objective methods to the study of man, but rather by the constitution of an empirico-transcendental doublet which was called *man*" (Foucault 1973, 318–19).

3   Not all of the stories told about AIDS "make sense." In particular, religious fundamentalist claims that AIDS is God's work are deemed unscientific, because they do not easily conform to the tropical or epidemiological models. Claims by various groups that AIDS is a genocidal U.S. biological warfare plot could fit either model: providing a motivation for vectorial movement or a referent for the apparent spatial specificity. However, both the tropical and epidemiological model view disease as a natural force, hence, neither is comfortable exporting the natural origin into a human plan.

4   The shift from people being provided the technology and information with which to imagine themselves a community called "nation," to a technology that takes over their imaginative activity and invents a more corporeal, but no less imagined community defined by the capacity to contract particular forms or sets of disease — "risk group" — is significant: capital interests shift away from the print-capitalism favored in Anderson's argument and toward medical research, also circulated through media technologies, and the icon toward which the imagining tends shifts from national flag to statistical index — homosexual, prostitute, etcetera. Instead of creating a stable nation, the communities imagined by epidemiology are perpetually reconstructed, contingent categories based largely on non-national traits (though for nearly a decade, donor deferral lists included sex with African nationals alongside sex with prostitutes). Epidemiology is *of* the nation but not *for* it.

5   However, projects between American epidemiologists and vaccine researchers work, and their Thai peers belie anything like universally held "Asian values" or "Western values." The proposed Thai vaccine trials were endorsed by local researchers eager to establish themselves, and developing countries' scientists in general, as scientific, a thoroughly un-Asian value. Their Western compatriots were eager to accommodate local standards of care and research conduct in a sham acquiescence to Asian values. Sex-worker advocates attempting to ensure fair treatment of the women who would be the research subjects relied heavily on the language and semi-secured requirements of human rights.

6   Condoms are highly problematic since they are associated with earlier eugenics campaigns under the guise of family planning. Dissociating the condom from family planning in order to let it read as disease prevention has been extremely difficult.

7 Multiculturalism has a rather different meaning in Australia, as compared to its contemporary U.S. usage. What began as an exclusionary immigrant policy has emerged in 1980s-speak as a paradigm for sustaining a nation in the face of radical ethnic difference. Of course, since Aboriginals were not immigrants, they are only a recent part of Australia's vision of a multicultural society. And, somewhat like the First Nations or Native Americans in North America, they are not so sure they want to erase the history of their brutal displacement in order to become one among many cultures occupying what they view as rightfully their land.

8 I'm suggesting that safe sex arose and was globalized as a penalty. For a longer discussion of the rise of prevention discourse, see my *Fatal Advice* (1996).

9 Morocco and Israel are not part of the African and Eastern Mediterranean regions, as one might guess, but are in the European region.

JENNIFER ROBERTSON

Dying to Tell: Sexuality and Suicide in Imperial Japan

[The Japanese] play up suicide as Americans play up crime and they have the same vicarious enjoyment of it. They choose to dwell on events of self-destruction instead of on destruction of others. . . . [Suicide] meets some need that cannot be filled by dwelling on other acts. (Benedict [1936] 1974, 167)

To mention suicide and Japan in the same sentence is to bring to bear a set of stereotypes that continue to shape Western perceptions of non-Western cultures. (Wolfe 1990, xiii)

Why are there so many lesbian double suicides reported in the society column of the daily newspapers? One can only infer that females these days are monopolizing homosexuality. (Yasuda 1935, 150)

Introduction: "Homosexual Elegy"

> Her love for a woman
> Was greater than her parents' love for her;
> And her older sister was cold-hearted.
> She blushed and her heart danced when first they met.

But because they are two women together,
The fan's life is short.

Dashing from east to west,
Theirs was a passionate love
In a baneful world
Only to succumb to nihilism.
When will it fade, the anger in her heart?
For lesbians, the answer is suicide.
Because they are not man and woman,
The fan's grief is deep.

These verses, titled "Homosexual Elegy" (*Dōseiai hika*), were submitted by an amateur songwriter to the humor column of the February 17, 1935, edition of the *Asahi Shinbun,* a nationally distributed daily newspaper in Japan. That day, the column was devoted to spoofing an attempted lesbian double-suicide that had taken place about three weeks earlier. The "feminine" partner was Saijō Eriko, a twenty-three-year-old "woman's-role-player" (*musumeyaku*) in a popular all-female revue, and the "masculine" partner, Masuda Yasumare, an affluent and zealous twenty-seven-year-old fan of the actress (figs. 1, 2, and 3).[1] (Yasumare was a masculine name that she chose for herself; her parents had named her Fumiko.)

As the masculine partner, Masuda was singled out as aggressive and deviant, and cast as the more pathetic of the two, owing to her "unladylike" appearance and behavior. She belonged to the urban upper class whose female constituents were expected to epitomize the "good wife and wise mother" gender role sanctioned by the Meiji Civil Code, based on the German model and operative from 1898 to 1947. Moreover, as a "masculinized" (*danseika*) female, Masuda was one of the "problem women" associated with the so-called woman problem (*fujin mondai*), a term coined around 1900 as a euphemism for issues related to females' civil rights and the struggle of the New Woman (*atarashii onna*) for full citizenship and equality, including voting rights and autonomy (or agency) (see Koyama 1982, 1986; Nolte and Hastings 1991; Sievers 1983). Obviously, not all New Women were lesbians, but all were castigated by conservative pundits as problematic and "masculine" females in contrast to the codified model of femaleness.

In addition to these verses, readers submitted different genres of satirical

Figure 1. The all-female Takarazuka Revue, founded in 1913, in a scene from *Rosarita* (*Rosariita*, 1936) (from Hagiwara 1954, 13). Saijō was a member of the rival Shōchiku Revue, modeled after Takarazuka.

commentary on the incident, including ballad dramas and comic dialogues ("Modan otona tōsei manga yose" 1935). A pun-filled ballad titled "Suicide Journey of a Flapper and a Mannish Woman" (*Datemusume dansō michiyuki*), referred to the feminine partner as a "flapper" and a "revue girl" whose last dance (*dansu*) was with a female cross-dresser (*dansō*). The couple's suicide attempt was sensationalized widely in the mass media, including in the *Fujin Kōron* (Women's Review) and *Chūō Kōron* (Central Review), two of the most prominent mainstream magazines in which articles addressing the intersection of sexuality, sexology, and modernity appeared on a regular basis.[2]

Three years before Masuda and Saijō tempted fate, the successful double suicide of a heterosexual couple, a Keio University student and the daughter of a wealthy (Christian) household, was similarly sensationalized, and elegies were published in the mass media memorializing the exquisite purity of their love — needless to say, the poems were not submitted to humor columns.

Figure 2. Saijō Eriko onstage (left) and offstage (right) (from Saijō 1935).

Figure 3. Masuda Yasumare (Fumiko) with and without her "Lloyd" spectacles (from Saijō 1935 and Nakano 1935, respectively).

The two had decided to commit suicide together by drowning (in a mountain lake southwest of Tokyo) after the woman's parents took steps to force her into an arranged marriage. As I discuss later, arranged marriage preparations motivated many women (and men) to commit, or attempt to commit, suicide regardless of their sexual orientation. A comparison of "Homosexual Elegy" with a poem on the heterosexual couple's suicide, titled "A Love Consummated in Heaven" (*Tengoku ni musubareru koi*),[3] suggests the differential narrative treatment of the psychological circumstances and (at least, initial) public reception of homosexual (*dōseiai*) and heterosexual (*iseiai*) double suicides. The differential treatment was also apparent in the Japanese social-scientific literature on double suicide, as we shall see. The poem introduces the atmosphere defining the incident, followed by first, the man's lament, and second, the woman's, and ends in a joint declaration by the couple.

> This evening's farewell, the moon also
> Dims with grief; in Sagami Bay
> The fire lures of fishermen are damp with tears.
> So fleeting is love in this life.
>
> With you the bride of another,
> How will I live? How can I live?
> I too will go. There where Mother is,
> There beside her,
> I will take your hand.
>
> God alone knows
> That our love has been pure.
> We die, and in [Heaven],
> I will be your bride.
>
> Soon, we will fade away happily:
> Spring flowers on Mount Sakada.[4]

It is quite clear that this poem was not intended as a spoof or critique of the practice of double suicide, and the incident inspired a popular movie of the same title (Seidensticker 1990, 35). The pristine love of the couple is celebrated, and all of nature, from the moon to the fishermen, weeps with grief tinged with bittersweet joy for their union in Heaven. The lesbian couple, on the other hand, and specifically the "masculine" partner, was portrayed as a casualty of, to use today's jargon, a dysfunctional family, represented by insufficient parental love and a cold-hearted older sister. Their attempted suicide was characterized as an act provoked by nihilistic anger, as opposed to visions of conjugal bliss in another life.

Masculinized Females as Social Disorder

Juxtaposed, these two cases underscore the commonsense or dominant notion in Japan past and present about the dichotomous construction of sex, gender, and sexuality. In modern Japan, as in the United States, a person's gender is assigned, and (hetero)sexuality assumed, at birth on the initial basis of genital type, but this is neither an immutable assignment nor an unproblematic assumption.[5] Although, in the case of Japan, the existence of two sexes and two genders is taken for granted, "female" gender (femininity) and "male" gender (masculinity) are not ultimately regarded as the exclusive province of female- and male-sexed bodies, respectively. Sex, gender, and sexuality may be popularly perceived as irreducibly joined, but this remains a situational, and not a permanently fixed, condition.

The introduction and coinage in the late nineteenth century of the new social-scientific terms "homosexual" (*homosekushuaru,* also *dōseiai*) and "heterosexual" (*heterosekushuaru,* also *iseiai*) obfuscated actual sexual practices, which were far more complex and boundary-blurring than the models of and for them. "Homosexual" and "heterosexual" were conveniently superimposed on the existing dominant dichotomous construction of sex, gender, and sexuality, and stimulated a new, psychoanalytic exploration of their relationship. However, these terms, especially in their official Japanese translations of *dōseiai* and *iseiai,* were not used consistently and were qualified on the basis of extenuating circumstances and definition-stretching practices. For example, depending on the context, *dōseiai* was used to describe either a relationship that involved a same-gender, same-sex couple (e.g., two feminine females, or two masculine males), or a same-sex, different-gender couple (e.g., a "butch-femme" female couple, or a "butch-nellie" male couple). Masuda and Saijō clearly were constructed in the mass media as an *ome* or "butch-femme" couple—that is, a couple consisting of what was perceived as a masculine woman and a feminine woman.[6] Initially, they were ridiculed openly—as in the instance of the humor column—not for the simple fact of their unconventional relationship, but for other reasons, including their public and publicized conduct, their celebrity and affluence, and, most importantly, their apparent eschewal of (heterosexual) marriage and motherhood.

Japanese pundits have been adept at selectively adapting for domestic and often dominant purposes institutions and terminologies that were first established and coined outside of Japan. One of the earliest such sources was China, and since the sixteenth century, Europe has served as an important antecedent. It was in the late nineteenth century that Euro-American loanwords and Japanese neologisms in the new field of sexology rapidly made their way into professional and lay parlance alike, evidenced not only in a wide range of printed media, including translations of foreign texts, but also by the many dictionaries devoted to introducing and defining such words. Among the loanwords and Japanese social-scientific neologisms that were household words by the early 1900s were, in addition to "homosexual" and "heterosexual," "fan" (*fuan*), "love letter" (*rabu retā*), "lesbian" (*rezubian*), and *gyaruson* (from the French, garçon), in reference to a mannish woman. Other somewhat less conspicuous loanwords referring to same-sex sexual practices were "sapphism" (*saffuo*), "tribadism" (*tsuribadeizumu*), and "uranism" (*uranizumu*), among others (Hayashi 1926; Ōsumi 1931).

Obviously, social and sexual practices labeled and categorized in the "feudal" Edo period (1603–1867) were undertaken and perceived differently in the succeeding Meiji period (1868–1911) and onward, when the country was embarked on a course of modernization, industrialization, and selective Westernization. In fact, a growing if grudging acknowledgment, and new interpretation, of sexual relations between females prompted the introduction of the term *dōseiai* to distinguish their activities from those of males, although before long the neologism became a standard word for homosexuality in general, regardless of the sex of the individuals involved (Furukawa 1994, 115). Among the "indigenous" terms for lesbians and lesbianism are *aniki* (older brother), *dansō no reijin* (beautiful person [female] in men's clothes), *gōin* (joint licentiousness), *imoto* (younger sister), *join* (female licentiousness), *joshoku* (female eroticism), *kaiawase* (matching shells), *mesu* (female [animal]), *musumeyaku* (woman's role-player), *neko* (pussy[cat], similar in meaning to "femme"), *onēsama* (older sister), *osu* (male [animal]), *otokoyaku* (man's role-player), *shirojiro* (pure white, with etymological implications of falseness and feigned ignorance), *tachi* (an abbreviation of *tachiyaku,* or "leading man," similar in meaning to "butch"), and *tomogui* ("eat each other") (Robertson 1988b, 19–20; Sugahara 1971, 4–5). Japanese lesbian feminists today translate butch and femme as *tachi* and *neko,* and often use the loanwords *butchi* and *fuemu* (Minakawa 1987, 23). Another Japanese term for "butch" often encountered today is *onabe,* or shallow pot, a play on *okama,* or deep pot, a slang word for a "feminine" homosexual male (i.e., a "bottom"). In short, indigenous and foreign-derived words alike were and are historically and culturally specific to the Japanese discourse of sexuality.

The works of Freud, Krafft-Ebing, Carpenter, Ellis, Hirschfeld, Weininger, and others were imported directly to Japan where they were translated, often by Japanese scholars who had studied abroad, and employed immediately in the identification of social problems and their analysis and resolution, exercises in which the state became increasingly invested (Frühstück 1996, 1998; Furukawa 1994). For Japanese social scientists and critics, the loanwords "homosexual" and "heterosexual" helped to explain historical phenomena in a new way, and to devise new categories of pathological phenomena, such as "female" psychology, neurasthenia, and fandom. Like all other methods of classification and analysis, these terms and their definitions both opened up new insights and closed off others.

For many critics, "moral depravity" accompanying the growth of the modernizing (or Westernizing) city seemed to be the only viable "explanation" for *ome* or "butch-femme" relationships among bourgeois urban women, at least until the advent of all-female revues, whose man's-role-players (*otoko-yaku*) inspired new ideas to account for the increasingly visible masculinized female (Robertson 1992). Whereas the Japanese "good wife, wise mother" was praised by conservatives as the embodiment of social stability and cultural integrity, her alter ego, the "Western" masculinized female — and New Woman in general — was perceived as the embodiment of social instability. As Sharon Sievers has shown, national cultural identity in Imperial Japan was premised on a sexual division of symbolic labor, where crew-cut males in dark suits evinced the nation's modernization program, and kimono-clad females with chignons represented the longevity and continuity of Japanese "tradition," itself a modern product. (In fact, short hair for women was made illegal in 1872, although this law was routinely flouted and rarely enforced [Sievers 1983, 14–15].)

The place of class in the overlapping discourses of sex, gender, and nation-ness cannot be underestimated. Some females, in the first half of the twen-tieth century at least, "passed" as men in order to secure employment as rickshaw drivers, construction supervisors and laborers, fishers, department store managers, grocers, and so on (Tomioka 1938, 103). "Passing" was as-sociated unequivocally with sexual deviancy in the case of urban middle-and upper-class girls and women who, it was argued, wore masculine attire not to secure a livelihood but as an outward expression of their "moral de-pravity." As privileged and educated — in short, bourgeois — girls and women, they were supposed to fulfill the state-sanctioned "good wife, wise mother" gender role. Consequently, those who resisted were vilified in journal and newspaper articles on mannish women, and roundly critiqued in texts and treatises on "female" psychology (Sakabe 1924; Sugita 1929, 1935; Ushijima 1943; Yasuda 1935).

The modern(izing) state discouraged gender ambivalence and sexual con-fusion, which were associated with social disorder (Watanabe and Iwata 1989, 127), and the steady militarization of the society heightened the delineation of sex and gender. On the surface at least, it seems that the state got its way: a one-day survey of 1,180 people in Ginza, Tokyo's premier boulevard, con-ducted by culture critic Kon Wajirō in 1925, revealed that 67 percent of males wore Western-style outfits, while all but 1 percent of females appeared in Japa-nese dress (cited in Silverberg 1992, 38). Nevertheless, the 1 percent (and prob-ably more) of females who did wear "modern" clothes rankled critics who believed that one dreadful effect of the select Westernization of social, politi-cal, and economic institutions was the apparent masculinization of the Japa-nese woman and the neglect of Japanese customs (Nogami 1920; Tachibana 1890; see also Roden 1990; Silverberg 1991). Moreover, as Donald Roden re-ports, "the expression and representation of gender ambivalence captured the imagination of the literate urban populace" in the 1910s and 1920s, spark-ing a heated debate in the media between conservatives and liberals (Roden 1990, 43).

Whereas Roden claims that debates about gender and sexual ambivalence were directed at males and females equally, my extensive perusal of hundreds of contemporary newspaper, magazine, and journal articles leads me to dif-ferent conclusions: females almost exclusively were singled out as the source of sexual deviance and social disorder, and as the target of acrimonious debates about the relationships among sex, gender, and sexuality.[7] If the sexes were converging, as some pundits argued (e.g., Nogami 1920), it was because the masculinization of females was compromising the masculinity of males, who appeared more feminine in contrast; that is, the markers distinguishing male from female, masculine from feminine were losing their polarity. The dialectical dynamics of sex-and-gender were experienced as a zero-sum game. Because the nation itself was personified in contrastive gendered terms, it would not do to have androgynous females (and males) wreaking symbolic havoc. Gendering "New Japan," as the imperial nation was called, was an ongoing project that constantly adapted to extenuating circumstances. As I have illustrated in an article on the culture of Japanese imperialism, when the martial spirit of the Japanese was at issue, the West and Euro-American cultural productions were cast as feminine and feminizing, in the "bad" sense of unmanly and emasculating. Contrarily, the nation was personified as feminine, in the "good" sense of traditional, when the superior cultural sensibility and artistic achievements of the Japanese were publicized (Robertson 1995, 974). Mannish girls and women in particular were therefore deemed un-Japanese.[8]

The press propagated a negative definition of the New Woman, describing her as "an indulgent and irresponsible young Japanese woman who used her overdeveloped sexuality to undermine the family and to manipulate others for her own selfish ends" (Sievers 1983, 175). Whether or not actual females claimed the label, the New Woman was a cultural construct—a trope of and for social disorder in the eyes of the state (Silverberg 1991; cf. Smith-Rosenberg 1985, 245–96). The "feminization of males" (*danshi no joseika*) was a consequence of the "masculinization of females" (*joshi no danseika*), and while the former was worrisome, it was the latter condition at which critics directed their fearful anger (see Roden 1990). For conservatives, whose collective voice was amplified in the press, the masculinized female (and the mannish lesbian) embodied social disorder: she eschewed conventional femininity, flouted the "Good Wife, Wise Mother" model of gender sanctioned by the civil code, and disrupted Japanese "tradition."

Siting Double Suicide

Suicide is a key component of a Japanese national allegory, as Alan Wolfe argues in his exploration of the relation between the concept of "national suicide" and autobiographical writing (Wolfe 1990, 14–15, 215–17). "Problem women" who, in the 1930s, chose suicide were squarely situated within this allegory. For female couples to commit or attempt double suicide was tantamount to their making a public(ized) claim for sexual citizenship and subjectivity through an act of ultimate resolve valorized for centuries in literature and reified as a quintessentially "Japanese" expression of sincerity and purity of intention. The suicide and parasuicide notes and letters of lesbians constituted an important voice in contested debates about the relationship between sexuality and nation-ness in a modern(izing) Japan (as remarked by Yasuda in the third epigraph to this article).[9] Moreover, lesbian suicide attempts effectively highlight the connection between self/social-destruction and self/social-reconstruction, as we shall see.

Before examining lesbian (double) suicide attempts in greater detail, the category and subcategories of "double suicide" must be placed, briefly, in historical and anthropological context. The several Anglophone works that deal analytically with "Japanese suicide" avoid mention of "homosexual double suicide" even though this particular category figures, quite prominently in some cases, in the Japanese social-scientific literature on suicide.[10] By the same token, whereas the long history in Japan of same-sex sexual relations between males (specifically Buddhist priests, samurai, and Kabuki actors) is well accounted for, if largely descriptively (e.g. Leupp 1995), until very recently sexual relations between females have remained largely unrecognized, unacknowledged, invisible, and inaccessible in the postwar scholarly literature in and on Japan.[11]

However, unlike the bridled Japanese and Anglophone scholarship of today, various types of lesbian practice, including double suicide, were widely and openly highlighted, discussed, sensationalized, and analyzed in the scholarly and popular media of early-twentieth-century Japan. The involuted complexities of sexual practices and the instability of categories thereof, together with a perceived and internalized stigma on lesbian subjects, jointly have induced Japan scholars to disregard *even what captivated the Japanese public and scholarly community at a given historical moment.* Ironically, the space of sociosexual (in)difference is evident *not* in the popular-cultural discourse shaping a specific period, but in the academic scholarship on Japan. The persistence of the dominant sex-gender ideology that females are objects of male desire and not the subjects of their own desire, effectively inhibits both naming that desire and identifying multiple modes of female *and* male sexualities in Japan. Attending to the early debates on sexuality, and conveying a sense of the contested rhetorical climate in which they took place, are a necessary beginning for a more complete (and more responsible) anthropology of sexuality, gender ideology, and associated practices today.

Double suicide is often translated as "love suicide" in keeping with the nuances of the Japanese terms *shinjū* (hearts contained) and *jōshi* (love death). As Takie Lebra notes, the "theme of inseparability stands out not only in the motivation or goal, but also in the method [of suicide]" (Lebra 1976, 195–96). Whereas prior to the seventeenth century *shinjū* denoted "milder pledges of love such as exchanging oaths or tearing out a fingernail," it has since meant both a double suicide by lovers and any suicide involving the death of more than one person, such as *oyako shinjū* (parent [mother]–child suicide), *fūfu shinjū* (married-couple suicide), *shimai jōshi* (sisters suicide), and *muri shinjū* (forced or coerced suicide) (Keene 1976, 253; Lebra 1976, 195). Since the early twentieth century, *dōseiai shinjū* and *dōseiai jōshi* have been the most common terms used for homosexual double suicide.[12]

Double suicide qua love suicide is distinguished from *junshi,* which denotes one or more persons' death as martyrs for a cause or to prove their loyalty to a deceased superior. *Seppuku* refers to ritual disembowelment and was used historically (albeit limitedly) not only for voluntary death but also as a penalty reserved for members of the elite samurai class. This largely proscribed yet much glamorized practice, along with the military's legitimation of institutionalized suicide during World War II, have informed the creation of a naturalizing link in the minds of Japanese and non-Japanese alike between suicide and Japaneseness.[13] Most of the literature on suicide on which such "copulative conjunctions" (Wolfe 1990, xiii) are made, however, is based on literary portrayals of suicide taken at face value and on the generalization of the "logic" of war, military strategy, and wartime xenophobia. Finally, all of the types of suicide noted above are, in turn, distinguished from the "ordinary" solitary suicide referred to generically as *jisatsu* (killing of the self).

Lesbian Double Suicide: The Practice

In his book on Tokyo since the great earthquake of 1923, Edward Seidensticker makes note of the "high" incidence of suicides and double suicides in the 1930s, and connects these acts to the "nervous and jumpy" national and international climate. The Japanese government withdrew from the League of Nations in 1933 after rejecting a demand for the Kwantung Army to withdraw from Manchuria, where they had established the puppet ("The Last Emperor") state of Manchukuo in 1932. Parts of Manchuria had been under Japanese control since 1906; the Kwantung Army plotted to occupy that country in 1931, which led to the outbreak of a full-scale war with China in 1937, a development marked as the "beginning" of World War II for Japan. Seidensticker suggests that the Japanese government's withdrawal from the League provoked feelings of isolation and apprehension among ordinary citizens, which, with the economic depression, exacerbated the despondency, illness, and family difficulties that motivate suicidal acts (Seidensticker 1990, 35, 37). The decision to withdraw from the League also appeared to have quickened the resolve of the Japanese state to pursue a zealous and aggressive course as an anticolonial colonizer. Okinawa, Taiwan, Korea, and Micronesia had already been under Japanese rule for decades by this time, and in 1940 the military state proclaimed the formation of a Greater East Asia Co-Prosperity Sphere, with Japan as the nucleus, as the key to the liberation of the rest of Asia and the Pacific from European and American imperialism.

We might productively interpret lesbian double suicides as both signifying and symptomatic of another dimension of national isolation and apprehension, not only on the part of the females involved, but also on the part of culture critics obsessed with the figure of the masculinized female, and especially the mannish lesbian (cf. Smith-Rosenberg 1983, 245–96). Yasuda Tokutarō's rhetorical question, in this essay's third epigraph, about females' monopoly on suicide and homosexuality points to this other dimension. Unlike the majority of his contemporaries, Yasuda was unusual in looking favorably upon Japanese lesbian practices as representing female and ultimately cultural emancipation, in that mutual cooperation between females and males would insure that neither would be reduced to servile status (Yasuda 1935, 152; see Roden 1990, 54). His interest, in his words, in the "widespread phenomenon of same-sex love among females" was provoked by press coverage of Masuda Yasumare and Saijō Eriko's attempted double suicide, to which I now return (Yasuda 1935, 146).

What were the circumstances of the female couple's attempted "love suicide"? The media focused mostly on Masuda, whose masculine appearance was perceived not only as a marker of aggression but also as subversive and dangerous. Saijō, on the other hand, was treated more leniently, for the likely reason that her comparatively feminine, if problematically "modern," appearance was perceived as less threatening than Masuda's blatantly maverick figure. It is also likely that as a "revue girl" (*rebyū gāru*), a vocation associated with wanton women, Saijō's conduct was already marked as beyond the pale (cf. Asagawa 1921; Ozaki 1986). Masuda, on the other hand, was singled out as proof of the "recent, disturbing increase in the 1920s and 1930s in lesbian affairs between upper-class girls and women"; affairs that presumably "in the past, were associated with lower-class status" ("Kore mo jidaisō ka" 1935).

Saijō, the feminine partner, published an autobiographical account of the suicide attempt two months after the event in *Fujin Kōron*.[14] I will recount most of Saijō's story to provide readers with a sense of its tone and colorful characterizations. Saijō begins by recalling how she first met Masuda backstage after a show in May 1934 at an Osaka theater: the actress was stepping out of her bath wrapped in a towel, when Masuda approached and struck up a short conversation. The cross-dressed fan's physical beauty, especially her straight, white teeth, round "Lloyd" spectacles, and "Eton crop" (a short hairstyle) impressed Saijō, and the visits became a daily affair (figs. 2 and 3). Come autumn, after half a year of constant contact at different venues in eastern and western Japan, Saijō reports that Masuda's letters to her grew intensely passionate; the handsome fan would write such things as, "I can't bear to be apart from you for even a moment." "Although these letters could be interpreted as expressions of lesbian love," the actress explains, "I viewed them as the confessions of a sincere fan" (Saijō 1935, 170).

Saijō's admission of the fuzzy boundary between fandom and lesbian desire played into the dominant perception of female fans of the all-female revue as pathological and socially problematic. "Fan" was often used as a euphemism for lesbian (or for a girl or woman with lesbian proclivities), and by the same token, fandom was identified as a serious illness marked by an inability to distinguish between sexual fantasies (themselves problematic phenomena in women) and actual lesbian practices ("Hogosha wa kokoro seyo" 1935; "Kore mo jidaisō ka" 1935; Robertson 1998b, chs. 4 and 5).

In her account, Saijō refers to herself by her first name, Eriko, and characterizes herself as a gullible actress—as highly impressionable and thus "naturally inclined" to become absorbed into Masuda's charismatic aura. She waxes nostalgic about their walks, hand in hand, along the bay: "for those who didn't know us, we probably looked just like [heterosexual] lovers" (Saijō 1935, 171). The couple traveled widely in the Kansai area, and New Year's Day 1935 found them together in bed in a Kyoto hotel. Saijō claims that by that point she had wearied of the intensity of their relationship and wanted to return to Tokyo, where she had a photo-shoot scheduled for the first week of January. But whenever she mentioned the word "return home" (kaeru), Masuda became deathly pale and stern, and Saijō would lose her courage to insist.

They spent the next several days on a ferryboat to Beppu on the island of Kyushu—a "gateway to death," as Saijō describes the experience (Saijō 1935, 172). Travel provided this and other same-sex couples an opportunity for extra-ordinary activities and practices that could not be practically sustained in the more mundane realm of everyday life (cf. Ōhara 1973, 244–45). A couple would often travel for several days to a particular suicide site, enjoying each other's intimate company to an unprecedented degree. It was on the trip to Beppu that Masuda first recited to Saijō the sad story about her sterile, dysfunctional, and fatherless family. Masuda's father had separated from his wife shortly after his brokerage firm went bankrupt and set up housekeeping with a mistress with whom he eventually produced six children ("Dansō reijō no kashutsu jiken" 1935).

Much to her apparent chagrin, Saijō's chronic appendicitis flared up shortly after they arrived in Beppu, and the actress was hospitalized for three days. The doctor encouraged her to return to Kyoto by train, which was faster and more comfortable than a ferryboat. Back in Kyoto, the tension between the two women escalated, although they "fought silently": When Saijō insisted on returning to Tokyo, Masuda threatened to commit suicide.

Meanwhile, Masuda's mother had hired a private investigator to locate the itinerant couple, at which point the press, alerted and ready to exploit the splashy story, filed daily reports on the couple's saga, noting that their real "suicide journey" (michiyuki) began on the night of January 23 ("Dansō no reijin" 1935), when, after a "storybook-like" chase involving trains and cars, the couple was apprehended in Nagoya by the private investigator. Masuda's mother and sister blamed the revue actress for the love-struck fan's transgressions, including the theft of money and stock certificates out of which their travels were paid and fancy gifts bought. Masuda was sent back to her mother's house in Osaka, and Saijō retired to her parents' home in Tokyo.

That was not the end of their relationship, however. Late at night on January 27, Saijō received a telephone call from Masuda, who had fled to Tokyo the previous night and was staying at a city hotel. (The press described her escape as a matter of "reentering the fickle world of sexual desire" ["Dansō no reijin" 1935].) Saijō went immediately to the hotel, her father in tow. Feeling sorry for her "special friend," Saijō, "at [her] father's urging," prepared to spend the night with Masuda, who recounted her escape.[15] Apparently Masuda had fooled her mother into thinking that she was asleep in bed by stuffing cushions under her blankets. Breaking open the terrace door, she climbed over a tall wall to freedom, cutting her hands badly in the process. Borrowing money from a neighbor, she made her way to Tokyo, vowing never to return to her family from hell. Before leaving, she left a note on her bed instructing her mother and sister not to pursue her—advice they ignored.

Masuda and Saijō conspired to move secretly to another city hotel in order to avoid the droves of pesky newspaper reporters who had tracked the handsome fan to Tokyo. At around midnight, they pushed their beds together and "went to sleep." No mention is made in Saijō's account of a double suicide pact or the ingestion of tranquilizers and sleeping pills. The narrative as a whole is crafted defensively, with the actress represented as a victim of her fan's willful passion. Acknowledging the widespread press coverage of the attempted double suicide, Saijō allows the reader to supply the missing details and notes simply that she was shocked to find herself awake in the morning.[16] Looking at Masuda's "peacefully sleeping form," Saijō read the masculine female's suicide note, which was reprinted in her *Fujin Kōron* article as follows:

> Eriko [Saijō's first name].
> Even though it seems as though we've known each other forever, ours was a very short-lived relationship. But you more than anyone have left a deep and everlasting impression on my heart. What this means not even I know for sure. What I do know is that I loved you [*suki deshita*] unconditionally. Now as I approach the end of my life, I can say that I never thought that I would become so profoundly indebted to you. In any case, thank you; thank you very very much. I don't know how I can thank you enough. No, it's not merely thanks, I will die indebted [*os-*

ewa] to you and that is a happy thought. My incorrigibly selfish ways have caused you much grief. Please forgive me. Once I had made the decision to die, I cried and cried thinking of all that we've shared and how much I would miss you. And I realized how sad it is to die alone. To be perfectly honest, I wanted you to die with me. But I am aware of your circumstances, and you always assumed a rational stance in contrast to my emotional one. So, I'll go alone after all. Goodbye.

Yasumare [Masuda's self-selected first name]

January 28, evening (Saijō 1935, 178)

Masuda's letter was likely edited by Saijō or someone else in a way that exonerated the revue actress from any complicity in a double suicide attempt. Saijō also appears as "rational," in contrast to Masuda's "emotional" self. Perhaps this was a strategy designed to minimize the incident's damage to her acting and modeling career? In any case, shortly after her double suicide attempt, Saijō left the Shōchiku Revue to pursue a career in film. She all but disappeared from that revue's fan magazines, where she had been featured regularly before the incident.

In concluding her tale of love and suicide, Saijō reveals that she was able to deal influentially with the Masuda family lawyer, requesting that her masculine partner be allowed the unprecedented step of forming a branch household (*bunke*) and living independently, as if Masuda were, in fact, male. And when Masuda's estranged father visited his daughter in the hospital, Saijō criticized him for being an absentee father. Saijō herself vows henceforth to keep a close watch on Masuda's behavior. Self-interest aside, Saijō's and others' accounts of the couple's ordeal in prominent mainstream magazines effectively parried the earlier disparaging treatment of their double suicide attempt in the humor column of the *Asahi Shinbun* (e.g., Tani 1935).

Lesbian Suicide: The Theories

Some Japanese scholars and clinicians have regarded the double or love suicide, in general, as a peculiarly Japanese practice informed by the Buddhist belief in reincarnation and the spirit of martyrdom in the way of the samurai (*bushidō*) (e.g., Isomura Eiichi and Sagami Mitsugu in Ōhara 1965, 187–88). Others have disagreed, providing historical evidence of the practice elsewhere in Asia and in Europe (e.g., Yamana Shōtarō in Ōhara 1965, 186–87). Still others, as we have seen, linked lesbian practices, including double suicide, to the more recent, insidious effects and social ramifications of Westernization.

Quite a few Japanese psychiatrists and social critics of the time assumed that females' "natural" passivity and hormone-provoked melancholia made them susceptible to neurasthenia (*shinkeishitsu*), which in turn occasioned a pessimism expressed in the form of homosexuality. Their melancholia was exacerbated, in turn, by homosexual practices that made them further susceptible to suicidal impulses (Fukushima [1935] 1984, 562; "Shōjo no hi no sei mondai" 1934; Tamura 1913). Pundits and critics also asserted that all-female revues on the subject of romantic love and its ephemerality, together with certain European films, such as the antipatriarchal *Mädchen in Uniform,* first shown in Japan in 1933 to sold-out audiences, valorized both lesbianism and suicide ("Shōjo no hi no sei mondai" 1934, 9).[17]

"Homosexual Elegy," translated at the start of this essay, parrots the various explanations for lesbian sexuality and double suicide popularized in the press. For example, a 1935 newspaper article on the recent fad among girls and women of dressing as men incorporated an interview with a physician, Saitō Shigeyoshi, who cited the theories of bisexuality proposed by Otto Weininger in explaining female transvestism in Japan ("Kore mo jidaisō ka" 1935). Weininger's formulations contributed to the "psychiatric style of reasoning" that emerged in the late nineteenth century in America, Europe, and Japan (see also Davidson 1987). Today, his *Sex and Character* (1903) is recognized as racism (anti-Semitism) and misogyny in the guise of scientific analysis.

On the one hand, Weininger, like many of his Japanese counterparts, linked female anatomy to such negative characteristics as chronic immaturity and emotionalism, and a preoccupation with sexuality. On the other hand, he alluded to the transformative effects of gender, suggesting that "[h]omosexuality in a woman is an outcome of her masculinity and presupposes a higher degree of development." He also claimed that "the degree of emancipation and the proportion of maleness in the composition of a woman are practically identical," an observation that was shared by his Japanese readers and counterparts (qtd. in Garber 1992, 225; cf. Sugita 1929).

In the newspaper article introducing Weininger, Saitō, the Japanese physician, acknowledges a long history of lesbian sexuality and mannish women in Japan, but claims that the permanent condition was "more prevalent in the West," implying, as did others, that an incorrigibly masculinized female (in this case, a mannish lesbian) was thoroughly Westernized and therefore un-Japanese ("Kore mo jidaisō ka" 1935). Doubtless, Saitō was also familiar with the work of Weininger's contemporary, Richard von Krafft-Ebing, whose *Psychopathia Sexualis* (1886) was standard reading for Japanese psychologists and sexologists. It was even appropriated as a template for *Hentai seiyokuron* (The theory of deviant sexual desire), coauthored by Habuto Eiji and Sawada Junjirō in 1915 (and reprinted eighteen times over the next decade) (Roden 1990, 45). Krafft-Ebing created a new "medico-sexual category, the Mannish Lesbian," in which he linked "women's rejection of traditional gender roles and their demands for social and economic equality to cross-dressing" (Smith-Rosenberg 1983, 272). What was a universal, if new, "medico-sexual" category for Krafft-Ebing was for Saitō a consequence of Westernization.

Masuda and Saijō were referred to disparagingly in the newspaper article as practicing a "deviant homosexual love" (*hentai dōseiai*). "Deviant," because same-sex, different-gender (e.g., "butch-femme") relationships were regarded as abnormal, while same-sex, same-gender relationships, or passionate friendships among outwardly feminine couples, were and are regarded as part of a normal and self-limited stage in the female life cycle (Tamura 1913; Mochizuki 1959; Robertson 1989, 1992). Lesbianism, broadly defined as eroticized, intimate relations between two females, was not itself an issue so long as it was self-limited and unmarked by the presence of a masculine partner. Provided sexual practices neither interfered with nor challenged the legitimacy of the twinned institutions of marriage and household, nor competed with heterosexist conventions in the public sphere, Japanese society accommodated (and still does) a diversity of sexual behaviors. To wit, social reproduction need not be synonymous with human reproduction (as in the case of adopted sons–*cum*–sons-in-law, a common strategy of household succession in Japan in the absence of a male heir), but the former must not be compromised by a politicized sexual identity that interferes with the latter.

Following their European and American counterparts, such as Havelock Ellis, some Japanese psychologists active in the early twentieth century drew a distinction between "real" or "permanent" (*shin*), and "provisional" or "transient" (*kari*) homosexuality in females. Unlike their European and American counterparts, they sometimes referred to the former condition as "Western" and the latter as "Japanese." Whereas the former condition, embodied by the masculine woman, was deemed "incurable," the latter condition, embodied by the feminine woman, supposedly resolved itself quickly once she married. Parents were reassured that "provisional lesbianism" was not the result of "mental insufficiency or illness," but rather should be perceived as a short-lived "spiritual hedonism" (*seishinteki kyōraku*) ("Kore mo jidaisō ka" 1935).

The works of the European and American sexologists named earlier "quickly captured the imagination of Japan's earliest students of psychology," amateurs and professionals alike (Roden 1990, 45; see also Hirschfeld 1935, 7–39). The application of these theories by Japanese scholars and clinicians was informed by an apparent contradiction: a subscription (sometimes on the level of academic lip-service) to the universality of Euro-American psychological theories and a belief in Japanese uniqueness, which in turn was typified by a lack of both awareness and theoretical engagement with everyday sexual and gendered practices in Japan (Yoshimoto 1989, 25; see also Yasuda 1935). In this connection, the German sexologist and advocate of homosexual rights, Magnus Hirschfeld, reported that during his lecture tour of Japan in 1931 he encountered among his Japanese colleagues, many of whom had studied in Europe, an apparently "widespread ignorance of intersexual male and female types off the stage, and especially of the extent of homosexuality in general" (Hirschfeld 1935, 30).[18] He recorded the following illuminating account of his conversation with Miyake Kōichi, a professor of psychiatry:

> Professor M[i]yaki . . . said when we first met: "Tell me, my dear Hirschfeld, how is it that one hears so much about homosexuality in Germany, England and Italy and nothing of it among us?"
>
> I answered: "That, my dear colleague, is because it is permitted by you and forbidden by us."
>
> "But it seems to be more prevalent in Europe," he continued. "In all my long practice I have never yet seen one single case."
>
> "I can scarcely believe that the phenomenon is rarer among you than among us," I replied, "but I shall be able to tell you better in a few weeks when I have done some investigating among specialists in the subject."

I gave him my opinion shortly before I left, after I had had a chance to find out, from letters written me by Japanese and particularly from people who came to see me after my presence was known, that every form of homosexuality, in tendency as well as in expression, is precisely the same in Japan as in Europe. My old observation was again completely confirmed: the *individual sex type* is a far more important factor than the *racial type* (Hirschfeld 1935, 30–31; original emphasis).

Despite a cultural history of same-sex sexual practices among males, not to mention the sensationalized coverage of homosexual love and its social implications, some of Hirschfeld's Japanese colleagues claimed to be unaware of the history and present situation of same-sex or homosexual practices in Japan — or they at least maintained a public posture of ignorance — as is obvious from their published works. In an article on "deviant sexual desire," for example, Ōsumi Tamezō focuses on homosexual practices *outside* of Japan, providing Japanese translations for English, French, and Latin terms (Ōsumi 1931). Roden suggests that Japanese sexologists writing for an educated but popular audience were obliged to grace their articles and books "with just enough pseudo-scientific information and prescriptive advice to limit government censorship without dampening the curiosity of their middle-class audience" (Roden 1990, 46). The use of Euro-American examples to illustrate allegedly universal (homo)sexual practices may have been, in part, a strategy to avoid official censure, which was considerable by the late 1930s. But what could account for earlier self-censoring practices?

Sabine Frühstück (1998) suggests that some German- and Austrian-trained sexologists, like Miyake, willfully dismissed those sexual practices that they felt would compromise Japan's international image as a "civilized" country, while others used new sexological categories to isolate and rebuke all types of New Women, and particularly the mannish lesbian. It might also be the case that Miyake and others like him simply did not recognize certain historical same-sex sexual practices in Japan as categorizable under the new sexological terminology adopted from Continental *Sexualwissenschaft*.

Finally, not a few Japanese scholars claimed that their knowledge of Japanese sexual practices was gained indirectly, if not tortuitously, through the study of, for instance, German. Thus, even the progressive psychologist Yasuda Tokutarō, in a 1935 article on historical perspectives on homosexuality, credits his knowledge about Japanese (male) homosexual practices to German texts lent to him by the late Iwaya Sazanami, who, Yasuda claims, first "informed the world about the history of homosexual love in Japan" despite being publicly acknowledged only as a specialist in children's folklore (Yasuda 1935, 147).

Although Hirschfeld focused only on male homosexuals in his investigation (for the obvious reason of accessibility), he did discuss the topic of homosexuality with the leaders of the Japanese women's movement, including Ishimoto Shizue and Ichikawa Fusae (Hirschfeld 1935, 12). If patriarchal critics regarded the New Woman and the mannish lesbian as examples of the worst ramifications of Westernization, Japanese feminists (and some male reformers) used "the West" in part as a rhetorical device to create a new discursive space in which to critique the patriarchal family-state system, sexual double standards, and political repression (see Sievers 1983). "The West," in short, was deployed as a foil in contradictory ways with respect to the sex-gender system: by traditionalists and state ideologues as subversive and detrimental to the androcentric status quo, and by their adversaries as a type of counter-discourse (whether registered in writing or in sartorial expression) through which to express what was otherwise politically difficult or even impossible and ideologically inconceivable. The evocation of "the West" was not about the specific countries and cultural areas grouped under that rubric, but about contemporary social transformations in Japan; it was invoked as a discursive space for a range of adversarial cultural and political critiques (cf. Chen 1992, 688).

Dying to Tell

Suicide and attempted suicide generated a variety of narratives representing a spectrum of genres, including social-scientific analyses, suicide notes, letters, wills, autobiographical accounts, magazine and newspaper articles, poems, dramatic chants, and so forth.[19] Masuda's suicide note to Saijō apparently was one of five she had prepared for members of her family, a close friend, and for the public (Nakano 1935, 164). Only the note to Saijō was made public, although it may have been doctored, as I have suggested. Significantly, the suicide and parasuicide narratives written by Japanese lesbians and published in the print media contradict the various dominant theories about both suicide and lesbianism, such as those ventured by Komine Shigeyuki, a prominent sexologist first writing in the 1930s. We are already familiar with the details of the Masuda-Saijō case; another prominent incident two years later, in 1937, was featured in the *Fujin Kōron*.

Briefly, the case involved a love triangle among three women (in their mid-twenties), one of whom was "malelike" and attractive. The mannish lesbian and the younger feminine partner regarded themselves as "spiritually, a perfect married couple." The latter's parents took it upon themselves to arrange a marriage for their maverick daughter, a unilateral act that occasioned the couple's decision to commit double suicide. The masculine partner failed to show up at the appointed time and place, and in frustration and disappointment the younger, feminine woman drank poison alone. Her solo attempt at self-destruction failed, for she vomited the poison and survived. She then received a suicide letter from her partner, which read, "Goodbye forever. I pray for your happiness. Please forgive my selfishness. My last wish is for you to return to the countryside and get married. 'D', forever beneath the ocean" (qtd. in Ōhara 1973, 244–45).

"D" had committed suicide with the other, older feminine partner. Enraged, the younger woman slashed her wrists but again did not succumb to her injuries. Her own suicide note (to her deceased lover) read: "I believed in you completely. . . . I can't let you sink alone into the frigid waters of the ocean." This incident was referred to in the newspapers as *shinjū sannin kurabu*, or "The Suicide Triangle Club" (qtd. in Ōhara 1973, 245).

Komine drew distinctions between heterosexual and homosexual double suicides. He claimed that whereas a heterosexual couple's double suicide was premeditated and often provoked by their inability to marry, a homosexual couple's decision to commit double suicide was spontaneous and carried out for apparently "trivial" reasons. While Komine did not discount entirely the possibility of sexual desire between females, he did insist that "empathy and commiseration" (*dōjō*), and not frustrated sexual desire (sometimes in the guise of resistance or opposition to an arranged marriage), was the catalyst for lesbian double suicides (Komine 1985, 197–98).

The various narratives generated by the Masuda-Saijō attempted double suicide and others, demonstrate that the women's decision to die was neither spontaneous nor motivated by petty concerns. Moreover, although a couple's frustration at the futility of maintaining their romantic relationship was underplayed, there seemed to be a public consensus about both the "causes" of lesbianism and the suicidal effects of melancholia, loneliness, a dysfunctional family, and/or parental efforts to force a woman into an arranged marriage—causes that were hardly trivial. This was a consensus that coexisted with attempts in the press to trivialize female couples and their tribulations.

Komine tabulates the numbers of "female same-sex double (or 'love' suicides)" (*joshi dōseijōshi*) reported in the daily press between 1925 and 1935, acknowledging that the actual figures were probably much higher (Komine 1985, 232).[20] The haphazard quality of suicide statistics in the early twentieth century, in terms of collection, categorization, and interpretation, makes it difficult to determine accurately both the number of suicides per se and which of the double suicides actually involved lesbian couples. Clearly, a proportion significant enough to attract critical attention were committed by lesbians. Komine himself suggests this in his study of homosexual double suicide, although he warns that not only are double suicides committed by female couples hidden in statistics for heterosexual suicides—in the event that a man and two women were involved—but not all female double suicides involved lesbians, as in some cases, siblings were involved (Komine 1985, 176). There are 342 incidents in Komine's data of "female same-sex double (or 'love') suicide" (totaling *at least* twice as many females) reported in the press between 1925 and 1935. His category *joshi dōseijōshi* is ambiguous: given the subject of his book, Komine most probably means "lesbian double suicides," although it is not entirely clear whether or not he adjusted his statistics for the possibility that some of these suicides (or attempts) involved female siblings or love triangles (e.g., two women in love with the same man).

Over half of these acts occurred during the "nervous and jumpy" years of 1932 and 1935. Komine claims that confirmed lesbian double suicides amounted to about 31 percent of all categories of suicides (Komine 1985, 174–75). The average age of the women at the time of their resolve to die was between twenty and twenty-five years. The vast majority of lesbian double suicides involved factory workers, waitresses, and nurses, in that order; prostitutes constituted the majority of female actors in the case of heterosexual double suicides (Komine 1985, 178, 174). Komine reports that whereas the actors in heterosexual double suicides tended to be of different social statuses and classes—for example, a male novelist and a prostitute, a wealthy housewife and a chauffeur—the vast majority (over 80 percent) of partners in homosexual double suicides were of the same social status, class, or occupation (Komine 1985, 175).

As I have noted, one reason why the Masuda-Saijō attempted suicide generated so much interest and attention was due in large part to their social prominence: Masuda's upper-class status and Saijō's celebrity status. However, their statuses alone did not clinch their notoriety, for the newspapers and magazines of those and earlier years were filled with accounts and analyses of female homosexual practices and their consequences. Widespread press and magazine coverage facilitated the public intertextuality of lesbian practices and attempts (both successful and unsuccessful) of double suicide, although the majority of actors in these incidents were but names and statistics without faces. Doubtless, a widely publicized lesbian double suicide attempt on June 12, 1934, was familiar to Masuda and Saijō, just as the partners in that attempt were inspired to die after reading an article about a female student from Tokyo who jumped into the crater of Mt. Mihara on the offshore island of Ōshima. The student "took along a friend to attest to the act and inform the world of it" (Seidensticker 1990, 36).[21]

The June 1934 case concerned a love triangle involving a so-called masculinized female (age twenty-three) to whom two feminine females (ages eighteen and twenty-three) were attracted. All three worked at a Tokyo coffeeshop where the cross-dressed, mannish partner was a manager and the other two waitresses.[22] The many newspaper articles on the case quoted the women as recognizing that in society at present a bona fide love relationship was only possible as a couple and not as a threesome. Acting upon that realization, the "kindhearted" older feminine partner decided to withdraw from the group to simplify matters. One morning in early June she left suicide notes at her sister's and brother's homes and proceeded to a park where she swallowed an overdose of tranquilizers. She later recovered ("Dōseiai no onna san'nin shinjū" 1934; "Dōseiai no seisan" 1934).

Meanwhile, the couple had resolved, independently, to die together, and set out on a two-day suicide journey to the offshore island of Ōshima, where they planned to throw themselves into the volcanic crater. The masculine partner had chosen this particular mode of death, inspired by the aforementioned student's suicide there a year ago — apparently most suicidal females elected either to drown themselves or to swallow tranquilizers or sleeping pills (Komine 1985, 183). In an autobiographical account summarized below, she

Figure 4. The lesbian couple dejected at the failure of their suicide mission (from *Watashi wa koi no shorisha* 1934).

recounts how the pair spent the night at an inn, "thinking only of death," and how she held her partner close to her as they stood in the thick fog that hugged the coast (Sakuma 1934, 82).

Alerted by the siblings of the estranged partner, the press trailed the couple to Ōshima, updating readers on their whereabouts and activities. The masculine partner was described as sporting short hair and dressed like a man's-role-player in the all-female revue theater. She cut a dapper figure in her white knickerbockers, red jacket, two-tone shoes, and panama hat. The feminine partner wore a "Western-style" dress, short socks, and straw thongs. Guided by the island's residents, who had easily spotted the two climbers, the paparazzi caught up with the couple shortly after the proprietor of a summit teahouse, sensing their melancholia, had grabbed them as they headed toward the crater. One of the several photographs of the couple published in the press shows them standing together, heads bowed in dejection at having failed in their mission (fig. 4). Only after their capture did they learn from reporters of their estranged partner's attempted suicide two days earlier ("Watashi wa koi no shorisha" 1934).

Two months later, Sakuma Hideka, the masculine partner, published an autobiographical account of the incident in *Fujin Gahō* (Women's Illustrated News), a mainstream women's magazine. A staff reporter prefaced the account by claiming that "everyone has experienced homosexual love at least once, but no one has written about its mysteries until now" (qtd. in Sakuma 1934, 82). After asking for everyone's forgiveness, Sakuma dismisses categorically the rumors that were spread like wildfire through the press of her "father's alcoholism," her grandmother's "geisha past," her impoverished, dysfunctional family, and her alleged "biological maleness" and "ability to impregnate women." She criticizes sharply the newspapers' role in trivializing her ordeal by inviting readers to submit satirical songs about the incident (as the press did a year later in the Masuda-Saijō case) (Sakuma 1934, 82).

It is clear that Sakuma understood the link between economic autonomy and self-representation and subjectivity, for she makes the radical argument that, provided they can support themselves, why shouldn't two women (much less three) in love with each other be able to live together in the same way that heterosexual couples can and do? "I don't hate men, I've just felt closer to women since graduating from girl's high school [*jogakkō*]," she declares.[23] As for her so-called masculine appearance, Sakuma explains that "although I may have assumed a man's role, I am neither physically nor mentally malelike." And she stresses that by wearing trousers, she is not impersonating males but rather wearing what is most convenient and comfortable given the demands of her managerial job. Sakuma closes her narrative by lamenting her loneliness (Sakuma 1934, 83). Meanwhile, notoriety was good for business, and large, expensive ads for the coffeeshop where Sakuma worked began appearing in the press (e.g., *Asahi Shinbun* 1934b, 3).

More vividly than the actress Saijō's autobiographical account, the manager Sakuma's account suggests an apparently ironic connection between the resolve to commit suicide and the resolve to challenge on some level a family-state system that rendered women docile and subservient. Historically in Japan, suicide or attempted suicide was recognized, and to some extent valorized, as an empowering act that illuminated the purity and sincerity of one's position and intentions. A suicide letter corroborated these virtues by documenting one's motives. In other words, suicide was a culturally intelligible act that turned a private condition into a public matter.

Obviously, attempted (or unsuccessful) suicides have more direct political capital for, as in this case, the women live to tell in greater complexity about the circumstances informing their resolve to die, and they live to act on their resolve, and to encourage action on the sometimes radical vision articulated in their suicide notes. Saijō, for example, claims in her account that she was able to deal influentially with the Masuda family lawyer regarding the unprecedented establishment of a branch household for her masculine partner. And Sakuma's article about her attempted double suicide introduces to mainstream audiences ideas and arguments about self-representation and the connection between economics and gender ideology that were (and still are) quite radical.

Lesbian suicide and parasuicide letters and accounts collectively constituted another voice, whether explicitly controversial or defensive, or both, in heated public debates about the articulation of sexuality, gender ideology, cultural identity, and (inter)national image. Moreover, like acts and attempts of suicide itself, these texts, including those which doubled as love letters, were both a private exploration and a public proclamation — "public" because the art of writing letters consists in making one's views known to a correspondent, whether that person be a lover, parent, sibling, or anonymous reader. Suicide notes in this sense were an extension of, and not a substitution for, lesbian practices. Largely on account of the cultural intelligibility of suicide in Japan, stories of suicide and attempted suicide seem to have served, even if by default, as an effective way to get controversial ideas into print and integrated with the popular discourse of sexuality. I have reviewed the circumstances of only several of the hundreds of cases of lesbian suicide and parasuicide reported, yet these several cases generated a significant number of newspaper and magazine articles and analyses, whether sympathetic or hostile.

Clearly there is more to suicide than simply the "cultural appeal [in Japan] of masochistic behavior" (Lebra 1976, 200). Lesbian double suicides and attempted suicides were predicated on — and both used and criticized as a trope for — a revolt against the normalizing functions of "tradition" (qua the "Good Wife, Wise Mother") as sanctioned by the civil code. Double suicide itself was a mode of death eulogized and allegorized in literature, particularly since the late seventeenth century, but when linked with women's unconventional sexual affinities and practices, lesbian suicide and parasuicide accounts drew attention to the symbolic death of the traditional Japanese Woman and the emergence on the public stage of new and more complex female actors.

Notes

Archival and field research in Japan for parts of this project were facilitated by the following grants and fellowships: Japan Foundation Professional Fellowship (June–September 1987); Northeast Asia Council of the Association for Asian Studies Grant (June–September 1987); Social Science Research Council Research Grant (June–September 1987); University of California, San Diego, Japanese Studies Program Travel Grant (Summer 1987); University of California, San Diego, Affirmative Action Faculty Career Development Grant (July–September and November–June 1990); Fulbright Research Grant (January–August 1990 and September–October 1991); University of Michigan, Faculty Research Grant, Center for International Business Education (June 1992); University of Michigan, Center for Japanese Studies Faculty Grant (June 1994); Wenner-Gren Foundation for Anthropological Research Regular Grant (Fall 1995); Social Science Research Council and the American Council of Learned Societies, Advanced Research Grant (Fall 1995), and the Wissenschaftskolleg zu Berlin (1996–97). A greatly truncated version of this paper was presented at the American Anthropology Association annual meeting, December 2, 1994, in Atlanta, Georgia. Parts of this paper appear in my new book, *Takarazuka: Sexual Politics and Popular Culture in Modern Japan* (Berkeley: University of California Press, 1998). I wish to extend special thanks to Celeste Brusati for her insightful comments, and to Cindy Patton and Benigno Sanchez-Eppler for their interest and perseverance. All translations from Japanese to English are mine except when noted otherwise. Japanese names and authors published in Japanese are presented with the family name followed by the given name.

1   Saijō was a member of the all-female Shōchiku Revue, founded in Tokyo in 1928, fifteen years after its archrival, the Takarazuka Revue, was established in the city of Takarazuka near Osaka. The Shōchiku Revue later established an Osaka branch, and the Takarazuka Revue opened a Tokyo theater in 1934.

2   By the 1930s, the population of sixty-five million purchased ten million copies of daily newspapers, and the number of registered magazines and journals was 11,118. Print culture was available to all classes of consumers (Silverberg 1993, 123–24), and the Masuda-Saijō "love story" was circulated countrywide.

Fiction writers also capitalized on the erotics of lesbian double suicide. Tanizaki Junichirō's serial novel *Manji* (1928–30) focused on an obsessive triangulated relationship involving a married woman, a bisexual femme fatale, and the former's husband, and their attempted double (actually triple) suicide (Tanizaki 1995). My essay reports on actual cases of lesbian suicide and not on its representation in fiction.

3   The poem was subtitled, "The Philosophy of Suicide" (*Shinjū no fuirosofui*).

4   The Japanese text is in Ōhara 1965, 210. Verses two and three appear in English in Seidensticker 1990, 35, and I have deferred to his translation, with one exception: I changed the original *tengoku* in the third verse from "paradise" to "Heaven," to underscore the woman's Christian faith. The remaining verses are my translations.

5   While this method of gender assignment is most typical of, but not limited to, Anglo-Americans, the lack of specific information on the assignment and assumption of "female" or "male" gender among non-Anglos makes me reluctant to generalize for all Americans. To generalize a "Japanese" notion of gender admittedly is problematic, given the various ethnic groups comprising that surficially "homogeneous" society, although "Japanese" arguably is a more inclusive signifier than is "American."

In this connection, I should also note that although I am familiar with much of the scholarly literature on the relationships among cross-dressing, sexuality, and gender ideology, and cite some relevant sources, I have kept comparisons to a minimum, partly for reasons of space, but also because I am in a better position to provide otherwise inaccessible and stereotype-bending information about Japan that augments the larger — mostly Eurocentric — scholarly literature.

6   *Ome* or *ome no kankei* (male-female relations) were the expressions often used to identify lesbian couples. *Ome* is an abbreviation of *osu* and *mesu*, terms reserved to distinguish between male and female animals. They become pejorative when used to label humans, as in this case.

7   Roden does acknowledge in passing that it was the New Woman and not her male counterpart who "triggered" the debates about the relationships among sex, gender, and sexuality, although his essay as a whole suggests that unconventional males and females were criticized to equal degrees in the media (Roden 1990, 43).

The one exception to the overwhelming focus on the "woman problem" and its "problem women" was a Manichaean debate in the mass media about the place of the Kabuki *onnagata*, or woman's-role-player, in modern Japan: was he a naturalized and necessary tradition or unnatural, perverse, and anachronistic? As I discuss elsewhere (Robertson 1998b, 56–59), "tradition" won out over charges of perversity. Briefly, the valorization of "tradition" as part of the spiritual mobilization of the people during the wartime period (roughly 1931–45) included the promotion of Kabuki as a classical Japanese theater arts form, a status that insured its central place in the cultural archive of the Japanese Empire as a living symbol of Japanese cultural superiority.

8   I discuss at length the feminine and maternal personification of "Japanese tradition" in Robertson 1998a.

9   Parasuicide refers both to the attempted suicide and the "suicide gesture," usually in reference to individuals who are not actually trying to kill themselves (Buhrich and Loke 1988).

10   Among the major Anglophone works dealing with Japanese suicide are Benedict [1946] 1974; De Vos 1973; Lebra 1976; Pinguet [1984] 1993; and Seward 1968. Japanese works in which homosexual double suicide figures quite prominently include Komine 1985; Ōhara 1965, 1973; Tatai and Katō 1974; and Yamana 1931.

11   Recent works addressing lesbian practices include the "lesbian special issues" of the "alternative" journals *Bessatsu Takarajima* (1987) and *Imago* (1994); Furukawa 1994; Roden 1990; and Yoshitake 1986. Privately circulated newsletters (printed by women's/feminist/lesbian groups, for example) are another source of information about Japanese female sexualities.

12   For additional terminology, see Ōhara 1965, 186–87. I am not interested here in reviewing the sociopsychological literature on suicide, or in exploring the sociology of suicide per se. If the suicide actors were female, the prefix *joshi* or *josei* (female) preceded the generic (androcentric) expression. Another term used, albeit inconsistently, for ostensibly non-lesbian female same-sex suicide is *onna dōshi shinjū* (double suicide of like-minded girls/women).

13   This "naturalized link" was symbolized vividly by the brief deployment at the end of the war of kamikaze and suicide submarines (*raiden*), and by the mass suicides of Japanese civilians in Saipan (1944) and Okinawa (1945).

14   The details of this incident are drawn from Saijō's account unless otherwise indicated (Saijō 1935).

15   Saijō claims that her father urged her to stay close to Masuda, whom they felt was suicidal, until someone from the Masuda family could come and fetch her. Although Saijō's parents are rarely mentioned in the various accounts of the double suicide attempt, when they are, it is always in a kindly light.

16   If the story filed by a veteran reporter for the *Fujin Kōron* and friend of Saijō's father is accurate, then the actress's account is disingenuous. Apparently, the reporter interviewed a woozy Saijō after she had swallowed an overdose of sleeping pills. Following her back to her room, he found Masuda in a near coma and called for medical help (Nakano 1935).

17   *Mädchen in Uniform* was filmed by Leontine Sagan in Germany in 1931, based upon the play, *Yesterday and Today,* by Christa Winsloe, who also republished it as a novel, *The Child Manuela.* Ruby Rich interprets *Mädchen,* which takes place in a girls' boarding school, as a "film about sexual repression in the name of social harmony, about the absent patriarchy and its forms of presence, about bonds between women which represent attraction instead of repulsion, and about the release of powers that can accompany the identification of a lesbian sexuality. . . . [The film] offers a particularly clear example of the interplay between personal and collective politics — and the revolutionary potential inherent in the conjunction of the two" (Rich 1983, 44). A Japanese critic writing in 1935 declared that "the film [*Mädchen*] offers clues as to why female sexual perversion [*josei no seiteki tōsaku*] is increasing" ("Shōjo no hi no sei mondai" 1935).

18   The lectures in Japan during the months of March and April were part of Hirschfeld's world tour that year. While in Japan, Hirschfeld lectured at scholarly conferences on the "status of sex pathology," one of which was the first sexological lecture at the University of Tokyo, and gave public lectures in Tokyo and Osaka, which were sponsored by the *Asahi Shinbun,* a leading newspaper. Not only were all his lectures translated directly into Japanese, but Japanese abstracts of his talks were distributed to the audiences, and "long illustrated reports" of the University of Tokyo lecture were published in several medical journals (Hirschfeld 1935, 10–11). Hirschfeld's explorations and theories about homosexuality continue to be employed by Japanese social scientists, sexologists, and critics writing today (e.g., Watanabe 1990).

The "stage" in question is both the all-male Kabuki theater, and specifically the *onnagata,* or "woman's-role-player," and the all-female revue theater's *otokoyaku,* or "man's-role-player."

19   There are several Japanese books specifically on the subject of wills and suicide notes, including Ōhara 1963 and Yamana 1931.

20   Komine also tabulates the number of male homosexual double suicides (Komine 1985, 202–32). I have focused exclusively on lesbian double suicides.

21   Seidensticker writes that this particular suicide triggered a vogue for jumping into the same crater, and by the end of 1933, about a thousand people had plunged into it, the majority of whom were male (Seidensticker 1990, 36). Suicide and attempted suicide venues seem to follow trends, and in the 1930s a disproportionate number of people attempted to end their lives by hurling themselves into Mt. Mihara.

22   The press noted that the fact that all three lived with seventeen others in an attached dorm increased the likelihood of their lesbianism — an argument prem-

ised on a type of demographic determinism ("Dōseiai no onna san'nin shinjū" 1934).

23   Girls' schools and the all-female revues, along with their (unmarried) teachers and members, were singled out by sexologists and social critics as the sites and agents of homosexuality among females (Sugita 1935; Tamura 1913; Ushijima 1943; cf. Smith-Rosenberg 1985, 266, and Vicinus 1989) — thus, the critics' perception of the deleterious effects of the German film, *Mädchen in Uniform*, on girls and women.

DANIEL BOYARIN

Outing Freud's Zionism, or, the Bitextuality of the Diaspora Jew

Psychoanalysis is the Rashi-commentary on the present generation of Jews.
—Franz Kafka

On January 5, 1898, Sigmund Freud went to the theater (Masson 1985, 293). The play was Theodor Herzl's *Das neue Ghetto.* Very soon thereafter—if not that very night—he dreamed the dream that he later called "My Son the Myops."[1] Until now the significance of this marvelous conjunction of texts has been primarily "exploited" in readings of Freud's individual psychobiography. But its significance is much broader. The intertextual meeting of Freud and Herzl in Freud's dream constitutes a singularly illuminating moment in that multifold psychopolitical phenomenon known as the "Emancipation of the Jews," and the event is crucial for understanding not just that phenomenon but also psychoanalysis and Zionism as materially implicated in the history of sexuality, indeed in the invention of sexuality at the fin de siècle (Davidson 1992).

Freud recorded his dream as follows:

> On account of certain events which had occurred in the city of Rome, it had become necessary to remove the children to safety, and this was done. The scene was then in front of a gateway, double doors in the an-

cient style (the 'Porta Romana' at Siena, as I was aware during the dream itself). I was sitting on the edge of a fountain and was greatly depressed and almost in tears. A female figure—an attendant or nun—brought two boys out and handed them over to their father, who was not myself. The elder of the two was clearly my eldest son. I did not see the other one's face. The woman who brought out the boy asked him to kiss her good-bye. She was noticeable for having a red nose. The boy refused to kiss her, but, holding out his hand in farewell, said 'AUF GESERES' to her, and then 'AUF UNGESERES' to the two of us (or to one of us). I had a notion that the last phrase denoted a preference. (Freud 1955d, 269)

One of the most significant aspects of the "My Son the Myops" dream is the way that it produces a conjunction of political and sexual meanings. Freud's dream of a safe haven clearly thematizes a positive affect for Zionism (Frieden 1989, 120), but Zionism for Freud, and indeed for Herzl, was not simply a political program.[2] It was not even an alternative to assimilation with the culture of western Europe, but rather a fulfillment of the project of assimilation, as I have argued elsewhere (D. Boyarin 1997). Assimilation for these Jews was a sexual and gendered enterprise, an overcoming of the political and cultural characteristics that marked Jewish men as a "third sex," as queer in their world. For Freud, Zionism was motivated as much by the Oscar Wilde trials as by the Dreyfus trial.[3] It was a return to Phallustine, not to Palestine. Freud's sexualized politics is not so much about freedom from oppression as about passing. It is impossible to separate the question of Jewishness from the question of homosexuality in Freud's symbolic, textual world. In that world, passing, for Jews, entailed homosexual panic, internalized homophobia, and ultimately, aggression. The aggression, however, was turned in a surprising direction, as we shall see via a reading of Freud's most explicit text of Jewish politics, *Moses and Monotheism*.

The political meanings of the "Myops" dream are explicitly thematized in Freud's associations to it. After noting the connection with Herzl's play, Freud writes: "The Jewish problem, concern about the future of one's children, to whom one cannot give a country of their own, concern about educating them in such a way that they can move freely across frontiers" (Freud 1955e, 573). The phrase that provides the clearest associations with Herzl's play is "concern about educating them [the children] in such a way that they can move freely across frontiers."[4] The play, *The New Ghetto,* is explicitly founded on the premise that although physical walls have broken down between Jew and German, spiritual, cultural, and social walls are still in place. The "double doors in the ancient style," can be taken to refer to Jewish life in the ancient style, since, after all, Freud's word for *doors* is *Tore,* that is, via a typical dream-work pun, *Torah.* This verbal association would be strengthened by a visual connection with the double doors of the Holy Ark within which the Torah is kept in the Synagogue.

The dual doors, the Torah, are the gates of the new ghetto, the ghetto without walls in Herzl's play, that from which they must be able to escape. The phrase reflects Freud's conflicted desire that he educate his children in such a way that the borders between them and the gentiles would be broken down, that they would be able to cross freely that frontier — whether by conversion or, more likely, by assimilation. Freud, like Herzl, at a deep level wished to be recognized as a complete and authentic member of German *Kultur,* in no way different from others. At the same time, though, like Herzl he wished to remain Jewish while abandoning Judaism — not only the religion itself but all the cultural practices that divide Jews from gentiles.

Such a wish is, of course, a highly ambivalent one, and it is no wonder, therefore, that "My Son the Myops" is a highly ambivalent dream. The most obvious site (literally) of ambivalence in the dream is the role of "Rome" in it. "On account of certain events which had occurred in the city of Rome, it had become necessary to remove the children to safety, and this was done. The scene was then in front of a gateway, double doors in the ancient style (the 'Porta Romana' at Siena, as I was aware during the dream itself). I was sitting on the edge of a fountain and was greatly depressed and almost in tears." To this part of the dream, Freud contributes the association: "By the waters of Babylon, there we sat down, and there we wept when we remembered Zion." This verse from Psalm 137 refers to the exile from Jerusalem, and it is clearly this association that provides the occasion of sitting by the fountain and weeping. But Jerusalem has been "converted" in Freud's dream-wishes into Rome. The waters of Babylon are the fountain at Siena, at the Porta Romana, the gates that lead to Rome. By the waters of Siena, there we sat down, and there we wept, when we remembered Roma. It is Rome that is the object of desire here. Freud's next associations to his desire to educate the children so that they can freely cross frontiers would mean, then, to educate them so that they can return to Rome, the locale of the gentile oppressor as well. It is, after all, not surprising that Rome should function in this way for Freud, given the role that classical learning, *Bildung,* played in his cultural aspirations and achievements, as in those of most Viennese Jews. The salvation of the Jews will come when they are no longer distinguishable as Jews.

There is more evidence for this conflation of Jerusalem and Rome in Freud's thoughts, that is, for his desire for a Jewishness that would be indistinguishable from gentility. In the dream, Freud refers to taking the children to safety, and through one set of associations to "GESERES"/"UNGESERES," via *ungesäurt,* unleavened bread, to the flight to safety from Egypt. But in his interpretative associations, Freud supplies a reference to another threat to the safety of children. He writes that he and Fliess had passed the door of a physician called Dr. Herodes, and Freud had jokingly remarked, "Let us hope that our colleague does not happen to be a children's doctor" (Freud 1955e, 574). In the Gospel of Matthew, Joseph saw in a dream that Herod was going to kill the baby Jesus, and fled *into* Egypt. Herod flew into a rage, and had all of the male children in the region of Bethlehem killed, and thus "was fulfilled what was spoken by the prophet Jeremiah: 'A voice was heard in Ramah, wailing and loud lamentation' " (Matt. 2:13–18). Obviously, the Matthew pericope is itself a Christian typological reading of the slaughter of the innocents in Egypt by Pharaoh, and the threat to the Christ child by the ambiguously Jewish king and a flight into Egypt from Palestine are a typological, reversed rewriting of that story. (For Matthew in general, as is well known, Jesus is a Moses antitype). Freud himself refers to the etymology of GESERES, from the Hebrew/Yiddish *goiser,* "to decree evil." Pharaoh's determination to kill all the male Israelite infants is named by this verb in the Pesach liturgy, and this returns as well in the Matthew allusion, for GESERES, as Freud himself reveals, was (Viennese? Galician?) Yiddish slang for weeping and wailing.

It is, however, of a piece with the rest of the evidence brought forward here that for Freud, the Christian version and the "Jewish" version of the salvation of children through flight, through crossing borders, are completely conflated, paralleling the conflation of Rome and Jerusalem. This assimilation of Jewish to Christian allusions is, moreover, doubled by Freud's repeated reference to Pesach as Easter in his text: "In their flight out of Egypt the Children of Israel had not time to allow their dough to rise and, in memory of this, they eat unleavened bread to this day *at Easter*" (Freud 1955e, 574; emphasis added; cf. Frieden 1989, 124–25).[5] Freud's famous parapractic confusion of when his meeting with Fliess had taken place, whether at Christmas or Easter, seems also related to his confounding of the Exodus flight from Egypt at Pesach/Easter with the Gospel flight into Egypt at Christmas.

It is no wonder that such dream-thoughts were stimulated by a day residue of Herzl's play.[6] As Jacques Kornberg has written, "Herzl experienced intense Jewish self-disdain and feelings of inferiority, but he was also animated by feelings of Jewish pride, loyalty, and solidarity. In this sense the contempt for Jews Herzl was struggling with was, not least, his own. That he struggled with it instead of succumbing to it makes the term *ambivalence* the operative one in describing Herzl's attitude" (Kornberg 1993, 2).

The ambivalence underlying wishes for Jewish assimilation, like other performances of colonial mimicry, is deeply embedded in issues of both gender and sexuality. Pressures to assimilate were exacerbated in the case of the fin-de-siècle Jews by the invention of heterosexuality, and thus of homosexual panic, that was proceeding in just that chronotope. Gerard Beritela, accordingly, reads the "Myops" dream as about conflicted homoeroticism. Going to Rome represents desire directed originally toward his nephew John, whom Freud explicitly identifies with his "martial ideals" and Hannibal fantasies (Freud 1955d, 196–97), and then toward Fliess (Beritela 1993). Strong support for Beritela's argument can be offered from a different dream reported in another of the Fliess letters, written several months before the "Myops" dream, in which Freud writes quite explicitly:

> Thus the dream had fulfilled my wish to meet you in Rome rather than in Prague. My longing for Rome is, by the way, deeply neurotic. It is connected with my high school hero worship of the Semitic Hannibal, and this year in fact I did not reach Rome any more than he did from Lake Trasimeno. Since I have been studying the unconscious, I have become so interesting to myself. A pity that one always keeps one's mouth shut about the most intimate things.
>
> Das Beste was Du weisst,
>
> Darfst Du den *Buben* doch nicht sagen.
>
> [The best that you know, you may not tell the boys.] (Masson 1985, 285; original emphasis)

This "*meshugene* letter," as Freud dubbed it, is riveting. Freud recognizes that his dream of meeting Fliess in Rome is based in some deep and hidden range of his psyche. He connects it with Hannibal's desire for Rome and with his own identification with Hannibal. Hannibal is explicitly marked as a figure for the Jew (Semitic) in the text, and his desire (like Freud's) is to possess — and perhaps destroy — Rome, the gentile (Freud 1955d, 196). Rome thus occupies a highly equivocal position within the economy of desires that this letter projects, the ambivalence of possessing and being possessed that is eroticism itself.

Finally, we have the revealing segue into the quotation from Goethe, an allusion to an explicitly pederastic context; the speaker is Mephistopheles, "that old pederast" (Heller 1981, 95). The secret, then, that Freud cannot reveal, that most intimate thing, seems very likely to be the secret of his desire for Fliess. This interpretation is further confirmed by Freud's own reflections in *The Interpretation of Dreams,* where he writes that his Hannibal fantasies were traceable back to the very early relationship with his nephew John, an attraction whose erotic dimensions Freud himself remarked (1955d, 198) and that he himself connected with his later need to have "an intimate friend and a hated enemy," which ideally "come together in a single individual" (Freud 1955e, 483). The "official" oedipal interpretation of Grinstein (1980, 90–91) rewrites the homoerotic components of the Rome ambivalence as screens for desire for the mother, thus, like Freud himself repressing his homoerotic desire. Furthermore, Jones, anticipating Eve Sedgwick (1985), already realized that the "hunting in couples" aspect of Freud's connection with John is homoerotic in nature; the two of them used to engage in mutual sex play with John's sister Pauline (Jones 1953, 1:11). Finally, as McGrath sagely remarks, the Hannibal story itself has a well-known homosexual component in the guise of a Livian story of homosexual relationships between Hannibal and Hasdrubal (McGrath 1986, 66).

Late in the "Myops" dream, two boys are presented by a female figure. Freud writes: "[She] handed them over to their father, who was not myself. The elder of the two was clearly my eldest son" (Freud 1955e, 441). Freud is not their father, but at least one of them is Freud's son. The simplest resolution of this paradox is that Freud is their mother. The denial represents, then, an assertion. These boys have two male parents. As Beritela notes, this proposition is doubled at the end of the dream, when Freud writes that the boy greets "the two of us (or [the] one of us)." Since a child cannot—both "in reality" and because of censorship—have two male parents, the two have to be collapsed into one: "who was not myself/or the one of us." Beritela explains the otherwise unexplained association with Fliess in the text, one that Freud himself refers to as a "sudden association" (Freud 1955e, 443): "I remembered how, during the previous Easter, my Berlin friend and I had been walking through the streets of Breslau." It is thus Fliess who is the unnamed father of Freud's child in the Rome dream, which also takes place at "Easter."

But of course we must once more pay attention to Freud's famous confounding of Easter and Christmas. The meeting had actually taken place, not at Easter at all, but at Christmas. Above I have read this as the product of a conflation of the flight *from* Egypt—Easter (read Passover)—with the flight *into* Egypt—Christmas. Under the sign of the sexual interpretation, however, this confusion is further overdetermined. On this reading, it is more to the point that Freud has suppressed "Christmas" than that he has mentioned "Easter."[7] As Luxon suggests (1995), since, as Geller and others have shown, Freud's desire is to bear Fliess's baby (Geller 1992, 265–66), then if "Easter" is a slip for "Christmas," Freud has already "sublimated" his desire to have Fliess's baby into a fantasy of bypassing sex with Fliess—of conceiving miraculously. If we read Freud's letter to Fliess, it becomes clear that such conception would be through the ear, just as the Immaculate Conception of Mary was through the ear: "I am looking forward to our congress as to the slaking of hunger and thirst. I bring nothing but two open ears and one temporal lobe lubricated for reception" (Masson 1985, 193; cf. Jones 1951).[8] Beritela's sexual reading of "My Son the Myops" is very well-grounded indeed.

Given the "racialized" construction of sexuality—or is it a sexualized construction of race?—prevalent in fin de siècle central Europe, it is not surprising to find that in Freud's text the sexual and the political are so perfectly superimposed on one another. In confluence of the erotic and political themes in the "My Son the Myops" dream, the ambivalence about homoeroticism that it manifests is directly and intimately related to the theme of Jewish assimilation that Freud himself read in it.

Beritela argues that Freud's insistence in the dream that the city is both Rome and not-Rome cannot be explained convincingly, as Freud himself did, by the fact that he had never seen the actual Rome—a city for which a multitude of images existed—but must, in fact, be a screen for ambivalence. And

Rome indeed would have carried a whole set of complicated associations for
Freud, ranging from the original Roman Empire to the hegemony of Christian culture (the nun in the "Myops" dream) within his life-world (Masson
1985, 449).[9] These signifiers were both objects of enormous desire—culture,
learning, *Bildung*—as well as enemies and oppressors. This very nun, moreover, is transparently a figure for the elderly Catholic woman whom Freud
claims stimulated him sexually in early childhood and thus, on his own interpretation, made him queer (D. Boyarin 1994a). Note the ambivalence in
the portrait of this nun. On the one hand, she was a nurturing figure; on the
other, she has the prototypical red nose of the stereotyped drunken gentile of
eastern European Jews. She wants to kiss the boy, but he refuses. Rome is thus
overdetermined as both the site of desired homoerotic congress and the location of the gentile oppressor. Rome is split into the good, male, "Protestant"
Rome (*Bildung*, "the head of a Roman citizen" in Freud's study [Torgovnick
1990, 196–97]) and the bad, female, Catholic Rome (the nun).[10]

The situation of the European Diaspora male Jew—frequently elided as
"the Jew," tout court (in this essay, when I use the term "Jew," read European, male Jew)—as politically disempowered produced a sexualized interpretation of him as queer, because political passivity was in Freud's world
equated precisely with homosexuality. As John Fout has written, "The male
homosexual was portrayed as sickly, effeminate, perverse, and out of control, just the opposite of the 'normal' male, who was physically strong and
active, the head of the family, dominant in the public world of politics at home
and abroad, and in complete control of his sexuality and his emotions. The
male homosexual only personified female characteristics, such as passivity
and physical and emotional weaknesses" (Fout 1992, 413). These "female characteristics" are, as well, of course, the very characteristics that were identified
as belonging to the Jew—by anti-Semites and Zionists.

Diaspora is accordingly queer, and an end to Diaspora would be the equivalent of becoming straight. The fact, then, that political Zionism was invented
precisely at the time of the invention of heterosexuality is entirely legible.
The dominant male of Europe, the "Aryan," is the one who is already "physically strong and active, the head of the family, dominant in the public world
of politics at home and abroad," and thus not queer, so an assimilation that
would lend the male Jew these characteristics would accomplish the same
heterosexualizing project as Zionism. Freud himself seems to conflate these

two schemes for inventing straight, male, modern Jews. It is, according to this view, no accident that *Moses and Monotheism* was written at the same moment in Freud's life when he was identifying the "repudiation of femininity" as the "bedrock of psychoanalysis"—but I anticipate my argument below. The "Zionist" elements of the dream thus fit perfectly with the homoerotic ones, that is, as their negation. Freud's Zionism outs itself as homophobia.

Freud himself drew the analogy between the sexual and the political, between the situation of the individual, sexually passive, "inverted," humiliated Jew and the Jewish people as a whole—and between himself and the collective status of Jews. Associations between "passivity" and humiliation were all-pervasive in the culture of Europe.[11] In a passage from the "Wolf Man" case history, Freud describes an incident in which the Wolf Man's sister had played with his penis when he was "still very small." Freud concludes that the patient had developed fantasies of active sexual aggression toward his sister that "were meant to efface the memory of an event which later on seemed offensive to the patient's masculine self-esteem, and they reached this end by putting an imaginary and desirable converse in the place of the historical truth. . . . *These phantasies, therefore, corresponded exactly to the legends by means of which a nation that has become great and proud tries to conceal the insignificance and failure of its beginnings*" (Freud 1955c, 20; emphasis added). As Madelon Sprengnether has remarked, "Freud's comment on this episode reveals the extent to which he associates it with the kind of sexual humiliation he had experienced at the hands of his own nannie" (Sprengnether 1990, 72).

This passage provides the hermeneutic key for a deeper understanding of the political/cultural situation of the Jews within which psychoanalysis was produced: the memory of a situation that seemed offensive to Freud's masculine self-esteem was effaced by putting an imaginary and desirable converse in place of the historical truth. "Feminine" Jewish passivity coded as homosexual and experienced as shameful for "real men," was to be rewritten as an originary, "manly" aggressiveness, an imaginary and desirable converse indeed. And Freud's gratuitous political remark is a perfect précis for *Moses and Monotheism.* This is Freud's "family Romance," writ large as the family romance of the Jewish people.

"Male" was encoded within this culture as spiritual, "abstractly sublime," incorporeal, powerful, and universal, and this is precisely how Freud (and others of his time and place) described the "true" Judaism, directly counter to those representations of it as a feminine religion, primitive, physical, carnal, and weak. One such account of the time has it that "Semites are like women in that they lack the Indo-German capacity for philosophy, art, science, warfare, and politics. They nevertheless have a monopoly on one sublime quality: religion, or love of God. This Semitic monism goes hand in hand with a deep commitment to female monogamy. The masculine behavior of the Indo-German, who masters the arts and sciences in order to dominate the natural world, is met with the Semite's feminine response of passivity and receptivity. As the wife is subject to her husband, so the Semites are absolutely permeable to the God who chose them" (Olender 1992, 110, paraphrasing Rudolph Friedrich Grau [1835–93]).

The religiosity and spirituality of the "Semite" are depicted here as a female sexuality. Monotheism equals "natural" female monogamy. The early Nazi theologian, Reinhold Seeberg, held similar views, writing of "the essential Semite character in its leaning toward religion, whereas the Indo-Europeans lean more to critical scholarly thought. The latter would, so to speak, represent the masculine element, the Semites the feminine" (Seeberg 1923, 111; qtd. in Briggs 1985, 250).[12]

Freud's *Moses and Monotheism* is best read as part of a massive sociocultural attempt by German-speaking Jews in the nineteenth century to rewrite themselves and particularly their male selves as Aryans, and especially as Teutons.[13] In order to do so, they engaged in a rereading of the biblical and postbiblical past, emphasizing in that past exactly what traditional rabbinic Judaism had deemphasized, namely, its martial aspects. These Jews were caught in a terrible double bind, most eloquently described by Gilman: "Become like us — abandon your difference — and you may be one with us," but "[t]he more you are like me, the more I know the true value of my power, which you wish to share, and the more I am aware that you are but a shoddy counterfeit" (Gilman 1986, 2). Since they were vilified as female and opportunistic because of their Jewishness, conversion to Christianity was no escape for these Jews, because it only confirmed the stereotype of opportunism and lack of manliness. The solution that they hit on was to reconstruct themselves, via a reconstruction of the Jewish past, as virtual Aryans, thus providing the impetus for the mimicry that I have been discussing. An entire Jewish collective — including its Orthodox members (Ellenson 1994) — engaged in a project of the assimilation of Jewish culture to *Kultur,* and this included an assimilation of

Judaism itself to Protestantism, the sublime faith, and much of this assimilation of Judaism involved the reconstruction of gendered roles.[14] A striking confirmation of this interpretation has recently been provided by Paula E. Hyman, who argues that the retained and even deepening religious loyalty of German Jewish women in comparison to their husbands, was not a counter to assimilation but a form of assimilation, because "[m]en and women alike within Western Jewish communities adopted the dominant middle-class view that women were responsible for inculcating moral and religious consciousness in their children and within the home more generally. According to this view, women were also the primary factor in the formation of their children's Jewish identity. *The conservative role of maternal keeper of the domestic flame of Judaism became a fundamental aspect of the project of assimilation*" (Hyman 1995, 27; emphasis added).[15] Rather than the conversion of the Jews, the total conversion of Judaism was the solution. As Hyman stunningly concludes, "the Mother in Israel" was but "a Jewish version of the American 'True Woman' " (28).

Without in any way denying that Jewish culture, like any other, was subject to critique and "modernization," I would categorically assert that the efforts of German-speaking Jews at a "purposeful, even programmatic dissociation from traditional Jewish cultural and national moorings" was a form of colonial mimicry, such as best anatomized in Frantz Fanon's *Black Skin, White Masks,* and one that was predicated on an "Orientalist" reification of traditional Jewish culture as a mere "social pathology" (Aschheim 1982, 5–6).[16]

As the terms of anti-Semitism would predict, the conversion of Judaism involved primarily a gendered discourse, a massive attempt to rewrite the Jewish male of the past as indeed a man. Among the traits that Goethe considered that the Jew would have to give up in order to be acceptable to German society were "wild [read hysterical] gesticulations" and "effeminate movements" (Aschheim 1982, 7). Freud's original title for *Moses and Monotheism,* "The Man Moses and Monotheist Religion," was much closer to its cultural import (Van Herik 1982, 175), for Freud's whole point was to argue that Hebrew monotheism was a religion of manliness, self-defense, and self-control, in order to efface the "effeminate" Jewish difference of Judaism and rewrite it as "manly" Protestantism *avant la lettre*.[17] The analogy between the autobiographical and the political is compelling. Shades of the Wolf Man.[18]

Let us begin as Freud does, with Moses himself and his name. Echoing the plausible philological reading of the name as a reflex of the Egyptian *Mose* that forms theophoric names such as *Thutmose* and so on, Freud then makes a very strange move. He writes: "Now we should have expected that one of the many people who have recognized that 'Moses' is an Egyptian name would also have drawn the conclusion or would at least have considered the possibility that the person who bore this Egyptian name may himself have been an Egyptian. In relation to modern times we have no hesitation in drawing such conclusions, . . . though a change of name or the adoption of a similar one in fresh circumstances is not beyond possibility" (Freud 1955f, 9). Freud himself bore an "Aryan" name. His name had been changed, to be sure, but the "original," Sigismund, the name of an early modern Polish king known for his friendliness toward Jews (Klein 1985, 46), was *historically* just as gentile as Sigmund—although in Freud's time it was a stereotypically Jewish name (Gilman 1993b, 70; see also Pellegrini forthcoming). "In relation to modern times we have no hesitation in drawing such conclusions," ergo, Sigmund must have been an Aryan. Freud's sublimation of the Jewish child Moses into the Egyptian prince Mose, via the forgetting of his own name, strongly supports the readings of this text as Freud's own family novel—he actually called it *ein Roman*—his own fantasy that he is not the child of the abject Schelomo ben Jakob but Oedipus, son of Laius, or Hannibal, son of Hamilcar. The implication of Freud's own argument, then, is that he himself "may have been" an Aryan. This family romance for Freud and for the entire Jewish people is borne out throughout the work.

Freud's descriptions of biblical religion are tendentious, to say the least. Thus, near the beginning of the second essay, he writes: "Some of these differences [between the Jewish religion attributed to Moses and the religion of Egypt] may easily be derived from the fundamental contrast between a strict monotheism and an unrestricted polytheism. Others are evidently the result of a difference in spiritual and intellectual [the German word for both is *geistig*] level, since one of these religions is very close to primitive phases [of development], while the other has risen to the heights of sublime abstraction" (Freud 1955f, 19). It is not often noted how wildly inappropriate either of these adjectives is when attributed to biblical religion, which was neither a "strict" monotheism, nor had it risen to the "heights of sublime abstraction."[19] Take, for instance, the common misapprehensions that the Bible forbids pictorial representation of any kind and that God is necessarily invisible because wholly spiritual. Neither of these two popular dogmas corresponds to what we actually find in the biblical text, as a result of which the obvious meaning of that text is typically revised by its readers (D. Boyarin 1990).

The rewriting of the history of Judaism, Kantian, Hegelian, and Platonic-Pauline in its impulses, has been going on for so long and been so successful that we think we recognize Judaism in such descriptions. Thus, typically, Judaism is thought of as the religion of abstract thought and as indifferent or hostile to aesthetics. Renan, however, only a little more than a century ago thought differently. For him the "Aryan" was characterized by "abstract metaphysics," while the "Semite" represented poetry; the Aryan scientific reason, the Semite religious feeling; the Aryan philosophy, the Semite music (Olender 1992, 78). It is clear how this maps onto Rousseau's and Kant's distinction between the female beautiful and the male sublime (Lloyd 1993, 75). Moreover, as Lloyd further remarks (without noticing the theological subtext), for Hegel, "Divine Law" (i.e., the Jew), insofar as it is concerned with "duties and affections towards blood relatives," is the "nether world" and "is also the domain of women" (81). Freud's narrative both accepts and contests this picture. To be sure, the Jews of Freud's day are "atavistic," "fossilized," caught in a world of superstitious ritual, feminized, but it was not always so; once they were as sublime as Aryans, and it is that sublime, Aryan-like, true Mosaic tradition that Freud seeks to recover and revive.

As Eric Santner notes, Weininger had written that "[i]t is, however, this Kantian rationality, this Spirit, which above all appears to be lacking in the Jew and the woman" (Weininger 1975, 411; qtd. in Santner 1996, 185 n. 35). Weininger, of course, was right. Traditional Judaism has very little to do with Kantianism. The desperation to make this not be so becomes nearly an obsession in the writings of Freud's Jewish contemporaries (Ellenson 1994, 15), as in Derrida's paraphrase of Hermann Cohen: "Let us go directly, by way of a beginning, to the clearest proposition, the firmest and, for us, the most interesting one: the close, deep internal kinship (*die innerste Verwandschaft*) between Judaism and Kantianism. That is to say also between Judaism and the historical culmination (*geschichtliche Höhepunkt*) of idealism as the essence of German philosophy, namely, the Kantian moment, the inner sanctum (*innerste Heiligtum*) which Kantianism is, with its fundamental concepts (the autonomy of universal law, liberty, and duty)" (Derrida 1991, 48–49). Whatever its other parameters, Kant's sublime comprises also the move toward abstraction that Freud would refer to as sublimation (*Sublimierung*) and Lacan as *Aufhebung* (Lacan 1985, 82). Kant himself had written that the commandment against making graven images or idols (Exod. 20:4) is "the most sublime passage in the Jews' book of laws" (qtd. in Olender 1992, 160).[20] In Kant's definition, the "sublime is directly concerned with the unrepresentable. It calls for detachment from sensibility (from perceptible forms) in order to accede to the experience of a supersensible faculty within us" (Goux 1990, 141). But as I—and others—have shown in earlier work, the prohibition on graven images of God in biblical religion has little or nothing to do with a putative unrepresentability of God. If, as Goux writes, "nothing that can be the object of the senses can, strictly speaking, be considered sublime," then the biblical God, the seeing of Whom is the *summum bonum* of religious life, can hardly be described as sublime (D. Boyarin 1990).

Kant may have been in some ways "the Jewish philosopher" as is sometimes claimed, but his "Jewishness" is only so by virtue of the Kantianism of German Judaism (Ellenson 1994).[21] One German ultra-Orthodox leader wrote, "Blessed be God, who in His wisdom created Kant! Every real Jew who seriously and honestly studies the 'Critique of Pure Reason' is bound to pronounce his 'Amen' on it" (qtd. in Ellenson 1994, 23). This sublimation of Judaism is, however, a sort of fetish, recognizing and disavowing at the same time the connections between Judaism and the religions of "primitives," especially insofar as rites like circumcision are shared among these (see Geller 1993, 55).[22] Eilberg-Schwartz, in *The Savage in Judaism* (1990), has both exposed how inadequate such descriptions of Judaism are and described the cultural processes by which Judaism came to be so rewritten in modernity. Among their tendentious characteristics, such descriptions of the history of Judaism require an assumption—explicit in the work of Wellhausen—that the "priestly" aspects of the Bible, such as food taboos and purity rituals, were the products of a late degeneration of Israelite religion and not its pure fountainhead.[23] It follows, of course, that Orthodox Jewish adherence to such ritual behavior marks Judaism as both "degenerate" and primitive with respect to Christianity, but according to these scholars this is only true of the "late corrupt form" of Judaism.[24] Freud at once accepts and defends against this Protestant interpretation of Judaism. For him, as for the German Protestant Bible scholars, the "true Jew" was nothing like the priest-ridden ritualist projected in the

Torah. Freud's defense of Judaism ends up almost identical to the anti-Semitic denunciation of it.

Masculine renunciation and its links to the putative triumph of spirituality over the senses is the essence of Freud's argument in *Moses and Monotheism.* It is the sublimation of the sensible penis in the unrepresentable — thus sublime — (veiled; cf. 2 Cor. 3:13) phallus that is at issue here, and this implies the sublimation of the Jewish people.[25] Where the Jews have been accused of carnality and, therefore of being like women, Freud (like Philo before him) would demonstrate that they are more spiritual, and more rational, than the Others, and therefore more masculine than the accusers themselves (Lloyd 1993). In other words, Freud did not set out to explain the prohibition on images of God in a psychoanalytical framework; Freud set out to counter anti-Semitic charges that Jews are not spiritual but carnal, female and not male. Moreover, after the turn of the century, Freud was very busily, almost frantically, engaged in disavowing his own homosexual desires (D. Boyarin 1994a). This "repression" was produced in the context of the virulent anti-Semitism and homophobia, which were one and the same movement, Adolph Stoecker's "Christian Values" movement, in Germany in his time (Fout 1992, 405; see also Gilman 1991b, 180). The last thing Freud would have wanted to do, at the onset of the Nazi genocide of Jews and homosexuals (Moeller 1994), was to confront the feminization/homoeroticization of the male Jew in relation to God. Eilberg-Schwartz has provided dramatic confirmation for this reading of Freud's work (Eilberg-Schwartz 1994, 39). He shows that Freud drew back from a conclusion that seems ineluctable from his argument, namely that monotheism predicts representations of the male worshipper as feminized vis-à-vis the male God and as a fantasized erotic object for the male God, thus producing the tension that leads eventually to the de-anthropomorphizing — the unmanning, if you will — of the deity. Eilberg-Schwartz explains Freud's reluctance to come to this conclusion as a product of his fear that it would amount to representing Jewish men as feminized, thus playing into the hands of that representation of himself as Jewish male that he was trying so hard to avoid.

I wish to pursue this reading further. It is not only the case, as Eilberg-Schwartz has it, that Freud seems to hold back from a conclusion to which his own theory leads him, namely, the avoidance of homoeroticism giving rise to the abstraction of God, but more: there is an active contradiction within his discourse. Renunciation of the fulfillment of desire, which is encoded in Freud's text as masculine, is occasioned by a submissiveness vis-à-vis a male Other, whether it be the "great man" Moses or the deity. But that very submissiveness, the mark of the religious person, was itself feminizing in the terms of nineteenth-century culture. The "higher," that is, the more "masculine," that Judaism gets, the "lower," that is, the more "feminine," its adherents become. Freud's constant skirting and finessing of this issue are the mark of the true tension that generates the text.

The Jewish male, having been vilified for hundreds of European years as feminized, and this no longer — after the rise of heterosexuality — being readable as a mark of resistance and honor by the "emancipated" Jew, set out to reinstate himself as manly, in the terms of the masculinist European culture that had rejected and abused him (Hoberman 1994). He sought "manliness." And perhaps the most revealing part of *Moses and Monotheism* is the disquisition on the qualities of the "great man" that Freud delivers in the third essay (Freud 1955f, 107–11). This passage introduces his section on "The Advance in Intellectuality" — his term for the historical situation of Judaism. In his various attempts to define what it is to be a "great man," Freud immediately discards chess masters, virtuosi on musical instruments, distinguished artists, and scientists, but unhesitatingly declares, nevertheless, that Goethe, Leonardo da Vinci, and Beethoven were great men (108).[26] He believes that a closer approximation to the category will be found among "men of action — conquerors, generals, rulers" (109), but ultimately decides that "all the characteristics with which we equipped the great man are paternal characteristics, and that the essence of great men for which we vainly searched lies in this conformity. The decisiveness of thought, the strength of will, the energy of action are part of the picture of a father — but above all the autonomy and independence of the great man, his divine unconcern which may grow into ruthlessness" (109–10). Whatever else is going on here, it is precisely the modes of achievement characteristic of Jews in Freud's world — science, performing music, and chess — that are excluded as defining of "greatness." Strikingly enough, artists are left out as well, but somehow the Aryan artists Goethe and Beethoven are in. It would be very hard, indeed, to imagine a Jewish cultural paradigm within which "autonomy, independence, and divine unconcern" not to speak of "ruthlessness" are ideal characteristics of the male.

In his study of the Schreber case, in a chapter entitled "Schreber's Jewish Question," Eric Santner has focused on yet another aporia of *Moses and
Monotheism*. He writes that "for Freud, the ethically oriented monotheism
of the Jews and the historical condition of diaspora are linked by a series of
traumatic cuts: of the deity from plastic representation; of spirituality from
magic, animism, and sexual excess; of the passions from their violent enact-
ments; of the people from a territory conceived as proper to them. These various modalities of loss, separation, and departure, which Freud views as so
many forms of the instinctual renunciation (*Triebverzicht*) that undergirds the
rule of law in the most general sense, procure for the Jews what he calls 'their
secret treasure,' namely a sense of self-confidence and superiority with regard
to pagan cultures whose spirituality has remained, as he puts it, 'under the
spell of sensuality' [Freud 1955f, 115]" (Santner 1996, 122). Santner points out
that Freud has a great deal of difficulty, however, in accounting for this "secret
treasure," not being able to clearly articulate just why a "set-back to sensuality" should have such a powerful effect in raising the self-regard of individuals or peoples. Freud writes that "[w]e are faced by the phenomenon that
in the course of the development of humanity sensuality is gradually overpowered by intellectuality and that men feel proud and exalted by every such
advance. But we are unable to say why this should be so" (Freud 1955f, 118).
Freud's final response to this aporia is to discover an "uncanny secretion of
jouissance within the precincts of the moral law" (Santner 1996, 124), a sensual ascetic rapture (*einem neuen Rausch moralischer Askese*) in the very renunciations of sensuality. Santner keenly comments:

> What Freud discovers as a paradoxical kernel of jouissance within the
> domain of an otherwise austere, Kantian moral universe is, as Boyarin
> has rightly noted, occasioned, *in Freud's narrative,* by submissiveness to
> a "great man." But that narrative construction was itself generated by
> an impasse in his argument apropos of the Jewish valuation of *Geistig-
> keit.* Freud was unable to imagine a resolution of that impasse—the im-
> possibility of accounting for the value of this value—outside the terms
> of the "father complex." Freud's "great man" fills a gap, a missing link
> in his argumentation about the emergence of a new cultural value. But
> to follow Freud here, as I think Boyarin does, is to miss, once more,
> the encounter with this missing link. To interpret Freud's failure as the

avoidance of a homoeroticism implied by his own narrative domesticates the impasse on which Freud's interpretation founders, the impasse
that called his narrative into being in the first place. (Santner 1996, 124;
original emphasis)

Santner's comment is profoundly cogent, revealing a dimension in the
European imaginary of the Jew, the woman, and the queer as an "abjection,
the experience of something rotten within" that "signifies a cursed knowledge
of jouissance, which only by way of a kind of secondary revision becomes
legible as 'homosexuality,' 'femininity,' or 'Jewishness'" (Santner 1996, 125).
This "secondary revision," however, is only for Schreber the Aryan, for the
one to whom femininity and Jewishness can be put on and taken off. The Jew
Freud is mostly too busy trying to get the Aryan phallus, to get "invested"
with it to experience such cursed knowledges — except, of course, for the one
very significant moment that Santner spotlights, that brief gap when *Jewissance* is glimpsed by Freud.

Freud's impasse is occasioned by his very assumption that Judaism is to be
characterized as a compelling renunciation of the senses (the mother) for the
spirit (the father, phallus, logos), and that this renunciation has generated in
the Jew, from the time of Moses, a sense of superiority with respect to pagans,
that is, a sense of profound well-being in a world that is hostile and threatening to Jews. But there is hardly any reason to think that this was the way
ancient Israelites imagined themselves — neither as superior by reason of renunciation nor as particularly threatened. I think, rather, that it is, if anything,
a parental or erotic intimacy with God, being the object of God's desire, that
would have described their sense of being special — *Gott der Tatte,* not *Gott
der Vater.* In other words, the first point that should be absolutely clear and
obvious is that Freud is concerned not at all with Moses or the Bible but with
the situation of Jews in his own time.

Freud's very description of Moses's "advances" and the aporia that it produces for him is, in the first instance, a desperate grab for this Spirit (phallus)
that Weininger had denied the Jew, a signifier of his profound need to ward
off, not so much homoeroticism, as in Eilberg-Schwartz's account, but femininity. Freud is then genuinely troubled by the question of why, having mis-
read Judaism as such an austere, desiccated, incorporeal renunciation of the
senses, Jews should feel good about it at all, why they should not be denied all

jouissance. But he knows, of course, that they do, that at least for the *Ostjude* being Jewish is a source of secret joy. He had written to his fiancée Martha Bernays, "The form wherein the old Jews were happy no longer offers us any shelter" (Freud 1960, 318). And then through this misprision of the "essence of Judaism," Freud reveals/conceals the secret of abject *jouissance* that Santner saves in Schreber's discourse from Freud's attempt to hide it again. But at the first level, the question remains what it is that occasioned the originary misreading, and I conclude that it is Freud's dire need to be manly, to discover a manliness at the origins of Jewishness, Moses, and the Bible.

As Jay Geller has put it, "[Freud's] crucial problem was to understand how the Jews 'have been able to retain their individuality till the present day' ([1955f], 136–37). . . . Freud himself appears to be resisting the solution to this problem" (Geller 1993, 50–51). Geller goes on to locate the source of Freud's resistance in the *Leitfossil* of *Moses and Monotheism:* circumcision. The very act that enables the resistance (*Widerstand*) of the Jewish people, the mark of repression/sublimation that releases the "uncanny secretion," is precisely that which feminizes the Jewish man: "After the *Leitfossil* circumcision is unearthed, this analysis reconstructs the traumatic knowledge [Santner's "cursed knowledge"], which Freud seeks to repress, of a source of the anti-Semitism jeopardizing his situation as a Jew: in the Central European cultural imagination, male Jews are identified with men without penises, that is, with women, thereby problematizing sexual difference in a society in which individual identity and social cohesion are determined by the sexual division of labor" (Geller 1993, 52). At the site of the penis, the overdetermined mark of gendered and "racial" anomaly, circumcision concentrates for Freud the "castration" — political and sexual — of the male Jew, the Jew as female (penisless), queer (perverse and passive), and homeless (in Diaspora). All of these motifs come together in *Jewissance,* as I shall now try to show by expanding the opening that Geller's work has furnished.

The sexual and political themes, first concatenated in "My Son the Myops," come together in one stunningly overdetermined moment of *Moses and Monotheism*. Immediately after his discourse on the great man as Aryan father, Freud produces the following utterance:

> Why the people of Israel, however, clung more and more submissively to their God the worse they were treated by him — that is a prob-

lem which for the moment we must leave on one side. It may encourage us to enquire whether the religion of Moses brought the people nothing else besides an enhancement of their self-esteem owing to their consciousness of having been chosen. And indeed another factor can easily be found. That religion also brought the Jews a far grander conception of God, or, as we might put it more modestly, the conception of a grander God. Anyone who believed in this God had some kind of share in his greatness, might feel exalted himself. For an unbeliever this is not entirely self-evident; but we may perhaps make it easier to understand if we point to the sense of superiority felt by a Briton in a foreign country which has been made insecure owing to an insurrection—a feeling that is completely absent in a citizen of any small continental state. For the Briton counts on the fact that his Government will send along a warship if a hair of his head is hurt, and that the rebels understand that very well—whereas the small state possesses no warship at all. Thus, pride in the greatness of the British Empire has a root as well in the consciousness of the greater security—the protection—enjoyed by the individual Briton. This may resemble the conception of a grand God. (Freud 1955f, 112)

This bizarre analogy provides the climactic moment in Freud's attempted appropriation of the sublime phallus for Jews, and it renders crystal clear what the political background for that attempt is. The Jew is the epitome of the citizen of the small state with no warships, indeed "he" is not a citizen of any state at all. Freud is arguing that the Jews' "grander [more sublime] conception of God," their sublimation (masculinization) of physicality and desire, the vaunted "advance in *Geistigkeit*," provides them with an alternative asset for the warships and state power that they do not possess. At this point it is obvious that the Zionism of Freud's contemporary, Theodor Herzl, was another answer—more direct and more responsive to new and emerging paradigms of the masculine, namely, "Muscular Christianity"—to this same Jewish question. Where Freud sought for Jews a compensation for the lack of imperial power, Herzl pursued imperial power itself (D. Boyarin 1997). It is immediately in the next paragraph after this encomium to imperial power that Freud invokes the prohibition against making images of God as a sign of the "triumph of *Geistigkeit* over sensuality, or strictly speaking, an instinctual renunciation." These are the characteristics encoded as sublime, male, and Protestant in Freud's cultural world. In the next paragraphs Freud writes of "our children, adults who are neurotic, and primitive peoples," and, together with these, of the succession of the matriarchal social order by the patriarchal one. The connections between these expressions are clear, but it is vital to remember that it was the Jews who were branded as neurotic, primitive, sensual, and female in fin-de-siècle central Europe.

We can now see Freud's claims for the "superiority" of the Jews in a different light. Key to my interpretation is the recoding of "submissive" from feminine to masculine within the space of this passage. By reading the "inclination to intellectual interests" as a product of the dematerialization or sublimation of God, Freud accomplished another brilliant defensive move. What has been stigmatized as the femaleness of the Jewish male, both his circumcision and his devotion to the interior, "female" pursuits of study, actually marks him as more masculine than the Greek, who in his very muscularity is less restrained, less able to "renounce instincts" (Freud 1955f, 115, and especially 116), and thus paradoxically less "male" — than the male Jew.[27] Jewish carnality, adherence to a law characterized by its passionate attachment to blood and flesh and thus described by anti-Semites (Hegel) as feminine, is transvalued by Freud precisely into a very masculinist *Geistigkeit* or denial of the body itself. The very binary oppositions of maleness and femaleness, renunciation and submission, civilization and oppression, have been destabilized in Freud's text. This instability has to do, in part at least, with the vacillating "racial" positioning of the fin-de-siècle Jew.

An early disciple of Freud's and the founder of psychoanalysis in India, G. Bose once sent Freud a depiction of an English gentleman, remarking that he imagined that was how Freud himself appeared. Freud responded that Bose had not paid attention to certain "racial" differences between him and the English, which, of course, can only be a reference to his Jewishness (Seshadri-Crooks 1994, 185, 211 n. 19). As this wonderful anecdote suggests, Freud's origins as *Ostjude* constantly crossed his aspirations as a bourgeois European. He was both the object and the subject of racism at the same time. Seen from the perspective of the colonized, Freud might look like a white man; from his own perspective, as from that of the dominating Christian white, he was a Jew, every bit as racially marked as the Indian. In the racist imaginary of the late nineteenth century, in fact, Jews were most often designated mulattos. The best denotation, then, for the "race" of the European Jew seems to be off-white: *Ecru Homo.*

Two modalities of reading the "race" of Freud's discourse have emerged in recent years: one — the "colonial" — would read this passage, and by extension Freud's other "ethnological" comments and texts, as being about "black" men and thus as having been produced by a "white" man (Bhabha 1994, 89; Kazanjian 1993, 103–5). The other would read "white" and "black" here as barely disguised ciphers for Aryan and Jew (Gilman 1991a, 175; 1993b, 21). In the first, Freud is the colonizer; in the second, the colonized.

These disparate ways of reading Freud on race are not, in fact, mutually exclusive, but two equally crucial aspects of the peculiar racial situation of the European Jew, who is "white" — but not quite. Jews are not white/not quite in Homi Bhabha's felicitous formulation for other colonial subjects. Freud was at once the other and the metropolitan, the "Semite" among "Aryans" and also the Jew desperately constructing his own whiteness through an othering of the colonized blacks.[28] The results of this double condition are virtually indistinguishable in Freud's texts, because Jews were a genuinely racialized other (just as much as African Americans are in the United States) and, paradoxically, because of his identification with his own oppressors. I mean that Jewishness functioned racially in Austro-Germany substantially as "blackness" does in the United States. The "one drop" theory was operative for Jewishness. For instance, a typical anti-Semite of Freud's time stated: "Jewishness is like a concentrated dye; a minute quantity suffices to give a specific character — or at least, some traces of it — to an incomparably greater mass" (qtd. in Gilman 1991a, 175). Another representative nineteenth-century savant refers to "the African character of the Jew," while Houston Stewart Chamberlain, Wagner's son-in-law and Hitler's hero, wrote that the Jews are a mongrel race that had interbred with Africans.[29] The Jew was the mulatto, quite literally, as W. E. B. Du Bois found out one night in Slovenia when a taxi driver took him to the Jewish ghetto (Gilroy 1993, 212). Since Freud feared that some feature would always betray his thinking as "of Jewish descent" and his discourse as merely a "Jewish science," the "individuals of mixed race" are certainly Jews; and yet, it cannot be denied that he wrote explicitly about "whites" and "coloured."[30] The "colonial" reading of Freud cannot easily be dismissed.[31] I would claim the equivocal racial positioning of the fin-de-siècle Jew as one more locus for Freud's ambivalence, for his *bitextuality.*

Freud remained ambivalent about the civilizing mission of colonialism almost to the very end, and his ambivalence is marked by a series of equivocations in his writing. In 1908 he described female neurosis as being the product of libidinal renunciation occasioned by civilization: "Anyone who is able to penetrate the determinants of nervous illness will soon become convinced that its increase in our society arises from the intensification of sexual restrictions" (Freud 1955b, 194), and even: "The cure for nervous illness arising from marriage would be marital unfaithfulness" (195).[32] In this text, then, the primitive is written as the healthy libido unrepressed by civilization — Gauguin's Tahiti. At the same time, however, a parallel and opposite tectonic movement takes place in Freud's writing. As Marianna Torgovnick has remarked, Freud fathomed in a text published in 1915, "Thoughts for the Times on Life and Death," the deleterious aspects of civilization but still claimed that "the great ruling powers among the white nations" should, in fact, rule over the others in order to "civilize" them (Torgovnick 1990, 197). The year 1913 saw the publication of *Totem and Taboo,* which concerns itself with "some points of agreement between the mental lives of savages and neurotics" (Freud 1955i).[33] In the late 1920s, when *Civilization and Its Discontents* was being written, civilization, with its demanded instinctual renunciations, was seen as the source of neuroses (Freud 1955a, 87, 97, esp. 139), and Freud could write that "civilization behaves towards sexuality as a people or a stratum of its population does which has subjected another one to its exploitation" (104).

The negative evaluation of the civilizing mission in this last comment that "civilization behaves towards sexuality as a people or a stratum of its population does which has subjected another one to its exploitation" supports the hypothesis that Freud's ambivalence about repression versus sublimation parallels and opens up to the uncertainties of his political situation. Freud's critique of civilization (and male domination) goes hand in hand with his understanding of the evils of colonialism itself, and his sanction of colonialism goes in unison with his self-contradicting championing of renunciation and sublimation as male virtues. In other words, I am suggesting that Freud as the object of racism — and particularly one that configures him as "female" — finds it perhaps easier as well to identify with women than he does later on when it is crucial that he ally himself with the male. In the earlier text (Freud 1955b, 199) the female incapacity for intellectual thought is a social product caused by repression by male civilization of the sexual instinct in girls of modern society, while in the later text this incapacity is a sign of primitivity. In 1908 Freud contests Moebius's view that "women's physiological feeble-mindedness [Freud's scare quotes]" is caused by an opposition between sexuality and intellectuality and argues that "the undoubted intellectual inferiority of so many women can rather be traced back to the inhibition of thought necessitated by sexual suppression" (199), but by the late 1930s his views seem more similar to Moebius's. This conflict is an index of the ambivalent, middle-man position of the Jew as both object and subject of the racism of the civilizing mission.[34]

The ambivalence in Freud's disposition vis-à-vis civilization and the primitive is generated precisely by the ambiguity of his position as "white male." Freud as the Jew, the "black," the unacknowledged (by him) object of the racist discourse of evolution, sees well the horror of colonial domination, but when Freud identifies himself with the "white man," then he perceives the great virtues of the civilizing mission. Seshadri-Crooks writes that "Freud had certainly assumed an implicit identity for the analyst as a white European man" (Seshadri-Crooks 1994, 194), an assertion with which I can only agree. I would interpret this very sentence, however, in a sense perhaps unintended by its author but which nevertheless resides within the syntax, reading it as: Freud had certainly assumed (put on) an identity (mask) for the analyst (himself: not quite white, "Hottentot," Jewish sissy) as a white European man.[35]

Freud, however, remains forever equivocal about this, as one can easily see by his dual comments within the space of a page about "more and more instinctual renunciations" as leading "in doctrine and precept at least—[to] ethical heights which had remained inaccessible to the other peoples of antiquity," but these very same renunciations "possess the characteristic of obsessional reaction-formations" (Freud 1955f 134–35).[36] Moreover, we can locate this fault line in his psychodynamic theory itself at the site of the ambiguity surrounding the term *sublimation* vis-à-vis reaction-formation, aim-inhibition, and repression. Laplanche and Pontalis note somewhat dryly that in Freud's writings, "there are only the vaguest hints of dividing lines between sublimation" and repression, obsession, and aim-inhibition, but "the capacity to sublimate is an essential factor in successful treatment" (Laplanche and Pontalis 1973, 433). Since obsession and repression are part of what there is to be treated in a successful treatment, the cure and the disease become hard to distinguish. This famous moment of incoherence in the dynamic theory is the product, I suggest, of the pervasive ambivalences I have been exploring as products of Freud's fin-de-siècle sexual-political situation, indeed, almost emblematic of a liminality that Freud manifests.

Seen in this light, Freud's apparent (if ambivalent) rapport with the civilizing mission, as well as his acceptance of the bromide that ontogeny recapitulates phylogeny, is a much more complex political move than it might first appear, for the "primitives" to which he addresses himself are as much Jewish primitives — indeed, first and foremost Jewish primitives, primitives within — and only secondarily the contemporary objects of the civilizing mission of colonialism. Freud's apparently guileless use of the phrase "a state within a state" as a metaphor for "pathological phenomena" (Freud 1955f, 76) is telling here, as, of course, that phrase was coined for women and Jews, the twin primitive Others within the German state (Geller 1993, 56). Freud had apparently, almost against his will, internalized the anti-Semitic ideology that Jews were a people both out of time and out of place. Other Jews in his milieu had also incorporated such views, most notably the western European Zionists of Herzl's movement.

Although Freud was not, certainly by 1939, a Zionist in the sense of being a supporter of Jewish settlement in Palestine and the founding of a Jewish state there, his interpretation of Jewish history was exactly the same as the Zionist interpretation — ancient glory followed by thousands of years of degradation producing moral, spiritual, and aesthetic distortions in the oppressed people. The "high" religion of the Egyptian Moses, the purely spiritual monotheism, was the production of a "fortunate period of established possession"; that is, "[i]n Egypt, so far as we can understand, monotheism grew up as a by-product of imperialism" (Freud 1955f, 65), but as the Jewish people underwent the trials and sufferings of the Diaspora, "their god became harsh and severe, and, as it were, wrapped in gloom. . . . they increased their own sense of guilt in order to stifle their doubts of God" (64). Freud explicitly echoes the best of German Protestant Bible scholarship: "Institutions such as the ritual ordinances, which date unmistakably from later times, are given out as Mosaic commandments with the plain intention of lending them authority" (65). The great ideals of the true Mosaic religion remained dormant within the people, but the priests with their "ceremonials" became increasingly the dominant force.

Freud went beyond most of his contemporaries, however, by actually split-ting Moses and thus Judaism into two different antithetical and antagonis-tic groups with two different Moseses and two different religious traditions. The "true" Moses, the Egyptian one, is remarkably like the ideal Protestant. Freud's Moses fantasies and dreams provide important backing for this thesis. When he dreams he is on a mountain looking yearningly at "the Promised Land," it is not, however, the Land of Israel, but Rome, like Hannibal at Lake Trasimeno (Freud 1955d, 194; cf. Masson 1985, 285), and this is emblematic of the metamorphosis of the man Moses at his hands. In the early essay on the *Moses* of Michelangelo, Freud discovers that Moses is not about to throw down the tablets of the Law, but is, in fact, checking that impulse and that, therefore, Michelangelo has "added something new and more than human to the figure of Moses; so that the giant frame with its tremendous physi-cal power becomes only a concrete expression of the highest mental achieve-ment that is possible in a man, that of struggling successfully against an in-ward passion for the sake of a cause to which he has devoted himself" (Freud 1955g, 233). Moses is now the very model of a masculine spirituality and re-nunciation—as well as a "manly" aggressiveness—"in contrast to the medi-tative king, he was energetic and passionate" (Freud 1955f, 60).

Bluma Goldstein has shown how identified Freud was himself with this gentilified Moses: "In 1900 Freud characterized his own adventurous nature in terms of conquest: 'I am actually not at all a man of science, not an ob-server, not an experimenter, not a thinker. I am by temperament nothing but a *conquistador,* an adventurer, if you wish to translate this term—with all the inquisitiveness, daring, and tenacity characteristic of such a man.' Whether in the guise of conquistador or Semitic warrior, Freud apparently conceived of himself at that time as conquering Rome in the name of Jewry, which the Ro-man Church, in his view, had persecuted and continued to threaten. But what did happen when he finally reached Rome?" (Goldstein 1992, 76). According to Goldstein's exemplary reading of Freud's essay on Michelangelo's *Moses,* what happened was that Freud discovered a Moses who embodied all of the values and traits of European Christians, indeed who was a central monument of European Christianity in the heart of Rome itself, another, like Hannibal, un-Jewish Jew (not the same thing, of course, as a *non*-Jewish Jew).

The other Moses, the second Moses was, on the other hand, all-too-Jewish, and the religion that he founded was obsessed with "neurotic" ritual observances and not with "sublime abstractions." "Everything in the [Egyptian] Mosaic god that deserved admiration was quite beyond the comprehension of the primitive masses" (Freud 1955f, 63). On Freud's own theory that such ancient fault lines reappear in later splits within a people (38), could we not read this as a covert (perhaps unconscious) representation of the distinction between German Jews and their embarrassingly primitive relatives, the *Ostjuden,* the "black" Jews, the Jews who spoke a language one converted German Jew referred to as "Hottentot" (Gilman 1986, 99)? Such a "family romance" was not unprecedented among Viennese Jews of Freud's generation. Theodor Herzl went so far as to write explicitly that the *Ostjude* was of a different "race" from the "evolved" German Jew. Freud's account of how the ideas of the original Moses, "the idea of a single god, as well as the rejection of magically effective ceremonial and the stress upon ethical demands made in his name" (Freud 1955f, 66), were suppressed but reappeared hundreds of years later would be an allegory of the reappearance of such "high" ideas of religion among the German Jews after centuries of their abeyance among the *Ostjuden.* As one of Freud's Bnai Brith lodge brothers couched it: "We Jews . . . are not constrained by dogma. In his inner being the Jew, the true Jew, feels only one eternal guide, one lawgiver, one law, and that is morality" (Ludwig Braun, 1926; qtd. in Gilman 1993a, 75). Gilman appropriately glosses this: "This image of the Jews as following only 'natural law,' rather than the complicated rules and rituals of traditional Judaism, imagines them as the ultimate rationalists, at one with God and nature" (Gilman 1993a, 75). Hiding behind the second, "too Jewish," ritualist Moses is none other than Mauschel, "little Moses" or ("Ikey"), the malicious name that German anti-Semites, both Jewish and gentile, applied to eastern European Jews (Gilman 1986, passim). Mauschel is obsessed with his primitive, atavistic, and irrational rituals. If the first Moses is Mendelssohn, the second is Mauschel. Indeed, one might almost wish to rename the work *Mauschel and Monotheism.*

The crisis of the early 1930s so heightened this strain that it gave way finally in a "personality split" within Moses and the Jewish people: *Moses and Monotheism.*[37] Each of the "religious" categories that Freud projects is, like Rome, split and doubled. Judaism is not identical with itself, and neither is Christianity. The split between the "queer effeminate" *Ostjude* and the "straight male modern" Jew (Brenkman 1993), between Mauschel and Mendelssohn, seems to be repeated in a split between the Austrian Catholic and the German

Protestant as well, suggesting further Freud's complicated identifications of self and other — all within. Another way of saying this would be that the evolutionary narrative is from Catholic to Protestant Christian — and from Catholic to Protestant Jew (with some temporary devolutions along the way). "Maimonides is, within Medieval Judaism, the revealing mark of Protestantism" wrote Hermann Cohen (qtd. in Derrida 1991, 53, 65), and Freud's description of the religion of sublime abstraction is surely much more like that of Moses Maimonides — and Hermann Cohen — than like that of the biblical Moses.

It is clear now which border, which frontier it was that Freud desired to cross. When he has crossed it, however, he has lost something. As Bram Dijkstra has perceptively written, "The truly psychotic, rather than merely neurotic, idealization of a supremely evolved white male and the concomitant assumption that somehow all others were 'degenerate' had, as Freud was writing [*Civilization and Its Discontents*], begun to reap its most evil harvest. Even the most casual reader of the theoretical disquisitions of the later nineteenth-century exponents of the science of man must at once perceive the intimate correlation between their evolutionist conclusions and the scientific justification of patterns of 'inherent' superiority and inferiority in the relations between the sexes, various races, and the different classes in society" (Dijkstra 1986, 160). The ambivalence in Freud's disposition vis-à-vis civilization and the primitive is generated precisely by the ambiguity of his position as "white male." Freud as the Jew, the "black," the unacknowledged (by him) object of the racist discourse of evolution, sees well the horror of colonial domination, but when Freud identifies himself with the "white man," then he perceives the great virtues of the civilizing mission. This tension was always present, but resolves itself most definitely in the gap between *Civilization and Its Discontents* and *Moses and Monotheism*. While still in the killing field of the "evil harvest," Freud perceives the violence of civilization. Safe, however, in the "great[est] ruling power among the white nations," in *Moses and Monotheism* Freud ruminates that it is the "primitive" who has not (yet) undertaken renunciation of libidinal strivings who is most similar to the neurotic and the female, and renunciation thus has become a sign of greater psychic health. Now the "Jew" has to be demonstrably on the side of civilization, the father, masculinity, and heterosexuality.[38] This is not a sign of bad faith on Freud's part but rather an instance of "persecution and the art of writing." Read this way, these texts form almost an uncanny inchoate preliminary draft for the *Dialectic of En-*

lightenment.[39] I suggest that the off-whiteness, queerness, and feminization of the male Jew is productive of a kind of insight. The aporia, or set of aporias, in the Freudian text is best read as built into the heart of modernity, and the personal (sexual) in Freud is, therefore, political in ways only adumbrated in previous contexts, precisely for the ways that the Jew (male and female) was equivocally sexualized, racialized, and gendered in Freud's life-world. Freud's ambivalence, his bitextuality—sexual, gendered, racial—finally is a kind of knowledge.

Notes

1   The dream was given this name owing to a passage within it that I will not read here. There is a great deal of unclarity about whether or not Freud dreamed the dream after seeing the play or perhaps even before it (McGrath 1986, 236). He could have heard about it, or even read it, for it was published in Vienna in 1897. For my argument this does not matter at all, since I am reading the two texts as elements in a certain discourse, as synchronic intertexts. It makes a better opening anecdote, however, if we assume that Freud saw the play and then dreamed the dream.

2   Loewenberg, followed by McGrath, detects in this dream a "hidden Zionist theme." The main evidence for this interpretation lies in the phrase in Freud's commentary about "one's children, to whom one cannot give a country of their own." In fact, there is a great deal of ambiguity in this interpretative move itself, since for Loewenberg it would seem the dream represents "a latent attraction to, and envy of, the world of Jewish salvation through politics" (1970, 132), while for McGrath, the dream constitutes an assertion that "directly dismissed Herzl's new cause" (1986, 237).

3   The latter itself was, moreover, as we learn clearly from Proust (and might have surmised anyway) as much a matter of Jewish manliness as of Jewish safety. The appropriate response to the Dreyfus affair was to fight duels with anti-Semites (Proust 1993, 11; 20–21).

4   The "standard" psychoanalytical readings of this sentence all seem inadequate to me. The best that Grinstein can offer, for example, is that "[i]t will be recalled how many of Freud's references in *The Interpretation of Dreams* deal with his wish to attain the rank of Professor and with the anti-Semitic prejudices to which he was constantly exposed. Quite understandably he wanted to spare his children this kind of treatment and wanted to move to another country, such as England, where his children and he himself could enjoy greater freedom and tolerance"

(Grinstein 1980, 321). This seems to me hardly an adequate gloss for "educating the children in such a way that they can freely move across frontiers." The emphasis here is surely on the mode of the children's education and not on the freedom or intolerance of the place in which they are being educated. It is still less obvious to conclude that the meaning of this sentence has to do with Freud's dream of being a professor and its frustration at the hands of anti-Semites. McGrath accepts Grinstein's reading, similarly ignoring the fact that Freud's concern is not with the crossing of frontiers but with educating the children so that they could cross frontiers (McGrath 1986, 243). Anzieu's only allusion to this sentence is in a denial, when he writes, "Nothing in this dream justifies the interpretation formulated by Maylan (1930), who, writing from an anti-Semitic point of view, claims that Freud's neurosis was the result of a repressed wish to be converted to Christianity" (Anzieu 1986, 261). I find Maylan's view compelling.

5 To the best of my knowledge, garnered from native informants, Viennese Jews did not refer to Pesach as "Easter."

6 This is so, on Freud's own account, whether he had actually seen the play then or read it or even read a plot summary of it. See note 1 above.

7 Of course, the two readings do not contradict but supplement each other.

8 Luxon (1995) suggests: "Maybe Fliess is a Joseph type of father and Freud's 'real' desire is to be 'visited' by a bigger Father?"—thus rendering Freud a type of Schreber (Craft 1995, 100)! This is suggestive of further support for a point of Freud's identification with/as Schreber that I have made elsewhere (D. Boyarin 1994a), namely an explanation for Freud's own "paranoid" tendencies directed at male lover/rivals, from Fliess to Jung. This should not be read reductively. Even paranoids have real enemies, and Jung, at any rate, was certainly an enemy to Freud (and to his people).

9 The very insightful comments of Bluma Goldstein are very relevant here (1992, 72–74).

10 It seems indeed worth noting that in totally Catholic Vienna, only a half of the Jews who converted, converted to that faith, and the rest declared themselves either Protestant or "konfessionslos" (Le Rider 1993, 187–88). For the association of Protestantism with manliness by another Jewish, queer writer in a Catholic country, see Proust 1993, 31.

11 With respect to the "division of people into 'active' and 'passive' races by Gustav Klemm," Efron writes: "In his General History of Civilization (1843) Klemm posited that the active races were masculine, thriving in cold climates, while the passive ones, residing in warm climates, were effeminate" (Efron 1994, 15).

12 For Seeberg's Nazi sympathies, see Briggs 1985, 251.

13 Note Freud's comment that the Jews were in Cologne, where he fantasized his own ancestors came from, before the Germans (1955f, 90)!

14 To be sure, Freud lived in Catholic Vienna, but I think it is not inaccurate to suggest that the kind of religiosity that he admires and constructs as originally "Jewish" in *Moses and Monotheism* is more like German Protestantism than Austrian Catholicism. For discussion, see below.

15 Fanny Neuda, in *Studen der Andacht* (1862), provides an elegant proof-text for her thesis. If one takes away the minimally, specific Jewish content, it could have been produced by any advocate for domesticated bourgeois sentimental religiosity of the period, but it was written by an Orthodox Jewish woman! On Neuda, see Hyman 1995, 34. It should be noted that although this book of prayers for women was translated and published in English, the appendix to which I am referring, in which the pleas for women's education in order that they might more fully perform their "angel in the house" role, was not included in the English version.

16 In other words, I agree completely with Seshadri-Crooks when she writes that "[Freud's] easy condensation of totemic rites as being 'the same thing' as present day neuroses also elides the glib pathologization of non-Western cultures" (1994, 192). My intervention is to claim that, for Freud, the traditional Judaism of the *Ostjude* is in the same category of the non-Western and primitive as totemic rites and equally as pathologized.

17 I do believe that it was the Protestantism of high German *Kultur*, understood as *Aufhebung* of all previous cultures, that was Freud's model, in spite of his dwelling in Catholic Austria, or perhaps because of it. But again, let me emphasize, Freud's was an assimilationism like Herzl's Zionism (for which, see D. Boyarin 1997), one that sought not to erase the name "Jew" but rather to reconfigure Jews as identical to gentiles and as such in origin. The "Egyptian" Moses is a perfect figure for this move. Therefore, arguments that Freud was not "ashamed" of his Jewishness or was pugnacious against anti-Semites are precisely beside the point.

18 Freud returned to this view in his analysis of the Schreber case, in which he argued that Schreber's fantasies of being the Redeemer followed his feminization, *Entmannung*. "For we learn that the idea of being transformed into a woman (that is, of being emasculated) was the primary delusion, that he began by regarding that act as constituting a serious injury and persecution, and that it only became related to his playing the part of Redeemer in a secondary way. There can be no doubt, moreover, that originally he believed that the transformation was to be effected for the purpose of sexual abuse and not so as to serve higher designs. The position may be formulated by saying that a sexual delusion of persecution was later on converted in the patient's mind into a religious delusion of grandeur"

(Freud 1955h, 18). The two passages provide striking commentary on each other and together a hermeneutic key for the reading of *Moses and Monotheism*.

19   Freud himself realized how malapropos these descriptions are of actual biblical religion, but ascribed all of the "primitive" characteristics to the religion of the "Midianite Moses," as opposed to the spiritual religion of the "Egyptian Moses [who] had given to one portion of the people a more highly spiritualized notion of god, the idea of a single deity embracing the whole world, who was not less all-loving than all-powerful, who was averse to all ceremonial and magic and set before men as their highest aim a life in truth and justice" (Freud 1955f, 50).

20   Hegel's description of Judaism as "the religion of the sublime," of which Jay Geller has reminded me, seemingly follows from this point.

21   This provides quite a different spin on Kant's alleged "innermost affinity with Judaism," as recently discussed by Harpham 1994, 530. Precisely the point of the construction of such an affinity by figures like Hermann Cohen would be to produce identity between "Judaism" and the German Spirit. Harpham also quite curiously seems to dramatically underplay Kant's own quite spectacular expressions of anti-Semitism. On the other hand, he fathoms acutely that "from serene thoughts of reason it is but a short step to critical terrorism in the service of revolutionary fantasies of the essential unity of mankind" (Harpham 1994, 531–32). Harpham explores the contiguities between Inquisition and Enlightenment; I would locate the sources of the Kantian Universal—with both its light and dark aspects—further back, in Paul (D. Boyarin 1994b). My point is that Enlightenment and Difference are structurally, systemically antithetical, which does not yet mean that we can do without either Enlightenment or some kind of Universal. For further articulation of the paradox see Boyarin and Boyarin 1995.

22   Gilman 1993b, 188, should be compared here both for the ways that my reading of *Moses and Monotheism* is similar to his and for the equally considerable ways that we differ.

23   This view, which was the scholarly consensus about the history of Judaism among German Protestant scholars, is directly evinced in Freud 1955f, 51. This historiography of Judaism was enshrined in German Reform Judaism as well.

24   It is for this reason that Solomon Shechter referred to the Higher Criticism of the Bible as the Higher Anti-Semitism.

25   Gilroy, on the other hand, remarks the "dangers for both blacks and Jews in accepting their historic and unsought association with sublimity" (1993, 215–16). See also on this Boyarin and Boyarin 1995.

26   Cf. Gilman's point that in his discussions of creativity, Freud never once mentions a Jewish writer or painter (Gilman 1995, 119).

27 It is symptomatic that when Freud writes of the legendary founding of rabbinic Judaism in R. Yohanan ben Zakkai's escape from besieged Jerusalem, he mentions only the "masculine" pursuit of intellectuality that it presaged and not the notoriously "feminine" mode of the escape through trickery, in a coffin (Freud 1955f, 124).

28 For analogous processes in American culture, see Rogin 1992; Gilman 1994.

29 Freud had read Chamberlain (Gilman 1993b, 236). For extensive documentation of the "blackness" of Jews, see Gilman 1986, 172–75; 1993a, 19–21. For a fascinating explanation of the functions of such discourse, see Cheyette 1995.

30 And "Jewish science" was definitely a racist/anti-Semitic term of art, a fact brought out clearly in Gilman 1995, 112–13.

31 For an exemplarily thoughtful version, see Seshadri-Crooks 1994. Seshadri-Crooks inquires as to whether certain descriptions of Freud as contemptuously patronizing of Indian psychoanalysts (the same Bose) do not reproduce such contempt, since Bose and his fellows seem unaware of Freud's contempt and patronization (186). A version of this question could be asked here as well. If Freud's work is as irretrievably tainted with racism and colonialist ideology as some would have it, how is it that a Fanon did not indict this corruption?

32 See discussion also in Gay 1986, 351.

33 Freud is certainly aware that "savages" hedge sexual life with prohibitions and taboos, as he explicitly writes in the first chapter of *Totem and Taboo*. I think, nevertheless, that he not infrequently imagines the "primitive" as a space of unrepressed libido, as in Gauguin and Douanier Rousseau.

34 For a somewhat different, brief take on this matter, see Scheman 1993, 26.

35 It is not difficult to understand why the victims of British imperialism—the "rebels"—might read this passage differently. Freud, in seeking desperately to escape the characterization of his own people as feminine, accomplished this by stigmatizing those others. Bose was not entirely wrong to see in Freud a representative of the British colonial order (Seshadri-Crooks 1994), and for me to pretend otherwise would be to abandon redemptive critique for apologetic. In future work I hope to articulate historically the role of the "Aryan" myth in the production of Freud's affect about India.

36 Cf. the somewhat similar reading of another aporia in Freud's text by Geller 1993, 62.

37 Torgovnick shrewdly sees the same split in the 1930 preface to the new edition of *Totem and Taboo,* not associating it, however, with *Moses and Monotheism.* The difference between my reading and Torgovnick's is that where she sees a rather simple contrast between the way that the Jew is portrayed by the anti-Semite and

Freud's attempt to counter it, I see much more equivocation within Freud himself. Torgovnick does not cite the very early valorization of the "primitive" in "'Civilized' Sexual Morality" (Freud 1955b), and thus misses, I think, an opportunity to see a layer of identification with the "primitive" Eastern Jew long before "the pressure of Nazism" (Torgovnick 1990, 201). Otto Rank was more consistent than Freud. For him the "essence of Judaism" was in its avoidance of repression and its "stress on primitive sexuality," which was a positively marked term for Rank (Rank 1985; see discussion in Gilman 1993a, 176).

38   These two orientations of the Jew for Freud almost mirror the differential relations of nineteenth-century German and British anthropology toward Jews, as described by Efron 1994, 35–36.

39   For readings of this text appropriate to this context, see J. Boyarin 1992, 108–10; Harpham 1994, 532. For a different analogy between Freud and Adorno, see Gilman 1995, 108; Stieg 1995, 196.

SYLVIA MOLLOY

Of Queens and Castanets: Hispanidad, *Orientalism,*

and Sexual Difference

For our generation and the one following it, D'Halmar points out the way from Loti to Proust. — Montenegro 1934, 15

I really regret not being able to dress up as a Turk in Santiago.
— Augusto d'Halmar, in Edwards Bello 1966, 10

Describing the cultural climate of early-twentieth-century Spanish America (while disingenuously trying to justify his own affair with a gypsy dancer), the Mexican writer José Vasconcelos wrote: "In those days Spanish dancing was the filter for a Dionysian reconciliation with our Hispanic past. In the midst of a wave of invasive Yankee customs, and after nearly a century of resentful isolation, we avidly drank the waters of a common lineage. What diplomacy could not achieve, what philosophers would not even try, was accomplished in an instant with *Flamenco* dancing. . . . In one strike, the much maligned castanet-clacking Spain united nations of common descent in a way that had proved impossible to politicians and intellectuals" (Vasconcelos 1982, 305).

So much did castanet-clacking Spain captivate Spanish America (or some sectors of Spanish America) that I remember, while growing up in Argentina in the 1940s, the noise of castanets and *zapateo* seeping out of shabby suburban dance academies into the streets. They usually advertised *Baile clásico y español,* but the true vitality and verve, if one was to judge from the noise, came from the latter, performed with more gusto than finesse, and not from the vapid renditions of *Swan Lake* or *Coppélia.* I also remember, in newspaper advertisements for Mardi Gras costumes for children, alongside "The Pirate," "The Gaucho," and "The Marquise," the inevitable fiery red dress of the Spanish dancer, ages six to twelve. All this took place, of course, in very cosmopolitan Buenos Aires, more inclined to identify culturally with Paris or London than with its past metropolis; a Buenos Aires whose snobbish élite would rather die than be thought of in terms of castanets, flowing trains, and red dancing shoes, and where Spaniards, no longer *conquistadores* but turn-of-the-century immigrants and their descendants, were the object of unflattering ethnic jokes. What was true in this Buenos Aires of the 1940s, was true, I suspect, in more than one Spanish American capital: the heroic powers of *flamenco* as a barrier against Yankee invasion (if indeed it ever worked that way), the aura of Spanish dancers and their castanets evocative of a mythical, Hispanic tradition, had certainly dimmed. Yes, every now and then, excellent *flamenco* companies toured Latin America, yes, people still spoke admiringly of the mythical performer "La Argentina," yes, García Lorca had endowed Spanish gypsies with an unquestionable, if ephemeral, vogue, but Spanish dancing, castanets, and things *flamenco* had entered, once and for all, the realm of the tacky. Not only had they lost their aesthetic appeal, they had definitely lost the quality that Vasconcelos wished on them, that of a continental, Hispanic, rallying symbol.

I want to stay for a moment with the notion of *flamenco* as a degraded cultural icon (a degradation that had begun long before Vasconcelos, in nineteenth-century Spain itself), and explore the notion of binding through tackiness. For by the 1940s — even as dutiful petit bourgeois girls were learning the difficult art of castanets — *flamenco,* and Spanish dancing in general, had become, at least in Argentina, a secret rallying symbol for a very different constituency. In Buenos Aires, for example, the Teatro Avenida, where *flamenco* performances and *zarzuelas* (or Spanish operettas), were regularly staged, had become one of the principal cruising spots for gays in the city and indeed, was the site, in 1943, of the second most important homosexual scandal of the century (the first involving military school cadets a few years earlier), a *razzia* that resulted in the deportation of an entire Spanish company directed by the celebrated dancer Miguel de Molina and, concomitantly, in the unexpected outing of a hitherto silenced subculture.[1] As little girls dressed up as "the Spanish Dancer" so did little boys: the gypsy dancer in the billowing red dress became one of the preferred roles for drag queens throughout Spanish America, as the unforgettable Manuela, in José Donoso's hellish vision of rural Chile, flamboyantly and tragically shows.[2]

Within this vertiginous movement from heroic to tacky, the subversive import of which seems evident—the mystical bonding figure, "our transterritorial Spain" as Unamuno called it (1925, 429), turned into a campy, subversive icon—let me recapitulate the ideological import (and the ideological ambivalence) of *lo hispano,* a heterogeneous composite of considerable effectiveness, from the turn of the century through the 1920s. With the exception of Puerto Rico and Cuba, newly independent from Spain, where *lo hispano* was still perhaps too close for comfort, most Latin American countries, by the end of the century, had sufficiently dissociated the political from the aesthetic in the domain of things Spanish so as to see both, political and aesthetic, in a new light. Even *before* political independence from Spain, a Cuban, Martí, was capable of teasing apart the two, as in the memorable evocation of the Spanish dancer in poem 10 of *Versos sencillos.*[3] In the realm of the aesthetic, Spain's cultural artifacts, thanks to the revisionary poetics of turn-of-the-century *modernismo* and its reappropriation of the French *espagnolade,* took on new life. In the realm of the political, a more complex recasting was necessary. While it is true that centennial commemorations of independence, celebrated throughout Latin America in 1910, recreated the scene of rupture with Spain and renewed a rhetoric of origins,[4] it is no less true that Spain, this time, was incorporated into those very commemorations, allowed a friendly place at the table. This was literally the case in Argentina, where already in 1900, by presidential decree, the national anthem was "cleansed" of stanzas offensive to Spain; where, in addition, the Spanish Infanta herself, Doña Isabel de Borbón, presided over the celebration of independence. Thus Spain is recuperated in the centennial rhetoric of independence not so much as the colonial power from which Latin America had seceded, but as a simulacrum of origins, as the phantasmatic roots that bound Latin American nations together and provided them with a common "tradition" that would set them apart both from decadent Europe and from their pragmatic northern neighbours. *Lo hispano* was Latin America's way into a quasi-mystical *Latinity*.[5] It became synonymous with the open-ended (though by no means nondiscriminatory) notion of *raza,* the latter signifying, to quote one critic, "hispanism, recognition of the essential belonging of America's being to the tradition of Latin culture, as expressed in Spanish language and in Spanish artistic creations" (Henríquez Ureña 1918, 47). It is not surprising that, in spite of the superficial paradox, some of the most ardent nationalists of the 1920s and 1930s, no longer seeing *lo hispano* as a sign of dependence, exalted it as a bonding figure.[6] It should be added that, in most of these cases, the ideological claim on hispanism, besides satisfying the hankering for a strong national (or continental) identity, fostered xenophobia, racism, and, quite specifically, anti-Semitism.

It is within this generally conservative reevaluation of *lo hispano* that one must read four novels published between 1908 and 1928, namely, Enrique Larreta's *La gloria de don Ramiro* (The glory of Don Ramiro) (1908), Carlos Reyles's *El embrujo de Sevilla* (The magic of Seville) (1922), Augusto D'Halmar's *La pasión y muerte del cura Deusto* (1924), and Joaquín Edwards Bello's *Un chileno en Madrid* (A Chilean in Madrid) (1928). All four take place in Spain, albeit in different regions, all four engage in resurrecting *lo hispano* as a vital (if violent) heritage. But only one, D'Halmar's *La pasión y muerte del cura Deusto* (The passion and death of the priest Deusto), has a specifically homoerotic content — an exception in itself, at the time, and, in the context of the programmatic reevaluation of *lo hispano,* a true aberration. It is this aberration, and the light it casts on the revisionist process of things Spanish, that I wish to consider in this essay. To do so, I must first consider some aspects of Augusto D'Halmar's background that I find useful for my argument.

Although hailed by influential Chilean critic Hernán Díaz Arrieta as one of "*los cuatro grandes,*" "the four great ones" in Chilean literature, Augusto D'Halmar is virtually unknown except to Chileans, students of Chilean literature, and a few cognoscenti. Díaz Arrieta does not hesitate to state that "[i]t is not excessive to speak of a generation in literature before D'Halmar and another after D'Halmar, which he himself inspired, at least in the beginning, when it was necessary to open doors, point to new horizons, go out in the world" (Díaz Arrieta 1963, 18). Yet the precise nature of D'Halmar's innovations — *which* doors were opened, *what* horizons were pointed to — is never spelled out, even when it may be hinted at in fairly transparent statements: "For our generation and the one following it, D'Halmar points out the way from Loti to Proust" (Montenegro 1934, 15). Díaz Arrieta does speak of D'Halmar's homosexuality, ambivalently: it is, he writes, "something that no one till now has spoken of clearly, although everybody knows: D'Halmar's uranism does not explain everything, but without it you understand nothing" (Díaz Arrieta 1963, 19). Calling D'Halmar's homosexuality a "private drama" and a "secret abyss," Díaz Arrieta speaks of it in exculpatory fashion, reducing it to a personal, shameful secret: "[D'Halmar's] social standing hushed the rumors. And also his physical appearance, his virile tone of voice, his audacious disposition" (Díaz Arrieta 1963, 12). And yet, I would argue, it is precisely that homosexuality, provocatively voiced throughout D'Halmar's work, either directly as in *La pasión y muerte del cura Deusto* and *Los alucinados* (The Hallucinations), or obliquely, as in the rest of his oeuvre, that constitutes his most important contribution to literature.

Born in Chile in 1882, Augusto Goémmine Thomson (in at least one version of his life) was the illegitimate son of a well-to-do Chilean woman named Thomson and a French sailor (Goémmine), passing through Chile, who never returned. A rebel and a dandy, who invested his literary poses and flashy mimicry with the weight of political statements, the young Thomson must be credited for what is surely one of the most interesting experiments in turn-of-the-century Latin America, the foundation of a small, all-male, utopian commune (or "*colonia tolstoyana*") in the south of Chile. The members of the *colonia* were Thomson, the leader, a younger writer named Fernando Santiván, who became, for Thomson, "the friend, the disciple, the reverent protégé" (Santiván 1965, 1460), and two painters. The commune lasted barely more than a year, for reasons I shall not consider in detail here, and it was during that time, from 1904 to 1905, that Thomson took on the name D'Halmar. He would later say that it was the name of a Swedish ancestor; more interesting, perhaps, is the fact that it was, at the beginning, a *shared* pseudonym, the one he and Fernando Santiván chose for a joint collaboration: Augusto and Fernando Halmar.[7] As the commune dissolved so did the friendship between the two men, following a scenario that recurs in D'Halmar's later fiction, most notably in his transparently allusive *La lampara en el molino* (The lamp in the mill): two men, bound by loving friendship, are torn asunder when one of them falls in love with the other's sister. Santiván did indeed marry Thomson's sister and broke the bond between the two men. Thomson was left with the

pseudonym and, we may speculate, added the aristocratic particle, with a survivor's exquisite irony, as he reclaimed it for himself: *D'Halmar.* The pseudonym that had marked the plenitude of male collaboration, the "perfect friendship," was now a sign perpetually half-vacant, a reminder of loss.[8]

Out of that loss D'Halmar the writer was born, a product of canny self-
fabrication or, as he himself states in a mock interview with himself, "an author who has achieved the miracle of 'recreating himself,' both in the sense
of creating himself again or engendering himself, and in the sense of finding
pleasure in his own creations" (D'Halmar 1963, 234).[9] This careful, programmatic self-fashioning, consolidated by the choice of the pseudonymous persona, is viewed somewhat uneasily by critics as a fraudulent process through
which the "real" D'Halmar—a contradiction in terms—disappears: "As if
D'Halmar, before creating his works of art, had created a D'Halmar in such
perfect a manner that the real one, the man, the author of a technique, van-
ishes" (Eduardo Barrios, qtd. in Espinoza 1963, 13). I would argue instead
that the pseudonym, *D'Halmar,* should be seen as the author's first queer
fiction, one that encodes loss and the impossibility of reunion, male desire
and (failed) male collaboration, into the very fabric of D'Halmar's oeuvre
and literary persona. A founding text, the pseudonym is also, I would add,
D'Halmar's first fiction of displacement, the beginning of the unceasing *errancia,* or wandering, that is the subject of most of his books. D'Halmar may
well be the name of a Swedish ancestor of Thomson but it is also, in Spanish, *al mar,* to the sea—a call that Thomson, after his break with Santiván,
heeded with a vengeance both in his life and his texts. It is striking that after a
first, conventionally realistic novel squarely set in Chile, *Juana Lucero,* which
he wrote before the *colonia tolstoyana* venture and before the change in name,
D'Halmar would never again choose Chile for a setting.[10] Nor, for that matter, would he live much in Chile after 1905. Through connections, in 1907
he was named consul general in Calcutta and lived in India for a year. He
was then sent to northern Peru in 1908, where he spent the next seven years,
also in a consular post. In 1916, "for obscure reasons," as one critic delicately
puts it (Acevedo 1976, 35), he was discharged from the service and moved to
Paris, where he covered World War I as a foreign correspondent. Then (again
after intimations of a homosexual affair gone wrong [Díaz Arrieta 1963, 33;
Espinoza 1963, 22]), he moved to Madrid, where he spent sixteen years and
wrote his best work. In 1934, an impoverished D'Halmar returned to Chile,

devoted himself to revising hitherto unpublished material for publication in his *Obras completas*, and occupied minor government positions procured by friends. At first acclaimed by the literary establishment as a long-lost brother, the *hermano errante*, the errant brother (and, perhaps, the *erring* brother?) finally come home, D'Halmar nevertheless seemed to have outlived his celebrity, or at least his notoriety: "Despite having managed his fame so wisely, as a charmer, a mesmerizer, a hypnotist, back in Chile D'Halmar was unable to prevent the gradual waning of the prestige given to him in the past by distance" (Díaz Arrieta 1963, 3). In 1942 he was awarded the first *Premio Nacional de Literatura*—but no one remembered to invite him to the awards ceremony. In 1950, he died.

The prestige given by distance (and patiently nourished by the author himself) was not simply that of the eternal voyager, fired with an indeterminate wanderlust, but, more precisely that of the exotic traveler, affecting the conventional attitudes of Eurocentric orientalism, in its more familiar, French version.[11] D'Halmar's frequent references to the Near and Far East, his purported familiarity with Arab customs, and his proclaimed direct contact with a world to which Chileans, and Latin Americans in general, had only indirect access through literature (with the exception of a few turn-of-the-century travelers), earned him a solid reputation as an exotic world traveler, a sort of Latin American Pierre Loti. While all orientalism is a *chose mentale,* Loti's was supported by extensive geographic displacements throughout his years as an officer of the French navy. By contrast, D'Halmar's travels were more modest; his orientalism seems to have been incorporated at one blow, with the strength of sudden conversion, during the trip in 1907 that took him to Asia via England, France, and Egypt. D'Halmar was in India only briefly, fell unromantically ill as soon as he arrived, and got himself shipped back to Chile and named to another consular post. (Indeed, so desperate was he to move that he accepted the only other post available in the foreign service, the consulate at Etén, in the northern Peruvian desert, doubly undesirable for its location and its promise of political discomfort, since Peru had just lost a war over boundaries to Chile.) A case of translated exoticism learned from European writers, indeed mostly from Loti, with whom D'Halmar liked to think he had a lot in common and whose semi-mystical presence in his life and work he acknowledged more than once,[12] D'Halmar's orientalism has a particular flavor. It is of course directly evident in those texts inspired by his voyage to Egypt and India, such as *Nirvana, Mi otro yo* (My other self), and *La sombra del humo en el espejo* (Shadow of smoke in the mirror), but it is not necessarily tied to location. Indeed, one might argue that D'Halmar's initial orientalist fiction is *Gatita* (Kitten), a novella set in northern Peru. The first to deal with what would become D'Halmar's preferred erotic relation, that of the older man of authority with the colonized, gender-ambiguous child—a homoerotic, pederastic version of Said's "Oriental sex"[13]—*Gatita* is set in a little town in the Andean desert that gives the impression "that it could just as well have been in Palestine, or that the hamlet could be in Mahé, in the Indies, or in Jibuti, in Africa" (D'Halmar 1970, 174); a town where "the white-washed walls were as bright as those of a Casbah slum" (176) and whose *mestizo* inhabitants are found to be full of "that mournful lassitude left by the Arabs in Spain and by the Spanish in America" (182). This shifting orientalism, loosely projected on the not strictly oriental but certainly racially diverse, finds its most elaborate form in *La pasión y muerte del cura Deusto,* the novel D'Halmar wrote in, and about, that other Arab country, Spain; a novel with which, I will argue, he both rejoins and subverts attempts to reclaim *lo hispano* in the Latin America of the 1920s and 30s.

D'Halmar, we are told by his friends and critics, liked to dress up, even before becoming D'Halmar. His preference seems to have gone to flowing robes: "Augusto spent the day dressed only in his nightgown, which made him look like a young Muslim fakir," writes Santiván, orientalizing in turn, of their early days in the *colonia tolstoyana* (Santiván 1965, 1401). In "Pequeños pensamientos del destierro" (Brief thoughts from exile), musing on his need to change costume (*mudar de disfraz*), D'Halmar himself writes: "It is not the puerile exoticism of playing the Mameluke that makes me insist on wearing oriental dress. If I do so, it is to conjure I don't quite know what dark destiny which I hardly dare think of" (D'Halmar n.d., 106). D'Halmar seems to have been especially partial to "native" headdress, according to his imaginary interviewer: "It is known that he has worn the Osmanli fez in the Orient of the Sultans, the Hindu [*sic*] turban in the Far East, and that in Spain he wears a cape and a Cordovan hat in Andalusia" (D'Halmar 1963, 234). The verb tenses D'Halmar uses here are interesting. Dressing up as "Oriental" is in the past tense, dressing up as "Spanish" in the present; the latter, as it were, continues the former, *Carmen* follows (finally, coincides with) "the chic of Araby," to use Marjorie Garber's felicitous phrase (1992, 304). Does D'Halmar dress up as "Spanish" also "to conjure I don't quite know what dark destiny which I hardly dare think of?" What, after all, *is* Spain for D'Halmar?

D'Halmar describes his conscious decision to take up residence in Spain, for what would be his longest stay in any country other than Chile, in significant terms: "Having less foresight than a wild animal, than an insect even, I did not have a lair I could call home, a burrow that I could call my country [*patria*]. I for whom no one waited anywhere, who had all the world and all my life at my disposal, the sky for my only flag, and the desolate freedom of a man from nowhere, I chose to set boundaries, to retire to a place that would be favorable to me. Under the terrible sun of India I had learned, at my own expense, that climate is the first requisite for well-being and that . . . moral climate was as indispensable as physical climate. It was then that I thought of Spain (D'Halmar 1963, 222). Further down he adds: "I have renewed myself morally [*me he rehecho*], or to be exact, Spain has renewed me morally. Because in Spain I have found peace within myself" (222).

Spain is a site of moral restoration, of personal renewal, where D'Halmar —he who liked to stress the self-engendering qualities of his literary persona—makes himself over, or as he literally writes in Spanish: *Me he rehecho.* This refashioning of self, signified on one level by the cape and the Andalusian hat, goes together with the notion of setting boundaries and finding "moral . . . well-being" and "peace within myself," a desire for stability quite atypical in D'Halmar, who repeatedly expressed his preference for movement, erasure of limits, fleeting identities.[14] It is obvious, then, that whatever role orientalism plays in D'Halmar's Spain—and it does—it is accompanied by the rhetoric of a moral and national quest: the refashioned self settles down in a renovated *patria.*

Recourse to the notion of Spain as *patria* is, as I have indicated, very much a part of Latin America's continued reflection on origins at the time. D'Halmar is definitely aware of this movement and up to a point buys into it, as his journalistic writing of the period makes clear.[15] In his review of *Un chileno en Madrid,* a novel by his compatriot Joaquín Edwards Bello, he praises Edwards Bello for writing on "the *idée fixe* of the Latin American who, for love of the country of his future, looks back to the country of his past, like one who, going back to the source, not only sees that it still flows but that the water is purer there than in the river lower down" (D'Halmar 1929, 500). Yet it is in that very Spain, converted into a phantasmatic *heimat,* a Hispanic common abode, that D'Halmar sets his most explicitly homoerotic fiction. It is as if, having uprooted himself from his native Chile and opted for a life abroad, orientalizing himself as he went along, D'Halmar needed to rethink *lo hispano* as did other Latin Americans, but needed to do so on his own terms. Of course, the precise terms in which he did this — namely, by projecting homosexual desire into the very heart of the *patria,* thus questioning exemplary Hispanic constructions of gender — attest to the limitations of that very *patria* and to D'Halmar's tentative place within it.

Like Carlos Reyles's *El embrujo de Sevilla,* D'Halmar's novel takes place in Seville. Unlike Reyles, "a staunch believer in the potential of that land of heroism and dreams" (Rodríguez Mallarini 1980, 18), who projects his plot back to a fiery nineteenth century, D'Halmar places his story squarely in the twentieth, achieving that exquisite, sickly effect (also found in D'Annunzio's descriptions of Rome in *Il Piacere*) brought by the contact between two worlds, the pastoral and the technological — a child on a donkey next to a Hispano-Suiza. D'Halmar's *La pasión y muerte del cura Deusto* tells the story of a Basque priest who, distraught because his best and dearest friend, also a seminarian, marries his sister (a by now familiar scenario), requests to be sent to a faraway parish and ends up in Seville. There he becomes increasingly attached to Pedro Miguel, also called *El Aceitunita,* "Little Olive," a young gypsy boy of *morisco* and Jewish ancestry who introduces him to things Andalusian; who also becomes a singer in his choir, a sexton in his church, and — D'Halmar here repeats the pattern of *Gatita* and *La sombra del humo en el espejo,* while taking it one step further in explicitness — becomes the object of a love that the priest cannot confess even to himself *but that everybody around him can see.* Crucial to the novel, as its two main structuring lines, are Deusto's persistent denial of the nature of this love and the boy's growing awareness of his own beauty and power to seduce. Sem Rubí, a roué Jewish painter who reads like an Andalusian combination of *Dorian Gray*'s Basil Hallward and Lord Henry Wotton, talks the boy into posing for him and introduces him to the world of *flamenco,* bullfighting, fast living, and sexual ambiguity. When the boy, grown weary of his new life, returns to Deusto, aware of the strength of his bond with the older man, the full recognition takes place: "Then the black eyes and the green eyes, as if they had never looked at each other before, understood. And it was delightful, and it was terrible. Whoever has looked that way, once, in the shadows, should not see the light again" (D'Halmar 1969, 200).[16] The young man decides to leave, finally realizing that "lo nuestro," our thing, has no future. ("Lo nuestro" is as far as the text goes in naming the unnameable, which is—given the bond implied in the use of the possessive—considerably far.) Then, in a memorable station scene, the priest, refusing the young man's pleas to accompany him to Madrid and start a new life together, runs onto the tracks and lets himself be crushed by the very train that takes the young man away from him. The scene surely owes quite a bit to Tolstoy, the master who had inspired the *colonia tolstoyana* of D'Halmar's youth. Curiously enough, an identical Anna Karenina–effect may be found at the end of *El ángel de Sodoma* (The angel of Sodom) (1929), another Latin American homoerotic novel by the Cuban Hernández Catá. There the protagonist, as guilty and desperate as D'Halmar's priest, throws himself in the path of an approaching subway car.

As a homoerotic novel, *La pasión y muerte del cura Deusto* doubtless belongs to the tragic modality: there is much anguish, much soul-searching, much naming-while-not-naming ("How could we stay here when everybody says we are . . . what we are not!" [D'Halmar 1969, 221]), much shame, and a suicide at the end. This suicide actually allows us to measure the progression with respect to D'Halmar's previous homoerotic fictions. *Gatita* and *La sombra del humo en el espejo* are basically elegiac texts celebrating man-boy love;[17] they skirt homosexual conflict and end in separation (*La sombra* very much in the vein of the Athman episode in Gide's *If It Die*), but not in death. Instead, in texts like *La pasión y muerte,* or certain stories in *Los alucinados,* which out homosexual conflict (although never directly named it), the result is, of necessity, death: the queer becomes the sacrificial victim. To ask for a different treatment of homosexuality, from a Latin American writer in the 1920s, would be anachronistic.[18] That D'Halmar has taken care to assure a "good" response on the part of the larger public is shown by the ambivalent treatment afforded the young boy, who at times is treated like a calculating *viborilla,* and at others like an upright, loving human being. It is as if the book counted on two different receptions: the one, judgmental, from those who need to see the queer as a "little viper"; the other, complicitous, from readers "entre nous."

But what most interests me here is how this tale of thwarted homosexual love fits into D'Halmar's new *patria.* Spain, for D'Halmar, is a much more complex construct than, say, for his fellow Latin Americans Enrique Larreta or Carlos Reyles, literary archaeologists whose recuperation of *lo his-*

pano, steeped as it was in conservative ideology, is fairly straightforward. D'Halmar's Spain, instead, is a map of conflicting geographies and conflicting desires. Not incidentally, the novel is set in Seville, a crossroads par excellence: not only Spain's original gateway to and from the Americas, but also a site of ethnic diversity and cultural hybridity, of mixture and general ambiguity.[19] *El Aceitunita* comes from a gypsy mother and a Jewish father; a marginal mixture par excellence, he has olive skin, chestnut hair, and improbably blue eyes (which, later on in the text, D'Halmar inadvertently calls green). He is a "youngster who, although circumcised, babbled litanies to the Christian Virgin" (D'Halmar 1969, 41), and who, when singing the *Angelus,* "retained an Islamic something, it was the voice of a neophyte ephebe, ambiguous, and, for that very reason, full of a mysterious charm" (33). Posed against a window, *El Aceitunita* looks precisely like "that Andalusian ephebe a Cordovan caliph had named *Sword* because he said the boy's eyes had pierced his heart" (135). The orientalization of Seville extends to the city itself, its buildings, memorably evoked in the heat of the afternoon:

> The nostalgia with which the Basque often remembered his native Basque country could well be a warning of his senses. The heat had inflamed the sapphire of the Seville sky turning it into a garnet. The palms did not give shade, the white facades reverberated, Sierpes street was covered with ship sails. Africa had crossed the straits and, through Algeciras, had stolen into its ancient possessions. Like crackling red coals inside tiny incense burners, poppies burnt up their opium, carnations distilled musk, roses dripped vanilla. But what prevailed was the smell of honey, as if the honeycombs had melted. Surely it was the bees, left without hives, that made that deafening murmur, like the noise of breakers in seashells, a noise that was probably only in the ears of those suffering from overexposure to the heat.
>
> With their canvas screens and rope hammocks, patios felt like covered decks on ships crossing the Red Sea. Even the waterspout grew sleepy. With drawn shutters, in the suffocating penumbra of the stuccoed rooms with their tiled floors, the inhabitants tried to barricade themselves against the torrid assault of summer. (45)

Just as D'Halmar changes into cape and Cordovan hat when in Andalusia, so also do his characters dress up, cross-dress, and undress with surprising frequency. Pedro Miguel—whose nickname, *El* (masculine) *Aceitunita* (feminine), is already, quite casually, a gender composite—dresses up as the Jesus child for Deusto's Easter pageant; as an Arab for the carnival party given by the poet Giraldo (a shadowy character explicitly compared to Dorian Gray); and as a gypsy when he performs *flamenco* for the first time on stage. For his part, the Basque priest, in his feeble attempts at erotic damage-control, tries to dress up the South as North, to re-dress the "Muslim tolerance" (D'Halmar 1969, 16) by simplifying church ritual, banning ornaments, and—incidentally—banning all women (i.e., the nosy church ladies in charge of decorations) from the parish house.[20] This parish house, in turn, is re-dressed to look like Algorta, the priest's spartan Basque home: "objects had taken on a vague look of *over there* . . . and in reality the priest Deusto hoped to see this transformation extend to other things" (16; original emphasis). But "other things" are not so easily transformed, and re-dressing, dressing up, and cross-dressing go both ways. Allowing himself to be tempted by his protégé into an outing to the circus, Deusto sheds his northern priestly skirts for a southern *señorito* suit: "By candlelight, before the small mirror, a trim young man, dressed in black, knotted his tie. When, armed with hat and cape, he met the boy outside, the little gypsy could not believe that his young and handsome companion was the adult priest whom he had always considered old" (122).

One may speculate why D'Halmar chose Seville as the setting in which to rethink *lo hispano* and not, for instance, Castile (where *lo hispano* had been and was still being rethought by Spaniards themselves). It was, perhaps, a nod toward the *espagnolade,* the acknowledgment of an old and tried recipe. *La pasión y muerte* inevitably brings Mérimée's *Carmen* to mind, even in its ethnic attributions: the desirer is Basque,[21] the desired, Andalusian; the North is economical and repressed, the South wasteful, equivocal, and untrustworthy. Or one could say, I suppose, that D'Halmar, in choosing Seville, the gateway to America, is inverting Spain's gesture of colonization, submitting the *madre patria* he claimed to have rediscovered to a defamiliarizing, orientalist gaze, and doing so at the original site of Spain's imperial enterprise. Or is it perhaps something else? I would propose, instead, that D'Halmar is creating a different *patria* by the very recourse to orientalism, that the choice of Seville, of exotic, tacky, castanet-clacking, and incense-burning Seville, allows him to carve out a space of *very visible* difference wherein to speak what cannot be spoken elsewhere in Hispanic literature, an extra-ordinary place where homoeroticism and homosexuality not only "pass" (albeit marginally) but can be made to pass into fiction.[22] To paraphrase D'Halmar, orientalism, most especially in the case of *La pasión y muerte del cura Deusto*, "is not the puerile exoticism of playing the Spaniard" (or not *only* that) but a cultural necessity, a way of conjuring an otherwise "dark destiny which I hardly dare think of" by outing it, by advertising it, even when disguising it — precisely by not keeping it in the "secret abyss" to which critics would doom it. By orientalizing the *patria*, D'Halmar can both speak of homosexual desire *out there* and, in the same movement, bring it back home.[23] Thus, he not only problematizes a univocal "straight" reading of *lo hispano*, but highlights as well the inevitable repression of normative national(istic) cultural discourses (the Latin American ones included), discourses into which sexual divergence did not, does not, must not, fit.

Notes

Unless otherwise noted, all translations are my own.

1   Interestingly, General Ramírez's repressive, pro-Nazi regime contributed to the unexpected publicization of the incident: "The strict censorship of the press that was prevalent in the country kept the case from the newspapers; however, it was gossiped about throughout the country, to the point that, for the first time and at all social levels, the 'homosexual phenomenon' was openly discussed. Dubious jokes and allusive songs were heard in the street and the workplace, in schools and cafés, even in the most prudish households" (Sebreli 1983, 11).

2   For provocative readings of Donoso's *El lugar sin limites* (Hell has no limits), see Sarduy 1987; Sifuentes-Jáuregui, 1997.

3   "El alma trémula y sola/Padece al anochecer:/Hay baile; vamos a ver/La bailarina española./Han hecho bien en quitar/El banderón de la acera:/Porque si está la bandera,/No sé, yo no puedo entrar" (My soul, quivering and alone / Suffers as night falls: / There's a show; let's go and see / The Spanish dancer. / They were right to remove / The big flag from the sidewalk: / If the flag were still there, / I don't feel I could enter) (Martí 1982, 189).

4   For intelligent views on the import of these centennial celebrations throughout Latin America, see Alonso 1990, 52-56.

5   Spain itself had prepared the way for this Latinity early on, especially after the war between the United States and Mexico, using it as an argument against Cuba's independence. As a journalist of the period writes, with much fire and mixed meta-

phors: "Woe unto Spanish American republics if Cuba ever ceases to be Spanish! Woe unto the Latin race in the New World, if our sentinel advancing into the Atlantic were to fall, wounded and betrayed! Today that rock is the shield of a whole race, and on her battered ramparts it would seem that Cortés and Pizarro still wander, encouraging our soldiers" (Asquerino 1857, 2).

6   "Nationalism without Hispanism is an absurd claim in our American countries since it would mean reversing a biological process. . . . Hispanism should be the assimilating and bonding agent of our national transformations" (Suárez 1929, 22).

7   "Augusto convinced me that we should collaborate, like the famous Goncourt brothers or the Savoyards Erckmann-Chatrain: a perfect friendship in disinterested, literary harmony. It was then that we abandoned our names, Augusto G. Thomson and Fernando Sant-Iván, in order to adopt the common pseudonym D'Halmar, preceded by the names Augusto and Fernando. I managed to write some stories and articles under this name. But I did not feel satisfied" (Santiván 1965, 1515). Santiván writes *D'Halmar,* but the early, shared pseudonym seems to have been simply *Halmar.*

8   For an illuminating consideration of male collaboration that helps understand this precise case, see Koestenbaum 1989.

9   In that same mock interview, "El reportaje que nadie nos hace nunca" (The interview no one ever asks us to give), D'Halmar imagines the following exchange: "Q: Name? A: The one I have created for myself. Q: Family? A: The one I have adopted" (D'Halmar 1963, 235).

10 In fact, he will more or less disavow *Juana Lucero* in his mock interview: "[*Juana Lucero*] does not belong to me. It was written, during an earlier life of mine that lasted twenty-one years, by that ill-fated Thomson, whose mere executor I am. May both book and author rest in peace" (D'Halmar 1963, 236).

11 Emily Apter's description appropriately summarizes D'Halmar's orientalism: "French colonial literature is made up of a nasty tissue of Orientalist clichés; romantic physiognomical and characterological typologies, racist sexual fantasies, and frozen, "postcarded" images of native subjects indiscriminately shuffled between black, brown, métis, Asiatic, Arab, Kabylian, Moorish, Ottoman, Bedouin, Islamic, and Byzantine cultural frames" (Apter 1992, 207).

12 For specific references to Loti in D'Halmar, see: "Alrededor de Loti," "La vaga fecha," "Año Nuevo en Constantinopla" in *Antología* (D'Halmar 1963); "Navidad en el mar" (which Díaz Arrieta rightly interprets as a mystical reunion with Loti) and "La vaga fecha" in *Nirvana* (D'Halmar n.d.); and "Valerio Dux" in *Los alucinados* (D'Halmar 1935).

13   For a critique of Said's erasure of homoerotics from his construction of orientalism, see Boone 1995. "[T]he possibility of sexual contact with and between men," Boone reminds us, "underwrites and at times even explains the historical appeal of orientalism as an occidental mode of male perception, appropriation, and control" (90).

14   To the question "What do you find overwhelming?" that he asks of himself in his mock interview, he replies: "The obsession with the 'I,' with the specific name. The impossibility of losing myself, of dissolving . . ." (D'Halmar 1963, 238).

15   During his stay in Spain, D'Halmar writes regularly for the Spanish journal *Informaciones*. Between 1925 and 1928, he also writes for *La Nación* of Santiago, contributing impassioned descriptions of his travels through Spain that are later published in a volume, *La Mancha de Don Quijote* (1934).

16   The male-to-male gaze is omnipresent in D'Halmar's fiction. To give but one example, also from *La pasión y muerte:* "At that moment, it was as if fire had run through his body. His eyes stopped and stared, because he had just picked up Deusto's gaze, fixed on him, from the balcony. He hesitated for an instant, then with a mournful voice he improvised the final sorrowful song that was addressed only to him . . ." (D'Halmar 1969, 163).

17   I choose to consider *Gatita* a homoerotic fiction despite the quite obvious fact that Gatita is a young girl. The author's particular treatment of this "girl," his emphasis on her androgyny, his calling her "una niña, un niño" and likening her to a page, his stress on sensual *attouchement* and lack of heterosexual encounters (she is presumably his lover) so reminiscent of Loti's chaste eroticism, his comparing her to Zahir, the Arab servant boy in *La sombra del humo en el espejo,* I think, justify my decision.

18   I can think of only one Latin American text of the period in which homosexuality, once outed, is not met with violence or death. I refer to the surprise ending of Enrique Gómez Carrillo's "Marta y Hortensia": "Why would I open the door when I have never been capable of killing two women?" (Gómez Carrillo 1919, 80). The fact that it is a story about lesbians may well account for its benign ending.

19   As James Fernández writes, "Throughout the sixteenth and seventeenth centuries, the city was praised and censured for its diversity and promiscuity. 'A new Babylon' was a common epithet for Seville; Saint Teresa de Avila, among others, called the city an 'infierno' " (Fernández 1994, 978). There are obvious echoes of that reputation in D'Halmar's description of the city.

20   The only female figure left in the parish house is that of the faithful nanny-housekeeper, a protective figure initially developed by D'Halmar in *Gatita*. Not

incidentally, this one is called Monica, in keeping with her saintly, motherly qualities.

21 Deusto's Basque descent and fond evocation of his province, besides referring to *Carmen*'s Don José, point also in the direction of Loti, who had made Hendaye his second home.

22 The other homoerotic novel I have mentioned, *El ángel de Sodoma* by Alfonso Hernández Catá, is presented as a case history, framed by a prologue by Dr. Gregorio Marañon, the Spanish philosopher and doctor of medicine, and an epilogue by Dr. Luis Giménez de Azua, both of whom attempt to medicalize the text and channel its reception. That homosexual desire can only be spoken of when "safely" ascribed to the exotic is clear in all of D'Halmar's fiction. Even those narratives that do not take place in exotic settings are given an exotic twist. In "Valerio Dux," one of the stories in *Los alucinados* that takes place in Paris, the androgynous boy who steals the protagonist's heart (and leads him to suicide) is from Brittany, a region presented as the capital's "exotic" other (D'Halmar 1935).

23 Interestingly, the Argentine Manuel Gálvez, in his attempt to recover Spain for Latin America, takes pains to deny Arab influence in Spain, even (rather incredibly) in Andalusia: "Today the Arab world only exists in Spain as an archaeological ruin" (Gálvez 1986, 248); and, "In Seville, usually considered an African city, Arab influence is insignificant" (249). Gálvez (a right-wing, militant Catholic writer) concludes his vehement denial of the Arab presence in Spain with a telling reference to gender: "But those of us who feel the soul of our race, who have seen that soul wandering along the narrow streets of cities in Castile, look upon the arabesques of the Alhambra, the gardens of the Generalife, all those delights that reveal a *sensual and effeminate* people, as exotic things. Castilian Spain, although old and impoverished, we carry within us; African Spain is very far removed. It is a poetic legend, practically a story of the *Thousand and One Nights*" (258; emphasis added).

RHONDA COBHAM

Jekyll and Claude: The Erotics of Patronage

in Claude McKay's Banana Bottom

Two "unnatural" acts occur in *Banana Bottom,* both of which seem shockingly inappropriate in this bucolic narrative. Claude McKay (1890–1948) mentions the first almost parenthetically on the second page of the novel when the heroine, Bita Plant, successfully completes her debut as accompanist to the church choir of Banana Bottom: "Bita was a girl with a past. Between the years of twelve and thirteen she had been raped. She had been raped by Crazy Bow Adair" (McKay 1961, 2).

Crazy Bow is a gifted, near-white youth—a genetic throwback to European stock within a mixed-race family—whose brilliant academic career is cut short when his obsession with music and musical instruments turns his head. There is no suggestion that Bita feels traumatized by his action, and she remains bewitched by his uncanny musical talent. However, Bita's rape is the narrative pretext that brings her to the attention of the English missionaries, Malcolm and Priscilla Craig. In an effort to compensate for what they view as a heinous crime of violation, the Craigs adopt Bita and pay for her education in England. Their intervention equips her for the role of sentient protagonist in McKay's story. The villagers, on the other hand, see nothing unnatural in the connection between Bita's rape and her improved status, and McKay notes that "there was not a dark family in Banana Bottom and that gorgeous stretch of tropical country that did not wish one of their children had been in Bita's shoes and had been instead the victim of Crazy Bow" (McKay 1961, 29).

The second "unnatural" act has more dire consequences. Halfway through the novel the young deacon, Herald Newton Day, whom the Craigs have handpicked to marry Bita, is discovered in flagrante delicto with Sister Christy's nanny goat. Unlike Bita's loss of innocence, Herald Day's action sends him tumbling into disrepute in the eyes of his fellow villagers. His disgrace is not so much on account of attitudes towards bestiality — a not uncommon pastime in this agricultural village. Rather, the deacon's act is aberrant because of who — or what — he claims to be. He fails to live up to the moral codes appropriate to his social aspirations, and is therefore returned to the cultural and social obscurity from which he originally was plucked.

In narrating these incidents, McKay shifts between a critique of the peasants' desire to distance themselves from a state of nature, and a concern with the lines of patronage through which such aspirations were controlled. These were important issues for McKay, as his own access to an intellectual life, which took him far beyond the limits of his Jamaican peasant village, was a consequence of his unusual relationship with a wealthy English recluse, Walter Jekyll. McKay reproduces many aspects of their relationship in *Banana Bottom* through his account of the friendship between his heroine, Bita, and her English mentor, Squire Gensir, as if to demonstrate that there were ways of acknowledging the tensions and tendernesses of cross-racial patronage without reducing the protégé to a sign of his patron's desire. But the excesses of the sexual relations that hedge in the chaste minuet between Gensir and Bita in *Banana Bottom* speak to the anxieties that belied McKay's posture of self-assurance in his own dealings with white patrons. This essay situates McKay's Jamaican novel against the backdrop of the textual and sexual expectations around patronage that McKay encountered in Jamaica and abroad — especially the fascination with African primitivism in Europe and the white enthusiasm for black creativity in America during the Harlem Renaissance. It reads the effects of these expectations on the distinctions McKay struggles to enforce between natural and unnatural acts, dialect and "straight" English, and action and utterance. Against the grain of conventional readings of Bita as resolving the conflict between body and intellect in McKay's writing, I argue that McKay's attempt to refigure racial inequalities as gender hierarchies offers a troubling commentary on the personal and cultural liabilities of patronage.

At the age of eighteen, McKay ran away from home and joined the police force in order to be nearer to Jekyll, who had offered to educate him (McKay 1979, 67). Jekyll introduced McKay to European literature, languages, and philosophy, gave the youth access to an audience among the Jamaican elite for his poetry, and organized the British publication in 1912 of McKay's first two volumes of dialect poetry, *Songs of Jamaica* and *Constab Ballads*.[1] That same year, he arranged McKay's release from his police commission and financed McKay's migration to America. Over the next five years, Jekyll supported McKay's academic and business ventures generously (Cooper 1987, 67, 70). McKay never forgot his mentor's "gentleness and otherworldliness" (McKay 1979, 17). He wrote *Banana Bottom* after Jekyll's death in 1928, eulogizing him in the portrayal of Squire Gensir, and in the novel's dedication to "Pacjo" — the peasants' affectionate nickname for the eccentric little Englishman.

The relationship between Bita and Gensir in *Banana Bottom* reproduces the relationship between McKay and Jekyll, down to the books they share and the conversations in which they engage. Given Jekyll's background and the historical context of his friendship with McKay, there may have been a homoerotic dimension to their relationship. Jekyll is widely presumed to have been sexually attracted to men, and he had a long history of mentoring promising youths to whom he had taken a fancy.[2] But although McKay changes the sex of the protégé in his story, a move that could have allowed for a heterosexual rearticulation of any erotic undertones in his relationship with Jekyll, he assiduously avoids any suggestion that the friendship between Bita and Squire Gensir is anything but platonic. All the other characters in the novel seem to be throwing themselves passionately into relationships with every conceivable object, but at the point in the text when Bita's adult sexual needs assert themselves, McKay has her swept away from Gensir by the insistent throbbing of the drums at a revival meeting. From here she is snatched by her father's mule driver, Jubban, who eventually becomes her lover and husband.

To understand this evasion we need to look more carefully at the expectations about patronage that Jekyll as mentor and McKay as his protégé brought to their unusual (unnatural?) friendship. Jekyll was a fin-de-siècle bohemian with agnostic leanings and an aristocratic background (McKay 1970, 17; McKay 1979, 70; Cooper 1987, 23n.77). An ardent disciple of Schopen-

hauer, whose work he translated into English, Jekyll deplored the enerva-
tion of modern Western civilization. He made his retreat into the Jamaican
countryside in an attempt to reconnect with some form of unspoiled "natural" life. Jekyll collected Jamaican folklore and shunned what he considered
the philistine society of the Jamaican social elite. McKay first came to the English collector's attention when Jekyll stopped to have his carriage repaired
by a wheelwright to whom McKay was apprenticed. The wheelwright mentioned that his apprentice fancied himself a poet. Jekyll was intrigued by the
notion of a peasant poet who, from his perspective, may have epitomized the
Enlightenment ideal of the noble savage. McKay recounts Jekyll's initial response to his work:

> He read my poetry one day. Then he laughed a lot, and I became
> angry at the laughing because I thought he was laughing at me. All
> these poems that I gave him to read had been done in straight English,
> but there was one short one about an ass that was laden for the mar-
> ket—laden with native vegetables—who had suddenly sat down in the
> middle of the road and wouldn't get up. Its owner was talking to it in the
> Jamaican dialect, telling it to get up. That was the poem that Mr. Jekyll
> was laughing about. He then told me that he did not like my poems in
> straight English—they were repetitious. "But this," said he, holding up
> the donkey poem, "this is the real thing. The Jamaican dialect has never
> been put into literary form except in my [*sic*] Anancy stories. Now is
> your chance as a native boy to put the Jamaican dialect into literary lan-
> guage. I am sure that your poems will sell." (McKay 1979, 66–67)

Notwithstanding the momentary dread he expresses that Jekyll may have
confused him with the driver of donkeys in his poem—or even with the donkey itself—McKay, in his recollection of the incident, does not present himself
as a noble savage. He understood that he was "Mr. Jekyll's" social inferior but
claimed the Englishman as a friend and intellectual peer.

Jekyll was not McKay's only source of erudition or nonconformist ideas.
Many black townships in rural Jamaica at the turn of the century could boast
small circles of well-read school teachers and professionals, and McKay encountered a wide range of books and ideas through such people.[3] His older
brother, U. Theo McKay, had declared himself an agnostic at a time when the
majority of educated Jamaicans were deeply God-fearing. Moreover, McKay

claims that many of the peasant boys who were his friends were notorious for their skepticism and iconoclasm (McKay 1970, 12). McKay was probably open to Jekyll's "pagan" ideas because of this antiestablishment peasant tradition. However, his early exposure in his brother's home to the "freethinking" debates raging in Britain at the turn of the century — debates that were followed avidly in the colonies — encouraged him to associate progressive ideas with a world beyond the limitations of colonial society and made him peculiarly receptive to someone like Jekyll. McKay identified with all Jekyll's postures — including his mentor's sense of being cut off from the "spontaneous" peasant culture that, ironically, McKay probably embodied for Jekyll. The paradox becomes clear in McKay's initial response to Jekyll's suggestion that he write in dialect: "to us who were getting an education in the English schools the Jamaican dialect was considered a vulgar tongue. It was the language of the peasants. All cultivated people spoke English, straight English" (McKay 1979, 67).

McKay's response dramatizes the distinction that many progressive colonials drew between the legitimacy of the challenge to the status quo contained in the British freethinking tradition and that expressed in the equally iconoclastic but socially devalued native tradition. Jekyll's championing of the native tradition increased its esteem in McKay's eyes and led him subsequently to rethink his opposition to using dialect. But Jekyll's appreciation of Jamaican speech did not mean that he considered it intellectually sophisticated or that he approved of its subversive potential. His typecasting of McKay as a native boy who ought to write in dialect may have been prescriptive, and there remained for the young poet a lingering desire to prove that, in spite of his peasant origins, he too could write verse in "elevated language." As McKay himself puts it, "I used to think I would show them something. Someday I would write poetry in straight English and amaze and confound them" (McKay 1979, 87).

"Them," in the passage quoted, refers to the literati among the "wealthy near whites and the British and American residents" of Jamaica for whom, according to McKay, Jekyll occasionally "trotted out" his protégé (McKay, 76). McKay directs his frustration with the limitations of his role of noble savage at "them," rather than taking issue with his mentor who had encouraged him to exploit this role. But elsewhere he registers his awareness of the structure that Jekyll's perspective imposed on their relationship. On one occasion

Jekyll, who considered Sydney Olivier, the governor of Jamaica, a middle-class upstart, lost his temper when Olivier attempted to invite himself to stay overnight under Jekyll's roof. McKay recalls how Jekyll's strongly stated class bias on this occasion prompted him to ask: " 'But Mr. Jekyll, how can you tolerate me? I am merely the son of a peasant.' 'Oh,' said he, 'English gentlemen have always liked their peasants, it's the ambitious middle class that we cannot tolerate' " (McKay 1979, 71).

There are many layers of ironic silence in McKay's retelling of this incident. For instance, we can almost feel the infinitesimal hesitation covered over by Jekyll's "Oh," as he tries to decide how to allay the fear of rejection implicit in his protégé's question. Faced with the choice of sentimentalizing their relationship in a way that might name its homoerotic possibilities, or patronizing the youth, he opts for patronage, but manages in doing so to parody himself in the role of patron, thus drawing any hint of ridicule away from McKay and onto himself. McKay returns the favor in retelling the story by passing over Jekyll's self-presentation in silence and allowing the multiple ironies of the words he ascribes to Jekyll to stand in for any reservations he may have wished to register about Jekyll's attitudes. The strategy enables McKay to show us Jekyll's limitations without discounting the wit and genuine affection that he felt motivated his mentor's response.

For all this deft self-parody, Jekyll remained firmly ensconced in his aristocratic notions of class and racial hierarchy. He distrusted the new professional middle class in England, to which the Fabian socialist governor Sydney Olivier belonged, and his relationships with "his" peasants were cordial only as long as they recognized his feudal rights as lord of the castle. Jekyll was quick to condemn any violation of the social order. Writing in *The Bible Untrustworthy*, an agnostic publication, he faults Jesus for "not car[ing] about social order; he disliked the upper classes and railed at them in words of astonishing rancor." In the same tract, Jekyll associates Christ's iconoclasm with the violent, hyperbolic language of Jamaican peasants and warns that "obeying Christ's literal injunctions would lead to anarchy" (Jekyll 1904, 259). In his collection of *Jamaica Song and Story*, Jekyll's otherwise neutral or appreciative comments about a broad range of folk customs acquire a punitive edge when he comments on folk songs connected with the Morant Bay Rebellion of 1865. The local uprising resulted in the death of three white functionaries and about four hundred black and brown Jamaicans. However, in a note to a folk song about the rebellion that he collected, Jekyll characterizes it as a near carnage of whites that was averted only by the "prompt action of Governor Eyre" (187–88).

Jekyll's comments suggest that, in spite of his desire for contact with nature and spiritual community with the tillers of the soil, he still felt threatened by the possibility that the feral energies of the lower classes could be turned against him or his class. Jekyll's ambivalence may have had its effect on his mentorship of McKay. Under his tutelage, McKay wrote poems in dialect in which masters castigated their mules, or prostitutes vilified policemen and other "upstart" members of the new black middle class. However, Jekyll appears to have encouraged his protégé to censor any militancy that might have threatened what he considered the status quo. For example, McKay never anthologized his poem "Gordon to the Oppressed Natives," in which (in contrast to Jekyll) he celebrated the militancy of the Morant Bay rebels.[4] This was one of McKay's best-known early poems. It had appeared in the *Jamaica Times* in 1912, alongside other poems that were published subsequently in *Constab Ballads*. In the same year, the poem won a prize in an Empire poetry contest, and it was a favorite recitation piece at local concerts and debating societies.[5] Nevertheless, it is conspicuously absent from both of the collections Jekyll facilitated.

Clearly there were limits to the freedom McKay's mentor was prepared to allow him in their unequal relationship. McKay began to divest himself of this element of Jekyll's patronage when he moved to America, where he felt freer to work in "straight English," as well as to express his views on social and racial injustice in stridently militant poems like the famous anti-lynching sonnet "If We Must Die." But even at this remove, the desire to ally himself with his patron's notions of "good taste" still lingered. In his autobiography, McKay records how, on the advice of an unnamed English friend, he omitted "If We Must Die," in spite of its popularity, when he published *Spring in New Hampshire* (1920), his first collection of American poems. McKay's self-censorship aroused the ire of one of his newer white patrons, Frank Harris, editor of *Pearson's Magazine*. McKay took to heart Harris's accusation that he cared more for his mentor's sensibilities than for the people whose sacrifices his poem celebrated, and he remembers vowing not to allow such false inhibitions to influence his future decisions (McKay 1970, 97–99).

Whatever the sincerity of the bonds of friendship between Jekyll and Mc-

Kay, therefore, there were obvious strains in the structure of their relationship. It placed McKay in Jekyll's power even as it allowed him that access to an intellectual life and artistic sensibility he coveted. We can better understand something of the complexity of McKay's dilemma in writing about this relationship if we compare it to the issues at stake in Foucault's discussion of the dynamics of erotic friendships between boys and men in classical Greece in *The Use of Pleasure*. Foucault remarks on the oscillation between a concern with the "natural or 'unnatural' character of that type of love" (Foucault 1985, 221): natural because it united two masculine intellects and affections in a friendship superior to the love of women, but unnatural because it placed the youthful, receptive partner in a passive, and therefore potentially shameful, relationship with another man. According to Foucault, "[s]exual relations thus demanded particular behaviors on the part of both partners. A consequence of the fact that the boy could not identify with the part he had to play [*sic*]; he was supposed to refuse, resist, flee, escape. He was also supposed to make his consent, if he finally gave it, subject to conditions relating to the man to whom he yielded (his merit, his status, his virtue) and to the benefit he could expect to gain from him (a benefit that was rather shameful if it was only a question of money, but honorable if it involved training for manhood, social connections for the future, or a lasting friendship)" (224). As Foucault describes it, there is a degree of instability built into such transactions on account of the need for both parties to maintain an understanding of their relationship as both an act of reluctant acquiescence on the part of the youth and a form of ideal fellowship between two mutually consenting parties. But neither Foucault nor the classical Greek texts he cites succeed in conveying a sense of what the youth could consider pleasurable about the sexual aspect of such an exchange. Foucault's own account, quoted above, is littered with evasions, qualifications, and ellipses, which suggest that the physical acts by which the older man appropriated the youth's body could not be named— that is, not as long as the perceived passivity of the youth in the relationship remained a marked term, opposed to the active role prescribed for a potential full citizen of the Greek democracy.[6]

Instead, by a series of substitutions that recalls the parenthetical insertion of Bita's rape into the record of her educational accomplishments, intellectual pleasure becomes both the enabling pretext and the consequence of physical penetration. The passage quoted from Foucault demonstrates how the migration of the locus of sexual pleasure from the body to the mind has the effect of sublimating the physical and of eroticizing the intellectual elements in the exchange between mentor and protégé: it blurs the distinction between carnal knowledge and intellectual stimulation; between physical penetration and discursive appropriation; between body and text; between action and utterance. Even if we assume, therefore, that the erotic aspects of the relationship between McKay and Jekyll were not expressed through sexual acts, Jekyll's discursive appropriation of his protégé's identity placed McKay in a position of vulnerability homologous to that experienced by the Greek youth in Foucault's account. Like Foucault's hypothetical youth, McKay could rationalize his status only if he could somehow read Jekyll's appropriation of his identity as a benign act in which he acquiesced so as to achieve ultimately a status that equaled or eclipsed that of his mentor. But whereas the Greek youth could look forward to growing into full enfranchisement as a citizen within the Greek democracy, there was no such structural guarantee to diffuse the racial and social inequalities between McKay and his patron. Indeed, while the issue for the Greeks was that eventually the boy would be a citizen and therefore he could not be allowed to take pleasure in an act of bodily submission, the issue for the colonizer in a relationship of cross-racial patronage may have been the fear that the boy could become an equal: that the peasant could aspire to the status of middle-class upstart. From this perspective, the colonized body/boy would be required to take pleasure in his receptive position in order for his patron to re-mark him as subordinate—as happened, for example, when the peasant poet was expected to share his patron's pleasure in the dialect poem that marked his exclusion from the power associated with the speaking of "straight" English. There can be little doubt that McKay and Jekyll took pleasure in their friendship in ways that transcended the limitations of their social and historical context. But McKay ran the risk of being demeaned by his association with Jekyll whenever any representation of their relationship obscured the distinction between his allowing Jekyll to assign him the role of his desired object, the noble savage, and his sense of himself as inhabiting that role.

In relation to Jekyll and in his later life, McKay constantly walked the tightrope between exploiting and being exploited by the meanings assigned to him by his mentors. Within the colonial system of meaning, he embodied the savage, one step away from regressive sexuality, whose body linked the colonizers to (or separated them from) a state of nature they both desired and feared. But in his self-representation, McKay remained the youth who acquiesced to his mentor's desire—a desire whose physical object could never be named—in exchange for the intellectual pleasures denied him by an unjust social system.

Such distinctions must have seemed all the more urgent in New York, where McKay became involved in the literary activity leading up to the Harlem Renaissance.[7] In early-twentieth-century America there was still a palpable tension between the ideal of democratic debate and persuasion, upon which public forms of rhetoric relied, and the reality of black silence, which had its origins in the earlier suppression of slave speech and writing.[8] The dominant culture also mediated black access to the word in the Jamaican context, but the white population there was a minority. A more fully enfranchised black majority could articulate desires (like those contained in the folk songs Jekyll collected) that threatened the dominant class enough to generate defensive editorial responses. In turn-of-the-century America, by contrast, it was still not unusual for whites, drawing on the traditions of minstrelsy and the abolitionist novel,[9] to appropriate the prerogative of voicing black desire in a variety of texts. In *The Sage in Harlem,* Charles Scruggs lists over a dozen white novelists of the 1920s who wrote on blacks or wished to do so, including Charles Van Vetchen, whose *Nigger Heaven* epitomized the white fascination with a decadent, "oversexed" Harlem. Scruggs points out that "by 1925, this situation of 'Whites writing up Blacks' had become such a cliché that Hemingway could make fun of it in *The Torrents of Spring:* 'Could that be the laughter of the Negro?' Hemingway's hero wonders. Hemingway is satirizing not only Sherwood Anderson's *Dark Laughter* but the tendency to romanticize blacks as if they were a Greek chorus and the key to discovering mysterious, inchoate America" (Scruggs 1984, 143).[10]

The shift from aesthetic appropriation to financial patronage of blacks during the Harlem Renaissance introduced further tensions. Powerful white patrons were able to exploit simultaneously the bodies and voices of a range of black artists.[11] McKay felt repulsed by the apparent ease with which many of his black peers accepted these arrangements, or misinterpreted their intimacy with white patrons as "a token of Negroes breaking into upper-class white society" (McKay 1970, 321). Furthermore, the caste lines that separated black and white were much more clearly drawn in North America than was the case in Jamaica. Indeed, one could argue, as the character Trumper does at the end of George Lamming's novel *In the Castle of My Skin,* that finely differentiated gradations of color in the West Indies were so much a part of the status quo that race had become invisible within West Indian social discourse or was mediated purely by class.[12] In Harlem, Paris, and London during the interwar years, a single, well-demarcated racial boundary was not only more visible than it would have been in Jamaica, but it was being transgressed flagrantly in the highly charged atmosphere of racial intimacy within radical and bohemian circles.

McKay may have felt insecure because distinctions he took for granted in Jamaica but never was forced to name had to be reasserted or refigured in this more volatile social situation. For him, the explicit intimacies of the cross-racial patronage he observed in America did not signal greater personal freedom for black artists. Instead, he saw many of the patrons as "white lice crawling on black bodies" (McKay 1970, 337), whose power and largesse exacerbated the violability of their protégés' bodies and intellects.

In this exploitative environment, McKay clung to a version of his Jamaican experience in which blacks were proud and independent, and the "best" blacks and whites observed unstated rules of social discretion in their often cordial interaction with each other. In the chapter of his autobiography entitled "White Friends," McKay contrasts what he considered the sycophancy of black writers to white patrons in America with the friendship between his father and a white missionary in Jamaica, a friendship that McKay maintains was based on true affection and mutual respect. He compares his father's kindness to this missionary friend with the contempt the elder McKay displayed toward another white cleric whom he considered an opportunist and a thief. In concluding McKay explains: "I make this digression about white friendship and my father, because, like him, I have also had some white friends in my life, friends from the upper class, the middle class, the lower and the very lowest class. Maybe I have had more white than colored friends. Perhaps I have been impractical in putting the emotional above the social value of friendship, but neither the color of my friends, nor the color of their money, nor the color of their class has ever been of much significance to me. It was more the color of their minds, the warmth and depth of their sensibility and affection, that influenced me" (McKay 1970, 37–38).

If in this passage McKay seems to protest too much, it may have been because he, too, found it difficult to control the effects on his own work and its reception of the versions of patronage he claimed to despise. Much of McKay's writing was completed under the aegis of one form of white patronage or another.[13] When *Home to Harlem* appeared, McKay was accused by other black intellectuals of pandering to the prurient tastes of his patrons by writing without restraint about black sexuality.[14] Conversely, in his autobiography, McKay rails against white critics who combed through his poetry for evidence of sexual excess in his life (McKay 1970, 89–90).

McKay's need to shield himself from the prurience and emotional violence of white patronage, while at the same time availing himself of its financial resources, undoubtedly contributed to his ambivalence about representing his own sexuality in his writing. Yet he fully identified with Jekyll's view that the ubiquity of sexual repression, which led to the displacement of the erotic from the body to the mind, was precisely the "problem" of modern white society. In both *Home to Harlem* and *Banjo,* McKay presents us with pairs of male protagonists who function as each other's Jekyll-and-Hyde alter egos:[15] the one characteristically being sentient, intellectual, and culturally self-assured, but lacking in the capacity for spontaneous hedonism evinced by his less respectable alter ego. The "Jekyll" figure in the dyad is typically a black West Indian with a background similar to McKay's, but McKay made a point of distancing himself from "Hyde" characters, like the American Negro Jake in *Home to Harlem,* who some critics assumed were meant as self-portraits. Although he claimed he was "unobsessed by sex" and saw no reason to avoid the topic in his novels "like the preaching black prudes wrapped up in the borrowed robes of hypocritical white respectability," McKay nonetheless maintains, "I couldn't indulge in such self-flattery as to claim Jake in *Home to Harlem* as a portrait of myself. My damned white education has robbed me of much of the primitive vitality, the pure stamina, the simple unswaggering strength of the Jakes of the Negro race" (McKay 1970, 228–29). Time and again, the West Indian character's desire for the unfettered eroticism of his American friend is played off against his revulsion at his friend's coarseness and seeming lack of intellectual depth. The dichotomy is anticipated in one of McKay's early dia-

lect poems, where the reader overhears with the narrator the rebellious outburst of a "whoppin' big-tree boy," who has been engaged to carry the wares
of an itinerant Syrian peddler:

> Nummo wuk at all fe me is my determination still;
> Me no care damn wha' you say an' you can jes' do wha' you will
> Me deh go right back to to'n, yah, underneat' me old big-tree
> All dem boys wid eboe-light dem, dem is waitin' deh fe me.
> (McKay 1912, 48)

The boy's outburst is framed by McKay's presentation of himself, the frustrated policeman on duty, who finds he grudges the "big-tree boy" his lack
of inhibition in dealing with authority and his assertion of a right to pleasure:
"Ah! I wish I knew a little, jes' a little of de joy/Dat nature has bestowed on you,
my whoppin' big-tree boy" (McKay 1912, 48). In a phrase like "a little of de
joy/Dat nature has bestowed on you," it is difficult to decide whether McKay,
under the guise of writing in dialect, is merely imitating the air of world-weary
nostalgia that his mentor affected or whether, by this time, he did feel robbed
through his special education and mentorship of a connection to the rebellious aspects of the folk culture Jekyll so vehemently castigated. Here, as in
the Jekyll-and-Hyde relationships of the novels, the object of McKay's desire
seems to be equally some ideal identification with nature, and his mentor's
power to assign to the Other the role of nature's child.[16]

Banana Bottom represents McKay's attempt to work through his early experience as a protégé from the vantage point of his later encounters with patronage in North America and Europe. The novel plays out the fiction that the
relationship between Bita and her mentor transcends the restrictive norms
of its time, by representing their friendship as purely platonic and (therefore) free of exploitative intent. Yet in every other relationship, both social
and sexual, to which McKay exposes his young heroine, the inequalities of patronage that dogged McKay's relationship to Jekyll, and threatened even in
retrospect to undermine its equilibrium, reassert themselves, overwhelming
the narrative at times in their urgency, obscenity, and violence.

The friendship between Bita and her rapist, Crazy Bow, constitutes one re
writing of the relational dynamic between patron and protégé. Here McKay
reverses the process by which he acquiesced to Jekyll's discursive appropriation of his body as a semiotic marker for "nature"—as the intuitively wise

savage, in touch with the earth and with his emotions. McKay inverts the racially and socially overdetermined role of the protégé in relation to his mentor by making his black character the cerebral one and his white and near-white characters intuitive. Thus, the near-white eccentric, Crazy Bow, embodies all the qualities of savagery, intuition, and communion with nature that Jekyll celebrated in the Jamaican peasantry and assigned implicitly to McKay. McKay's tenderness and rueful affection in his account of Jekyll's foibles in the story "My Green Hills of Jamaica" resonate with Bita's memories of her rapist, who suddenly reappears one day when she is playing the organ and indicates that he wishes to play:

> . . . [W]hen he stretched out his hands and touched the organ, she vacated the stool and he sat down and immediately began playing. Bita had never really felt any resentment towards him at any time, but now she was gripped by a deep sorrow that a human being, a rare artist, should be deprived of the ordinary faculties. But the thought came to her that perhaps he did not realize the lack of them and was possibly a greater performer for that.
>
> How bewitching was his playing! No wonder he had magnetized her into that trouble of his adolescence. If only she possessed a little of the magic of his natural genius. (McKay 1961, 257)

Bita's later response to that other white eccentric, Squire Gensir, who McKay tells us is a fictionalized version of Jekyll, is conveyed through a parallel evocation of intuitive genius and musical seduction:

> Perhaps Squire Gensir, because of the disparity of background, tradition, and race between him and Bita, was more susceptible than the circumstances warranted to the affinity of her mind with his, *considering that she was also a member of the human family.* . . . He marvelled that Bita was devouring his profoundest books on religions and their origins and scientific treatises — the theory of the universe, the beginning of life, the history of civilizations and the physiology of man and nature, and that she did not merely parrot the ideas she picked up but interpreted them intelligently.
>
> On her side Bita appreciated him more for his sensitive feeling and interpretation of music. Although his knowledge of the famous great

composers was exhaustive and discriminating he was none the less enthusiastic about the lesser and sometimes anonymous ones. He was ever alert and quick to seize on the best, the original in popular songs, simple melodic strains and spontaneous chants, and he was the first to write down the folk songs of the peasants.

His ear was as keen as his memory was prodigious. (McKay 1961, 240–41; emphasis added)

In McKay's rewriting of the relationship between mentor and protégé, Bita is attracted to Gensir's musical intuition, so similar to that of Crazy Bow, rather than to his greater knowledge or social prestige. Moreover, McKay's presentation of Bita's interaction with both men confers agency on Bita rather than Crazy Bow or Squire Gensir. Bita's rape becomes, inexplicably, "that trouble of his [Crazy Bow's] adolescence," although elsewhere we are told that Bita was thirteen and Crazy Bow twenty-five when it occurred. Squire Gensir also is described as "susceptible" to the affinity he discovers between himself and Bita, an affinity based on the latter's intellectual abilities rather than her intuitive faculties. Bita draws both men to herself, because through them she can gain access to a culture of sensibility.

The symmetry in McKay's presentation of the two men would seem to anticipate a moment of consummation between Gensir and Bita, similar in spirit if not in detail to the sexual encounter between Bita and Crazy Bow. But rather than acknowledging a physical dimension to Gensir's response to Bita, McKay refers out of the blue to the fact that Bita "was also a member of the human family." The almost Freudian slip reestablishes the huge social gulf that McKay's conferral of agency on Bita would have us evade: in relation to Gensir, Bita is barely a member of the human family, in the same way that, in relation to Crazy Bow, she remains ultimately a victim of abuse. Moreover, although Bita enjoys the same kinds of freedoms to wander unsupervised with Gensir as she did as a child with Crazy Bow due to the difference in their ages, Bita is no longer a child and Gensir is no village idiot. No amount of finessing could produce a consummation of their relationship that did not undermine in some way Bita's claims to equality and human dignity in relation to Gensir. The defensive reference to Bita's claim to membership in the human race from the cultural perspective of Gensir's world also elicits the memory of Herald Day's bestiality, a playing out of desire that did indeed go beyond the boundaries of the human family. Through this association McKay warns that Gensir would risk reducing himself to the level of Herald Day if his attraction to Bita expressed itself in a form that did not respect her claim to human equality.

In displacing his mentor as the voice of authority in this narrative of their relationship, McKay seems to want to have it both ways: on the one hand, he reduces Gensir to a mirror image of Crazy Bow, associating by implication the patron's appropriation of his protégé's identity with the violence of rape; on the other hand, he makes Bita's rueful affection for both her patron and her rapist signs of her agency and largesse rather than a response to their exploitation or magnanimity. But McKay's inversion works only if he displaces any physical response Gensir may have evoked in Bita from her body to her mind. The one occasion in the text where the platonic quality of their friendship seems to verge on something more overtly erotic is a purely cerebral moment. It occurs shortly after Bita's betrothal to Herald Day, when she asks Squire Gensir if he has ever been in love. Squire Gensir admits to one early passion and mentions that the woman he loved had married a friend who was the son of a well-known poet. Bita is a great admirer of that poet's work, and the effect of Gensir's information is instantaneous:

> She had never imagined that she would have any knowledge other than out of books of the reality of [that poet]. Yet here in her obscure island home conversing with her was a man who had known him in the flesh. Right then a change took place in her idea of the squire. There was a transfiguration and a romantic cloud seemed to descend and envelope him before her eyes. She began practising a minuet from Mozart that he had open on the piano.
>
> But all the time her head was full of the thought: How strange he is! How strange he is! No white person had ever touched her with such a feeling of otherworldliness as this man. (McKay 1961, 127)

Like the description of Bita's early attraction to Crazy Bow because of the way he plays a sweet love song at a tea meeting, the scene for this seduction is set against a background of music. But although the language of her encounter with Gensir stresses the palpable ("the reality of that poet"; knowing "in the flesh"; being "touched" by feeling), the object of Bita's desire remains intangible. What eroticizes Gensir for Bita in this exchange is not his prowess with other women or his success in competition against other men, but his association, albeit at a great remove, with a British literary icon who embodies for Bita the object of her cultural desire. This is as close to a moment of consummation as we experience in the novel. It is analogous to that elusive moment in Foucault's narrative when the youth could honorably consider giving himself to his mentor, not merely on account of his desire for material wealth or personal prestige but because, in the protégé's eyes, his mentor was now synonymous with merit, virtue, and status, and because the consummation of their relationship could identify the youth with the noblest manifestations of culture his society had to offer.

McKay's introduction to music and intellectual ideas was in part a consequence of his friendship with Jekyll, but in the novel Bita's education takes place before Squire Gensir enters the narrative. The time shift facilitates the introduction of two other white mentors: the missionaries, Malcolm and Priscilla Craig. Malcolm Craig is clearly modeled on the missionary whose friendship with his father McKay makes the centerpiece of his reflections on "White Friends" in his autobiography, and he shares many of the gentle characteristics McKay associates with Squire Gensir in his novel. However, the portrayal of the white woman, Priscilla Craig, allows McKay to transpose his unease about the social and racial inequalities that undergirded the economy of patronage onto a less sympathetically drawn white character. Here, too, issues of power and social control are worked out around competing attitudes toward sexuality. McKay is merciless in his satire of Mrs. Craig, whose over-refined sense of decorum compels her to hide from her maid the "evidence" (her bedroom slippers) that she has spent the night in her husband's bed. The missionary's association of sensuality with barbarism has its effect on Bita, who must decide how much to reveal of her participation in a village tea meeting—a social activity the Englishwoman considers primitive. Although she need not submit her social life to Mrs. Craig's censure, the idea of not saying where she has been makes Bita feel "uncomfortably little and cheap": "It was ugly. Not her idea of living. To do things of which she was ashamed. Her native pride rose against that. And also her education. There was a great pride of tradition behind that education. It was a code that an imperial proud nation had prepared and authorized for her selectest and most favoured sons and daughters. And by a strange fate she, an alien child of enslaved people, had been trained in its principles" (McKay 1961, 205).

McKay presents Bita's spirited independence evenhandedly, as the product of her British education and her native pride. The hypocrisy that Priscilla Craig evinces, however, suggests that Bita's inherent good breeding rather than the British example has been the more salient influence. It is symptomatic of the novel's ambivalent discourse on nature that McKay in this instance seems anxious to claim for his heroine precisely that intuitive sensibility from which he distances Bita in his representation of her friendships with Gensir and Crazy Bow. On this occasion, Priscilla Craig is mollified by the information that Squire Gensir had chaperoned Bita at the tea meeting. But her response dramatizes the extent to which Bita's need for a mentor to supervise or validate her social interactions is created by the devaluation of her culture vis-à-vis that of her patrons. Trapped within her patrons' definition of culture, Bita must either cut her ties to the folk or approach them through the aegis of a white mentor.

It is hardly surprising that McKay connects Mrs. Craig, even more explicitly than Gensir, with Herald Day's sins of presumption and hypocrisy. Priscilla Craig pushes the match between Deacon Day and Bita, and she is appropriately mortified by the deacon's fall from grace. Moreover, McKay goes even further, redirecting at Mrs. Craig the charge of "unnaturalness" through which Day's aspirations are undermined. Once more, he drives his critique home by evoking an aberrant sexuality that links the patron with the object of her patronage. This time, however, aberrance is configured as the displacement of "natural" bodily responses by "unnatural" mental responses to the erotic. At a lecture by a fellow missionary on African masks, Mrs. Craig's internal reverie on the divine wisdom that ensures her race its place among the elect is shattered when the "primitive" African masks on the walls seem to detach themselves and begin dancing around her: "Priscilla remained transfixed, deprived of voice to shriek her utter terror among those bodiless barbaric faces circling and darting towards her and bobbing up and down with that mad grinning. And now it seemed that Patou was among them, Patou shrunken to a grinning face, and suddenly she too was in motion and madly whirling round and round with the weird dancing masks (McKay 1961, 199). Priscilla's fantasy expresses her anxiety about being overwhelmed by the black creative energy she seeks to control, epitomized by the presence among the dancing heads of her retarded son Patou, and her own inability to resist the erotic pull of the dance. But the masks and faces in Priscilla Craig's fantasy are eroticized by their very disembodiment. They recall McKay's critique, in his other novels and in his autobiography, of the European fascination with African primitivism and the displacement of the body by the intellect as an erotic object in Western culture. From this perspective, Crazy Bow's desire for Bita's body can be revalued as a "natural" act, while Mrs. Craig's desire for Bita's head is represented as "unnatural."

While the parables of Crazy Bow and Priscilla Craig rewrite the narrative of patronage so as to undercut the power of the mentor, the cautionary tales of Herald Day's career and a number of other sexual encounters to which McKay exposes Bita explore the anxieties inherent in the role of the protégé. Day doubles for Bita in the role of protégé in much the same way that Priscilla Craig doubles for Gensir in the role of patron, since his presence allows McKay to distance the less savory aspects of the dependent role from the person of his ideal protégé. The Craigs adopt Bita rather than Herald because they are uneasy with the contrast created between their idiot son, Patou, and an intelligent black boy. Clearly, Day's potential achievement is infinitely more threatening to the dominant culture than Bita's, since he is both male and black. What seems less clear, however, is why his potential should have seemed so threatening to his creator—so much so, that McKay subjects him to the most punitive forms of retribution meted out to any character in the novel.

One way to explain Day's characterization may be to approach him via Foucault's distinction between the youth who occupies a certain role in relation to his mentor and the youth who internalizes or enjoys that role. Unlike Bita, Day embraces his position of social and intellectual inferiority in relation to his white patrons. Day accepts Gensir's agnosticism, for instance, as appropriate in a white person, but when Bita suggests that she shares these views he responds, "You're not a white person to go crazy from education." Rather than a defense of her agnosticism, Day's comment elicits from Bita an impassioned critique of the assumption behind his words: " 'Mr Day!' cried Bita. 'This is not the first time you've used that "white person" phrase to me in that invidious sense. Let me tell you right now that a white person is just like any other human being to me. I thank God that although I was brought up and educated among white people, I have never wanted to be anything but myself' " (McKay 1961, 169). Bita's diatribe is reminiscent of McKay's claims to independence and equality in his friendships with whites. Yet Day's subsequent fall from grace lends credibility to the arguments for white superiority.

Significantly, Squire Gensir speculates that Day's aberration may have been the result of excessive intellectual effort, for which the young deacon is not "naturally" endowed.

And yet, given what we know of the blurred lines McKay draws and re-draws in the novel around what constitutes the "natural" and what the "un-natural," it is difficult to be sure how he would have us read this incident. On the one hand, Day's arousal by the nanny goat is the "natural" act par excellence: like Crazy Bow's rape of Bita, it could be considered an "unmediated" physical response to a material stimulus, and no less a person than the village schoolteacher reminds us that such acts were not uncommon in agricultural villages. On the other hand, Day's actions occur during his preparation for a sermon on the text "Wherewithal shall a young man cleanse his ways?" There is more than a hint in the narrative that his inappropriate behavior is a response to the fantasies elicited by the biblical allusions to "unclean" practices he encounters in preparing his sermon—fantasies that are heightened by the heady access to power over the word occasioned by his first public ascent to the pulpit. If this is indeed the case, then Day's fall is the result of both his internalizing a sense of himself as less than his patrons—symbolized in his desire for and fear of public access to the word—and his having embraced too literally Western civilization's eroticization of the word. Day becomes what McKay in the American context most feared to be: the racial sycophant willing to sell himself to any white friend who would confer meaning on his existence, as well as the deracinated black man who, like his prurient white patrons, is capable of sexual arousal only through the intellectual voyeurism of reading about transgressive acts. His end is, of necessity, ignominious.

McKay's blurring of the distinctions between natural and unnatural acts begs the question of whether transcendence of the physical in the relationship between Bita and Gensir may not also be read as "unnatural." Certainly there are a whole series of "unnatural" substitutions between Crazy Bow's piano-playing scene, during which Bita recalls her rape with nostalgia, and the second piano-playing episode, in which she falls for the idea of Gensir's proximity to greatness. McKay may wish to make a distinction between the desire for whiteness displayed by Bita and Herald Day respectively (an appreciation of "the color of the mind" rather than the color of class or money?). Yet his strictures on the transgressive nature of the erotic when displaced from the body to the mind—the very displacement on which the integrity of his protégé's identity depends—prepare us to read Bita's fleeting indulgence of her infatuation with Gensir as a moment of grave narrative anxiety.

Bita herself makes no move to express her desire for Gensir through a physical act on this occasion. Nevertheless, as she leaves his house, Gensir is accosted by a boorish local white planter, Busha Glengley, who, watching Bita's retreating figure, says "with a leer: 'Nice girl, eh?' " (McKay 1961, 128). Glengley's innuendo places the most obvious construction that a person of his class and race would have put on the friendship between a white man and a young black girl at the time: that Bita was no more than a black body to be violated at will by white men like Gensir and Glengley. Gensir defends Bita's honor in the iciest tones he can muster, but later in the novel Bita narrowly escapes a second rape when Glengley's son attempts to exercise his droit de seigneur as she takes a shortcut through his family's estate. We are left with the impression that Bita avoids Herald Day's fate only because she does not allow the desire for the idea of Gensir to express itself as sexual pleasure in her physical submission to an "actual" white man.[17]

McKay's anxiety that any attempt to unite physical and intellectual desire could reduce him to that status of savage that he sometimes felt his white patrons needed him to occupy, is played out in the discovery and humiliation of Herald Day's bestiality and in Bita's near violation at Glengley's hands. But there remained a longing, already present in his dialect poems, and reasserted in his description of the relationship between Bita and Crazy Bow, for a spiritual state that could connect him without moral blight to an earlier state of "natural" sensuality. Critics have read Bita's marriage to Jubban as McKay's attempt to reconcile the cerebral and physical aspects of his desire.[18] But if we suppress for a moment the easy identification of McKay with Bita, it becomes clear that the attributes McKay associates with his sensuous American Negro characters in *Home to Harlem* and *Banjo* are distributed in *Banana Bottom* between two characters: the debonair and suggestively named Hopping Dick, who throws around his "Panama money" and flirts outrageously with Bita; and the taciturn intuitive man of the soil, Jubban, whom Bita eventually marries.

However, the role of the ascetic voyeur that we associate in the other novels with McKay himself is occupied at the outset of *Banana Bottom* by Squire Gensir. Within this configuration, Bita's body serves to unite the sensuous

Jubban and the sensual Hopping Dick with the sentient Gensir. Bita's marriage to Jubban is the most striking enactment of this multiple relationship with three competing aspects of her creator's personality. Gensir gives her away to Jubban at a double wedding at which the other groom is Hopping Dick. In the speeches following the formalizing of their vows, Hopping Dick speaks on behalf of both grooms since Jubban, as always, is silent. Like Gensir, who as "father giver" divests himself of his symbolic rights in Bita, Hopping Dick takes the opportunity in his toast to the brides to give over to Jubban any rights he may still feel over Bita. But since Jubban stakes no linguistic claims of his own, we are left with the sense of a precarious truce between the three men, based on their agreement for the moment to forego their claims on Bita's body or mind. Rather than resolving any internal conflict within the psyche of Bita, the arrangement functions to stabilize without challenging the competing claims of all three men.

In the geometry of this figure, the character of Bita stands as an empty signifier within the text, the space enclosed by the lines of desire that triangulate the opposing instincts within the person of McKay. She provides a connection to Jubban and the land for that alienated, cerebral aspect of McKay represented at moments in the novel by the figure of Gensir. Moreover, Bita's education is the symbol of gentility that legitimates the transition from peasant to proprietor for her husband, Jubban — in much the same way that black Jamaican cultivators of McKay's generation used their new access to education and claims to intellectual maturity to demand the transfer of political power from their colonial "patrons" to themselves. Lastly, Bita's good-natured tolerance for the feckless Hopping Dick validates the Dionysian and picaresque elements in peasant society increasingly associated with an emergent urban proletariat in Jamaica and New York, to which McKay actually belonged when he was not in the company of his powerful patrons. Deprived of language, Jubban can become the land without having to play the role of noble savage or voice the iconoclastic hyperbolic sentiments Jekyll disapproved of in the peasantry. Removed from the physical, Gensir can make love to Bita through words without succumbing to the weaknesses of the flesh that he found so diverting in a character like Hopping Dick but which, in a man of education and culture, would have seemed as aberrant as Herald Day's adventure. Relieved of the necessity to think, Hopping Dick can escape the deacon's fate and enjoy the "natural" sensuality for which both McKay and his mentor claimed they longed. Through the mediation of Bita's presence, each of these men is able to evade the contradictions inherent in the roles they play in relation to each other.

This careful stalemate is undermined by the erotic excess in the relationship between Bita and Gensir; compared to it, there seems to be precious little sexual energy in the relationship Bita has with Jubban. Nor, for that matter, is there anything particularly passionate about Bita's stubborn flirtation with Hopping Dick. It is Squire Gensir whose presence or absence stirs Bita to the core; whose opinion she treasures most; who worries out loud about her; and who is distressed when he cannot protect her. His books and music and conversation delight her; and once she marries, he wastes away and dies, as if his continued living presence would have compromised her tepid union with Jubban too severely. After his death, Bita mourns him by ascribing almost phallic properties to his voice, "that finest thing about his insignificant little body, which had opened the way for him into the deep obscure heart of the black peasantry" (McKay 1961, 310).

There is a particularly telling moment during the wedding procession, when Bita's horse bolts and all three men are forced to give chase. In a passage so laden with sublimated sexuality that it seems almost obtrusive within the text, Gensir explains his decision after this event to bequeath his horse, a fine-bred animal, to Jubban, the driver of mules:

> He explained to Bita, in making the gift, that riding so hard the day of the wedding had stirred up memories of his fox-hunting days. They were disturbing and he had decided that he did not need a horse any more. No doubt Jubban could make better use of the horse than he.
>
> Bita replied that if the memories were pleasant ones, she thought it was fine to remember them. But Squire Gensir replied that he did not want to be in constant contact with things that reminded him too forcibly of a past he had renounced. (McKay 1961, 307)

The subversive power of this barely repressed mutual attraction constantly threatens to overwhelm the ostensible romantic thread within the narrative, and we are left wondering once more why McKay did not simply provide some sort of closure or consummation to this relationship, even at the cost of making his story a tragedy of forbidden desire.

Perhaps McKay remained unable to move beyond his contradictory needs to be embraced by his mentor's culture while striving to eclipse its power to define him; for like Foucault's unequal partners, both McKay and his patron, despite their divergent social status, shared a common acceptance of the structural terms that defined their relationship. Jekyll may have celebrated the unencumbered sensuality of the distant infancy of his race, but, like Schopenhauer and the post-Enlightenment philosophers who preceded him, he ultimately accepted the loss of innocence as a necessary loss, a painfully inflicted tribal scar that marked the intellectual maturity and cultural superiority of Western civilization. So, too, McKay: for all his nostalgia for the Jamaican peasantry, McKay's desire for a return to a state of nature never seems more urgent than his need to affirm its loss. He professed to feel contempt for that racially defined circle of status and power that other black artists clamored to enter, yet he guarded fiercely his right to speak from within its protective ambit. Even at the point in the novel where he pours scorn on the hypocrisy and "unnaturalness" of Priscilla Craig, she remains associated in his mind with the "great tradition" of an "imperial proud nation." For a brief moment, when Bita is snatched from Gensir's protective ambit by the whips of the supplejackers and the insistent throbbing of the drums at the revival meeting, we glimpse another force that "assault[s] [Gensir's] emotional senses like a magic tempest" (McKay 1961, 253) and seems potentially stronger than the cultural tradition he represents. But Bita is quickly claimed by Jubban before she can come under its sway.

Lacking a fully articulated alternative to the best that Gensir's world represents, McKay's novel remains dominated by the very forces of cultural hegemony that Bita's characterization as a sentient black intellectual calls into question. Like Foucault in his description of erotic friendships between Greek men and youth, McKay must constantly defer naming the moment of consummation in the relationship between mentor and protégé, or risk confronting the assumptions about power and powerlessness built into such opposing categories as active/passive, black/white, or natural/unnatural. His narrative strategy allows him to maintain that his protagonists can transcend the hierarchies through which their respective societies construct meaning without challenging the ways in which such hierarchies situated whole cultures in relation to each other. Had he allowed Bita and Gensir to articulate their desire for each other in overtly physical terms, McKay would have been forced to affirm even more directly than he does how superior he considered Gensir's culture and, by extension, how unattainable the ideal of the perfect relationship between patron and protégé remained.

As it is, despite Gensir's death and his displacement in Bita's affections by Jubban, the squire nevertheless has the last word in her story. Bita symbolically eclipses Gensir in the village hierarchy when she inherits his house and library after his death, thus taking control of the cultural space he had formerly occupied. But the silent, essential peasant she marries can be read as the embodiment of all Gensir's fantasies about the unspoiled native. Rather than challenging the terms of his mentor's discourse, McKay, by allowing Bita to assume Gensir's place, in fact facilitates the consummation of the relationship with an idealized notion of the folk for which his own patron had longed. Indeed, since Jubban is effectively deprived of language, there is no discourse within the novel that could have allowed for the consummation of this relationship on terms other than Gensir's.

McKay's choice of the silent Jubban as Bita's deus ex machina suggests that, although McKay may have appreciated the vitality of the peasant's language, which Jekyll urged him to exploit in his early dialect poems, he had yet to find a way of claiming it as a vehicle through which to challenge or subvert Jekyll's cultural assumptions when writing about their relationship. Without recourse to Jubban's language, McKay is foiled by the poststructuralist double bind in Western discourse whereby, as Jacques Derrida writes in "Structure, Sign, and Play," "we have no language—no syntax and lexicon—which is alien to this history; we cannot utter a single destructive proposition which has not already slipped into the form, the logic, and the implicit postulations of precisely what it seeks to contest" (Derrida 1972, 8).

And yet such a reading seems unnecessarily reductive, as it makes Jubban's silence tantamount to a denial of his agency within the text. Jubban rarely speaks, and it is hard to imagine that a character like Bita, who is so irresistibly drawn to the seductive power of her mentor's discourse, could be aroused by Jubban's silence. Indeed our own enamourment with language as readers and the eroticization of the word makes it difficult for us to take seriously the ambivalent arguments McKay offers in support of this "natural" man.[19] Yet, as Homi Bhabha points out in "Signs Taken for Wonders," the inscrutability of the native may be his strongest suit, since the colonial subject can never be fully defined or accounted for in the terms of his master's discourse (Bhabha 1985, 173).

Jubban acts. And through his actions he supplants all rivals for Bita's affection. He rescues Bita from the supple-jackers' whips and from young Glengley's assault; he buys the right to her kiss at the tea meeting; he claims her body on their trip to bring home her father's corpse; and he curbs her runaway horse on the day of their wedding. Moreover, he is the only character in the novel whose sexuality remains unmediated by the language of the master. Jubban's most erotically charged utterance is McKay's description of him singing folk songs to the horses and mules that belong to Bita's father as he grooms them, and McKay makes a point of telling us that Jubban alone can pick ticks from under the tail of one particularly bad-tempered horse without being kicked in the groin (McKay 1961, 252). Compared to Herald Day's grotesque penetration of the nanny goat and Gensir's hysterical fear of the excitement he experiences while riding his horse, Jubban's relationship to this animal exudes both tenderness and mastery, and these are the qualities through which he domesticates Bita's colonial intellect and passion for the word.

McKay's engendering of his protégé as feminine allows him to accommodate this alternative resolution of the drama of thwarted desire between patron and protégé. But the textual parallel it sets up between the woman's position and that of Jubban's mules relegates Bita as definitively to a space beyond the human family as any discursive appropriation of her body by her patron would have done. McKay circumvents the politics of race through the hierarchies of gender.

For late-twentieth-century readers, McKay's *Banana Bottom* provokes contradictory responses to unresolved conflicts. Bita's substitution for McKay initiates a complicated exchange that links Gensir to Jubban in the relationship of patronage it rewrites through the body of Bita. If we read the novel as a triumph of the imagination over mundane social codes, then Gensir's discourse wins out over Jubban, and the text demonstrates how the marriage of true minds transcends the boundaries of race and class. If we read Jubban's silence as "natural" and subversive, then Jubban's action wins out over Gensir, and the invincibility of the native psyche in the face of colonial appropriation is reaffirmed. But both readings blot out the material female body of Bita, just as Bita's very inscription in the text erases the material male body of McKay.

McKay wrote *Banana Bottom* while living in North Africa, shortly after receiving the news that Jekyll had died and left his considerable library to his latest protégé—an "ignorant" and "unworthy" peasant boy, whom McKay also displaces conveniently via the cultivated Bita from his fantasy of the ideal protégé. Positioned temporarily outside the cultural space of Europe and North America and free, at last, of the emotional ties that bound him to Jekyll, McKay finally may have felt independent enough to explore the complex dynamic of his relationship with his mentor. Yet each of the worlds that McKay inhabited contributes to the instability of the elusive distinctions around which the competing desires of patron and protégé construct themselves in his text: the patron's desire for unmediated contact with a "natural" world; the protégé's yearning for the power of "straight" English; the unspeakability of the body; the unattainability of the word; the inscrutability of action. In articulating the erotics of patronage, the slippage between body and text — and body as text — is exacerbated by every new geographical location. Read from these shifting vantage points, *Banana Bottom* stands as a passionate paean to the one man who, more than anyone in McKay's experience, seemed willing to affirm his cultural worth and grant him access to the worlds and words he desired — and who seemed to ask nothing in return but McKay's own self.

Notes

1   Under Jekyll's tutelage, McKay read Pope, Milton, the Elizabethan lyricists, the late Victorian poets, Dante, Leopardi, Goethe, Baudelaire, Wilde, and Whitman, as well as a wide range of nineteenth-century philosophers, including Jekyll's favorites: Nietzsche, Hegel, Schopenhauer, and Spinoza (McKay 1970, 13–14; McKay 1979, 70).

2   McKay's later bisexuality is well-documented by Cooper (Cooper 1987, 75, 150) and Cooper concedes that Jekyll was almost certainly homosexual. He notes Jekyll's long, intimate friendship with Ernest Boyle, who followed Jekyll to Jamaica after he settled there permanently in 1895. Cooper also points out that, in a 1918 essay discussing Jekyll's influence on his education, McKay singles out Oscar Wilde, Edward Carpenter, and Walt Whitman as three of the writers whose work he discussed with Jekyll. Cooper reads this grouping as an indirect acknowledgement on McKay's part that homosexuality was at least a theme in his education through Jekyll (Cooper 1987, 23–25). In addition, there was a well-established tradition of men of Jekyll's station in the colonies taking homosexual lovers of subordinate social status (Hyam 1976, 135–47). Cooper points out that Jekyll had another mentoring relationship with a promising singer, Johnny Lyons, after

McKay left Jamaica, and that when he died he left his entire library to an unnamed Jamaican peasant whom McKay's brother describes as "an ignorant fellow from Hanover Parish." However, McKay stresses that Jekyll's lifestyle was extremely ascetic, and it would be completely in character for a late Victorian of
his eccentricity—whatever his sexual preferences—to have eschewed all forms of
overt sexual expression.

3 McKay lists Arnold's *Literature and Dogma,* Draper's *The Conflict Between Reli-*
gion and Science, Haeckel's *The Riddle of the Universe,* and a number of Herbert
Spencer's works among those he first encountered in his brother's library (McKay
1979, 19). Periodicals and novels carried by the village library included *The Spec-*
tator, The Windsor, the weekly *Times,* the *New York Herald,* and the novels of Mrs.
Gaskell, Charles Dickens, Walter Scott, Mrs. Humphrey Ward, Marie Corelli, and
Mrs. Henry Ward, whose *East Lynne* was a favorite of McKay's (McKay 1979, 44;
McKay 1970, 12). McKay also mentions having encountered several turn-of-the-
century treatises on sexuality in his brother's library, but he does not identify
these by name (McKay 1970, 245).

4 See *Jamaica Times,* 4 March 1912, 20. McKay's poem anticipates many of the sentiments expressed in his later sonnets on racial injustice. I quote the first and two
last stanzas from "Gordon to the Oppressed Natives" here for comparison with
the middle quatrains of "If We Must Die":

> O you sons of Afric's soil,
> Dyin' in a foreign land,
> Crushed beneat' de moil and toil,
> Break, break de oppressor's hand . . .
>
> Shake de burden off your backs,
> Show de tyrants dat you're strong;
> Fight for freedom's rights, you blacks!
> Ring de slaves' old battle-song!
>
> Gordon's heart here bleeds for you,
> He will lead to victory;
> We will conquer every foe
> Or togeder gladly die.

The middle quatrains of "If We Must Die" read:

> If we must die, O let us nobly die
> So that our precious blood may not be shed
> In vain; then even the monsters we defy

Shall be constrained to honor us though dead!
O kinsmen! we must meet the common foe!
Though far outnumbered let us show us brave,
And for their thousand blows deal one death blow
What though before us lies the open grave?

5   See Tom Redcam's review of "An All-Jamaican Entertainment," *Jamaica Times,*
15 June 1912, 11, for a description of one such performance at the James Hill literary society in Clarendon. The announcement of McKay's first prize in "T. P.'s
Federal Band of Song," a competition run from England for aspiring poets scattered throughout the Empire, appears in *Jamaica Times,* 4 May 1912, 20.

6   Halperin's essay on "The Democratic Body: Prostitution and Citizenship in Classical Athens" goes even further than I do here, as he reads the shame that was
associated with the receptive partner in a homosexual relationship as well as the
disenfranchisement of homosexual prostitutes in classical Greece as evidence of
the way in which the idea of full citizenship in Athens was worked out around
the notion of the inviolability of the full citizen's body. Conversely, he reads the
ubiquity of affordable prostitutes of both sexes as affirming the citizen's right to
exercise his phallic prerogative with respect to the bodies of non-citizens (Halperin 1990, 1–28).

I am indebted to my colleague, classicist Rick Griffiths, for further insights on
this point. He supports my analogies in his written response to my essay, dated
12 August 1991, by pointing out that inattention to the experience of the *eromenos*
in Foucault and Halperin is to be distrusted:

> What they can ignore is what the pederasts, and pot makers, and Plato
> could easily ignore, namely, the vastly more frequent range of sexual objects
> (not problematic or necessarily very interesting to dominate): wives, hetairai,
> and above all slaves. The cultivated difficulty (risk, expense, publicness, and
> built-in ephemerality) of pederastic success must pay tribute to the ease
> and gratification otherwise available for the free male, as well as to the women
> and slaves from whom defeat at any level of symbolism would not be accept-
> able. Pederasty may be a reflex of a slave-holding society, not so much elevating
> one partner over another (since, as I argued, the sport may have been in the
> unique mutability and uncertainty of the power relationship) but withdrawing
> both partners from a sexual marketplace filled with people unlike and beneath
> themselves. Pederasty in Athens and elsewhere had a strong link to political
> reaction. It had particular ties to Sparta, the nearest model of a closed society
> with a rigid system of segregation.

If Griffiths is correct, McKay's struggle to achieve a self-representation as "youth" rather than as "slave" is even more suggestive as, in order to achieve it, McKay must be able to represent himself as the youth, approached only through cultivated ritual difficulty rather than as the slave, whose body is there for the taking.

7 Douglas argues for a general instability in signification among African American participants in the Harlem Renaissance from a similar premise. Pointing out that African Americans who imitated whites in blackface in the theater were part of a complex system of performative doubling, she nevertheless notes that "[i]t is one thing to be in search of the 'primitive' as white artists of the 1920s were; another thing to be told, as the black New Yorkers were, that you are the primitive, the savage 'id' of Freud's psychoanalytical discourse, trailing clouds of barbaric, prehistoric, pre-literate folk culture wherever you go" (Douglas 1995, 98). She suggests that "disguise was so necessary to the black performer that final unmasking, stasis, telling it 'straight' . . . —even if presented, as it was in white art, as an artificial and theatrical gesture—became the ultimate taboo" (105–6).

8 Logue's discussion of "Rhetorical Ridicule of Reconstruction Blacks" shows how selective excerpting and distortion of statements by black political aspirants by white southern legislators and journalists—as well as sheer invention—were used to reestablish a stereotype of blacks during reconstruction as "barbaric, immoral and incapable of self-government" (Logue 1975, 401). Many of these rhetorical strategies found their way into literary representations of blacks.

9 K. Sánchez-Eppler's discussion of several pro-abolitionist novels, including Stowe's *Uncle Tom's Cabin,* explores how the black bodies in these texts speak/work on behalf of a white female agenda (K. Sánchez-Eppler 1993, 14–49). Conversely, in a later chapter, she examines the cost for black women writers if/when they attempted to represent themselves (83–104).

10 Scruggs's list includes Edna Ferber, Joseph Hergesheimer, DuBose Heyward, Roark Bradford, Clement Wood, Vera Caspery, I. A. R. Wylie, Gertrude Sanborn, Maxwell Bodenheim, Waldo Frank, T. S. Stribling, Sherwood Anderson, and Carl Van Vetchen as well as several playwrights. And he points out that "Hemingway was to do a bit of romanticizing himself in *The Sun Also Rises;* Bill Gorton's tale of the 'splendid nigger' could quite easily have found its way into Claude McKay's *Banjo:* the natural man versus corrupt Western civilization" (Scruggs 1984, 143).

11 See Lewis 1979, 98–103, for a survey of the major white patrons of black culture during the 1920s and 1930s and a discussion of their motives. Lewis discusses the many misgivings expressed by McKay and W. E. B. Du Bois about the literary implications of such patronage (175–78), while Garber 1990 cites many examples of its sexual implications.

12   See Tillery 1992, 3–20, for a full discussion of class and color distinctions in Jamaica and their effect on McKay.

13   The editor Max Eastman was a faithful friend and financial supporter of McKay for decades. John Reed's wealthy widow, Louise Bryant Bullit, supplied McKay with the funds to live in Europe and North Africa while he was writing *Home to Harlem* (McKay 1970, 253–54). McKay also received generous handouts from cinema magnate Rex Ingram while he was in Europe (McKay 1970, 272). His first trip to England was financed by a Mr. Gray, an associate of Jekyll's who was trying to found a utopian colony for artists and intellectuals in Singapore (McKay 1970, 38–39). And, of course, Jekyll himself completely financed McKay's first few years in America, giving him a generous lump sum when he left college to set up a business of his own.

14   See for example Du Bois's vitriolic attack on *Home to Harlem,* in "The Browsing Reader," in which he claims that after reading McKay's novel he felt distinctly unclean and in need of a bath (Du Bois 1928, 202). He accuses McKay of writing a sensational book about blacks to please a voyeuristic white readership. Alain Locke, Du Bois's archrival on many issues also concurred, accusing McKay in an article entitled "Spiritual Truancy" of pandering to "decadent aestheticism" to please the tastes of his white readers (Locke 1976, 404).

15   The pun may not be entirely fortuitous. Cooper quotes from a letter from Jekyll's brother Herbert to the archivist Frank Cundall in Jamaica, in which Herbert claims that Walter was friendly with Robert Louis Stevenson in the 1890s and that Stevenson would have been aware that he was using his name for his fictional Dr. Jekyll. Cooper implies that the real Jekyll may have left England when he did in order to avoid the notoriety created by possible parallels between his eccentricities and those of Stevenson's character (Cooper 1987, 23 n. 77, 78).

16   Bhabha anticipates my argument here when he points out the difference between what he calls the "colonial articulation of man and his doubles and that which Foucault describes [in *The Order of Things* II, chap. 9] as 'thinking the unthought,' which for nineteenth-century Europe is the ending of man's alienation by reconciling him with his essence" (Bhabha 1984, 132). Bhabha uses this distinction to argue that colonial discourse about the nature of the colonized subject articulates the colonizer's desire for an authentic historical consciousness. My argument takes his notion of mimicry a step further, as it sees the ways in which the native's discourse refracts and attempts to appropriate the colonizer's desire for authenticity as articulating the colonized's desire for the colonizer's power.

17   McKay makes Glengley fils, "near white" like Crazy Bow. Thus, even as he allows Bita to describe her persecutor as a "slimy white hog" (McKay 1961, 263), McKay

seems to imply that a "pure" white man might have acted, or been received, differently.

18   Morris's discussion of the two poles of behavior represented by Ray and Jake in *Home to Harlem* connects the unresolved conflict in their relationship with McKay's later presentation of Bita (Morris 1975, 36–42, 52). Giles calls *Banana Bottom* McKay's "best artistic statement of the ideal wedding of instinct with intellect" and sees its main character, Bita, as making "a believable commitment to such an ideal" (Giles 1976, 20). Diedrich argues that because she is a woman, Bita, in McKay's eyes, cannot suppress her sexuality, so "the spiritual conflict is ultimately resolved through her sexuality—a solution in keeping with the ideals of the Harlem Renaissance, which points to the influences of Dadaism, Expressionism, and Freudianism on McKay" (Diedrich 1976, 93; my translation). Lewis and Lewis 1977 see Bita's marriage to Jubban as an unsuccessful attempt by McKay to resolve class and race contradictions in his own experience. Even Stoff, who addresses directly McKay's problematic relationship to the noble savage, sees McKay's recourse to a single protagonist in *Banana Bottom* as McKay's most successful strategy for "free[ing] himself from the limitations imposed by the rigid polarizations of instinct and intellect in separate characters" (Stoff 1972, 39).

19   One such ambivalent argument is introduced after the death of Bita's father when she recalls: "When she was raped by Crazy Bow how strange and terrible her father's face had been, yet he had been so kind and more fatherly than ever to her. A fine father. And she had loved him deeply with a love rooted in respect. All the men she really respected had something of his character: Malcolm Craig, Squire Gensir, Jubban" (McKay 1969, 288). The insertion of Jubban's name in this list of father figures seems a strange way to validate a woman's attraction to her lover. If it succeeds at all, then the bizarre logic of inversions and substitutions that structure this narrative suggests that the juxtaposition also works to eroticize the father figures. Perhaps I am fastidious about these things, but there has always been something creepy to me about the way Bita and Jubban first make love on top of her father's coffin!

BENIGNO SÁNCHEZ-EPPLER

Reinaldo Arenas, Re-writer Revenant, and the Re-patriation

of Cuban Homoerotic Desire

When we move we tell ourselves the reasons why in the only terms we have. For many, and at the point of departure, those are the terms—the desires—of the place we leave. As time moves on and places take us in, the backward glances may illustrate more voluptuously the *why* and *what* we left; but such re-desiring will be a product of what we have picked up where we have been. If we differentiate between "exiles" and other kinds of "immigrants" it is because in the exile the vectors of displacement remain poised to return. The life and writings of Cuban exiled novelist Reinaldo Arenas (1943–90) provide a very pointed example of how sexuality makes people move and how moving affects the practices of the representation of sexuality and the investment in some sort of return. In the case of Arenas that return is staged with the auto-biographical creation of a demand for one more displacement after death: the exiled queer nationalist turns himself into a monument and awaits re-entry as a sexually charged, cultural and political presence back in the Cuba he left.

Ports Passed

Reinaldo Arenas's life can be summarized roughly as a succession of decades lived in different cultural or social spaces, and with different levels of exclusion from social and/or political enfranchisement.[1] Born in Eastern Cuba in 1943, the 1940s and 1950s include twelve years of childhood living with his mother and his grandparents in rural isolation and poverty, and, after 1955, six years of adolescence and poverty and boredom in the provincial city of Holguín. While no writings from this period have survived, all of his representations of childhood have their roots in these years lived in rural or provincial Cuba.

The 1950s end as Arenas reaches age seventeen, and as Cuba enters into its Revolution. Initially sharing in the revolutionary hopes and ferment, he migrates to Havana where he spends the 1960s taking on the life of the writer, passing through a world of university, National Library, and official literary periodicals, all substantially reinvigorated and politicized by revolutionary cultural activism. It is also during this period that he makes the transition from the world of early rural or provincial homoerotic encounters into a set of practices clearly discernible as part of a Cuban urban gay culture. By the end of the 1960s and the beginning of the 1970s the increasingly explicit dissonance of his writing, particularly with respect to homoeroticism and its discontents in an increasingly Stalinized socialist order, force him to bypass Cuban publishing restrictions. He starts to publish outside of Cuba without the requisite official imprimatur.[2] By then both his own homosexuality, and the nature of his writing, made him the perfect target of surveillance, prosecution, imprisonment, alleged rehabilitation, and a postpenal return to a social limbo of unemployment, substandard housing, and homelessness. Throughout the end of the 1960s and the 1970s Arenas produces a continuous flow of frankly antirevolutionary writing inflected with homoeroticism, which also includes the accompanying denunciation of state homophobia as an important component, with no hope of ever publishing any of it inside of Cuba, and under the perpetual fear of having his texts confiscated. This limbo ends abruptly with the onset of another one.

The same criminal record that puts Arenas in jail in 1973, puts him in one of the boats leaving for the United States through the port of Mariel in 1980: "counterrevolutionary activities" or "attitudes," which included "ideological diversionism" with reference to his writing, "public scandal" and "corruption of minors" with reference to his homosexuality. He enters into his last decade as a Cuban exile very much ill at ease within the Miami exiled community, and as a Cuban homosexual within the relative freedom and territorial unspecificity of U.S. gay culture. He also becomes the highly visible anticommunist cold warrior capable of opening Ronald Reagan's Cuban gay front. In 1990 Reinaldo Arenas commits suicide, a complication related to AIDS.

Displacement emerges as an important constant in the life lived, and in the writing career adopted in flight, or as flight, while Arenas moves with his queerness through a succession of Cuban and un-Cuban territories. Needless to say, as he moves he experiences different modalities of same-sex practices and homophobia, but more suggestively, the displacements also provide the writer with diverse emplacements from which to take differently structured backward glances at the life-quarry of his narrations.

This essay focuses on Arenas's posthumously released autobiography (*Antes que anochezca*, 1992; *Before Night Falls*, 1993) to illustrate how he keeps moving with his sexuality, and how the vector of his displacement out of Cuba, out of his past, and out of his closets, creates a corresponding vector of return in memory and narration, to both the places and the times left behind. Some would label this "nostalgia," deride it, and leave at that. Yet, if the life of the author plays itself out primarily under the pressure of the outward vector that pushes Arenas to his exile, the force exerted by the vector of return will continue to operate in the reader's response, structured then as the reader's return, and efficacious, both for the living reader and the posthumous author, as a manner of *repatriation*. The return of the child to a pansexualized Cuban countryside, the return of the young man to a repressively hypereroticized revolutionary Cuba, and Arenas's final framing of his Works and Figure as a monument demanding readmission back into Cuba, will all be discussed as repatriating performances staged by the queer Cuban nationalist in exile.

Re-writing in motion

In a troubled backward glance at the 1960s, written from the vantage point of 1980 and at the very beginning of his U.S. exile, Arenas alludes to the dubious privilege of those who move. He focuses on the weight of moving while carrying all the baggage accumulated during his passage through all previous stations, and he reflects on the difficulties of reusing, and reworking it all again from each site and condition of relocation.

> Pero [los cubanos], con la lucidez abrumadora del que viene del infierno, no podemos hacernos . . . ilusiones. El envilecimiento de la miseria durante la llamada tiranía de Batista, el envilecimiento del poder bajo el sistema actual. Somos el doble y hasta el triple de nosotros mismos. Vivimos querámoslo o no, en dos y hasta tres tiempos a la vez, lo cual quiere decir que no vivimos en ninguno.

> [But (Cubans), with the overwhelming lucidity of those who come from hell, cannot harbor . . . any illusions. The debasement of misery during the so-called tyranny of Batista, the debasement of power under the present system. We are the duplicate and even the triplicate of ourselves. We live, whether we want it or not, in two, and even in three times at once, which means that we do not live in either.] (Arenas 1991, 30; my translation)

Cuban displacements come through as a process of leaving hell to go nowhere, in a succession that creates a simultaneity of layered memories and experiences that leave the subject both out of time and out of place. Arenas is just attesting, with all the urgency of his Cuban victimizations both behind him and before him, that being immersed in the act of writing down the self is to live an intensified simultaneity of the past retrieved and the present of retrieval.

But this documentation of confusion is also an assertion of the lucidity of those who come from hell, and it has much to do with Arenas's obsessive capacity for rewriting his life to produce many of his books. This rewriting happens both in the sense of revisiting the same scenes in different books throughout his writing career, and recomposing the same book, after successive losses, confiscations and complicated smuggling, and reunification with his manuscripts. In the late 1980s, all fragments of life already used in a variety of different books written and rewritten during the 1960s and 1970s start to make their ways into the last rewrite. Because they are performed from exile, all the rememorations of Cuba in *Before Night Falls* constitute returns to the territory from which the writer is excluded. Even if the narrative can only return him to the Cuba of his past, I will argue that this nevertheless stands as a narrative self-repatriation in the face of the impossibility of an actual return.

What kind of an act (Bruss 1976) is Reinaldo Arenas's *Before Night Falls: A Memoir*? What does this text do—for or to its readers? What does it do to the world it revisits, to the historical record, or to the national culture reported in it as lived? How does it stand as the last instance in which Arenas went back to work up his past? How does it light up the other moments of creation in which he had engaged his backward glance?

The Child, Again and Never Twice, in the Same River

What does Arenas put back in his Cuban *patria* with this narration? Mostly he repatriates memories of social and political marginalization with a strong sexual component. Even if he goes back, to take us back, to what he wants to document as hell, the most erotic remembrances both in childhood and beyond will deploy much of the taste of paradise.

In Arenas's case, it has to be acknowledged that the autobiographical retour will not be the first instance of a narrative deployment of his own past. Arenas's fictional output always developed stories widely recognized as explicitly autobiographical. Yet, there are crucial differences between his fiction, which is adjectivally "autobiographical," and the presumptively nonfictional "autobiography." Accepting the established dates of composition for most of his works (see Ette 1992, 111), Arenas's trajectory shows a marked progression from a relatively closeted, barely sexualized or occluded queerness in his earliest novel, to an out and provocative, graphic and politically parodic representation of same-sex encounters in his subsequent works.

When he writes, in the early 1960s, a novel on his rural childhood of the 1940s (*Celestino antes del alba* [translated in English as *Singing from the Well*]), or when he writes, in the late 1960s and early 1970s a novel about his provincial adolescence of the 1950s (*El palacio de las blanquísimas mofetas* [The palace of the white skunks]), the return to the violence of the family and the boredom of the provincial capital hardly savors anything beyond the tender moments of surviving the horror. These two novels are suffused with explicit enough denunciations of homophobic abuse of the sensitive future poets that are the children they portray, but they are quite reticent about any kind of openly affirmed joy in homoerotic activity.

Celestino antes del alba was circulated as a manuscript in 1964 by a twenty-one-year-old Arenas, was awarded a national prize in 1965, and was published by the UNEAC (National Union of Cuban Writers and Artists) in 1967. This is the story of a visionary boy, living with his tyrannical grandparents and his ambivalent mother, deep in the poverty and isolation of an undated — but clearly prerevolutionary — Cuban rural setting. The novel starts to deploy Arenas's fascination with cousins, a fascination he will draw upon again and again. Celestino is sometimes a cousin of the nameless child narrator, and at other times the narrator's alter ego. The two children, or the two modalities of the same child, are extremely close: they sleep together and share the full spectrum of children's play, children's tenderness, and child abuse. The adults inflict the abuse for all sorts of reasons, but most emblematically to discipline Celestino's recalcitrant insistence on writing an unending flow of what the adults around him see as dangerously weird signs, and what the readers of the novel soon recognize as poetry.

Before the grandfather launches his campaign to chop down every tree on which Celestino has scratched out his poems, the narrative registers the following response from the narrator's mother:

> Escribiendo. Escribiendo. Y cuando no queda ni una hoja de magüey por enmarañar. Ni el lomo de una y[a]gua. Ni las libretas de anotaciones del abuelo: Celestino comienza a escribir entonces en los troncos de las matas.
>
> "Eso es mariconería," dijo mi madre cuando se enteró de la escribidera de Celestino. Y esa fue la primera vez que se tiró al pozo.
>
> "Antes de tener un hijo así, prefiero la muerte." Y el agua del pozo subió de nivel.

> [Writing. Writing. And when not a single yucca leaf is left to mess up — or a single palm leaf husk, or Grandpa's ledger books — Celestino starts writing on the trunks of trees.
>
> "That's [faggotry (*mariconería*)]," said my mother, when she [found out about Celestino's writery (*escribidera*)]. And that was the first time she jumped down the well.

"I'd rather die than have a son like that," and the water level in the well rose.] (Arenas 1980, 16; 1987d, 4–5)[3]

Here the issue of homosexuality comes into the work as an exploration of that Cuban cultural truism that asserts that all artists are queer, or that even if all Cuban artists are not queer, no one would deny that the count is high (cf. Ette 1992, 100). In *Celestino antes del alba* what can be read as a denunciation of homophobia, can also, and much more safely in line with the expectations of the revolutionary cultural machinery, be read as a denunciation of prerevo-lutionary boorish anti-intellectualism. On the political front, those in a posi-tion to emit official appraisals from the cultural institutions of the Revolution during the mid-1960s can read the anti-intellectual, anticultural tyranny of the Grandpa-deforester, for instance, as a critique of the cultural wasteland in which many Cuban artists suffocated before revolutionary cultural poli-cies provided much improved means for the production and dissemination of—ideologically instrumental—culture. With all its references to "*marico-nería*," *Celestino* remains substantially a closet text. Yet, even where he avoids the sexual explicitness of later texts, Arenas is still articulating that an artistic sensibility had started to develop under the label of *queer*.

The experience of violence both at the hands of peers, and at the hands of the family, becomes articulated in a choral imprecation, as if the commu-nity needed to contain the children's emergent queerness by inflicting pun-ishment, both physically and verbally.[4]

— ¡Celestino! ¡Celestino!
— El hijo de Carmelina se ha vuelto loco!
— ¡Se ha vuelto loco! ¡Se ha vuelto loco!
— Está haciendo garabatos en los troncos de las matas.
— ¡Está loco de remate!
— ¡Qué vergüenza! ¡Dios mío! ¡A mí nada más me pasan estas cosas!
— ¡Qué vergüenza!

["Celestino! Celestino!"
"Carmelina's child has gone crazy!"
"He's gone crazy! He's gone crazy!"
"He's scribbling on the trunks of the trees!"
"He's batty as a loon!"

"What a disgrace! My God! This kind of thing could only happen to me!"
"What a disgrace!"] (Arenas 1980, 17; 1987d, 5)

Thus far, the nature of the craziness (always *loco;* not quite *loca*) is not marked as necessarily sexual. But that shame, voiced by the mother as much as by the communal uproar, is not really associated with a psychological disorder as much as with something unspecified, yet contrary to social propriety. What follows does not fully disambiguate the shame or the craziness in order to turn it into an explicit admission of homosexuality, but it does make the exclusion specifically feminizing and the violence overspecifically rear-ended:

> Fuimos al río. Las voces de los muchachos se fueron haciendo cada vez más gritonas. A él lo sacaron del agua y le dijeron que se fuera a bañar con las mujeres. Yo salí también detrás de Celestino y entonces los muchachos me cogieron y me dieron ocho patadas contadas: cuatro en cada nalga.

> [We went down to the river. The boys' voices kept getting louder, and finally they were yelling. They pushed Celestino out of the water and told him to go swim with the women. I got out of the water too, right behind Celestino, and then the boys caught me and kicked my behind eight times — four on each [buttock].] (Arenas 1980, 17; 1987d, 5)

The strongest marker of the enormity of the shame that has to be hidden, comes in a masterfully hyperrealist recovery of dialogue between children. Arenas mercilessly documents the pain of not being able to resort to the family for redress of the abuses the world inflicts, thus providing a thorough record of the collusion between a homophobic social order and family discipline:

> "Que en la casa no se enteren de lo que me han hecho los muchachos", me dijo Celestino, y se secó los ojos con una hoja de guayaba. Pero al llegar a la casa, ya ellos nos estaban esperando en la puerta. Nadie dijo nada. Ni media palabra. Llegamos. Entramos en el comedor y ella salió por la puerta de la cocina. Dio un grito detrás del fogón y echó a correr por todo el patio, lanzándose de nuevo al pozo. . . .

> ["When we get to the house, don't let them find out what the boys did," Celestino said, and he dried his eyes with a guava leaf. But when

we got to the house they were already waiting for us at the door. Nobody said a word. Not a peep. We came to the house, went into the dining room, and at that, she ran out through the kitchen door. She gave a shriek behind the cookstove and started running all over the yard, and finally she jumped down the well again. . . .] (Arenas 1980, 18; 1987d, 6)

The mother's suicidal reaction is the ultimate endorsement of the communal rejection, intensifying the family's more than tacit agreement with the abusive group. Just in case we have been losing sight of the Cubaness of this representation, the lyrical—or the realistically unlikely—interpolation of the guava leaf for the dabbing of tears, immediately relocates this narrative as Cuban, which otherwise could have taken place anywhere that bullies and families collude to discipline and create queerness.

This river full of young men must have been very important for Arenas. He returns to it in different books and every time he returns he provides a different emphasis, a different valence to the sexual components of the scene. It is very difficult to ascertain exactly when any fragment of *Otra vez el mar* (Farewell to the sea) may have been written. This is the work most often rewritten, both in Cuba throughout the underground 1970s and out of Cuba between 1980 and its release in 1982. Héctor, the central character of the novel is a young writer, and this is the lyrical record of how he remembers the river:

Ayer
fue el día de San Juan
y tú detrás de los árboles,
escondido
viste a los muchachos desnudos
lanzarse al agua
flotar boca arriba
y otra vez lanzarse.
Ayer
fue el día de San Juan
y tú,
escondido,
oíste el estruendo de los hombres
bañándose en el río,
viste la espuma provocada

por sus cuerpos
escuchaste sus risas
observaste sus juegos.
Atónito escudriñaste sus figuras
relucientes.
Viste sus saltos.
Ayer
fue el día de San Juan
y tú corriste solo por el monte,
te revolcaste en la yerba,
regresaste al oscurecer (tías,
abuelos, madres, te aguardaban),
llevaste los terneros al corral,
te sentaste con los demás a la mesa.
Solo quedaste en la sala
bajo el quinqué. (Arenas 1982, 341–42)

[Yesterday
was San Juan Day
and you were hiding
behind the trees
you saw the young men naked
leaping into the water
floating on their backs
[and once more leaping.]
Yesterday
was San Juan Day, [...]⁵
and you,
hiding,
heard the noise of the men
bathing in the river,
you saw the foam
their bodies whipped up
you listened to their laughter
you watched their games.
In awe you ran your eyes down

their shining figures.
You saw their leaps.
Yesterday
was San Juan Day
and you ran alone across the mountain
you rolled over and over through the grass
you returned at nightfall (aunts
grandparents mothers awaited you)
you drove the yearlings to the corral
you sat down with the rest at the table.
You stayed alone in the parlor
under the kerosene lantern.] (Arenas 1986a, 331–32)

In *Otra vez el mar* Arenas does depict a very open and picaresque account of the homosexual frenzies of early adulthood in 1960s Havana and on Cuba's beaches. But the focus here at the childhood river is on the experience of barely acknowledging a child's same-sex desire, and feeling overwhelmed by adolescent lonesomeness. The correlatives of sexual activity—just looking and rolling in the grass—remain overshadowed by the pervasive sense of entrapment and separation projected by the young man's task of rounding up of the calves into the corral, together with the alienated demeanor at the family table.

Among the many things that happened between the *Celestino* version of the river and the rendition in *Otra vez el mar* seems to be a strong, enabling reading of Whitman's bathers in *Song of Myself.* If in *Celestino* poetry and queerness appear to be collapsed into the stigma of *mariconería,* the invocation of Whitman allows this pairing to become mutually supportive; it is poetry that allows Héctor, and Arenas, to frame desire, just as much as desire makes them the poets they are. When Arenas goes back to this river again to rewrite it into the autobiography from his emplacement in late-1980s New York, the river where Celestino and his cousin had found themselves excluded and abused, and the place where Héctor had hid behind a tree to watch overwhelmed, will be re-membered in *Before Night Falls* through a gay celebration as the "site of the grand mysteries," "lugar de los misterios mayores":

> . . . era el día de San Juan, fecha en que todo el mundo en el campo debe ir a bañarse al río. La antigua ceremonia del bautismo se convertía

en una fiesta para los nadadores. Yo iba caminando por la orilla acompañado por mi abuela y otros primos de mi edad cuando descubrí a más de treinta hombres bañándose desnudos. Todos jóvenes del barrio que estaban allí, lanzándose al agua desde una piedra.

Ver aquellos cuerpos, aquellos sexos, fue para mí una revelación: indiscutiblemente, me gustaban los hombres; me gustaba verlos salir del agua, correr por entre los troncos, subir a las piedras y lanzarse: me gustaba ver aquellos cuerpos chorreando, empapados, con los sexos relucientes. . . . Con mis seis años, yo los contemplaba embelesado y permanecía extático ante el misterio glorioso de la belleza. Al día siguiente, descubrí el "misterio" de la masturbación.

[. . . It was June 24, Saint John's Day, when everyone around would come and bathe in the river. The ancient baptism ritual had turned into a festival for swimmers. I was walking along the river bank with my grandmother and some cousins my own age when I saw over thirty men bathing in the nude. All the young men of the neighborhood were there, jumping from a rock into the water.

To see all those naked bodies, all those exposed genitals, was a revelation to me: I realized, without a doubt, that I liked men. I enjoyed seeing them come out of the water, run among the trees, climb the rocks, and jump. I loved to see their bodies dripping wet, their penises shining. . . . I was only six years old, but I watched them spellbound, in ecstasy before the glorious mystery of beauty. The following day I discovered another "mystery": masturbation.] (Arenas 1992, 25; 1993, 8)

In the latter days of the autobiographical rememorations, the river is transformed by a radically gay-affirming focus into a liturgical parody with validated religious resonances not previously used. In this retrospective, out and exiled in the relative freedom of 1980s New York, the Cuban river is remembered as a real site of the uplifting revelations of homoerotic beauty and pleasure. There is a tension between the nostalgia of what was—childhood, rural Cuba, and their queer pleasure—and the gay-affirming post-Stonewall discourses, which allows Arenas to remake a scene, previously framed as a site of homophobic enforcement and lonesome perception of difference, into a site of unabashed homoerotic discovery and fulfillment. It also must be acknowledged that the latter river scene is only about sex, while the two earlier renditions were more intricate in their exploration of the emergence of artistic and sexual identity under the signs and struggles of *mariconería*.

Moving provokes or enables *refocusing*. Arenas's trajectory takes his work through the same scene: from an early emphasis on the shame and rejection heaped on by communal and familial homophobia; through the emerging resilience of the poet who will struggle to articulate the mix of sexual excitement, social confusion, and political frustration; and all the way to the final gay-emancipated reclamation of the bodies in the country—*cuerpos en campiña*—making and sharing sexual pleasure in a Cuba re-figured as ubiquitously queer despite its norms.

Queering the Normal Back Home

From the emplacement of late-1980s New York, every bit of ostensibly marginalized Cuban sexuality will be paraded as the most often practiced thing in the world. Out in Arenas's rural home, sex with animals and sex with cousins of all genders, and even sex with uncles, will be represented as frequent, hardly exceptional, matter-of-fact. Traditional society will still mark all of that as deviant and depraved, and then the progressive Stalinization of the Cuban Socialist State will intensify the criminalization of all sorts of practices identified as deviant. But Arenas's representation of the frequency and the generalized involvement of obviously everybody, will insist on telling the lie on the systematic ideological occlusion.

There are two grand chapters that carry the same title, "El erotismo." The first one develops its topic in the prerevolutionary rural setting of Arenas's childhood (Arenas 1992, 39–40; 1993, 18–20). Arenas starts the chapter by asserting his first-person involvement: "Creo que siempre tuve una gran voracidad sexual" (I think I always had a huge sexual appetite). But after some very explicit description of the range of his "all-embracing" sexual experiences and satisfactions between the ages of seven and ten with both the animal and the vegetable kingdom, he engages the normalizing strategy of acknowledging that he was not the only one: "Era un gran placer templarse a un árbol; mis primos también lo hacían; se lo hacían a los melones, a las calabazas, a las guanábanas" (It was great fun to fuck a tree. My cousins also did it, with melons, pumpkins, and sour-sops) (1992, 39; 1993, 19).[6]

A three-page vignette under the rubric of "La escuela" (Arenas 1992, 27–29; 1993, 9–12) takes up only one page to talk about school itself, and then two pages to document a rich catalogue of sexual activities: the first looks at other boys, his relief discovering that others also masturbated, his individual forays with chickens, goats, and pigs, and the collective enterprise of making love to a mare, not ever quite knowing whether the pleasure was in the contact with the mare or in the sharing of group sexual spectacle (1992, 28; 1993, 10–11). He quickly glosses over his unpenetrative naked play with his cousin (*prima*) Dulce Ofelia (1992, 28–29; 1993, 11), and then pauses to relish in the page-long narration of his first proper intercourse with his cousin (*primo*) Orlando:

> El acto consumado, en este caso, la penetración recíproca, se realizó con mi primo Orlando. Yo tenía unos ocho años y él tenía doce. Me fascinaba el sexo de Orlando y él se complacía en mostrármelo cada vez que era posible; era algo grande, oscuro, cuya piel, una vez erecto, se descorría y mostraba un glande rosado que pedía, con pequeños saltos, ser acariciado. Una vez, mientras estábamos encaramados en una mata de ciruela, Orlando me mostraba su hermoso glande cuando se le cayó el sombrero; todos éramos guajiros con sombrero. Yo me apoderé del suyo, eché a correr y me escondí detrás de una planta, en un lugar apartado; él comprendió exactamente lo que yo quería; nos bajamos los pantalones y empezamos a masturbarnos. La cosa consistió en que él me la metió y después, a petición suya, yo se la metí a él; todo esto entre un vuelo de moscas y otros insectos que, al parecer, también querían participar del festín.
>
> Cuando terminamos, yo me sentía absolutamente culpable, pero no completamente satisfecho; sentía un enorme miedo y me parecía que habíamos hecho algo terrible, que de alguna forma me había condenado para el resto de mi vida. Orlando se tiró en la hierba y a los pocos minutos los dos estábamos de nuevo retozando. "Ahora sí que no tengo escapatoria," pensé o creo que pense, mientras, agachado, Orlando me cogía por detrás. Mientra Orlando me la metía, yo pensaba en mi madre, en todo aquello que ella durante tantos años jamás había hecho con un hombre y yo hacía allí mismo, en la arboleda, al alcance de su voz que ya me llamaba para comer. Corriendo me desenganché de Orlando y corrí para la casa. Desde luego, ninguno de los dos habíamos eyaculado.

[The *consummated* [emphasis only in translation] act, in this case reciprocal penetration, was performed with my cousin Orlando. I was about eight years old, and he was twelve. Orlando's penis was a source of fascination to me, and he took pleasure in showing it to me whenever he had a chance. It was somewhat large and dark, and once erect, its foreskin would slide back and reveal a pink glans that demanded, with little jerks, to be caressed. One day, up on a plum tree, Orlando was showing me his beautiful glans, when his hat landed on the ground. (Out in the country we all wore hats.) I grabbed his hat and ran off to hide behind a bush in a secluded place. Right away he understood exactly what I wanted; we dropped our pants and began to masturbate. What happened then was that he stuck his penis into me and later, at his request, I stuck mine into him while flies and other insects kept buzzing around us, apparently wanting to participate in the feast.

When it was all over I felt completely guilty, but not entirely satisfied; I could not help but feel very much afraid. It seemed to me that we had done something terrible, that in some way I had condemned myself for the rest of my life. Orlando laid down on the grass to rest, and in a few minutes we were romping around again. "Now there is definitely no way out for me!" I thought or I believe I thought, when I crouched and felt Orlando grabbing me from behind. While he was sticking it into me, I was thinking of my mother [abandoned by my father], and all the things that during all those years she never did with a man, which I was doing right there in the bushes within earshot of her voice, already calling me for dinner. In a rush I separated from Orlando and ran home. Of course, neither of us had ejaculated.] (Arenas 1992, 29; 1993, 11–12)

Arenas himself provides a very clear sign of his sense that memory is operating over a radical separation from a moment in which the narrated experience would have signified differently: to voice the double take he says, "I thought or I believe I thought." I would argue that this double take remains applicable to the entire autobiography.[7] His separation from the remembered scene is also marked by the charming exoticizing nod to his non-rural, non-Cuban audiences with insertions such as the parenthetical aside about hat wearing.

There is no reason to doubt the veracity of Arenas's report with respect to the reciprocity of the cousins' alternate penetrations. Yet it must be acknowledged that such specificity goes against the grain of the conventionally accepted modality of Cuban, or generally Latin, homosexual contact, in which the so-called passive and active roles are not supposed to be interchangeable (Almaguer 1991; Alonso and Koreck 1989; Carrier 1976; Lancaster 1988), and with the grain of the ostensibly mainstream reciprocity of Anglo-American gayness. Because of where he comes from, as Arenas articulates what he remembers, his text also proves quite capable of grating against the supposedly more enlightened sensibilities of his possibly homophile contemporary U.S. urban readership, especially with the documentation of sexual practices with animals and vegetables that are presented as commonplace in his rural setting (Arenas 1992, 39; 1993, 18–19). Despite the dark notes about the sense of guilt, the mother's tyrannical omnipresence, and the mock-Freudian detail of occupying her place while making love with the father, the vignette still comes through as a celebration of gayness spiced with its rural picaresque treatment of validated children's sex play.

To invoke the familiar categories of cousins in the Cuban countryside, is not so much a way of restricting the applicability of the findings, but rather an authoritative maneuver for claiming that the demographic sample selected for the analysis at hand is superbly representative. From the way the narration explores the activities of cousins, Arenas can intensify his assertion of the ubiquity of queer sexual practices. Here is the heavy-handed swipe he takes at repressive ideological formations with his own speculations on the normal and the natural, a strongly eroticized world-remaking pastoral:

> Es falsa esa teoría sostenida por algunos acerca de la inocencia sexual de los campesinos; en los medios campesinos hay una fuerza erótica que, generalmente, supera todos los prejuicios, represiones y castigos. Esa fuerza, la fuerza de la naturaleza, se impone. Creo que en el campo son pocos los hombres que no han tenido relaciones con otros hombres; en ellos los deseos del cuerpo están por encima de todos los sentimientos machistas que nuestros padres se encargaron de inculcarnos.

> [There is no truth to the theory, held by some, about the sexual innocence of peasants. In the country, sexual energy generally overcomes all prejudice, repression, and punishment. That force, the force of nature, dominates.

In the country, I think, it is a rare man who has not had sexual relations with another man. Physical desire overpowers whatever feeling of machismo our fathers take upon themselves to instill in us.] (Arenas 1992, 40; 1993, 19)

In the crescendo of grassroots testimonials of queer ubiquity opposed to the socially repressive norms, Arenas finally enlists for his argument even the authority of his grandmother, usually a figure hyperidentified in earlier narratives with family order and sexual repression:

Era sabia mi abuela; por eso conocía la noche y no me hacía muchas preguntas; sabía que nadie es perfecto. Seguramente, alguna vez me vio trasteándole el trasero a alguna puerca. . . . Pero nunca mi abuela me recriminó; sabía que eso en el campo era normal; quizá sus hijos y hasta su propio marido lo habían hecho.

[My grandmother was wise; that is why she understood the night and did not ask me too many questions; she knew that nobody is perfect. Surely there were times when she saw me playing with the behind of a sow. . . . But my grandmother never reproached me; she knew those things were normal in country life; perhaps her sons and even her husband had done them.] (Arenas 1992, 46; 1993, 25)

Arenas is very clear that the desire of males for males and the sexual satisfaction they bring to one another is very much part of that pansexual nature of the countryside he so relentlessly asserts. His narration of how his uncle Rigoberto, "the oldest of my uncles, a married serious man," used to take the eight-year-old Reinaldo on horseback stands as a comprehensive account of the silences that keep the evidence of homoerotic ubiquity from flying in the face of the socially repressive norm:

. . . inmediatamente que montábamos a caballo, el sexo de mi tío empezaba a crecer. A lo mejor una parte de mi tío no quería que fuese así, pero no podía evitarlo; me acomodaba de la mejor manera, me levantaba y ponía mis nalgas encima de su sexo y, al trote del caballo, durante un viaje que duraba una hora o más, yo iba saltando sobre aquel enorme sexo que yo cabalgaba, viajando así como si fuese transportado por dos animales a la vez. Creo que, finalmente, Rigoberto eyaculaba. Cuando regresábamos por la tarde, volvía a repetirse la misma ceremonia. Desde luego esto sucedía como si ninguno de los dos nos enteráramos; él silbaba o resoplaba mientras el caballo seguía trotando. Al llegar a la casa, Coralina, su esposa, lo recibía con los brazos abiertos y le daba un beso. En aquel momento, todos éramos muy felices.

[As soon as we were both in the saddle, he would begin to have an erection. Perhaps in some way my uncle did not want this to happen, but he could not help it. [I propped myself as best I could, I lifted up a bit and placed my buttocks on top of his sex], and during that ride, which would take an hour or so, I was bouncing on that huge penis, riding, as it were, on two animals at the same time. I think eventually Rigoberto would ejaculate. [We repeated the same ceremony in the afternoon] on the way back from town. Both of us, of course, acted as if we were not aware of what was happening. He would whistle and breathe hard while we trotted on. When he got back, Coralina, his wife, would welcome him with open arms and a kiss. At that moment we were all very happy.] (Arenas 1992, 40; 1993, 19–20)

This vignette demands to be read as the most tender lampooning of the ostensibly straight male who enjoys sexual contact with another male and nevertheless refuses to recognize it as a homoerotic encounter or practice. This is one of the many vignettes Arenas will provide to document that in Cuba, men like to have sexual contact with men, but do so hiding behind the cultural construction that lets the so-called active male keep his normative heterosexual identity intact, while the so-called passive or feminized participant carries all the stigma of their shared sexual activity.

There are other positions—subject positions—from which to arrive at a different reading, and Arenas leaves plenty of room for them with his careful attention to the articulation of the boy's, the uncle's, and—by extension—their society's willed or repressed, but at any rate, unquestioned lack of knowledge. Arenas, working from an authorial emplacement where he definitely knows, and from where he wants very much to include this "ceremony" among a set of practices unambiguously recognized as queer, still allows the boy, the uncle, and their society, back in their moment of the past, not to notice. The practice, the desire, and the achieved satisfaction remain fully enjoyed and socially untarnished because of the carefully reported lack of codes or vocabularies to label them *queer*. Arenas, in memory, is *framing* his straight uncle, but he is also reporting on a moment before language or social code come in to give name and label to a range of activities that since then have suffered both labeling and proscription. Many of the difficulties in mapping or accounting for nationally occluded sexual practices, or whatever identities may be grounded on such practices, have a great deal to do with the availability or unavailability of categories or vocabularies for their representation.

The mapping problem is as pronounced when the societies operate as if they lacked these vocabularies, as much as when the existing registers end up being different from those available at different cultural sites. When a story like the one Arenas tells to record his sexual contact with his uncle crosses the many borders he has crossed, such a story, and the nature of the event it represents, are exposed to a transnational and transcultural multiplicity of value judgments, very hard to disentangle. But whatever the outcome of the unexpected and unmanageable readers' responses, the image had affected — transnationally — the unassailable straightness of the serious and ostensibly hetero-macho Cuban male, as much as it has brought to the U.S. gay debates on intergenerational homosexuality one Cuban rural way of looking at it.

Re-writing Revolutionary Desire

The other chapter of *Before Night Falls* under the rubric of "El erotismo" (Arenas 1992, 120–140; 1993, 93–116) is longer, and it documents the wildest of the 1960s both in urban, still cosmopolitan Havana, and also in the revolutionary Cuba of the grand mobilizations — literacy campaign, civil militia national deployments, student brigades traveling to demonstrations in Havana, or to agricultural volunteer work in the fields. Everything that gave the 1960s their particular blend of politics and sexual freedom everywhere else in the West, was experienced as intensely in Cuba, even if, or as Arenas will argue, precisely because of the state's codification and ideologization of sexual mores.

In *Before Night Falls*, the sexual episodes set in the effervescent revolutionary heyday of the 1960s have less of the tableau quality we have seen in the prepubescent, prerevolutionary, pansexual pastoral of the Cuban countryside. But these episodes still document that everybody was doing it. In the sixties we have more of the tone of an interminable, sequential picaresque.

Here is a twentysomething Arenas, and in the place of his cousins we now see an array of friends and associates. The overwhelming number of sexual exploits that he claims for himself may be read as a boast, but they also carry the burden of a statistical assertion of queer ubiquity. First of all, Arenas does not assert any kind of singularity or supremacy. In fact, any other of the *locas* he regards as his peers sounds perfectly capable of as much activity as Arenas. With regard to sex, he depicts himself more as testimonially representative than as authorially or heroically idiosyncratic. All these *locas* seek an ostensible straight or sufficiently macho male as the preferred conquest. This turns Arenas's documentation into a comprehensive dialogue of queer conquests with ostensibly upright representatives of all the revolutionary institutions. As the *locas* enjoy their marginal sexuality, they provide essential sexual servicing to members of the armed forces and the police, to the prized athletes trained for Cuba's representation in international sporting events, or to the intellectual vanguard neatly concentrated in the new scholarship schools full of both elite students and professors. The bus- and truckloads of young bodies fueling the grand revolutionary mobilization turn into an ecstatic and uninterrupted homoerotic feast. Arenas also pays much attention to those involved in the older institution of matrimony, who, more periodically than sporadically, engaged Arenas and his friends in sex and even in relationships.

Arenas organizes the narration of his memories of satisfied homosexual desire as a compendium of couplings precisely with those men who, according to state rhetoric, were the bulwark of the Revolution. These makers of the *Patria* are then revealed acting out their same-sex desire, secure in the culture's tolerance of their *bugarronería* or active buggery, a practice that masks their homoerotic participation behind the imputed feminization of the *loca*, who then carries all the social stigma. Arenas thus unveils the whole nation, through its representative males, as forever intent on the marginalization of homosexuality while in the midst of a national frenzy where men don't shirk from having sex with men.

The adventures often enough end up in repressive disaster for the *locas*. But since the narrative has returned us to a Cuba with an authorially demonstrated homoerotic ubiquity, the victimization of the *locas*, as compared to the impunity of their *bugarrones*, emerges in the narrative as something logically untenable. It has to be recognized, however, that the exoneration of the *bugarrón* from the stigma of homosexuality, and the consequent denunciation of governmentally aligned *bugarronería,* is most untenable from an Anglo-American, or internationalizing, gay perspective that asserts either mutuality in sexual practices or shared identity under the rubric of homosexual for any modality of participation in same-sex practices. Together with this extra-Cuban emphasis on the equalization of all men involved in same-sex practices, regardless of their bodily — active/passive or masculinized/feminized — asymmetries, Arenas also makes a case for the recognition of the homoerotic in the very makeup of the socialist "new man," a man so male, so ideologically pure, and so socially useful as to be irresistibly lovable, especially by other new men.

In a remarkable interpretative moment Arenas puts everything on its head by making state repression itself the primary intensifier of everything it wanted to repress:

> Creo que si una cosa desarrolló la represión sexual en Cuba fue, precisamente, la liberación sexual. Quizás como una protesta contra el régimen, las prácticas homosexuales empezaron a proliferar cada vez con mayor desenfado. . . . Creo, francamente, que los campos de concentración homosexuales y los policías disfrazados como si fueran jóvenes obsequiosos, para descubrir y arrestar a los homosexuales, sólo trajeron como resultado un desarrollo de la actividad homosexual.

> [I think [sexual liberation] in Cuba actually [developed] as a result of the existing sexual repression. Perhaps as a protest against the regime, homosexuality began to flourish with ever-increasing defiance. . . . I honestly believe that the concentration camps for homosexuals, and the police officers disguised as willing young men to entrap and arrest homosexuals, actually resulted in the promotion of homosexual activities.] (Arenas 1992, 132–33; 1993, 107)

This cluster of Foucauldian propositions point to the proliferation of desire as a function of the very same mechanisms of repression. With this Arenas destabilizes the certainties in all the projections of Cuban masculinity. In doing so, he opens up in the sinews of the national identity the possibility — the definitive suspicion even — that this obsessive masculinist society shows structural evidence of rampant homosexuality, which at some point the nation is going to have to acknowledge, repatriate, and naturalize as its own.

Last Page of the Revenant

Now we have to change focus: from our discussion of Arenas's exilic trajectory and its effect on the re-presentation of sexual practices within a poetic
re-envisioning Cuban sexuality, to a discussion of Arenas's masterful textual staging of his own death in exile. We can easily imagine how his death,
marked both by AIDS and by suicide, might figure in any of the many homophobic registers available in the cultural settings where his life and work
have ever mattered. Against the grain of that, I would like to highlight how
Reinaldo Arenas uses the trope of defeating the disease to finish his works,
how he puts an autobiography at the end of those works, and how he produces
a remarkably self-assertive author's final seal to turn his last pages into a stage
for the delivery of his suicide note. This way of performing "the end" erects
a monument, and that monument, erected in exile and still unanchored, demands repatriation. This demand for the monumental repatriation of the
dead queer exile reinforces all those instances of quite lively queer desire that
are also demanding repatriation throughout the rest of the autobiography.
Just asking the question functions as a vehicle for a posthumous queer peregrination: where in La Habana, where in Guanabo, where in Holguín, are we
going to gather around to disseminate, to read, and to celebrate Reinaldo's
work? The first bust would have to go up somewhere in the vicinity of the spot
in Lenin Park where he was busted (Arenas 1992, 201; 1993, 176).

Arenas opens with an "Introduction," subtitled "The End" (Arenas 1992, 9;
1993, ix). The first paragraph does not say "I was born . . ." but rather it speaks
without details about the first bout with a clearly identified AIDS-related illness: "Yo pensaba morirme en el invierno de 1987" (9). The English translation does not quite get it. "I thought I was going to die in the winter of 1987"
(ix), projects more passivity than Arenas's Spanish, which could be rendered,
pushing in the other direction, as "I intended to die in the winter of 1987." In
the text, his first reaction when confronted with the facts, involves a decision
"to die close to the sea" (ix), for which he traveled south from New York, getting as close to Cuba as he could go: "Not exactly in Miami," another fraught
and homophobic place from which he also felt exiled, but in South Miami
Beach, a strip of sand in Cuban-like latitudes and just queer enough for him
to be able to breathe.

Arenas does not die in 1987, and he reports coming back to his apartment in New York from the hospital with a furious demand that he takes to a kind of altar, to a kind of saint, to the most explicitly homosexual of all major Cuban literary figure, one of Arenas's most enabling mentors:

> Cuando yo llegué del hospital a mi apartamento, me arrastré hasta una foto que tengo en la pared de Virgilio Piñera, muerto en 1979, y le hablé de este modo: "Oyeme lo que te voy a decir, necesito tres años más de vida para terminar mi obra, que es mi venganza contra casi todo el género humano." Creo que el rostro de Virgilio se ensombreció como si lo que le pedí hubiera sido algo desmesurado. Han pasado casi tres años de aquella petición desesperada. Mi fin es inminente. Espero mantener la ecuanimidad hasta el último instante.
> Gracias, Virgilio.

> [On my return home from the hospital, I dragged myself towards a photograph I have on my wall of Virgilio Piñera (who died in 1979), and I spoke to him in this way:
> "[You listen to what I'm gonna tell you]: I need three more years of life to finish my work, which is my vengeance against most of the human race."
> I think Virgilio's face darkened, as if I had asked for something out-rageous. It is almost three years now since that desperate request. My end is near. I expect to keep myself calm and collected until the very end.
> Thank you, Virgilio.] (Arenas 1992, 16; 1993, xvii)

For those with any sense of Cuban letters, this iconographic moment, this angry and still prayerful appeal to the most notorious homosexual figure in the Cuban canon, emerges as a moving and desperate act of homage and as-sertion that queer literary masters deserve both Cuban altars, and the trust of their followers. With this iconographic strategy, Arenas also positions himself as a kind of Cuban Dante, with his own Cuban Virgilio to keep him company during his retrospective tour from Cuban hell to Cuban hell.[8]

Arenas's introductory "End" closes with place and date, "New York, Au-gust 1990." Not surprisingly, much of the introduction details how Arenas used all the time available to him after his diagnosis to prepare for publication two novels, some poetry, and the autobiography, not so much his "complete works," as his "works completed while lengthening a death sentence." The last page of the autobiography is not dated but is a text released and performed four months after the date of the introduction, and it ranks with the perfect apocalyptic circularity of Melquíades manuscripts in García Marquez's *Hundred Years of Solitude,* or with the inevitability of the end in Fuentes's *The Death of Artemio Cruz.* In the search for perfect closure for a text written by and about its author, the suicide note can hardly be surpassed. It enacts total mastery or willfulness as it performs the end of the story as a function of authorial agency. "Pongo fin a mi vida" (Arenas 1992, 343), not quite "I am ending my life" (Arenas 1993, 317) as the translation says, but "I put an end to my life," which is to say, "I set down 'the end' to my life," or paraphrasing the presidential motto of total and final accountability, "the book stops here."[9] Moreover, if all this writing actually works as an act of vengeance, the vengefully departed has managed to take himself—at least bodily—out of the cycle of retribution. In preparation for his suicide on December 1990, Arenas leaves many copies of this letter to his "Dear friends." Since the note is signed, and clearly marked "TO BE PUBLISHED," "PARA SER PUBLICADA," the life so masterfully ended is explicitly handed over fully self-inscribed into the *res publica.*

But which *res publica*? Arenas, living his AIDS and its denouement in a U.S. setting, sits down to write a memoir that is very much not a U.S. AIDS memoir. It has no interest whatever in transforming either the perception of AIDS victims, or the homophobic social conditions of the United States. It dwells neither on the scene of sickness, nor on the indisputable humanity and courage of sufferers and survivors, because, committed as Arenas is to suicide, he will exclude himself precisely from that scene. So the whole exercise of rememoration is focused on Cuban matters. The autobiography enacts the end of a life; therefore it also becomes the closing volume of the "completed works." If his works are the monument, then the autobiography will recapitulate the monument as epitaph (cf. de Man 1979). From that monument, only the first novel and a couple of stories have ever been "published" in Cuba. The rest, practically the sum of his works in fact, remains substantially unread in the island. All that work, so much of it smuggled out of the island, then rewritten and expanded or finished abroad, then demands to be republished in Cuba. When you say that in Spanish, the magnitude of the challenge becomes clearer, for his work has to be "re-publicado," which is almost to say, reentered into the consciousness of the Republic. That demand now requires the clearing of some national space, or even just a site, on which to let his monument stand. Arenas made sure that such a site would never come to be associated with some actual tomb in exile. At the margin of the autobiography, but still very much as a part of the performance of his death and memorialization, Arenas complicated matters by requesting to have his ashes scattered in front of the Havana Malecón after the liberation of Cuba (Dibble and Barkett 1990). The closest he has come to identifying a site for the monument, is his obsession during the last years of his life to have all his papers carefully archived in the Firestone Library at Princeton University. In my pilgrimages to his archive, I have never asked the curators whether Arenas left any stated set of conditions under which his papers could be repatriated to Cuba. Now I do want to speculate: what kind of transformations would have to occur in Cuba, for Cubans to decide that it is time to ask Princeton to send Arenas's papers home?

Both that desperate trip in 1987 to South Miami Beach to die in the United States but by a Cuban sea, and the primary thrust of the suicide note, with so many markers of desire for return, reframe all the Cuban scenes in the autobiography as returns, even if just in narrative. There is nothing new in this rather conventional account of the ways exilic nostalgia operates. But if we focus on the extreme conditions set up by the frame of the autobiography, and if we go to the text, and to Cuba with the text, recognizing that every restaging can be seen as Arenas's last repatriated re-cruising, then we can return to the question of what this narrative act does.

How do the returns operate? Let's look at one return that suffuses all others throughout the book. In a book that ends Cuban life with a suicide very much validated as courageous and exemplary, I have found twenty-seven separate mentions of suicide. *Hasta los gatos* (Arenas 1992, 252), even cats commit suicide, which is a very Cuban way of saying that everybody does it. The reasons vary, but the repetition installs in the text yet another sense of ubiquity. A few of the suicides are funny, many are government functionaries who find themselves either ashamed of their own exercise of totalitarian power, or simply disgraced and out of favor, many others kill themselves to flee from repression in jails, concentration camps, or enslaving plantations. The mother down the well in *Celestino,* and Héctor crashing his car at the mouth of the Havana Harbor Tunnel, are two more Cuban suicides. Through all these retellings, the conventionally homophobic association of homosexuality with suicide is complicated and deflected. In Arenas's rendering, suicide is a function of oppression, not a function of queerness, or to put it in other words, Cuban queers kill themselves because they are oppressed both as *Cuban* and as *queer*. Arenas also refigures this Cuban tendency retroactively, highlighting the suicidal Indians and slaves as foundational actors in this national tradition of final self-destructive noncollaboration (cf. Arenas 1981; Arenas and Barquet 1991; Fernández-Robaina 1992–93).

Other of Arenas's texts also end in suicide, including many among his autobiographical fictions. But here I want to highlight his collection of political essays, *Necesidad de libertad* (The need for freedom), which ends with a graphic moment as telling as the suicide note in the autobiography. The last page here is a United Nations chart of suicides, which places Cuba among the world leaders, and way ahead of all other Latin American nations. In an article on José Martí in this same collection, the final and fatal return to Cuba of the father of the Cuban nation, who dies in 1895 in a rash and unauthorized charge against the Spanish forces in his first military skirmish, prompts Arenas to remark "that return is a suicide," "ese regreso es un suicidio" (Arenas 1986b, 57).[10] In many ways, after the naturalization of Cuban suicide that Arenas undertakes, both his fiction and his auto-thanato-graphical performance open up the signifying possibility "that suicide is a return," "ese suicidio es un regreso."

Arenas's own death emerges from all this repetition as a very Cuban death. "Pongo fin a mi vida" (Arenas 1992, 343) "voluntarily because I cannot continue working. . . . There is only one person I hold accountable: Fidel Castro" (Arenas 1993, 317). Then the note flies off into overdetermined nationalistic, anti-Castro, patriotic rhetoric:

> Al pueblo cubano tanto en el exilio como en la Isla los exhorto a que sigan luchando por la libertad. Mi mensaje no es un mensaje de derrota, sino de lucha y esperanza.
> Cuba será libre. Yo ya lo soy.
>
> [I want to encourage the Cuban people out of the country as well as in the Island to continue fighting for freedom. I do not want to convey to you a message of defeat but of continued struggle and of hope.
> Cuba will be free. I already am.] (Arenas 1992, 343; 1993, 317)

If this is a suicide in exile, and at the end of a life truncated by AIDS, the re-framing of this death as a Cuban thing depends in great measure on Arenas's capacity to recast his death, not as just another in the U.S. epidemiological body count, but as death by participation in something Cuban—as a politically marked Cuban suicide, with undisputed access to a Cuban grandeur worthy of monumentalization. If slaves in the Cuban plantations were told that their death would take them back to Africa, a trope that Arenas developed in *La loma del ángel* (Graveyard of the angels) (1987b, 95–96), his own textually charted and carefully performed suicide is also an opening back to Cuba, through which he revisits a historically and culturally significant multiplicity of Cuban suicides, among which his own will have to be enshrined (cf. Cabrera Infante 1983).

The conceit of the repatriation of Reinaldo Arenas's memory works best in the future of Cuban national formations: not so much by establishing, historically or backward, that what he testifies to in his retrospective was actually there, but more politically, poetically, and forward, imagining a future for Cuba when the nation would gladly repatriate him. It remains to be seen how far non-Cubans will take *Before Night Falls,* this textual performance that both demands to reterritorialize desire, and sets forth a highly nationalistic deterritorialized dying. Arenas brought out his queer Cuba to re-write it in New York, to wrap it up, together with the rest of his *obra,* as a Cuban queer monument, which now demands most vividly that reflexive negation of exile, the peregrination of return.

Notes

Unless otherwise noted, all translations are my own.

1   Reinaldo Arenas writes through a period of Cuban history when Cuba's traditional homophobia becomes most visible and most virulently symptomatic. This period spans the 1960s, 1970s, and 1980s. It includes: the triumph of the Cuban Revolution, with its initial campaigns to eradicate all practices of the commodification of sex in the early 1960s; the internment in the Military Units for Aid of Production work camps (UMAP) of a long list of social undesirables, prominently featuring homosexuals during the mid-1960s; the intensified codification and criminalization of homosexuality in the new Constitution and the new Family Code in the 1970s; the expulsion through Mariel of people with compromised so-

cial standing in 1980; and the need throughout the 1980s, both in Cuba and U.S.-Cuban communities, to respond to the onslaught of AIDS. All these developments form the preeminent backdrop for Arenas's highly denunciatory testimonial narratives, which he develops with his own volatile proportions of fiction, history, and autobiography.

There is hardly any critic who works with the writings of Reinaldo Arenas who does not feel the need to address his life as well. For good overviews of Arenas's life, and a variety of commentaries on the correspondences between life and work see Rodríguez-Monegal 1990; Santí 1990; Ette 1992; and Fernández-Robaina 1992–93.

2   These works include: *El mundo alucinante* (translated into English as *Hallucinations*) (Paris 1968, Mexico 1969, London and New York 1971); *Con los ojos cerrados* (With the eyes closed) (Montevideo 1972); *El palacio de las blanquísimas mofetas* (The palace of the white skunks) (Paris 1975, Darmstadt 1977, no Spanish edition until 1980).

3   The text enclosed in interior brackets here and in subsequent translated passages register my divergences from the published English translations. Citations of *Celestino* refer to the pagination of the 1980 Monte Avila edition.

4   See Lugo-Ortiz 1995 for an excellent account of how the community constitutes itself as a function of its homophobic choral imprecations of the "sexual deviant."

5   The English translation here interpolates: "the day of cleansing" (Arenas 1986a, 332).

6   If a rooster dies after one of his cousins has pleasured himself with it, the culture still has space to wonder, through Arenas's own musing, whether the cock was less injured by the physical duress of penetration than victimized by the societal shame heaped upon the hyperemblematic male who is actually supposed to be defined by his own penetrativeness vis-à-vis the hens (Arenas 1992, 39; 1993, 19).

7   The following scene with his mother provides another extremely acute record of Arenas's double take, which rules the tension between the moment of experience and the moment of signification. The added emphasis highlights the time factor: "Una noche, cuando yo estaba ya en la cama, mi madre me hizo una pregunta que, *en aquel momento,* me desconcertó. Me preguntó si yo no me sentiría muy triste en el caso de que ella se muriera. Yo me abracé a ella y empecé a llorar; *creo que* ella lloró también y me dijo que olvidase la pregunta. *Más tarde, o quizás en aquel mismo momento,* me di cuenta que mi madre pensaba suicidarse y yo le frustré ese plan" (Arenas 1992, 19), (One night, when I was already in bed, my mother asked me a question that *at that time* disturbed me greatly. She wanted to know if I would feel really sad if she died. I hugged her and started to cry. *I*

think she cried too, and told me to forget she had ever asked. *I realized later, or perhaps even then,* that my mother was contemplating suicide but had refrained because of me) (Arenas 1993, 3). See also the dead fetus in "La arboleda" (The grove) (Arenas 1992, 22; 1993, 6).

8   For another exilic recasting of Dante as a Cuban just emerged from a Cuban hell, see the opening and closing pages of José Martí's "Presidio político en Cuba" (1992); "Political Prison in Cuba" (1977). The trope of Cuba as hell or parodic paradise is, after all, a combination of obsession and commonplace. Arenas writes a prologue for *Desertores del paraíso* (Deserters from paradise), by his friend and companion Lázaro Gómez Carriles, under the title of "Al resplandor del infierno" (Arenas 1987c).

9   Upon hearing the description of the suicide note as perfect closure, Susan Ramond-Fic spontaneously volunteered the altered Tru(man)ism.

10   For another reading of Martí's suicidal return to Cuba, see Cabrera Infante 1983, 14–15.

MARTIN F. MANALANSAN IV

Diasporic Deviants/Divas: How Filipino Gay

Transmigrants "Play with the World"

Gay bars, West Hollywood, men who look like fashion models and Hollywood stars, Christopher Street, gay pride parades, living in with a boyfriend . . . if I stayed in the Philippines, I will never have experienced all these.

I remember how different Manila's gay scene was then. . . . now, after having gone back on an extended visit, girl . . . it is happening. The latest music . . . good looking men — brown-skinned studs . . . and just fun, fun, fun . . .

I went to a gay bar in the Castro. One clone queen took one look at me and tried to haul me out the door. He thought I didn't belong there — and he wasn't even the bouncer. I broke free but I never went to that bar again.

—Interviews with gay Filipino performers of Santacruzan

This study, the result of two years of ethnographic fieldwork, presents a microanalysis of a multiply marginalized group, Filipino gay men living in New York City.[1] I elicited extensive life histories of fifty Filipino gay men who ranged in age from twenty-two to sixty. All but five of these men were born and raised in the Philippines. Most of them have lived in the United States for more than ten years, with a majority living in Manhattan, Queens, and Jersey City.[2]

I highlight a specific event, a performance of a Catholic ritual by a group of Filipino gay men and lesbians in order to showcase the poetics of the Filipino gay diasporic experience. I focus on Filipino males in this study because of my own research interests as well as the conditions of the performance of this ritual.[3] Through this specific ritual, I focus on the attempts of these men to resist, contest, and reconfigure hegemonic images, ideas, and practices. I argue that identity formation among this group of diasporic men involves engagement with and creative amalgamation of practices and ideas from different locations. I delineate the kinds of engagements and linkages maintained, transformed, and performed by these men in their attempts to represent themselves through dreams, fabulous presentations, and quotidian struggles.

To situate this Filipino ritual reenactment within larger historical and social contexts, we must acknowledge that travel, migration, and diasporas in the late twentieth century mark a significant turning point in immigration history, particularly in the way immigrants are perceived and portrayed. No longer prone to "permanent rupture" from the homeland or total subservience to the hegemonic practices of the adopted nation, these "transmigrants" are living lives that span and transgress borders and specific localities with new means of transportation and communication in what is now called a "global ethnoscape" (Appadurai 1991; 1993). They maintain links to their country of origin, which then shape their interactions to the country of settlement or residence (Glick Schiller, Basch, and Blanc-Szanton 1992).

Sexual marginals experience their displacements as part of this global ecumene in particular ways. Ken Plummer writes: "Certainly the late modern world cannot be understood without seeing the interpenetrations of countries: of their economics; their cultures, their technologies. There is a worldwide process in which modern technologies have quite simply made the global world a local one: one in which news can be simultaneously consumed in many countries across the world at the same time. . . . And homosexuality is part of this. . . . Indeed, the gay and lesbian movements house identities, politics, cultures, markets, intellectual programmes which nowadays quite simply know no national boundaries. Homosexualities have become global-ized" (Plummer 1992, 17).[4]

In an article for the *Advocate,* Urvashi Vaid (1993), a prominent gay and les-bian political activist and herself a second-generation Asian American, ana-lyzed the parallels between immigrants and gays and lesbians. In doing so, she raised the specific dilemma of the gay/lesbian immigrant. Until the late 1980s, people who wished to visit or migrate to the United States were required to sign a document stating that they were not convicted criminals, Communists, or homosexuals. Tales of harassment and exclusion of gay and lesbian immi-grants and travelers in embassies, airports, and border crossings abound. Mi-noritized in multiple ways, these groups of immigrants not only have to face cultural, political, and economic displacements as newcomers to the country, but they also confront another set of oppressive regimes that deny them the "American dream" both in mainstream and gay communities.

The United States today occupies a paradoxical space for transmigrant gays and lesbians in what has been touted as the "gay nineties." With the ushering in of a new "liberal" presidency, the media have proclaimed the political ascendancy of gays and lesbians. Yet the present has also been touted as an era of the "immigrant backlash." Given that most accounts rely on a monolithic view of the gay and lesbian transmigrant, it is important to look into the specificities and creative possibilities in the practices of one group of gay men and/or lesbians in order to better understand the complexity of the issues at hand and the enriching particularity of their differences.

I use the word "transmigrant" and not immigrant or migrant to focus on the "multi-stranded relationships" such mobile people "forge and sus-tain, linking their country of origin with their country of settlement" (Glick Schiller, Basch, and Blanc-Szanton 1993, 11). I use the term "identity" not as a fixed and stable category, but rather as one that is highly processual, mo-bile, fluid, and contingent (see Maalki 1992; Chow 1993; Bottomley 1992). Identities, both collective and individual, are also "imagined," meaning that they are formulated and re-presented in particular cultural forms or expres-sions, such as rituals. Clifford Geertz, paraphrasing Victor Turner, writes: "[I]t is with expressions — representations, objectifications, discourses, per-formances whatever — we traffic: a carnival, a mural, a curing rite, a revital-ization movement, a clay figurine, an account of a stay in the woods. What ever sense we have of how things stand with someone else's [or some other group's] inner life, we gain it through their expressions, not through some magical intrusion into their consciousness" (Geertz 1986, 373).

Rituals are important social practices not because they are reflective of the social milieu, but rather because they present a metacommentary on the world (Bruner 1986, 26). For an immigrant or exilic group, "rituals provide the terrain in which the consciousness of communal boundaries is heightened, thereby confirming and strengthening individual location and positionality as well as social identity" (Naficy 1991, 295). In a world where identity is not rooted or territorialized within a specific place, rituals become the signs at the crossroads.

The Santacruzan

In March 1991, an organization of Filipino gay men and lesbians called Kambal sa Lusog was established.[5] "Kambal sa Lusog" literally means "twins in health," but is interpreted as "comrades in the struggle." Kambal sa Lusog is a unique group because unlike most ethnically or racially based gay organizations, it includes gay men, lesbians, and bisexuals. It has a monthly newsletter, meets almost every month at the Lesbian and Gay Community Center in Manhattan, and holds numerous fund-raisers and other group activities.

The Santacruzan, held in August 1992, was such a fund-raising activity. This event was not only successful in attracting other Filipino gay men who were not members, but it also involved the (re)production of a traditional Filipino ritual that I argue is central to understanding processes of community building and identity formation in the Filipino gay diaspora.[6]

The Santacruzan is an important traditional Catholic celebration in the Philippines that originated with Spanish colonization. It is celebrated every May and has been appropriately called the "Queen of All Filipino Fiestas." It is a street procession that usually begins and ends in the church. In other productions of this ritual, the plaza or a town's social center is used instead of the church.

The procession is essentially a symbolic reenactment of the finding of Christ's cross by Queen Helena or Reyna Elena, the mother of Emperor Constantine of the Holy Roman Empire. The ritual is based on a pivotal event in

Emperor Constantine's life. According to popular lore, Emperor Constantine, who was then a non-Christian, had a dream that he would win a battle if his soldiers would mark their shields with the cross. When he did what his dream suggested, he won the battle. Grateful about the outcome, Constantine urged his mother, Queen Helena, to look for the cross. Accompanied by *sagalas,* or muses, who figure in the different periods of biblical myth and history, the queen set out on a mission that has been memorialized in this traditional religious practice.

The usual muses who accompanied Reyna Elena are: Reyna Sentenciada (Justice), the three Virtues (Fe, Esperanza, and Caridad, or Faith, Hope, and Charity), Reyna Banderada or Motherland (Queen of the Flag), the bishop of Jerusalem, Reyna Sheba (Queen of Sheba), Reyna Elena or the Empress/Emperatriz,[7] Rosa Mistica, Constantino (the young Emperor Constantine), and biblical characters such as Judith and Mary Magdalene. Among the different additions in the early part of the century was Reyna de la Libertad, or Liberty. He/she is usually dressed as the Statue of Liberty and/or carrying the American flag. This figure is construed as a symbolic concession to American colonial rule.

In some accounts of the ritual's history, there are reports of performances that portrayed the Aetas (or Agta/Ita), who are dark-skinned aborigines of the Philippines, as part of the procession. The ritual's flexibility to various historical and cultural contexts has enabled the procession to become more than a religious procession of biblical personages. It has been transformed into a pageant of Philippine history. This reality has facilitated the creation of new muses or personages, and the range of the ritual figures is constrained only by the imagination of the people staging the procession. However, the recurring character in this ritual is always Reyna Elena, or the Empress Helena.

In the Philippines, the important figures in the processions are usually portrayed by women with male escorts. Apart from the bishop of Jerusalem (who is not portrayed frequently), Constantino is the only named male figure and is usually played by a child (either male or female). In regular renditions of the ritual, young women from a particular town or city district are chosen to participate. Being chosen to be part of the procession is perceived as a singular honor for both the woman and her family. The procession is constructed to be a showcase of "distinguished elite families" in the area, who also may sponsor a feast afterward, as well as a public demonstration of a town's or district's pride and solidarity. The Santacruzan provides an arena in which such communal efforts and spirits are deployed.

Despite its foreign roots, many Filipinos regard the Santacruzan as the quintessential Filipino ritual. Nowhere among the rather strict Catholic practices inherited from Spain is the Filipino appreciation for spectacles such as beauty contests and costumes given more free rein as well as theological relevance.

In some areas, there have been cases in which cross-dressed men have participated in these processions. In fact, one of these "infamous" kinds of Santacruzan is held annually in Pasay City (one of the cities in the metropolitan Manila area). Some informants who participated in cross-dressing Santacruzan processions in the Philippines reported that the content and symbols of these performances were no different from the traditional women-lead processions. They also reported that the procession was a kind of popularity contest. The gauge of popularity was the number of people (especially young men) who followed each queen. They said that after the cross-dressing procession and the feast, they (together with their choice of men) would slip into a secluded area to have sex in their gowns.

These cross-dressing processions are possible because of a long tradition of male cross-dressers in other spectacles such as the *karnabal* and *perya* (carnival and fair). Moreover, the *bakla* (the Tagalog gloss for homosexual and transvestite) is seen as the ultimate mimic or an expert in physical transformation (Cannell 1991). Stereotypically, the *bakla* is regarded as an artisan in crafts that involve mimicry and transformation, such as lip-synching, cosmetology, and female impersonation. Therefore, the cross-dressing Santacruzan logically extends such views and ideas into the realm of practice.

The lineup of personages in this reenactment of the Santacruzan in New York City included the combination of reconfigured "traditional" figures and newly created characters. It is important to note that each personage, or *sagala,* was individually reconfigured by each performer. Everyone was simply assigned a character and instructed to bring in a dress or costume.

This particular Manhattan performance of the Santacruzan in August 1992 was not presented as a procession, but as a fashion show. The focal point of the show was the stage with a fashion runway. In the center of the stage, before the runway began, was a floral arch reminiscent of the mobile arches of flowers that were carried in the procession for each mythical or historical personage.

The audience during this performance was also different. During most Santacruzan processions, people who line the streets or who are part of the processions usually carry candles, sing religious hymns, and/or pray. However, in this gay rendition, the audience hollered and screamed phrases of encouragement for queens, phrases taken right out of the voguing house cultures, like "Work it girl."

A man clad in a bikini suit portrayed Emperor Constantine. This was a departure from the traditional procession where Constantino was usually portrayed by a little boy or sometimes a girl. In this case, Constantino remained on stage to escort the "queens" up and down the runway. He resembled the "macho dancers" or "exotic dancers" who perform in many gay bars in the Philippines and New York.

Reyna Banderada (Queen of the Flag), who usually carries the Philippine flag in mainstream Santacruzan productions, incorporated the symbols of the flag, such as the stars and the red and blue stripes, in a slinky outfit. In this deconstruction of the flag, the three stars were strategically placed on each nipple and in the crotch area. A mask of the sun was carried by this new version of the motherland. Instead of walking demurely, s/he pranced around in seductive and "slutty" poses.

Reyna de la Libertad (Liberty) was dressed in dominatrix garb, complete with a whip. This queen's attire was composed of straps and pieces of black leather that left strategic parts of the body, like the derriere, teasingly exposed. Liberty in this instance was construed to mean sexual freedom. During the performance, Reyna de la Libertad posed menacingly at the audience, and before stepping down from the stage, s/he simulated whipping the behind of Constantino.

Rosa Mistica (Mystical Rose) is a theological emblem and not an actual person. This queen was wearing a multicolored sequined cocktail dress. When someone in the audience shouted "Fourteenth Street Special," implying that the dress was bought in a bargain store, others started snickering.

A new kind of queen was created for this presentation, Reyna Chismosa, or Queen of Gossip. This queen came out in a tacky dressing gown and hair curlers while screaming on a cordless phone. S/he walked up and down the stage teasing people from the audience while they egged her/him on. S/he also worked the audience to a teetering frenzy by screaming bitchy remarks like "Your mother said that you should go home" to individuals s/he singled out in the crowd.

The three Virtues were the only figures who were portrayed by lesbians. Two of them were dressed in denim shorts, combat boots, and *barong tagalog* (the traditional Filipino male formal attire). The third was dressed in a cock-tail dress and was the only one of the three to walk the runway. The other two remained on one side, like Constantino, and acted as escorts.

Reyna Sentenciada is usually portrayed like the figure of Justice, either carrying the scales of justice or with hands tied in front of her and blind-folded. The "gay" Reyna Sentenciada was again dressed in leather (sadomas-ochistic) dominatrix garb and wearing dark sunglasses. While his/her hands were tied by a black leather strap as he/she took to the runway, he/she untied him/herself at the center of the stage. And before s/he left the stage, Reyna Sentenciada, lifted his wig to show his bald pate.

Another muse was the Infanta Judith, or Judith of Bethulia, who saved her people from the domination of the Assyrians. During this performance held during the 1992 presidential election campaigns, the character came out as a Greek goddess, and instead of the head of Holofernes (the tyrannical Assyrian ruler), the gay Judith revealed the decapitated head of George Bush.

However, the finale returned to tradition with Reyna Elena and Empera-triz dressed in traditional gowns and tiaras. The Reyna Elena carried an an-tique cross and flowers as all Reyna Elenas have done in the past. There was no attempt at camp, rather, there was an insistence toward the kind of "femme realness" developed in voguing houses or house culture.[8]

Nostalgia, Difference, and Transnational Imaginings: Cross-dressing and the Filipino Bakla

To fully understand the context of the ritual, it is important to see the role cross-dressing plays and how it is appropriate and deployed in Filipino gay men's everyday life. The *bakla*, which is a term that has multiple meanings from cross-dresser/transvestite to hermaphrodite, is also called a *pusong babae*, or one with the "female heart." The construction of the *bakla* (not exactly a cultural or linguistic parallel to the gay man), centers on epicene and interstitial qualities. Largely desexualized, he is seen mainly in transvestite terms. Therefore, unlike the Western construction of the gay man, which centers on sexual object-choice, the Filipino *bakla* is largely gender-coded.

The centrality of cross-dressing in the construction of the Filipino *bakla* has entailed a distinctive view of this practice. One of the phrases symbolic of Filipino gay men's construction of cross-dressing is *paglaruan ang mundo,* or to "play with the world." This phrase was often uttered by Filipino gay men who were in drag. For many of my informants, cross-dressing was one way of confronting the vicissitudes of diasporic living, from finding a sense of belonging in the gay community to engaging racist practices.

Many of my informants drew a distinction between their style of cross-dressing, which is akin to "femme realness," and the comedic drag of Caucasian and mainstream gay men. The success of a performance depended on one's ability to convince people into believing and/or admiring their femininity. They maintained that comedic drag popular among Caucasians revolves around the absurd juxtaposition of elements and is largely parodic in nature. Caucasians used drag, according to my informants, as a way to reveal the very constructiveness of the mimicry (see Taussig 1993). In this gay ritual production, there were shifts from a kind of drag that most Filipino cross-dressers see as their own, to the theatrical, "scandalous," or comedic form of cross-dressing that they see as a very white or Western practice.

The idiom of "playing with the world" transforms the feminine ideal as object of scrutiny and spectacle into a vital weapon deployed in negotiating the interplay of difference, borders, and hierarchies. In other words, Filipino gay performers may subscribe to an ideal "realness," but they possess the outlook of agents who set out to negotiate and manipulate their versions of the "real" with those held by their audience.

The Contingencies of Space, Difference, and Hierarchy

This ritual performance should not be seen as an idiosyncratic act or a fortuitously amusing entertainment. Rather, it is important to see it as a complex bundle of meanings, if you will, a "moment" of critical conjunctions that speak to the Filipino gay diasporic experience. The combination of secular/profane and religious imagery as well as the combination of Filipino and American gay/mainstream icons provided an arena where symbols from the two countries were contested, dismantled, and reassembled in a dazzling series of cross-contestatory statements. Let me attempt to unpack a few of these semantic layers.

I look at this ritual as a "perverse," "dissident," or transgressive performance of identities. By this I mean that not only do the elements of the ritual deviate from the dominant regimes of meaning, they do so in terms of inversion, subversion, and reversal (Dollimore 1991). Such a "perverse" or transgressive performance is structured according to the following multiple hierarchical or power arrangements that are mutually reinforcing:[9]

> God/Men
> Sacred/Profane
> Men/Women
> White/Non-white
> Colonizer/Colonized
> Adopted Land/Homeland

These hierarchies reflect both the colonial and postcolonial experiences of Filipinos with Spain and the United States. The images and practices in the ritual are in part due to "more than three hundred years in the convent [with Spain] and thirty years of Hollywood [with the United States]."[10] It is not surprising therefore that the main elements in the ritual's structure were the juxtapositions of religious icons with secularized, profane, and sexualized images. The elements involved in this ritual are partial inflections of these historical realities, as well as articulations of the experiences of diasporic movement.

This ritual can be properly located within the ambivalent attitude of Filipino gay men (and Filipinos in general) toward the Catholic Church. Among Filipino Catholics, it is possible to "split" or to separate acts and behavior from professed religious and moral beliefs.

The secularization of the ritual also allowed a wider range of social commentary. First, the head of George Bush allowed the group to make a political statement during the 1992 presidential election. It marks a territorializing point in the ritual performance by an allusion to this important American political event. Furthermore, it points to the putative citizenship status of the participants. In other words, while many studies on transnationalism and diaspora emphasize displacement and the unbounding of borders, transmigrants' experiences, in certain moments, point to some kind of provisional fixing or mooring that is necessary to a sense of belonging in a new land.

The performance enabled these men to make some provisional statements regarding their need to address the questions about sexual freedom. As we have seen in performers' translation and reinterpretation of the figure of Liberty, these provisional statements involved articulations of Filipino gay men's emancipation from the government's and established religion's inability to deal with issues of homosexuality. Moreover, this ritual's concession to American colonial rule becomes a complex icon of American imperial expansion, Filipinos' postcolonial reconfiguration, and gay transmigrants' idealization of the homophilic space of New York.

The characters of Reyna Banderada and Reyna Chismosa represent a kind of oscillation between idioms of "vulgar" sexuality and comedic domesticity. The spectacle of Reyna Banderada, flimsily garbed in the diaphanous colors of the Philippine flag, reconceptualizes *Inang Bayan,* or "the Motherland," by wresting it away from its virginal and maternal tropes. Together with the half-naked figure of Constantino, Reyna Banderada brings to mind the stringent rules in the Philippines regarding the representation and handling of the flag. With almost a similar kind of reverence reserved for religious tenets, these rules are learned by all schoolchildren and men in compulsory military training in college as one of the ways in which patriotism is properly displayed. Reyna Banderada then is an embodiment of transgression of "love of country."

Reyna Chismosa is an anomalous addition to a coterie of mythical and biblical characters. The persona combines the stereotypical dichotomy of housewife and whore prevalent in many cross-dressing events. However, the character is not just any housewife, but rather a Western or Westernized one who has the economic means to stay at home and gossip on the phone. Such a domestic persona is a counterpoint to the glamorous figures of the other queens. It subverts the "proper" notion of the Santacruzan *sagala,* or queen, and provides an ironic figure that puts into question the whole ritual. The phone, in part, symbolizes one of the main connections of diasporic Filipinos to their homeland.[11] More importantly, Reyna Chismosa provides an apt analogue to both church and government as instruments of surveillance. But gossip is perhaps one of the integral strategies of resistance of oppressed people against hegemonic structures and agents. The process of gossip, which according to my informants is one of the regular activities of Filipinos both gay and straight, provides one possible way of communication among equals in defiance of a superordinate arrangement.

Such tropic play emphasizes the shifting nature of locations and spaces. Implicit in the structure of this ritual performance were the mercurial notions of "here" and "there." The sexualized images re-locate the ritual from the religious domain to a "gay" terrain. The remapping achieved in this ritual establishes the tension between the nation of birth and the nation of settlement, thereby unraveling the exigencies of "home." Finally, many of the life narratives of Filipino gay men pointed to the gradual drifting away from established religion. In fact, in many of these narratives, there is a tendency to look at religion as rooted in the homeland and secular individualism as inherently "American."

As I noted before, there are oscillations between the theatrical or comedic form of drag and a kind of cross-dressing. The comedic figure of Reyna Sentenciada pulling off his/her wig to reveal a bald head is set against the demure, "femme real" Reyna Elena. One Filipino gay man who was a member of the audience said that Reyna Sentenciada's shocking act of pulling off the wig was not seen favorably by other Filipino gay men. While it was funny, he argued that to show the incongruity between dress and persona destroyed the entire purpose of cross-dressing. As he said, "The illusion died."

This pageant, this re-processed procession, provided the space in which differences were confronted, refigured, and juxtaposed. Many of the Filipino gay men present were able to recognize the division or borders between these two kinds of cross-dressing practices. It raised the very notion of racialized spaces in the gay community in New York, particularly where there are places called "rice bars," "dinge bars," and "cha-cha or bean" bars. Leather bars, a white-dominated space, do not have any significant presence of Filipino gay men. This performance, with its use of *bakla* and American gay icons, provided Filipino gay men symbolic access to spaces from which they have traditionally been excluded.

This was made more explicit by the icons from different American gay traditions. For example, the muscular Constantino can be construed as a paean to white mainstream gay culture's hypermasculine images. Additionally, the paraphernalia of the gay leather set, the use of linguistic devices and cross-dressing practices from black and Latino voguers, the use of shocking acts—pulling off the wig—from American camp modes, are among the diverse strategies in opening up gay spaces. As one informant said, "What is really interesting in this Santacruzan is how this can be seen like a contest or a debate. . . . which one is better, louder, and more successful." Indeed, while this performance can be seen as such, there were no real resolutions in this occasion, but rather it was a way of revivifying what makes people like "us" Filipino gay men different from the "others."

Moreover, the ritual performance mirrors the experience of displacement, dislocation, and discrimination felt by some Filipino gay informants. These informants are silenced by oppressive regimes and practices expressed in orientalist terms even within the gay community. Informants have reported being seen as passive, "exotic," and/or sexless creatures by other gay men. Many informants told me about how they felt awkward or uncomfortable in gay sites or occasions that celebrate muscular bodies or in traditions such as leather or sadomasochism. In many gay bars in New York City, race and ethnicity are clearly demarcated. As one informant said, "You just can't go anywhere. You have to know whether you will be the odd man out in bars. You have to know your place."

Invisible Baggage, Drag Persona, and Nostalgia

Apart from marking difference, nostalgia was an important element in the Santacruzan pageant. The pageant was a way of "resurrecting time and place" (Stewart 1992, 252) for the largely immigrant group of Filipinos present that evening, as well as a way of revivifying memory and feelings of reterritorialization. As one informant said, "It made me feel like I was in Manila again." Cross-dressing, therefore, was a vehicle for nostalgia. It accomplished this by shattering "the surface of an atemporal order" (252). While this production may have had its distinctive elements, it nevertheless enabled them to think of other Santacruzan productions in cities and towns of their childhood. To some extent, the Santacruzan is part of the invisible baggage that they brought with them from their childhood, and which propelled them to travel back through their memories of "being there." Even those who were born and raised in California talked about how the Santacruzan was a major event in their childhood, and one of the few times they felt they were "Filipinos."

The juxtaposition of religious elements with secularized, profane, and sexualized images not only allowed a wider range of social commentary (e.g., George Bush's head), but also enabled the men to construct shifting notions of "here" and "there." The sexualized images relocated the ritual from a religious domain to a "gay" terrain, thereby mimicking the movements and tensions between the nation of birth and the nation of settlement. Such shifts unravel the instability of the notion of "home." The shock of the familiar, particularly in the finale with Reyna Elena, had a tremendous impact on many of the Filipino gay men present. Nostalgia revivified the image and memory of the Filipino homeland while at the same time acknowledging being settled in a "new home" here in the United States. Paradoxically, nostalgia created an invigorating energy in which to imagine a "parallel comradeship" among these men (which was confirmed by my interviews of Filipino gay men after the performance).

The links between nostalgia and cross-dressing were further exemplified by a Filipino cross-dresser whose drag name was Sarsi Emmanuel. He came to the United States at age fourteen, and was twenty-four when I met him in the summer of 1992 at The Golden Oven, a Filipino-owned and -run restaurant in Queens, the site of a big Filipino enclave.

On this particular night, the usual karaoke segment was the first in a series of performances that highlighted sentimental folksy tunes by Simon and Garfunkel, such as "Homeward Bound" and the ballads of Barbra Streisand. Afterward, while tables filled with regular customers, families with children eating Filipino food, a special event took place, a talent and beauty contest involving cross-dressing Filipino gay men. I was able to interview two contestants and discuss their chosen drag names and personas.

One of the contestants was Sarsi. Sarsi's drag name comes from a Filipino B-movie actress of the late 1970s. He commented on the evening's events: "Aren't we Filipinos unique? . . . We are so good at imitating. Did you see that man sing Frank Sinatra? . . . I guess despite the lack of blue eyes, he was really great don't you think? He was singing that song which reminded me of the other popular English songs played in Manila radio stations . . . what was it? . . . I was getting homesick. Well, I think we *bakla* are even better. Take a look at me and my name. . . . *O di va?* [Isn't it?] Don't you feel nostalgic about Tagalog films? I don't just bring Filipinos here the memories of home—I embody those memories—I look like her [like Sarsi] don't I?"

The role of memories of the homeland and the issue of postcolonial cultural and psychic displacement represent a crucial space in many Filipino gay transmigrants' and in all transmigrants' lives. Sarsi's image of his/her drag persona as memory-invoking is also a potent testimony to the Santacruzan. It belies not only nostalgia but the very construction of the Santacruzan as multiply transplanted: Spain, the Philippines, America. More importantly, it calls to mind the cultural mimicry that is seen as both the boon and bane of Philippine and other postcolonial cultures and peoples. Sarsi's ironic and defiant statement, however, recognizes mimicry's potential for engaging with inherently unequal relationships, such as the relationship between hegemonic Hollywood icons and non-Western performers (Cannell 1991).

Sarsi's symptomatic, succinct, and brilliant statement of embodying memory or provoking homesickness is not an altogether isolated case. Other drag names and personas of Filipino gay men that I have encountered in different situations were again those of starlets or big Tagalog movie stars, as well as of specific places in the Philippines, such Maria Christina Falls, Anna de Manila, Cory Antipolo, Lily Ermita and the like. Except for Manila, only the well-traveled or geographically well-informed non-Filipino would be able to decipher these names.

For these Filipino gay men, names are like coded messages, which on the one hand locate them temporally and spatially, while on the other hand provide them with mnemonic fuses. Through the process of imitating familiar gestures—acting demure or bitchy, holding the butterfly sleeve of the *terno* (the female native costume)—or familiar physical characteristics (e.g., a mole or long hair in a bouffant), these men were able to evoke memories of people and events from another time and space.

R.E.: *Transmigrant Dreamings*

Besides demarcating the general features of this reconfigured ritual, I have recorded the ways in which individual performers perceived or experienced the event. An informant I will call R.E. was twenty-three years old when I interviewed him right before the Santacruzan. He was a student in an art school in Manhattan. The youngest in a large family, he came to the United States when he was eighteen. He was very excited about being designated as the Reyna Elena. To be chosen as the Reyna Elena was an honor for anyone (man or woman) either in the Philippines or in Filipino American communities in the United States.

He said that as a child he used to watch annual Santacruzan pageants in his hometown in the southern Philippines, and that one of his dreams, apart from eventually living in America, was to be Reyna Elena. He said: "Ever since I was a small kid, I used to watch those spectacular parades and the things that I always thought was, one day I will be wearing a spectacular gown and be not just any ordinary *sagala,* but be the center of attention — be the most stunning Reyna Elena of all time. When I went to the U.S. I thought I will never be able to fulfill that dream. I thought that I would need to visit the Philippines to realize this dream."[12]

R.E. had a dressmaker in the Philippines make a *maria clara,* a traditional Filipino costume, and borrowed his family's antique cross for the Santacruzan procession in Manhattan. These were then flown to New York a month before the event. After the Santacruzan at the Gay and Lesbian Community Center, I asked him whether he thought it could have been different had his dream been fulfilled in the Philippines. He replied: "It would have been very traditional and not a lot of campy behavior in the parade. You know, we take the Santacruzan seriously in the Philippines, especially in our hometown. As you saw, there were some of us who wanted to carry on with the tradition. I carried flowers and a cross."

However, he further remarked that, despite the difference in the performance of the pageant, it would not have been possible for him to join the pageant in the Philippines: "My family would not have approved. We are one of the more prominent families in the province. They may know that I am *bakla,* but it would have been shameful. You see unlike the straight Santacruzan where it is an honor to be a participant, the drag Santacruzan is more like a sideshow albeit with a religious element. I guess the distance between my family and me has allowed me the freedom to do this." I asked him how he felt when he was onstage in costume. He said: "I knew I was in Manhattan, in Greenwich Village, onstage at the Community Center, but in my mind I was back in the Philippines, in my hometown, walking through the streets where I used to play as a child. People I know and who I grew up with were singing hymns and lighting my way. I felt I was back home."

For R.E., the culmination of childhood dreams in America came as a delightful surprise. He saw these dreams as both continuous and discontinuous with his original ideals. He said: "I know I would never have the same opportunity in the Philippines, but then again, even if I was able to join the Santacruzan in Manila—it would not be the same thing. We are in America, darling, we have to make do. When I came here, I had to adjust to conditions like having no maids, living alone, and going to gay bars without hustlers. It is the same thing with my dreams, I needed to be a little flexible. If not, I will not survive. . . . I will be one lonely queen."

Rosemary George has suggested that it is the "search for a location where one can feel at home, in spite of the obvious foreignness of the space, that propels the discourses engendered by the experience of immigration" (George 1992, 79). R.E.'s words, his life trajectories, and his dreams present a rich source of insights on specific issues of immigration, specifically on the notion of "home." The seemingly ironic juxtaposition of dreams and home in R.E.'s words marks the contingency of these concepts' provenance and existence. Using the invisible baggage or gunny sack of dreams and cultural practices, R.E. and other transmigrants refigure their lives and selves within existing constraints.

R.E. points out that it is possible for a dream first hatched amidst the restrictions of a Philippine town and the (dis)comforts of family life to be realized in a foreign space. The realization of R.E.'s dream in America, the land of dreams for many Filipinos, unwittingly exposes the complexity of "the process of making oneself at home" (George 1992, 79). This process continues in several successive generations as part of the struggle to create some coherence among spaces, dreams, and bodies. Yet such a coherence will never be complete. R.E.'s flight from the potential "shame" and loss of family honor through cross-dressing back in the Philippines to "freedom" in America is tempered by the secularization of the ritual in New York City's gay mecca and the difficulties of living in a foreign land. As R.E. pointed out, one must "make do." I construe his words not as a kind of defeatism, but rather as an exhortation to engage with the contradictions of his transnational existence. Indeed, despite the physical absence of his townspeople and other familiar scenes of his childhood, R.E. gracefully traipsed down the runway in his/her gown in a rundown former school building in Manhattan and felt at home.

Reflections on the (Trans)Nation

The significance of this particular performance speaks to the larger issues of immigration and diaspora as well as the cultural struggle of the formerly colonized. In addition, it unwittingly disrupts various national narratives. The performance also demonstrates how transmigrants negotiate between the hegemonic imperative of assimilation and the subaltern option of total defiance.[13]

In this ritual, American and Philippine social idioms, icons, and symbols fuse in order to provide a structure to an implicit narrative of a gay diasporic community. Performers in the Santacruzan, and R.E. specifically, are actively fabricating selves from strands of competing "national" traditions. In a sense, this "syncretic dynamic" appropriates elements from hegemonic cultural forms and in the process "creolizes" them by "disarticulating given signs and re-articulating their symbolic meaning" (Mercer 1988, 57). By fusing and infusing ritual religious components with the mundane and the taboo, Filipino gay men are in a sense "translating" their dreams, visions, and practices in creating and representing their lives in their land of settlement. Stuart Hall (1990, 235) notes that experiences in the diaspora are neither essential nor pure but heterogeneous and diverse. He further argues that identity within the diasporic context is marked by its transformative nature and emphasis on difference.

Nowhere are Hall's ideas more profoundly evident than in the words of R.E., who, with a pragmatic tone, narrated how his own dreams were transported and configured according to the exigencies of transmigration. In many ways the elements involved in its fruition have changed it. The transportation technology that allowed his costume to be flown from the Philippines and the existing racial and sexual politics in the gay community are but a few of the transformative elements that reconfigured his dream. Furthermore, the simultaneous presence/absence of people, places, and events in his memories and dreams paradoxically enabled R.E. to "feel at home" in the enactment of the ritual.

It is not just individual identities that are implicated in this process. The "rescripted" Santacruzan can be seen as "a style of imagining" a community.[14] In other words, the performance can be seen as an attempt by Filipino gay men to negotiate and represent their collectivity to themselves and to (sometimes more powerful) others. Such a ritual showcases the complex alliances as well as the fluid and multiple fields of social relations and identities of this group of gay immigrants. In particular, the ritual coalesces the agency of this group of men as they reinvent, resist, and refigure hierarchies and hegemonic ideas and practices in various locations (Glick Schiller, Basch, and Blanc-Szanton 1992, 11).

Immigration, George argues, "unwrites the nation and national projects because it flagrantly displays a rejection of one national space for another more desirable location, albeit with some luggage carried over" (George 1992, 83). In this ritual, transplanted individuals reinvent meanings that interrogate the divergences and continuity of experiences and images between the nation of origin and the nation of settlement. As such, it is important to note that in the performance, the very idea of "the nation" is brought into question. Indeed, as the ritual, and its performers, like Reyna Banderada, have unwittingly asked: Which nation? Whose nation?

This ritual space allowed Filipino gay men to "return the gaze," that is, to reinvent themselves according to their own terms. Cross-dressing is a cultural practice that is both tolerated and ridiculed in the Philippines and the United States (Levine 1990). This ambivalence is manifested in New York City's mainstream gay community's belated avowal of cross-dressing gay men not as anachronistic relics of the past, but as vibrant and significant members of that community. Deterritorialized moments and sites such as the Santacruzan (an ancient rite handed on by Spain to the colonies and now, re-presented in metropolitan America) allow us to derive insights into how Filipino gay men and other diasporic deviants "author themselves," make sense of their transmigrant experience, and indeed, "play with the world."

Notes

Versions of this paper were presented in 1993 at the annual conferences of the American Studies Association and the American Anthropological Association, as well as at the University of California–San Diego's "Queer in the Nineties" lecture series. This paper benefited from comments and suggestions by Deborah Amory, Rosemary George, Chandan Reddy, Judith Halberstam, Rick Bonus, Lisa Lowe, David Beriss, Virginia Dominguez, Gerry Cuachon, and Joey Almoradie. I would like to thank Cindy Patton and Benigno Sánchez-Eppler for their support and critical insights. I am grateful to all the Filipino gay men who shared a part of their lives with me. This work is dedicated to the memory of Dario Marano, a former colleague at Gay Men's Health Crisis, and fellow traveler in a world of diasporas.

1   At the outset, I need to highlight the problematic nature of the term "gay," particularly when applied to men and/or women coming from minority emplacements or Third World locations. Therefore, I use the term "gay" provisionally.

2   Filipinos are projected to become the biggest immigrant national group in the United States by the next century (Bouvier and Agresta 1987). For excellent discussions of Filipino immigration to the United States and the need to couch Filipino immigration within a diasporic framework see Okamura 1993 and Cariño 1987.

3   Except for one segment of the performance, the Filipino lesbian group members were primarily involved in the technical and support activities of the event.

4   I recognize that homosexuality is a category primarily denoting sexual object-choice. Despite this limitation, I must acknowledge its popular use in Filipino discourses.

5   Some informants who were members of this organization said that the impetus for formating this group was in part due to the *Miss Saigon* controversy. The controversy revolved around alleged racist practices by the production company and the orientalist overtones of the text. Many Filipino gay men were ambivalent about the controversy because Lea Salonga, a Filipina, was the star of the show. However, after talking to one of the founders of the group, he said that there had been talk about such a group even before the *Miss Saigon* controversy. A large factor had to do with the fact, he said, that many Filipinos do not relate to other Asians or to an Asian identity.

This statement had been confirmed by my interviews with Filipino gay men. As mentioned above, many of the informants perceived Asia only in terms of geography, and noted that significant differences existed between other Asians and themselves. Furthermore, there was also a perception that "Asian" meant East Asians such as Japanese and Chinese. Due to these views, many felt that their interests as gay men would not be served by a group like GAPIMNY (Gay Asian Pacific Islander Men of New York).

6   In a earlier paper (Manalansan 1994), I briefly discuss this event in relation to Filipino gay men's other engagements in gay community politics in New York City.

7   While these names refer to Queen/Empress/Reyna Helena or Elena, they are sometimes portrayed separately in the procession.

8   Voguing houses or house culture are groups of Latino and African American

gay men and lesbians whose community life centers on large social gatherings or balls. The balls are essentially competitions for cross-dressing and modeling and have numerous categories, one of which is "femme realness." Femme realness requires participants to look like "real" women — to the point of asking participants to have their face and extremities examined by the board of judges for signs of unsightly facial hair, muscles, or blemishes.

9   I am aware that I am treading on the much contested concept of binary oppositions. I submit that these arrangements are only binary in nature if seen in isolation from each other, and not in their interconnectedness in theory and practice.

10   This is a popular cliché summary of Philippine colonial history that has been attributed to the Filipino writer, Nick Joaquin.

11   AT&T has created special programs targeting Filipinos in America and has recognized them as being one of their biggest clients in the long-distance telephone business (Okamura 1993).

12   This conversation was conducted in Taglish and translated into standard American English. Unfortunately, some of the vibrant tone and inflections of code-switching were lost.

13   Here, I am clearly influenced by Jose Esteban Muñoz's work, particularly his (1995) analysis of a Latina lesbian performance artist, which demonstrates his ideas on "disidentification."

14   In an earlier work (Manalansan 1994), I briefly discuss the ritual along with other political activities and struggles of New York–based Filipino gay men.

MICHÈLE AINA BARALE

Queer Urbanities: A Walk on the Wild Side

The ordinary practitioners of the city live "down below," below the thresholds at which visibility begins. They walk—an elementary form of this experience of the city; they are walkers, *Wandersmänner,* whose bodies follow the thicks and thins of an urban "text" they write without being able to read it. These practitioners make use of spaces that cannot be seen; their knowledge of them is as blind as that of lovers in each other's arms. The paths that correspond in this intertwining, unrecognized poems in which each body is an element signed by many others, elude legibility. It is as though the practices organizing a bustling city were characterized by their blindness. The networks of these moving, intersecting writings compose a manifold story that has neither author nor spectator, shaped out of fragments of trajectories and alterations of spaces: in relation to representations, it remains daily and indefinitely other.
(de Certeau 1988, 93)

On the cover of the original 1962 Gold Medal/Fawcett paperback edition of Ann Bannon's *Beebo Brinker,* a green-suited female figure leans against a city lamppost that supports not only a traffic light but both street and directional signs. ONE WAY, reads a traffic arrow pointing left (Bannon 1962). ONE WAY, reads a second arrow that has been bent from its original position to now point, in confusing demand, to the right. The figure stands distinctly to the left of the post, her body on the side of the unequivocally pointing, unbent sign: ONE WAY. The traffic light is on red. The sign directly above her head announces Gay Street. Facing away from the gaze of both the figure and cover's viewer is a rectangular sign whose message we cannot read. To the figure's left is a fire hydrant. This collection of civic information, control, and prevention, together with the city pavement that is their ground, form a four-sided, two-dimensional frame within and against which the female body stands, the city spread out around and beyond her (fig. 1).

The figure illustrated for us on this cover is clearly meant to represent the novel's eponymous hero (heroine being far too femme a title for the soon-to-discover-her-butchhood Beebo Brinker) whose arrival in New York, fresh from her Juniper Hills, Wisconsin, farm initiates her into the urban gay subculture of Greenwich Village in the late 1950s. Within moments of Beebo's entry into the city she gains a mentor, in the form of Jack Mann, a gay male currently between boys, and in short order also finds a job, a gay bar, and a girl — and then another girl — and then still another girl. Losing the first, leaving the second, dumped by the third, Beebo returns to the second — we've lost sight of the first — now older and appropriately wiser the novel leads us to presume.

As this description of Beebo's girlish and girl-ly adventures might lead you to suspect, the novel is a pulp lesbian romance. Hardly the stuff of high literary culture, *Beebo Brinker* is the kind of novel one might have found in the local drugstore paperback book racks, its cost a modest fifty cents, its cover blurb's promise of erotic adventure — "Lost, lonely, boyishly appealing — this is Beebo Brinker — who never really knew what she wanted — until she came to Greenwich Village and found the love that smoulders in the shadows of the twilight world" — somewhat muted by the illustrator's use of somber brown, green, and grey tones.

As I have argued elsewhere, it is not all that odd that a mainstream press could find it fitting to publish a lesbian novel, since the paperback industry's earliest offerings were divided between well-known classics and novels of a slightly dubious nature (both sorts of publications, however, wearing cover jackets that promised scintillations greater than were, in fact, to be found within) (Barale 1993). Moreover, *Beebo Brinker* makes use of rhetorical appeals, I have argued, aimed specifically at the heterosexual male. It does so

Figure 1. Cover of *Beebo Brinker* by Ann Bannon (photo by Frank Ward, Amherst College).

by inviting that reader into the text through the novel's opening presence of Jack Mann as a girl-watcher who has spied fresh-off-the-farm Beebo in her earliest moments in the city. Only after we have followed Jack as he follows Beebo across town is Jack's gayness revealed. And by that point not only has the book been bought but the reader has been promised that in place of what had been supposed to be Jack's "normal" heterosexuality, the reader will instead experience Close Encounters of the Queer Kind — if only the reader will hang in there and keep turning those pages. Thus, both this novel's appeal to a heterosexual audience — one primarily male — as well as the paperback industry's early history as publishers of novels whose content was sexually provocative, mean that this narrative's specific focus on lesbianism would not rule out its appearance among other mainstream offerings.

Despite its pulpily romantic nature, however, *Beebo Brinker* offers us the opportunity to speculate upon gay migrants' use of the city. In the novel, the pleasurable anonymity that a dense urban population promises someone whose every oddity was noticeable in her original small town setting, jostles in seeming contradiction to Beebo's desire to find a site of shared queerness. The narrative of this search and its success is one we learn from inside. Because Beebo arrives in the city both ignorant of her oddity's name and yet aware of its forceful presence within her, readers learn with her — with the subcultural subject — not only what her oddity is called but where it can be lived out and even enjoyed. We accompany Beebo into gay bars — the first she, and possibly some of her readers, have ever entered. And we cruise, observe, and try to make sense of what goes on there. We hunt for, and find, a job where a girl doesn't have to dress as such, and then see what the world looks like when we enter posh skyscrapers via the service door, carrying a pizza. In short, the novel offers its readers a carte blanche to accompany a strange girl in a strange land. After we have turned sufficient enough pages — and I would argue, fewer than twenty — we are free to cross the borders and stroll through queerer parts of town and tour its streets, drink in its bars, ogle its inhabitants, and learn its intimacies; we become one of the gang, just another "beebo," as it were.

The novel's cover, however, does something complexly different. Rather than gayly welcoming anyone who is willing to pay for the fifty-cent excursion, the cover instead displays all the anxiety of a city father marshaling touring dignitaries. If the text offers native guides and colorful but articulate locals, the cover promises that efficient municipal control will always be in force should tourists find the natives threatening. Like those African safaris conducted from within a bus, with good photographic sites itinerized, explanatory narratives and rest stops carefully sanitized, the cover shows us both where the action is and how to avoid it. As such, the cover provides a cartography of desire, mapping the city as a locale in which conflicting needs are both satisfied and denied, both permitted—which is to say controlled—and yet acknowledged as outside policed precincts.

It would be difficult to argue that the female figure of the Gold Medal/Fawcett cover is represented as anything other than innocent. No curve of hip or bosom, no hint of thigh betrays her; her lower legs are not only modestly covered by a skirt falling well below her knees but are further obscured by the large wicker suitcase she holds, only to conclude in pink fold-over ankle socks and sensible brown oxfords on rather large feet that distinctly toe out, but awkwardly, not ballet-dancer gracefully. Never mind cleavage: that green blazer is buttoned just as far as it can go and beneath it there is a blouse buttoned right up to the neck. Far from erotic, her gaze is distant and impersonal, her lips firmly closed; only the long dead display less affect. The hair is girlish: not quite bouncy enough for an authentic Annette Funicello flip but neither so unkempt as to suggest a slovenly lack of femininity. Except for the slight cant of one hip, a clumsy rather than provocative posture logically called for by the evident heft of her suitcase, the figure stands flat-footedly full-face, as unbeguiling as the lamppost behind her.

In these details, as in several others, the cover hews to the spirit, if not the exact particulars, of the text's description of Beebo as newly arrived and "uncommonly handsome" (Bannon 1962, 10), as "big, clean, healthy . . . bright and sensitive" (18), as "decent, intelligent . . . good-looking" (21) but never wildly or even subtly sexy. Here's our first glimpse of Beebo Brinker: "She wore a sporty jacket, the kind with a gold thread emblem on the breast pocket; a man's white shirt, open at the throat, tieless and gray with travel dust; a straight tan cotton skirt that hugged her small hips; white socks and tennis shoes. Her short hair had been combed without the manufactured curls and varnished waves that marked so many teen-agers. It was neat, but the natural curl was slowly fighting free of the imposed order"(15). Some of the discrepancies that we note—the change from a tan to a green skirt, the addition of a thin gold bangle bracelet on the figure's left wrist, for example—seem trifling. Other details have textual origins and important significance:

the wicker suitcase (with its suggestion of the country), and the small but clear hint of something yellow—identified in the novel as "a yellow 'Guide to Greenwich Village' with creased pages" (9)—protruding from her jacket's right hip pocket.

It is always tempting to overread covers, to find a hidden agenda behind every detail, whether that detail is a change from the text, an addition to it, or a depiction of Bannon's own description. Therefore, I am not going to suggest that the cover's every line, color, addition, and subtraction have been motivated by deeply hidden or malign or crafty purposes. What we *do* know about the rationale behind this cover's set of particulars is that they were chosen because it was presumed that they would sell copies of the book. In other words, part of the agenda here is hardly covert. What is not so clearly manifest, however, is why this set of details was thought to have mass-market appeal, why, for example, the novel's white socks were replaced by pink ones. But I can speculate.

There is a kind of color coordination apparent in the cover's use of pink (a nicety not visible, alas, in black-and-white reproduction). Not only are Beebo's socks pink, but so is the title of the book, both of whose colors are adumbrated by the presence of lengthy pink smears in the area, the pavement, around her feet and extending under the copy line, "A NOVEL BY ANN BANNON." There's pink, as well, in a few odd patches at the very base of the lamppost and the fire hydrant. It's a feminine color, pink, possibly even a girlish one since youthfulness is certainly evidenced in the supposedly hand-printed, and therefore irregular, typography of the title.[1] And, in fact, there may be nothing more than color coordination at stake here. Of course, had the color of socks, title, and smears and patches been red, we would read the use of color here as distinctly sexual, I think, as imputing a kind of scarlet ladyhood to the urban corner-loitering, female figure. But stepping down the color value, diluting its force, girl-ifying it, de-eroticizes its effect. It may be that the softer, milder hue signals a sexual potential as yet youthfully unachieved; and certainly the fact that the figure wears bobby socks rather than hosiery emphasizes the figure's status as teenager, even though such a status is not without its own erotic potential.[2]

As a milder, less provocatively sexual or even explicitly *gay* color, pink may begin to signal something slightly alarming. Although pastel colors are often associated with femininity, youth, and innocence, pink, despite its appeal to girlishness, can also suggest that the female figure of the cover can pose some risks.[3] I am more inclined to read the presence of pink as an advertisement for the figure's future specific *queerness* than I am to read it more generally, or even generously, as prophetic of nothing more than her future *adult* sexuality. And the positioning of the GAY STREET sign directly above her head only furthers my inclination, just as it appears to name Beebo's. The cover seems to be suggesting that not only will we find herein the not at all uncommon tale of a country youth's discovery of the urban erotic, but it hints as well that it will be a story of both adventures and an identity that are possibly *pinko* in nature: suspicious, dangerous, radical, possibly covert, certainly neither mainstream nor middle class—in a word, illegal. I need to keep pushing at pink's possibilities, even though I court some danger in doing so.

American idiomatic uses of *pinko,* and its source in slang usages of *pink,* situate the term in a dense and even contradictory interplay of meanings that are *racial* (blacks referring to whites), *political* (Communist), *class-bound* (hot-rodders lost their "pink," in the parlance, when ticketed for traffic violations), and *civic* (certification of car ownership was usually printed on pink paper, in which case, one had one's "pink" only to later lose it for wild driving). All are usages[4] that suggest an Otherness that is at once threatening to the social whole—as in "pinko hippies"[5]—hypervirile in its vehicular souped-up-ness and illegal derring-do, and also enviably denotative of Caucasian membership. To be pink(o) in this sense dismisses pastel-hued passivity and suggests, instead, someone "out of bounds," one who inhabits urban jungles rather than civic centers, one who can show us things we've never seen and places we've never been, but also one who, given her pink, rather than black or brown or "colored" status, is nonetheless part of the "proper" whole.

The dubious gender of the title's name, *Beebo Brinker,* now takes on distinctly sexual meaning: this is the name of one who is deliciously No-man and Everyman. Like every (heterosexual) man, Beebo desires women. Even though she is not male, she is not yet herself woman: not *yet,* because she is emphatically immature; yet *not,* because of the ease with which sexual difference gets elided with gender so that Beebo's femininity can be called into question by the fact of her queer sexuality. The whole point of Beebo's entry into the urban wilderness is to lose her "pink"—to engage in unlicensed desires for members of her own gender. Thus even as the presence of that pink-hued title seems to reinforce Beebo's femininity, it also casts it into doubt. Any white reader, of any sex or sexuality, might stand there—*with her or as her*. She offers a site where that reader can be both "lost" and "lonely," and yet "appealing," just as she figures for a narrative where certain kinds of confusions will be clarified ("never really knew what she wanted—") once that site is entered ("until she came to Greenwich Village and found the love that smoulders in the shadows of the twilight world"). The cover thus provides us with a lonesome, vulnerable, still innocent figure of ambiguous gender but queer potential who can serve as a naive guide—hence we get to learn everything she does—in an urban underworld.

And now I am really going to push at my reading still harder, extend it as far as I can make it go. I do have a purpose; there is a point to all this, a payoff. Given the fact of the cover's pink splashings, it appears that both the particulars and the generalities of the sexuality represented here do not limit themselves to the female body. Instead Beebo's pink is able to broadly cast its hue, reflecting itself in the space in which she is encompassed and coloring the objects nearby in a kind of sexual spillover whose pastel nature mitigates some of the dangers usually associated with such contamination but doesn't entirely deny the possibility that pinkness can be "caught" by those in proximity. And the cover, in fact, is prepared for this possibility. The traffic light above Beebo's head brightly signals STOP, although which precise citizen is to follow this directive is not entirely clear. The most obvious person whose travels are to be regulated, if not entirely prevented, is the newcomer, the "beebo," whose wanderings can benefit from the system's management of her—or his—movement. Placed at a crossroads, the light gives the traveler a moment to pause and make a decision as to exactly which of the two possible "one ways" will be taken: up GAY STREET or down the other street whose name, interestingly enough, is unreadable. Of course, that bent ONE WAY sign both produces and legitimizes confusion.

The putative city fathers originally placed the signs to point at ninety-degree angles from one another, thereby marking all of GAY STREET as one way, west, let us say, while the unidentified street points north. The bend now seems to indicate that GAY STREET's directions change, fall into two parts, at this particular traffic juncture. Should you travel west you cannot return except by means of another street; should you travel east, you cannot later reverse your direction and travel west. Were this the only corner in New York—

as it is here—it would then seem that one could turn GAY or one could not, but no change of mind after the fact were possible. It would also seem as though both homosexuality and heterosexuality occupy the same site, could be mapped along the same west-to-east line, bifurcated neatly in the middle by a helpful traffic light that enables a pause for a moment's reflection before an irreversible decision needs be made.

Had the signs been left in their "true" relation to one another—had they remained unbent by the forces of urban life—the newcomer could proceed ONE WAY up GAY STREET, make a right, and then another, and then with a left turn, travel down the street that is not GAY. And vice versa. Once you knew the topography, once you had a map, access to either street was entirely possible. In such a tour of the city, ONE WAY signs direct traffic, but they don't prevent travel. What I am suggesting, therefore, is that the city planners got it right the first time: rather than oppositional, the two sexualities can be entered, crossed, exited, and retraveled. But by some kind of *bonum peccatum*—happy mistake—what the city fathers didn't adequately prepare against, the destructive urban forces implied by the cover design do. East is east and west is west and never the twain shall meet . . . except at the traffic light where there is a sign we cannot read. Because that sign is a rectangle, convention suggests that it is offering some kind of directive, most probably a prohibition. Since this is New York, I will suggest that the sign's presence implies NO PARKING, the automotive equivalent of NO LOITERING. Move on, the sign seems to warn. Don't linger here. Keep going.

Thus, in their original position, the signs enabled easy sexual crossovers, creating no barriers or boundaries. GAY and its opposite, its Other Street, could each provide part of the pathway to one another. It would seem as though the willy-nilly growth of urban routings—a growth as much planned as uncontrolled—produces an environment in which all things can be reached, by one means or another. To put it another way, the vehicular specifics of municipal traffic control prevent such rules from regulating other kinds of traffic, traffic of the sexual sort. As the mechanisms of control exert their power in one place, they loose their grip on another. In turn, another set of (ir)regulations, this time enforced by Gold Medal/Fawcett's marketing needs, corrects the lack of the first. By bending the rules, literally and representationally, the cover seems to close the loopholes left by the original city planners. But it doesn't really, of course. What the cover does, in fact, is invite the book-minded traveler to approach a site where both the legal and the illicit are possible. The traveler can go GAY and still be Other. And just in case this is all too frightening, help is at hand.

Should neither the directive to move nor the legal pause offered by the traffic light not suffice to prevent the spread of a menacing pink, there is a fire hydrant nearby, just to the left, to the west, if you will, of GAY STREET's sign. I find it difficult not to read the common city sight of this humble gray fire-plug as uncommonly significant here. It seems to suggest that should pink intensify—to a flaming red, for instance—municipal authority has the matter under control. Unregulated fires can be properly quenched; civic safety can be maintained.

I would presume that all threats to the civic system would call for containment. That is to say, that threats to the institution of heterosexuality need to be checked. Since the fire hydrant stands on the GAY STREET side of the west-east division, it might be the case that we are to understand that while clear bifurcations of sexual territory are necessary in the interests of civic safety, there is some danger in such segregation; where the non-gay do not dwell is precisely where regulation is hardest to maintain and things get fired up. Thus, that hydrant might be so placed because it seems likely to be most needed there. However, just how seductive is the promise that by going west the reader will enter torrid zones and possibly come upon a "love that smoulders"?

The cover figure has a map in her pocket, one which the illustration does not quite reveal but which the text fills in for us. If she is our guide, newcomer though she is, she has a means at hand to find her way. And it would seem that we will have to follow her to her destination if we are to find out the contents of her still unopened suitcase. Whether mundane or exotic, what's within can only be known if we go her way.

Notes

1   In a conversation some years back, one interested reader of Bannon's novel pointed out to me that the title's crude, hand-drawn typography is meant to call to mind Greenwich Village's reputation as a gathering place for beatniks. This seems right on the mark. Art, particularly in its bohemian environs, offers a rich site for any variety of unconventional activities. Poetry and deviancy come to occupy the same

urban space in such a way that we cannot fully disentangle the creative imagination from sexuality, or aberration from new, lyric forms.

2   Nonetheless, I would argue against the presence of bobby socks as inevitably deny-ing sexiness. Paperback novel covers from the late 1950s felt quite free to depict bobby socks–wearing girls as already highly sexually knowledgeable. Moreover, it is likely that widespread concern with the growth of urban gangs and juvenile delinquency during this decade served to intensify cultural representations of the teenage female as titillatingly sexual.

3   So far as I can tell, knowledge of the pink triangle's use to designate homosexuals from other Nazi prison camp prisoners was not available to either the gay or the heterosexual community at the time this cover was designed, and hence pink itself had no gay-associative significance, although I would imagine that its pastel nature might have made it a distinctly non-virile color and hence one that straight men should eschew.

4   According to the *Dictionary of American Slang* (1975), "pinko" is an adjective de-rived from the slang noun *pink*, whose first usage is specified as predominant in Negro speech to identify a white person, and whose second usage denotes "a mild political radical; esp. one sympathetic to, but not actually working for, the inter-national Communist movement." The third meaning of the term is "Lit. and fig., the legal certificate of car ownership; fig., the right to drive one's car. *Thus, for the traffic law violations one may lose one's "pink." Orig. and mainly hot-rod use. Because such certificates of ownership are often printed on pink paper. adj. = pinko* (original emphasis).

5   The *New Dictionary of American Slang* (1986), cites *Ebony:* "How come those Niggers and those creepy pinko hippies call us names like 'pigs'?"

SANDRA BUCKLEY

Sexing the Kitchen: Okoge *and Other Tales*

of Contemporary Japan

I

The best known of the novels of the popular Japanese woman author Yoshimoto Banana is entitled *Kitchen* (1988). The story begins with the protagonist,
Sakurai Mikage, a young university student, sitting alone in the kitchen of her
home. It is three days since the funeral of her grandmother. Sakurai's parents
died when she was a small child, and she was then raised by her grandparents. Her grandfather died when she was about twelve. Now, with the death of
her last immediate kin, she reflects in and on the kitchen and her new condition of aloneness. The novel opens with the line: "I think the place I love most
in this world is the kitchen" (Yoshimoto 1988, 8). She continues: "It doesn't
matter where it is or what kind it is, so long as it's a kitchen, a place where
meals are made, then I'm at ease. If possible I prefer it to be functional and
well used. With several fresh dishcloths hanging in reach and white tiles sparkling brilliantly. I especially love an incredibly dirty kitchen With vegetable
peel lying scattered on a floor that leaves the soles of your slippers black with
grime. The more outrageously spacious it is the better. A large refrigerator
stacked with food enough for an entire winter, towers over the kitchen and

I prop myself up against its silver door. I lift my eyes from the rusty knives and the gas cooker splattered with oil stains, and a star is shining desolately beyond the window" (8).

With a gentle shift in verbal inflection Banana (as Yoshimoto prefers to be called) melts Sakurai's imagining of the ideal kitchen into time-present of the narrative, and we join her in the spacious, incredibly dirty, well-used kitchen that is the kitchen of her childhood: "All that remains is the kitchen and me. At least that's slightly less worrying than thinking that I am entirely alone. . . . When the time comes for me to die I want to draw my last breath in a kitchen. Whether it is a cold place and I am alone or I am with someone and it is warm, I want to face it fearlessly with my eyes open. If it can happen in a kitchen I'll be happy" (8). Sakurai then describes how for the three days since her grandmother's funeral she has been sleeping in the kitchen: "No matter where I was, somehow or other I just couldn't sleep and so I progressed from one room to the next moving gradually towards the most comfortable places and finally one evening I realized that it was beside the refrigerator that I could sleep best. . . . In pursuit of a gentle sleep wrapped in an almost tearless calm state of sadness I pulled my futon into the brightly lit kitchen. I slept Linus-like in my blanket. The continual hum of the refrigerator protected me from lonely thoughts" (8–9).

With the death of her grandmother Sakurai faces the erasure of her entire family: "All that is left is the kitchen and me" (8). She is not completely alone, for there is still the kitchen; in her reflections she embodies the kitchen and family within a single memoryscape. Here, the kitchen is no longer a mere location or physical setting for the movement and action of characters. As seen in the passage quoted above, tense fluctuates in the space of the kitchen, displacing linear progression with tension and conflation of time-past, -present and -future. The familiar space drawn and punctuated by walls, floor, appliances, dirt, stains, dishcloths, and the familial figures of mother, father, grandfather, and grandmother are re-membered and re-presented in a disorderly and unpredictable configuration of a multiplicity of memories and experiences of familial/iar bodies and spaces.

Today, politicians and marketing strategists echo Banana in their under standing that the way to the heart of the nation is through its kitchens. The kitchen that is the source of the protagonist Sakurai's comfort is not merely a fixed architectural space defined by four walls and the function of cooking. It has become a fantastic space. Here, official discourses of national identity, gender, sexuality, family, and motherhood are enacted against the imaginary landscape of real and found memories and images of individual lives, a landscape drawn from experience, historical narratives, family stories, television drama, advertising, fiction, comic books, and much else. This fantastic space exceeds the physical area that names it, just as its value exceeds its utilitarian function. It is inflated. It is overcoded. It is the kitchen. The hum of the kitchen reverberates across time-past, time-present, and time-future.

A Japanese slang word for a gay man is *okama*. It is also the polite form of the noun *kama*, meaning cauldron or cooking pot. Some recent mass-media commentaries on gay identity in Japan suggest that this term derives from the notion that the gay male is raised in an environment where he is too close to his mother—symbolized supposedly by the cauldron. According to such explanations, gay identity is attributed to a psychological overdependence in the mother-and-son relationship—being raised too close to the hearth. In Nakajima Takehiro's film *Okoge*, the nature versus nurture debate of the origins of gay identity are argued in some detail and with passion, by a group of gay friends gathered for dinner at the home of one of the main characters, Goh. There is no conclusion to the discussion, the content of which we'll come back to again. However, the recent popular appropriation of the term *okama* into a pro-nurture argument ignores the historical usage of the term and even goes against the grain of the physical composition of the character with which it is written. *Okama* is a composite of the characters *chichi* (father) and *kane* (metal or money)—an unexpected specularization of the designator of an everyday object symbolic of the traditional domestic duties of the female in the Japanese household. It would appear that the character for *kama* represents the power and economic wealth of the male head of household—an empty or full cauldron—rather than carrying the flavor of any feminine quality associated with its utilitarian and domestic function.

By early Edo times the term *okama* was in common usage as slang for buttocks; however, there is no standardized explanation for the emergence of the association of the name of this domestic household object with this part of the human anatomy. Once this usage was established it was a simple semantic relay from the use of the term for buttocks to an association with anal sex and male homosexuality. In the Edo period "same-sex love" (dooseiai) between males was not only condoned but also a potential source of status and rite of passage within the boundaries of specific, clearly designated, and ritualized male-to-male power relationships of the samurai and aristocratic classes. The multiple configurations of male homosexual relationships were clearly located within the traditional flows of power of dominant androcentric discourses, and did not exclude parallel or contiguous heterosexual relationships (Schalow 1990). Any suggestion of a symbolic connection between the domestic functions of the cauldron and an excess of the maternal or feminine is a product of more recent popular constructions (or misconstructions) of contemporary gay identity—a false recourse to history or a recourse to a false history.

The term *okoge* has gained wide currency in the wake of Nakajima's film. The young and attractive *okoge* has become a familiar character appearing frequently in the pages of magazines and comic books targeted at both teenage and adult female readers, as well as in cameo roles on adult soap operas, and television and print advertising for everything from menswear to soft drinks. It is difficult to establish at what point the term *okoge* became popularized as a designator for young women who prefer platonic friendships with gay men to sexual relationships with heterosexual men, but the derivation of the word is transparent. When Sayako, the female protagonist of *Okoge*, goes to a gay club she bumps into Goh and Tochi, the gay male couple at the center of the film, and quickly strikes up a friendship with the two, reminding them of the first time she met them at a gay beach. The bartender describes Sayako as an *okoge*, and goes on to explain to her that if gays are *okama*—the rice cauldron—then women who like to be with gay men are *okoge*—the rice crust that sticks to the pot. He then chides her good-humoredly for her lack of prejudice toward gays. He asserts that he prefers to be discriminated against because if gays are not treated differently then they end up just the same as everyone else.

II

In the early 1980s the then Prime Minister Nakasone, went on national television in a prime time commercial. In the advertisement Nakasone appeared
in a traditional Japanese farmhouse surrounded by three generations of
family, seated around a large cauldron simmering over a coal-fired sunken
hearth, and enjoying their evening meal. Although nostalgia and tradition
have become strong marketing vehicles for the endless proliferation of perishable and durable consumer goods in Japan (Ivy 1993), Nakasone was not there
to sell the latest flavor in instant noodles. Rather, he faced his prime-time
audience and appealed to them to emulate this traditional domestic scene.
He asked that, as often as possible, they gather together the three generations for the evening meal in the spirit of the Japanese tradition of the extended family. This was the launch of the LDP's platform for conservative welfare reform (Buckley and Mackie 1985). I talked about the advertisement with
a Japanese woman friend who was married with one child and pregnant again
at the time it went on air. We were sitting in her living room, at the table that
served as the dining table at meal times, her work surface during the day, and
her child's study desk after school. At night it was folded away in the cup-
board to make room for her and her husband's bedding. "How the fuck am
I supposed to build a hearth?" she joked, pointing out that she lived on the
eighth floor of a high-rise. "If we all hang iron cauldrons like that the place'll
collapse." Having escaped from the grips of a tyrannical mother-in-law to the
privacy of the 3DK (two rooms plus kitchen/living area) only a year earlier,
the prospect of sharing regular evening meals with grandma and grandpa was
less than appealing.

   The LDP policy document in question was entitled "Strengthening of the
Family Base." Nakasone was closely allied with some of the most conservative
elements within the ruling LDP and this policy was the backbone of what came
to be known as a "Japanese Style Welfare State." A key section in the document read: "From now on it will be necessary to develop the special character
of our own country's society. We will have to plan to implement a welfare system in which an appropriate share is met by a highly efficient government,
but which is based on the solidarity of home, neighbourhood, enterprise and
local society, which is in turn founded on the spirit of help and independence
of the individual" (qtd. in Buckley and Mackie 1985, 184).

The underlying principle of the new policy was the transfer of the welfare function from the State to the family (read mother/wife figure of the nuclear household) and then secondly to promote corporate, private-sector responsibility. Faced with the crisis of the greying of Japan (that is, an aging population), the government was moving swiftly to deal with its financial inability to bear the welfare bill. Nakasone's chosen point of entry into the family for this delicate renegotiation of social contract was, predictably, the kitchen — but not a modern designer kitchen, rather the traditional site of domestic cooking and eating, at the heart of the household, the hearth.

In a recent advertisement that *was* for the latest flavor in instant noodles, a Japanese grandmother walks into a kitchen where she finds her daughter standing at her state-of-the-art gas stove stirring a pot of noodles for her two young children, who sit expectantly at the low-level traditional Japanese table in the next room (a satisfactory balance of technology and tradition). The scene sends the older women into a black-and-white flashback to her own mother teaching her how to cook noodles in a rustic, farmhouse, while her daughter, then a child herself, sits watching. Time-past, -present, and -future conflate until the voice of her daughter asking "Are you okay?" calls the grandmother back to narrative time-present. "Yes I was just lost in delicious memories. . . ." A male voice-over ruptures the play of transhistorical nostalgia to locate the viewer firmly in consumer time-present: "Try the delicious taste of our country-style noodles . . . it'll take you back home." Both the political party and noodle manufacturer (and their respective advertising agencies) recognized the fantastic space of the kitchen as fertile ground for mobilizing the notion of family in the retro-structuring of memories and traditions — central components of marketing strategies for consumer goods and social reform alike. The incorporation of the mother/wife is essential to a successful staging. Such strategies "order" the individual, family institutions, and the State within a mobius-like continuum that renders unworkable any clear distinction of the public and the private. Within this continuum the kitchen acts as an essential valve for the control of the inward and outward flows that sustain this organic linkage, and it is the mother/wife who manages the processes of circulation of food, consumer goods, cash, waste, and much else.

In the opening scene of *Okoge*, Sayako arrives at the beach with two female friends, one of whom has also brought her two children. They finally find

a bare patch of sand and lay out their towels and begin to undress for a swim. It is the children who discover first the reason why this part of the beach is less crowded. "Even if you saw something you didn't," says the mother to her children, leading them hastily off to the water and away from the scene of gay couples hugging and caressing on the beach around them. A can of beer rolls down an embankment to where Sayako and her friend sit. Sayako picks it up and returns it to a young gay man sitting in a row with other men along the top of the embankment. To thank her for her kindness he carries a plate of food down to her and tells her she is welcome to it. Sayako begins to eat but her friend is disgusted by the very sight of the food and warns her she might get AIDS. Sayako, for her part, takes another bite and then walks over to the same young man and his lover to offer them a plastic container of rice balls (*onigiri*) from her lunch. Another of the gay men teases her that she shouldn't spoil "gay boys" this way. After accepting the gift of the rice balls the lovers, Goh and Tochi, walk off into the water together where they embrace and kiss playfully at first and then passionately. Sayako sits down again beside her friend and watches the lovers intently. Her friend demands she stop looking. "It's disgusting, horrid," she exhorts. Sayako continues to watch. The camera draws the viewer down the line of vision deeper into the embrace of the two men.

III

Some years ago when I was staying in Tokyo, I got a call from a friend with whom I'd been in graduate school. She was now married and living in Japan. She and her husband, both Americans and fluent in Japanese, were running a successful copyediting company together, living in a Japanese middle-class suburban high-rise, and sending their six-year-old son to the local school. I had always been struck by her level of confidence and self-assurance, but none of this was evident in her voice as we spoke that day. She had received a call from her son's teacher to say that she wanted to visit her at their home that night. My friend had gone into a state of total panic trying to fathom what her child could possibly have done that might have gone beyond the realm of his usual *gaijin* (foreigner) behavior to antagonize the teacher so as to warrant a home visit. She was desperate for advice on how to deal with the situation, and especially preoccupied with whether to serve Western-style cakes and coffee or Japanese tea and rice crackers. It seemed clear to her that protocol would play a large part in resolving the crisis, and we *gaijin* all had our individual repertoires of cultural faux pas to tell. Many of these tales had to do with inappropriate or untimely offerings of foods and refreshments. My friend was determined to get it right in order to create the best atmosphere for the catastrophic news she anticipated.

When the teacher arrived my friend was at first relieved, and then bemused, and finally outraged to discover that it was her own behavior and not that of her child that had prompted the home visit. The teacher explained to her that she had taken this step of approaching her pupil's mother because she felt that the child was suffering unnecessarily from his mother's lack of discipline and focus. The cause of concern was none other than my friend's failure to create innovative and attractive lunch boxes for her son to take to school. She had been sending him off every day with what she considered a nutritional lunch of sandwiches and fruit wrapped in a brown paper bag. This the teacher assured her was unacceptable. Her failure to produce a daily variation of a carefully arranged combination of rice and assorted crafted, color coordinated, and seasonally appropriate side dishes and condiments in a tastefully presented lunch box was not only effecting the young boy's sense of standing among his peers, but was also impacting on his academic performance in class. How could he be expected to commit his all to his classroom exercises and homework when his mother did not model application and dedication to her role? Sandwiches that had been cut into amusing or interesting shapes made a pleasant occasional variation from rice, but what was her son to think of the same square cut bread every day? She was the only mother who did not take the time to cook rice for the daily lunch box. What a joy it would be for her son if she sometimes would even take the time to hand roll that rice into small balls, shaped lovingly around tasty, thoughtfully selected morsels of pickle, meat, or fish (*onigiri*).

The issues involved in this situation are complex and many. The teacher's desire for the child's integration into the group was consistent with the situation described by the anthropologist Anne Allison in the analysis of her own very similar experience. Allison details the symbolic and practical role of the production and consumption of the lunch box (*obento*) in the insertion of the mother-child relationship into the ideological state apparatus (after Althus-ser) of the education system: "Significantly, David's teacher marked his suc-cessful integration into the school system by his mastery not of the language or other cultural skills, but of the school's daily routines. . . . My American child had to become, in some sense, Japanese, and where his teacher recog-nized this Japaneseness was in the daily routines such as finishing his *obento*" (Allison, 1996, 200). Differing notions of both the criteria of performance of motherhood and the role of the mother in the child's performance of his/her own status as "student" in a Japanese school are generating different expec-tations and criteria/measures. Again Allison captures this well: "The *obento* is thus a representation of what the mother is and what the child should be-come. A model for school is added to what is gift and reminder from home" (200).

Like their children at school, mothers are watched by not only the teacher but each other; they perfect what they create, at least partially, so as to be con-firmed as a good and dutiful mother in the eyes of other mothers (Allison 1996, 203). The *obento* is constructed as a performative opportunity for the mother, and through her performance the child also is positioned to perform (positively or negatively) his/her status in the context of the classroom. It is not insignificant that rice sits at the center of this performative relay. Ohnuki-Tierney has written a thorough account of the symbolic role of rice in the historical and contemporary construction of Japanese identity in Japan — at the level of both nation and self (Ohnuki-Tierney 1993). The preparation, pre-sentation and circulation of this intensely overcoded symbol of Japaneseness locates the *obento,* the child, and the mother securely within the dominant circulation of meaning that order everyday life.

The teacher assured my friend that "their problem" could be set right and that she had already consulted with three other mothers who lived in the same building — and who produced exemplary lunch boxes on a daily basis — and they were prepared to instruct this young American mother in the fundamen-tals of the Japanese *obento*, and in particular the preparation and presentation of rice, and the crafting of rice balls. My friend, who reported all of this to her husband and me over dinner that night, was furious at the intrusion and embarrassed at the involvement of her neighbors without prior consultation. She was also completely resigned to her first weekly lesson the next Saturday afternoon. The suggestion that her husband, who also regularly prepared their child's lunch, might join in the process had been greeted with a reaction that signaled this to be one more *gaijin* faux pas.

In her telling of a similar tale, Allison offers several wonderful examples of *obento* recipes by way of demonstrating the level of attention to detail and commitment of time (planning, shopping, cooking, and presenting) expected of mothers in this process. She describes the "sweetheart doll *obento*" made in a two-compartment lunch box with four rice balls, each containing a different center, arranged in one half and in the other half two doll figures created out of cucumber bodies with quail egg head and painted faces, lying on pillows of flowers shaped from cooked carrot slices. The doll figures are covered with a quilt of ham that has been decorated with spinach. The whole creation is then held together with colored plastic toothpicks (Allison 1996, 204). The name given to this lunch-box design in the original Japanese recipe is *abekku obento.* The recipe came from the popular married women's magazine *Shufunotomo* (The housewife's friend). The term *abekku* is reserved for the description of young sweethearts and lovers. It is not a term used to describe a married couple. In Japan the ideal of romantic love is as much a consumable as the lunch box itself. Survey data leaves little doubt that the reality of the contemporary Japanese family is a far cry from the popular images of romantic heterosexual love that pervade the daily imagescape of a young Japanese woman's life before and even after marriage. The *shufu* (housewife) magazines that carry endless formulas and recipes for contemporary motherhood overflow with images of mothers and their children. Occasionally the father joins the image to create a brief snapshot of the perfect family, but usually he is absent—a far more realistic picture. In the *shufu* magazines, romantic images of a loving couple are generally limited to the spaces of advertisements for luxury consumer goods and the illustrations of feature stories on the exotic lives of the famous and the foreign. The mother who painstakingly crafts the cucumber bodies of the sweetheart dolls for her child's lunch box knows that it will take more than plastic colored toothpicks to hold this ideal together.

Sayako's natural parents are not known to her. Her adoptive parents were a distant Japanese female blood relative and an American man, a reporter based in Japan. Her adoptive mother died when she was in sixth grade at

primary school, and her father chose to place her in the care of a Japanese foster family. She never saw him again. A series of flashback scenes recall an almost ideally happy early childhood with her adoptive parents, the sense of betrayal and confusion at the moment of parting with her father, the daily fear of life as an outsider in a violent foster family, and finally her anguish and humiliation when sexually assaulted by her foster father. The adult Sayako keeps three dolls stored in a chest in her bedroom. A large adult male doll with Western features and the same dark hair as her adoptive father, lies with his arms around the shoulders of a much smaller Japanese female doll and a still smaller, childlike Japanese doll resting one on either side of him. Their faces are less like dolls than death masks, and they are laid out in the chest like a family of corpses.

It is Tochi's wife who opens the lid of the chest to expose the faces of this bizarre doll family. She screams out in horror, "What kind of a place is this?" Sayako offered her apartment to Goh and Tochi as a regular place to rendezvous when she realized how difficult it could be for a gay couple to find a place to be alone together. Tochi is married. He explains that he chose to try and ignore his homosexuality but eventually understood that he could not suppress his need for the love of a man any longer. He had one bad relationship before he found happiness with Goh. He has continued to live with his wife and conceal his gay identity from his family and fellow office workers. In one scene early in the film he sits eating lunch with his colleagues, shoveling rice into his mouth as he listens to one gay-bashing joke after another. One colleague comments that now everyone is afraid of AIDS and then goes on to advocate that they should "gather up the gays from all over Japan, pour gasolene over them and burn the lot." Tochi laughs at the joke with his coworkers, almost choking on his food.

Tochi's wife, suspecting her husband of having a male lover, has hired a detective to follow him and that is how she comes to be in Sayako's apartment. Goh has escaped out the window. He had been in the apartment cooking cabbage rolls for Sayako. He and Tochi have tried to repay her in part for her kindness to them by cooking her meals since they discovered that she can't cook at all. "So you've never cooked rice?" Goh asks Sayako in amazement as they return from shopping at the supermarket. "No we never ate it . . . you can live on milk," she explains of her early childhood with her adoptive parents. "What a wonderful sight to see men cooking so

enthusiastically!" she exclaims as she watches Goh and Tochi prepare dinner for her. After a superb dinner she falls asleep listening to the laughter
of Goh and Tochi in the bedroom upstairs.

It is on this same night that she dreams the flashback scenes of her abusive foster family. In the first flashback she wakes in the night to find her
foster father lying over the top of her on the bed kissing her on the lips.
She screams out. In the next flashback the foster mother is shouting abuse
as the family sits eating around the table: "He was just trying to kiss you
because he cares about you so much. . . . Why do you have to think such
disgusting thoughts? . . . Eat your food . . ." Sayako clings to a Western-
faced doll with huge round eyes, refusing to pick up her chopsticks and
rice bowl. One of the other children snatches the doll away and throws it to
the floor. The Western doll and her refusal to eat rice both mark Sayako's
difference, her status as outsider. Distressed by these memories Sayako
gets out of bed and climbs to the top of the stairs where she looks in on
the scene of Goh and Tochi sleeping in each others arms. She smiles and
gently slides the bedroom door closed.

IV

Rice remains the staple of the contemporary Japanese diet even if an electric
rice-cooker has replaced the traditonal *okama*. The family hearth may have
become technologized, but the role of the mother remains tied to an idealized
memoryscape of the cauldron hanging in the farmhouse, "delicious memories" of the flavor of grandma's noodles, the nostalgic aroma of rice burnt onto
the edge of the pot. Of course, it is also important to remind ourselves that rice
and rice flour noodles were not the stuff of daily fare for the majority of non-
urban Japanese until the twentieth century. White, bleached rice was a luxury
of the wealthy and urban merchant class, produced by rice farmers who could
not afford to eat their own harvest (Ohnuki-Tierney 1993, 30–43). In the rural
communities of premodern and early modern Japan cooking was primarily
women's work and more particularly it was the work of older women. Without slipping into retro-nostalgic reconstructions of the past, some feminists
in Japan have suggested that there was a greater permeability in the gendering
of work within premodern rural and merchant households (Aoki in Buckley
1997). The emphasis was placed on maximizing available labor resources in

order to maximize production potential across the range of household activities. Periods of labor intensive work—planting, harvesting, spinning, weaving and so on—saw the elderly take on a higher proportion of the domestic work of cooking and child care while the able men and women of the household worked to meet the seasonal deadlines. There is, however, far more evidence for women moving across the gender divide of domestic and non-domestic work than was the case for men, suggesting that the greater burden of flexibility fell on women in these processes of labor maximization.

Ironically, it was industrialization and modernization (and one might also add to this list Christianity) that marked the emergence of the ideological prison house of the "good wife, wise mother" in the late nineteenth century. The introduction of modern domestic technologies corresponded directly with a thoroughly coordinated State policy of women's education designed explicitly to produce good wives and wise mothers for an emerging middle class, and healthy and hygenic households among the working class (Bernstein 1991). Women were trained in the use of modern (and generally imported) domestic technologies and educated into the dual status of household manager and consumer. One example of this process was the introduction of the cooker, or stove, to replace the traditional methods of cooking. This new domestic appliance generated a frenzy of commercial activity around the promotion not only of the appliance itself but also of new food products and utensils, as well as cookbooks and cooking schools. The promotion of the latest durable and perishable domestic consumer goods was frequently linked in this way to the flow of new technologies of knowledge in a reordering of everyday life. Over the twentieth century the trend toward an increasingly specialized and professionalized mother/wife role has continued. Performance is measured in terms of fluency in the most current fluctuations in the technologies of knowledge underpinning contemporary everyday domestic practice and demonstrated management of the consumer input and output flows of the household. From the outset the processes of professionalization of the domestic role have incorporated a highly performative dimension.

What is more organic or better represents the inward and outward flows of the household than garbage? The municipality of Otsu offers an excellent case in point. Located in the Osaka-Kyoto region, Otsu has a population of

250,000. The local government decided to introduce a new garbage disposal system over the 1980s aimed at streamlining the collection and recycling processes (Ben-Ari 1990). All households (read housewives) were supplied with five sets of colored garbage bags. Each color represented a different type of waste product—combustibles, glass, metals, plastics, and paper. Households were requested (which in this case is equivalent to "required") to sort all garbage into these five types and store it in the appropriate colored bag. There was a pickup scheduled from a central collection point in each neighbourhood each day. Each day of the week was designated as pickup day for one specific color of garbage bag. Each day the household was requested to carry the garbage type for that day to the collection point, which was often several blocks away. The pickup time for each area was scheduled and started just after dawn. Bags could not be left overnight at the collection point, but had to be delivered on the morning of the appointed day.

It would probably be safe to say that this would be nightmare enough (or a joke) for most households in North America, Australia, or Europe. While there was some minimal resistance, the Otsu program was successfully implemented with only one change, which amounted to no change at all: five types of garbage, five colors of bags, five collections. What protest there was focused on the bags. Not only were the bags colored, but they were also imprinted on both sides. On the one side was the definition of the type of garbage to be placed in this color of bag, followed by a list of instructions for the handling and treatment of the waste—for example, "please squeeze out fluids thoroughly"—and lastly a contact and information number. On the other side of the bag was written the following: "As a member of the local community, I am shouldering my responsibility and throwing away my garbage. I am participating in the Movement for the Reduction of Volume of Refuse" (Ben-Ari 1990, 275).

At the bottom of the bag were two logos, that of the Otsu City Council and beside it the very official-looking logo of the Otsu Garbage Zero Association for the Promotion of Reducing the Volume of Refuse and the Recycling of Resources. This last title was written in full below the logo. In a large space in the middle of the bag was a place for the household name to be written. Each family was thus expected to own both its garbage and its performance as a member of the community. In response to protests over the "naming" of the garbage bags, the label "Name" next to the empty space in the middle of the bag was removed several weeks into the project. Despite this, some 80 percent of households continued to write their name in the space originally provided for that purpose.

Why did so many families continue to "own" their garbage even after this was no longer officially requested/required? Anyone who has lived in a Japanese neighbourhood will understand the status accrued through household garbage. The collection of garbage from centralized pickup points is common. The trend is toward large numbers of small bags rather than large garbage bags in the North American style. One particularly astute Japanese company marketed a clear garbage bag with considerable success. The transparent bags allowed housewives to demonstrate not only the quality of their garbage (expensive brand names and food types) but also their level of professionalization. Perfectly peeled fruit skins, neatly compressed milk cartons, perfectly folded scraps of paper. One could also demonstrate the level of technological sophistication of the household — electronically opened cans, pre-shredded waste paper, cans compacted in an electronic crusher, assorted waste from brand name appliances — coffee filters, state-of-the-art Cuisinart scraps, and so on. Garbage is treated by the professional housewife as a serious opportunity to be judged by her peers.

The preference for small garbage bags reflects the lack of storage space and ease of transport to collection points. The crisis in many a Japanese home is where to store the garbage until collection day and where to put the garbage pail in an already overcrowded kitchen. The double standard underlying the professionalization and associated valorization of the mother/wife role is perhaps nowhere more apparent than in architectural floorplans of both pre- and postwar Japan. The kitchen space has been consistently the smallest dedicated area. Studies, bedrooms, garages, and occasionally even closets are allocated a greater proportion of total square footage than the kitchen. Contemporary glossy illustrated architecture magazines aimed at a professional, predominantly male readership still seldom show kitchen details. When the kitchen is shown in illustration it tends to represent a highly stylized design ideal rather than a functional norm. Even house-design magazines published by real estate developers, and aimed at both the prospective male and female buyer of a new home, tend to foreground the more formal spaces over informal, family spaces. These formal areas function as potential sites for the performance of financial and cultural capital: a Western-style living room, traditional and formal Japanese-style room, entertainment room (featuring state-of-the-art audio-visual equipment), the entrance way, and front garden. Needless to say there is a direct correlation between the existence, size, and number of dedicated formal spaces in a Japanese home and the household income. As the struggle continues to maximize limited space in the Japanese home, whether an inner city 3DK apartment or a suburban freestanding house, there has been a design trend over the last decade toward an open combined kitchen/dining/living area. The proportion of total floor area allocated to the designated kitchen still remains minimal. However, this architectural design shift is exposing the kitchen to a wider audience and re-placing it at center stage of a family's performance of itself.

The discreet storage of garbage remains a challenge in the cramped space of most kitchens and yet, of all the space-saving miniaturized domestic appliances designed for the Japanese domestic market, the kitchen sink garbage disposal unit continues to attract limited enthusiasm. While the inefficiencies of the sewage systems in Japanese cities may offer one explanation for the slow uptake of this particular technology, a less technical explanation may be the fact that it detracts from the performative potential of garbage disposal at both the level of household (good mother/wife) and community (good citizen). The move toward recycling and improved garbage collection and disposal grew out of citizen campaigns—primarily community-based women's action groups—responding to government plans for the construction of nationwide incineration plants during the late 1970s and into the 1980s. Environmental concerns and the possible impact on house resale value led local groups of women into action in what proved a highly effective chain of independent nationwide local protests. The effect was a redefinition of waste management goals and methods within a more environmentally friendly framework and a move toward community-based disposal initiatives. The Japanese incinerator campaign is frequently held up as a model of successful citizen action.

However, Ben-Ari's analysis of the Otsu garbage collection project expressed some reservations about such schemes: "Co-production schemes, which are often seen as means by which to overcome the almost total control bureaucratic agencies have over people's lives, may actually turn out to be devices for enhancing this very control" (Ben-Ari 1990, 278). With the Otsu system of colored and named garbage bags we see an example of how instruments of government can recuperate and contain community-based demands for localized strategies within an institutionalized flow of power in and out of the specific site of the household/family. Ben-Ari describes the process as "incipient totalitarianism" (278). The end result in the Otsu case was the formalization of the flow of garbage into one more potential performative site for the staging of the professionalization of the domestic role. Women who came together around a shared political agenda in a community movement that defied the isolation of suburban life, were finally re-located in a competitive relationship defined in terms of relative performance. The institutional rechanneling of women's management of the outward flow of consumer waste from the household functioned equally as a channel for the management of the women themselves—organ-izing disorderly desires and energy. Japanese women are intensely aware of the public nature of women's domestic work and the importance of the performative dimension of domestic labor to the definition of status and identity of both the individual woman and the family/household within the community. The head of one neighborhood women's association in Otsu summed up the situation well when she described the introduction of the new garbage regulations: ". . . responsibility . . . belongs to each individual. But anyway in our neighborhood everyone complies with new arrangements. You see, our women's association is noisy (*yakamashii*) and we'll make trouble for anyone who won't comply. We get something like 99 or 100% conformity" (Ben-Ari 1990, 290). Self-perception and self-valuation are negotiated communally and collectively judged. Choice and self-determination, fundamental concepts in grassroots Western feminisms, become highly problematic strategies in this environment. In family- and community-based systems of monitoring and self-policing it does indeed all come out in the wash—or the trash.

Tochi's wife finally satisfies herself that neither her husband nor his lover are in Sayako's apartment. While she rejects Sayako's claims that they are a heterosexual love triangle she admits that this would be a relief if it were only true. The discovery of her husband's favorite shirt hanging side by side with Goh's matching shirt confirms her suspicions of her husband's affair. She throws the shirt on the bed, smashes a bottle, and begins stabbing and tearing at it, screaming and sobbing in anger. The scene is protracted. When her emotions are finally spent she steps out into the

doorway and back into her public face, her identity as *okusan* (wife) of a senior *sarariman* (white-collar worker). She straightens her clothes and hair and, assuming a refined level of polite honorific speech, she apologizes for bothering Sayako, and requests that she pass on a message to Tochi that he must stop seeing his lover. If he ignores her demand she will divorce him and inform his superiors at work that he is homosexual. As the wife leaves and Sayako moves back into the apartment to search for signs of Goh's escape route, a car moves through the neighborhood broadcasting a public announcement that the water supply will be temporarily shut off that afternoon to allow repairs to the sewage system. The subtitles to the English version of the film ignore this announcement.

Much of the public discussion of *Okoge* in Japan around the time of its release came from cultural talk-show celebrities or from feminists and was focused primarily on the representation of Sayako and the popularization of the category of *okoge*. Feminists raised concerns that Nakajima's film valorized the *okoge*'s denial of female sexuality as the only alternative to the heterosexual norm while erasing the possibilities of a lesbian identity. The popular media was simply drawn to the potential for sensationalist discussions of both gay identity in Japan and the new status of *okoge*. Predictably, more conservative commentators worried over the impact of the film's international circulation on Japan's overseas image. Outside Japan the major criticism of the film has been that it finally cannot resist a recuperative strategy and draws Goh, Sayako, and her infant son into the standard nuclear family model grounded in the normative assumptions of heterosexual practice and associated gender roles. I want to argue that this last interpretation, at least in relation to English-speaking audiences, is in part the construction of mistranslations or silences in the English subtitles. In fact, it is Donald Ritchie's subtitles that recuperate the narrative within a heterosexual framing at key moments. The omission of the public broadcast is one such moment and we will return to two others. Nakajima's direction of the film is tight and acutely aware of details of background sound and movement. His foregrounding of the public broadcast immediately after the outburst of Tochi's wife in Sayako's apartment is rich with significance.

There are two other key scenes in the film where Nakajima links the disruption of the normative flow of body fluids and the contemporary condition of the heterosexual nuclear family. In an early scene in the gay night-club where Goh and Tochi are regulars, a friend is performing a cabaret act in drag. Seen only from the back it at first looks as if beer were being poured but it soon becomes clear as the camera pulls back that s/he is uri-nating into a glass. The final, familiar gesture of shaking the penis, in com-bination with a cute wiggle of the bottom, confirms the performative pun that this is a "woman" who has everything. S/he takes a drink from the glass and then moves through the audience, forcing one patron to swallow a mouthful and then continuing to offer the glass around. S/he joins Goh and Tochi at their table at the end of the act and downs the contents of the glass in one shot before going on to explain that drinking one's own urine purifies the liver and is good for the blood. From the nightclub Goh and Tochi return to Goh's apartment. Nakajima films their lovemaking with a constant slow and sweeping movement of the camera across the bodies of the two men. There are no sudden shifts in angle or distance, no dominant perspective. The camera seems to linger or move across skin in tandem with the gentle flow of hands. The scene is long and the viewer shares the sharp sense of intrusion at the sound of knocking at the door. Heterosexu-ality and the family burst into the storyline in the form of Goh's distressed mother fresh from an argument with her daughter-in-law.

The mother chooses not to comment on all the obvious signs that Tochi is more than just a traveling salesman who has missed his train home and is staying for the night. After moving in with Goh she leaps into action with the help of her elder son to trick Goh into a matchmaking session with a prospective bride and her family. He is outraged when he arrives at a restaurant for what he believes to be a family meal only to discover that he has been set up. After the meal he confronts his family for the first time with his gay identity. The family all ignore what he is telling them entirely and continue to discuss the weather, fashion, and the prospective bride. Only after Goh storms out of the room does his brother state simply, "so he is gay after all." The mother retorts angrily, "I have no memory what-soever of raising a sick child." It is not until much later in the film, as she slips further into what appears to be senile dementia, that she tries to come to terms with her son's gay identity. However, the only framework within which she can redefine her relationship to Goh is one of guilt or respon-sibility, but not within the usual terms of the nurture/nature debate. She explains to Sayako that it is her fault Goh is gay. She remembers when she was pregnant with him that she once cut her finger on a rusty knife. It was then she believes that gay bacteria got into the wound. Her explanation that her son's "abnormality" resulted from the infection that flowed via her blood into his body is one that she can live with. Sayako sits listening to the explanation while in the next room Goh is having a dinner party for a group of his gay friends. They are deep in a heated conversation over their mixed views of the "cause" of homosexuality. Goh's mother bursts into the dinner party, cutting short the debate that is raging to demand that Goh should marry Sayako. Goh and his friends dissolve into fits of laughter. "He's gay, he'll never marry a woman!" one of them exclaims.

V

In 1993 the popular Japanese house-design magazine *Housing* ran a serialized comic-book story that featured a family in architectural crisis. A middle-aged husband and wife were busy building their dream home when news arrived that the paternal grandfather had been in an accident. His injuries would leave him wheelchair-bound but healthy. It was clear that the frail grandmother could not cope alone. But what was to be done? There was no room in the new house for two more people. Enter the enterprising architect come to the rescue. A few minor design changes would create two independent living areas linked via a common eating and living space—a new architectural design for both the physical and social infrastructure of the family. The added advantage in this arrangement was that the grandparents would make a financial killing with the sale of their inner-city property and could finance a substantial part of the cost of the new structure thus reducing their son's mortgage. One half of the house could be designed to accommodate the specific needs of its elderly and invalid inhabitants and there would still be plenty left over to equip a spacious shared kitchen/living area with the latest in new domestic technologies. Since 1993 there has been a marked trend in Japanese domestic architectural design magazines and promotional materials toward this three-generation house with both its increased space and its massively increased consumer potential. It has been labeled with descriptive slogans such as "Dual house," "Heart-full," "Three floors for three generations," and "Free-size."

The commercial images in the glossy brochures depict state-of-the-art households with a particular emphasis on technology as an aid in elderly-care environments. The three-generation home frequently incorporates what is popularly known in Japan as an H.A. system. The name is derived from a Japanization of Home *Electronics* into H.A. These systems offer the Japanese top-end consumer market a fuzzy logic-based domestic electronics technology. An H.A. system consists of a coordinated and self-adjusting central computer network, which can be programmed directly or accessed by telephone to create the "perfect" domestic environment. The fuzzy-logic system monitors fluctuations in internal and external conditions and independently modifies programming in order to maintain stability. For example, sudden fluctuations in temperature due to unexpected weather conditions would lead to adjustments in lighting, air conditioning or heating levels, hot water temperature control, and so on. The system is linked directly to emergency services and sends an alarm in case of forced entry, flooding, or fire. Individual power sockets are automatically turned off after a preprogrammed period of time to avoid accidents from appliances that have been left plugged in. Stoves, heaters, and other appliances can be automatically preset or activated by a touch-phone signal or preprogrammed voice commands.

An apparently omnipresent figure is frequently featured in advertising for the three-generation home, lurking in every nook and cranny. She is the aging mother-in-law/granny. She seems to be everywhere, overseeing each aspect of the domestic role of her daughter-in-law and enjoying the company of her grandchildren. The level of automated technology is presented as creating a comfortable and risk-free environment for the elderly. H.A. systems can be adapted to perform various functions specifically related to elderly care. Readings of heart rate, temperature, blood pressure, and other vital life indicators can be networked via the H.A. system into a centralized hospital-monitoring program. Timed signals send a reminder to take medication. Sudden fluctuations can set off a warning alarm in the household or on a mobile beeper. Automated chairlifts on stairwells, elevator seats in and out of the deep Japanese-style bath, heated floor coverings, and temperature-controlled toilet seats and bidets, among others, are all promoted as easing the labor associated with elderly care in the home.

The new three-generation H.A. home with its spacious, well-equipped open kitchen/living plan is now within reach at a huge price tag and a small sacrifice—making room for grandma and grandpa. It's a long way from the sunken hearth of Nakasone's 1980s campaign to the new designer H.A.-systems kitchen. Or is it? The trend toward nuclear households continued across the eighties despite the moralistic exhortations of the policy of "Strengthening the Family Base." By 1987, 60 percent of Japanese households were nuclear. However, real estate trends indicate that the shift to nuclear family, freestanding structures and semidetached units that dominated the markets through the 1980s is beginning to lose ground rapidly in the 1990s to the new option of the "Heart-full" "Dual house." Where direct policy intervention failed to promote a significant transfer of welfare functions from the State to the family, changing demographics, economic slowdown, and a housing market where entry-level prices for first-time home buyers are ten times the annual household income (the average in North America is five times) have all combined to make what previously seemed an unattractive option at least worthy of a second look. The added disposable income in a three-generation household and access to luxury consumer goods are major considerations in a time of slow or negative income growth and reduced salary-bonus packages. The advertising agencies unabashedly foreground the increased consumer capacity of the three-generation middle- and upper-middle-class household. The family that lives together buys together. One can almost hear the sighs of relief from the depressed domestic retail sector as well as conservative politicians as the three-generation family contemplates setting up house together.

This revolution in domestic technologies may be sexy but it is not necessarily liberating. It is the daughter-in-law/wife who is usually depicted in the advertising images as the one in control of the H.A. system, reprogramming with a mere touch of a button or phoning in from outside the home to monitor or adjust the domestic environment, a form of distance management. With a reduced workload, the new "liberated" woman is now even freer to be away from home, secure in the knowledge that her house and family are protected in case of emergencies and she is still in control. Her domestic and elderly-care duties are just a touch-phone away. But is the message so unambiguously good news? Is the technology liberating, or does it merely reinforce the fact that whether she is at home or not, at home her primary responsibility is still toward the management of the domestic space now populated with another generation of family requiring intensive care and attention. There is no excuse and no escape now that she is linked by an umbilical telephone line to the household. The new technological and spatial configurations of the household create yet another level of professionalization of the domestic role, and yet at the same time, these innovations draw the mother/wife into a new performative role as technobody, permanently plugged in, one more station on the domestic systems map—monitor and monitored.

Goh's mother moves into his apartment permanently when tensions with her daughter-in-law reach breaking point. Nakajima captures the acidity of the relationship between the two women in his careful portrayal of their intensely polite dialogues on the occasion of the failed matchmaking dinner for Goh. The daughter-in-law states explicitly that Goh should marry someone his mother will like in order to make a happier home for her. She and Goh's brother have no intention of taking the old woman back into their home. Goh takes in his mother but gets none of the potential benefits, because the eldest son has already sold the family home. The elderly mother comes with just her own personal effects and a few pieces of furniture. The pressures created on Goh and Tochi's relationship by the presence of Goh's mother together with the threats from Tochi's wife lead to a final split. Goh is left with his work and the care of his mother, whose mental and physical health is deteriorating rapidly. His friendship with Sayako is also strained. The suggestion that they should marry has left them each uncomfortable. They have no doubt of the depth of the love they feel for each other, but they also seem to acknowledge that they have no framework within which to understand it or possibly even sustain it. Marriage is not an alternative. They find their way out of a period of awkwardness when Goh accepts Sayako's aid in attempting to make contact with a man he has become attracted to, and they are again, briefly, able to relate to one another as *okoge* and *okama* with Sayako attempting to mediate between the two men. But, things backfire and the man in question forces himself on Sayako, a scene we will return to. Sayako and Goh do not meet again until after the death of his mother and the birth of her son.

Goh's mother is hospitalized for a period of time prior to her death. Nakajima depicts two scenes of her hospital care. In the first scene Goh is shown washing his mother's body in the public bathhouse of the hospital. He soaps her body, rubs her down, and then rinses off the soap with extraordinary gentleness and tenderness before carrying her into the deep bathwater to soak. His mother shows no sign of emotion or even an awareness of his presence until he lowers her into the warmth of the bathwater and her face melts into an expression of sheer joy at the sensation. It is in the next hospital scene that we are allowed to see that even if she offers no sign of her feelings for Goh and his devotion to her, his mother knows in whose care she wishes to be. Her daughter-in-law and daughter come to visit her in the hospital. First it is revealed in the conversation between the two that while left in the care of the daughter-in-law she had developed bedsores. Then, in anger at the jokes they are telling about her condition, the mother signals with her hands that she wants them to leave. As they leave the hospital the two women discuss how unusual it is for a son to take such exceptional care of his mother and what a relief it is to them that he is there to carry the burden of her care. "How fortunate it is that he is gay," the two women conclude with an air of both gratitude and relief. Goh stays by his mother's bed into the night.

VI

In Yoshimoto's *Kitchen,* several days after her grandmother's funeral Sakurai receives a visit from a young man who worked in a florist's where her grandmother often shopped. She had been surprised by the depth of his apparent grief at the funeral but slowly recalled the fondness and familiarity with which her grandmother had spoken of this young man. Sakurai was pleased to realize that they had enjoyed such a good friendship. The young man invites her to go and stay with him in the apartment he shares with his mother. He explains that they are worried about her alone in her grief and that, even though she does not know them personally, she should feel free to use their home as a safe haven until she decides what to do next. At a loss for what else to do with herself and drawn to the gentle manner of this man, Tanabe, she decides to move her basic possessions to their apartment. The thing that impresses her most on her first visit is the kitchen. It is an open kitchen facing onto a spacious living area in which there is nothing but a large sofa. The focus of the entire apartment is the kitchen.

She is overwhelmed by the newness and high quality of everything from the Silverstone skillet to the German-made stainless steel peeler, Tanabe's immaculate designer slippers, the thick pile of the mat, the endless rows of plates and glasses, the sparkling clean refrigerator. "I nodded and mumbled hmm, hmm, as I wandered around. It was a splendid kitchen. I fell in love with it at a glance" (Yoshimoto 1988, 17). Sakurai's passion for the kitchen in the Tanabe household is matched only by her admiration for the extraordinary beauty of the mother when they finally meet: "I was overwhelmed and just stood there with my eyes wide open. . . . Is this his mother? I couldn't take my eyes off her I was so surprised. Her smooth shoulder length hair, the slant and sparkle of her dark eyes, the perfect lips, and fine nose . . . she was almost inhuman. I had never seen anyone like her" (19). Sakurai already understood that Tanabe's mother worked in a bar. When he returned that night from driving her to work Tanabe turned to Sakurai and asked:

> "So, were you impressed with my mother?"
> "Yes. I mean, she is just too beautiful." . . .
> "But, could you tell?" he continued in the most strange manner, "tell that she's a man?" (21).

Tanabe goes on to explain that his birth mother died when he was a baby. His father, who had loved her passionately even though she was a very ordinary looking woman and he was quite the dashing young man, was inconsolable after her death. He took refuge in his commitment to devoting himself to the raising of their son. Before too long though he realized the impossible obstacles to undertaking the task effectively as a man and made a decision to undergo the necessary surgery to become a woman and take up the role of mother. In this new identity as a woman he sought employment in one of the few worlds open to transsexuals in Japan—the bar world. Through a series of painful operations Tanabe's new mother sculpted herself into the perfect female beauty.

Over the ensuing days Sakurai becomes increasingly enthralled by Tanabe's mother, Eriko, and even begins to imagine that she might herself grow to love Tanabe. It is when she realizes this that she decides she must leave the Tanabe home. At the beginning of the second chapter we find Sakurai is living alone. She hasn't spoken with Tanabe in months when she receives a call from him in the middle of the night to tell her that his mother has been murdered. A customer at the bar who fell in love with her only to discover her secret reacted badly and after several days came back and viciously stabbed her to death.

In *Kitchen*, the body of Tanabe's mother/father, Eriko, is *too* beautiful, unlike any other, extra-ordinary. The desire of Tanabe's father to mother leads him into a new identity as a woman. However, Yoshimoto finally insists on reducing Eriko to the sum total of her biological past and present (she is a man). Within the dominant narratives of contemporary Japanese sexuality and motherhood, the excess of this equation precludes the possibility of a future for Eriko. No matter what playful tendencies can be wrestled from between the lines, Yoshimoto Banana's fictions remain firmly grounded in normative dominant discourses of sexuality and gender. While Banana enjoys, together with her wide readership, the transgressiveness of the dis-orderly bodies that leave their traces across her narratives, their deviations are eventually curtailed, their potential forestalled. It is not within Banana's narrative imaginary that Eriko could become anything more than an anomaly. Her grisly fate is prescribed.

We first hear of the death of Goh's mother in a scene where Sayako returns to the gay bar where she had spent so much time with Goh and Tochi. She is carrying her infant son and comes looking for Goh. The man Goh had once been so attracted to has turned into a violent partner, beating Sayako, gambling heavily, and leaving her alone to deal with the threats from gangsters to whom he owes money. She hasn't enough money to buy milk for her child. One night not long after Sayako's visit to the bar, Tochi and Goh meet there by chance. Tochi explains that his marriage is over and he is about to make a spectacular exit from his company. He has been asked to act as the go-between for the marriage of two of his colleagues at work and has chosen the occasion of the wedding ceremony as the opportunity to confirm the rumors of his homosexuality. As go-between it will be his job to host the wedding. He arrives at the ceremonies with the same friend who performed the cabaret act at the beginning of the film. S/he is dressed in the appropriate ceremonial black kimono and formal hairstyle of a wife at such an event. Tochi undertakes the formal welcome of guests and then introduces his "wife." They move to center stage and perform an outrageous and provocative rendition of a children's song, playing with the double entendre of the words, "Always smiling and always upstanding." The guests are horrified and angry. The groom insists that they stop the performance, at which point they offer a formal salutation to the bride and groom and depart. As they walk down the corridor Tochi's wife is waiting for them. His marriage and career are at an end as was his intention.

This "coming out" at a company-sponsored wedding ceremony, in front of his wife, her family and his boss marks Tochi's decision to refuse to continue to perform the roles of *sarariman* (white-collar worker) and household head/husband. His mockery of the wedding ceremony as the public perfomance of the confirmation of the contract of entry into the heterosexual nuclear family, structure is the final punctuation mark to the death sentence Nakajima has articulated across the film narrative. What has been on trial is neither homosexuality nor the rarified category of the *okoge* but rather the heterosexual contemporary family. Each of the main characters of the film had been damaged by the requirement to per-form a clearly scripted role within this singular, dominant narrative. The families Nakajima depicts are at best unattractive and often downright dysfunctional. The burlesque scene of Goh and his friends in drag in a street fight with gangsters in the middle of a rainstorm attempting to res-cue Sayako, is not simply a juxtaposition of homosexuality and hetero-sexuality—gays rescue innocent *okoge* from grips of violent straight men. Nor do Goh and Sayako walk off into the sunset a happy hetero nuclear family unit.

Nakajima's *Okoge*, unlike Yoshimoto's *Kitchen*, is not a narrative about disorderly bodies but is a disorder-ing body of narrative. Nakajima is not interested in recuperating Goh and Sayako's relationship into the dominant model; however, that heterosexual nuclear family model is at the heart of the film. To say this is not intended as just one more recu-peration of *Okoge*, but an attempt to complicate the reception of Naka-jima's project outside Japan. Nakajima explores certain dimensions of the lives of gay men in contemporary Japan in an attempt at demysti-fication rather than the more common process of exoticization. He also explodes the mythologies underpinning such idealized and ideologically overcoded images of the family as Nakasone's three-generational gath-ering around the hearth, or the contemporary architectural and techno-logical innovations of the H.A. "Heart-full" "Dual house." The most disturbing moments of the film are either in the context of the family or non-homosexual sex. There are two scenes of sex that might be described as non-homosexual, but neither is uncomplicatedly heterosexual.

In one of these scenes Sayako attempts to set up a rendezvous at her home for Goh and the man he is attracted to, but instead she finds herself physically overpowered. She fights at first but then allows the man to penetrate her after he slaps her and knocks her down on the bed. However, Sayako is not depicted simply as a victim succumbing to violence or as a willing partner in sex. She assumes the position of Goh, repeatedly telling the man to think of her as Goh. At one level this can be interpreted as a denial of her own sexuality or a conflation of her own sexual identity with a gay male position in a denial of the possibility of a lesbian identity as an alternative to female heterosexuality. Both criticisms have been widely leveled at the film. Chris Berry, in his excellent monograph, *A Bit on the Side: East-West Topographies of Desire*, has cautioned against reducing the potential formations of sexual identity in diverse Asian cultural contexts to a limited contemporary Western repertoire of identities and associated categorizations of sexual practices. Without resorting to a retro-orientalism or exoticism, he explores the notion of sexual practice and identity as a site for tactical disaggregations of gender, sex, culture, and nation in local contexts where this process of cultural resistance to dominant formations can create cracks in the totalizing discourse of progress and globalization. It is possible that Sayako's adoption of an identification with Goh in this scene functions as a short-circuiting of predictable identifications.

In the framing of the scene where Sayako and the man are having sex, the male character is frequently cut out of the frame almost entirely or obscured by heavy shadowing. The camera is focused in long close-up shots of Sayako's face. Her expression fluctuates between blankness and an uncertain or troubled pleasure. The man is absented and Sayako seems somehow not present, despite the fact that her upper torso fills the screen. That is to say, she appears to be elsewhere, experiencing something that is only tangentially linked to the body that is moving on top of her. In this moment she does not inhabit her own body but the pleasure that body is experiencing. The assumption that Sayako's status as *okoge* erases her own heterosexual and/or lesbian desire erases the possibility that Nakajima is himself rejecting a limited number of options within a range of existing roles. An absence does not always signify an erasure or denial. This scene leaves no doubt that Sayako's is a desiring sexual body, but her desire and pleasure fall outside the power of representation of Nakajima's narrative and filmic technologies. He seems content to represent the unrepresentable, merely articulating a potential. The other non-homosexual love scene is of Goh's brief sexual encounter with the woman he had rejected as an arranged marriage partner. She seeks him out and demands that he admit that he is gay and that this was the reason for his rejection of her rather than any shortcoming on her part. She jibes him into joining her in a hotel room and then taunts him to "prove himself." Goh performs heterosexual sex, at least to the point of vaginal penetration, but the experience only confirms his absolute sense of himself as gay.

Earlier in the film we see Sayako at work as a voice over artist for comic animations. Her choice of such a marginal occupation is commented on as one more indicator of her difference, her position outside the mainstream. In one segment she is scolded for her performance of the text in front of her, and we listen to her read and reread the same line for the heroine of the comic story, "If you turn my body into a tree who will perform the rites?" Nakajima's repetition is deliberate and unsubtle. The line, repeated out of context, arrests the predictable flow of meaning and yet the tension of the repetition creates an expectation of significance. Sayako and Goh each refuse to read the lines of the dominant script "correctly." Ironically, it is Donald Ritchie's translation in the subtitles that misreads key scenes between Goh and Sayako back into that dominant script. After the burlesque scene in which her gay nightclub friends rescue Sayako from a gangster kidnapping, she returns with Goh to his home. He asks her if she would like to live with him. He says she can stay "just as long as she likes." According to the subtitles Goh then tells her son, "I'll be your father." The literal translation of what he says is, "what if you become the child of your uncle's house?" He refers to himself as *ojisan*—a marker for either an uncle or a familiar male adult. He does not say "my child" but mediates the relationship through the spatial configuration of the house. He does not use the word "father."

In the final scene of the film, Goh and Sayako are walking down a well known street in Tokyo's central gay district. They are swinging Sayako's son between them. As they walk Goh's attention is obviously briefly caught by another gay man on the street. Sayako asks him if the man is "his type." Goh replies, "No, not really." The subtitles then render

Sayako's next comment as "I don't mind." In the context of the sequence of Ritchie's subtitles it appears that she is forgiving him for a temporary "slippage" in his new heterosexual identity as partner to Sayako and father to her child. In fact what Sayako says to Goh is "ii desu yo . . . watashi wa," which carries both the meaning of "It's okay with me" and "I'm alright." Goh acknowledges her words with a quiet "unn," which takes its semantic value of "I know" or "I understand" from his non-verbals and intonation. This final exchange of the film undermines any suggestion that Goh and Sayako have moved into a normative nuclear unit. Goh's gay identity remains explicit and acknowledged. This "family" has no predetermined boundaries or prescribed roles. The script is unwritten. Both Goh and Sayako are opting out of a systems map in which identity functions as a regulating and regulated node, rechanneling dis-orderly flows of potential into professonalized stagings. In the final scene of the movie, as Goh and Sayako swing the child between them, meaning rests on/in nobody (single state of being) but is rigged in-the-between of a scaffolding hinged on the memories and movements of two radically differentiated, desiring bodies (singular assemblage of becoming). The structure may be familial but not familiar. The flows are unpredictable.

MARCIE FRANK

"How Did I Get So Anal?": Queer Self-Authorization

at the Margins

Julie Doucet's comic book, *Dirty Plotte,* began in 1990, but as she indicates on the inside cover of the first issue, "Before being a comic book, *Dirty Plotte* was a fanzine so the really first issue of D.P. was in September 1988. I've put out 14 publications of it. Half the cartoons in here are reprints of the stuff from these old mini comics."

Doucet's title, *Dirty Plotte,* refers to her surreal, dreamlike narratives and autobiographical sketches of sexual adventure; her dirty plots pun on the Quebecois slang term for *cunt.* As its origin as a fanzine might suggest, *Dirty Plotte* generates many of its effects out of local Quebecois culture. It has, nonetheless, become an international success — by 1993, it had been discussed in the pages of *Art Forum* (1991, 23; 1992, 125) and *Sassy* (1993, 36) magazines.

The first frame of the first page of the first issue of *Dirty Plotte* features a map of French Canada held up by two scantily clad women (fig. 1). On the left is a curvaceous babe who primps in a standard sexy pose, her tongue seductively placed on her upper lip. "Let's talk about *it!*" she croons. On the right is her scruffy, flat-chested, tattooed counterpart who identifies herself as Zeezee, and is identified in the margins as the "dirty version." Zeezee is actually dirty: her stockings are falling down, her makeup is running, one of

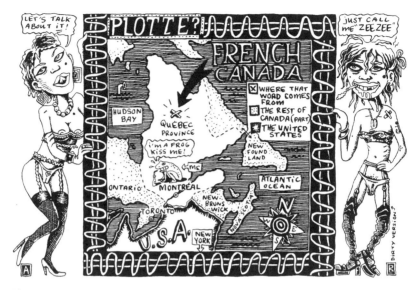

Figure 1

her teeth is missing, and her skin is filthy. This figure is Julie Doucet's alter
ego, a dirty plotte. But a pun on the name Zeezee, unlikely to be available to
the anglophone reader, evokes the common "infantile" term for penis (and
would translate roughly as "willy"). Doucet's "private" (to Anglos) joke on
Zeezee's privates suggests that the dirty plotte isn't a plotte at all in the ana-
tomical sense, but is rather a placeholder for the status of the francophone
cunt, the "plotte," in hegemonic, misogynist discourse.

   As pronounced by the woman on the right, the "it" we are invited to talk
about would seem to be sex, but the commodification of sex suggested by
her presentation is immediately complicated by her counterpart's bodily rendering of sex appeal as dirt. Doucet's literal uptake of "dirty," in a context
in which it is usually used to refer to sex, condenses the sublimations of the
metaphor; the literalization also deflates the anxieties that the metaphor sus-
tains, allowing Doucet to expose much of the ideological baggage that accom-
panies many representations of sex in general, and female sexuality in particular. Like Doucet's crosslinguistic puns on the term "plotte," and the name
"Zeezee," her literalization of "dirty" appropriates and subverts the term of
abuse; *Dirty Plotte* would thus appear to transform points of social and ideological pressure into points of resistance.

The map the women flank illustrates the place where the word "plotte" comes from, which is alternately identified as French Canada, and Quebec Province. If Doucet's self-representation as Zeezee works to resist colonizing and sexualizing discourses, it does so in ways that are underlined by another visual self-representation: the frog, who crouches above Montreal, says "I'm a frog. Kiss me!" and the arrow with "me" written in it identifies it as a figure for the author. "Frog" is an English term of derogation for francophones, but the self-identification, coupled with the imperative, "Kiss me," in which Doucet paraphrases Quebecois chansonnier Robert Charlebois, turns the insult into a declaration of pride even while the insistent autobiographical inscriptions (the repeated "me"s), comically deflate the potential erotic recognition of a kiss. Like the title, *Dirty Plotte,* the frog, who visually presides over the comic's unfolding, dramatizes the importance to Doucet's work of an ironic inscription of English in idiomatic French in Quebec.

Doucet's crosslinguistic and visual puns register her exploitation of the overlap of sexual and national discourses to fashion her own self-representation. The inside cover of the first issue of *Dirty Plotte,* with which this essay began, features miniature renditions of six of the old mini-comics' covers, which identify themselves and their contents primarily in French. Doucet thus overtly acknowledges the processes of linguistic translation that enable her national and international success.

Another Montreal comic strip, Rick Trembles's "How Did I Get So Anal?" could also be said to present and problematize minority sexual and national identities in a similar fashion to *Dirty Plotte,* although it does not (yet) circulate in the international arena. "How Did I Get So Anal?" appeared in Trembles's self-published fanzine, *Sugar Diet* no. 2 (1992). In "How Did I Get So Anal?" Trembles explores the narrator's highly personal understanding of the word "anal." As the narrator's asshole becomes the site through which he comes to terms with various erotic thrills and disappointments, the popular, vaguely psychoanalytic sense of the term that informs the sexualities Trembles describes is exploded.

However, Trembles's shaky self-representation, produced by the anglicized pun on his common Quebecois surname, Tremblay, is the only resemblance to Doucet's manipulation of national identities through crosslinguistic play. Trembles's work concentrates on questions of sexuality. For example, in one verbal gesture that illustrates the Foucauldian (Foucault 1978) insight that sexuality is produced through the discourses of confession paradigmatically exemplified by psychoanalysis, Trembles describes the piece as "thera-pee-yew-dick." In the comic, "anal" is thus detached from its ordinary contexts in therapeutic, medical, and sexual discourses and revalued. If such word-play is facilitated by the bilingual context of life in Montreal (and the syllabic breakup of "therapeutic" calls to mind an orthographic exercise), Trembles links them neither to politics nor to nation.

But if sexual and national identities are variously problematized in "How Did I Get So Anal?" and *Dirty Plotte,* by their recuperation of "plotte," "frog," "anal," and other terms of abuse, can these texts remain unimplicated in the scenes in which these terms operate as interpellations, from which they gain their shaming power? (Butler 1993, 223–42).[1] Like Queer Nation, which appropriates "queer" in order to subvert one of the accusations that enforces heterosexism and homophobia, don't these texts need to defer endlessly any stabilization of the reappropriated terms in order to signal their "affirmative resignification" without "reinstalling the abject at the site of its opposition" (240)? These are the sort of questions Butler directs to the strategies of appropriation and subversion that have been used primarily to expose the mutual imbrications of politics and sexualities.[2] But rather than exposing the sexual politics of nationhood, as does Queer Nation (Berlant and Freeman 1993, 193–229), *Dirty Plotte* and "How Did I Get So Anal?" question the relations between sexuality and politics. Instead of directly upending any particular sexual politics, these two texts open onto the many loopholes that are present in any — at least any current — politics of sexuality. And it is precisely their disruption of any alignment of genital sex, gender, sexual object-choice, and identity, and their registration of the pressures for such alignments that make these texts queer. As Eve Kosofsky Sedgwick points out, "queer" can refer to "the open mesh of possibilities gaps, overlaps, dissonances and resonances, lapses and excesses of meaning when the constituent elements of anyone's gender, of anyone's sexuality aren't made (or *can't be* made) to signify monolithically" (Sedgwick 1993b, 8; original emphasis).[3]

Like Butler, Sedgwick (1993a) is concerned to give an account of queer performativity, and like her, she begins with the leverage provided by the topic of shame. The suggestion that shame is something to be reversed by strategies that appropriate in order to subvert locates such interpellations as "queer" among others such as "black," or "Quebecois," although Butler makes clear that this process must secure an infinite deferral of stable meaning in order to avoid reproducing the structure it opposes. For Sedgwick, by contrast, shame is productive. In her account, shame directs attention away from the reductive understanding of politics that gets expressed in the critical evaluation — is this text subversive or hegemonic? — back toward the textual artifact and its possibly more complex politics both because it raises questions about identity without reifying the place of identity and because of its temporality: it is both a precondition for creative communication, sociability, and/or textuality, and their by-product. As Sedgwick puts it, "The place of identity, the structure 'identity,' marked by shame's threshold between sociability and introversion, may be established and naturalized in the first instance *through shame*" (Sedgwick 1993a, 12; original emphasis).[4]

For Sedgwick, shame reiterates the intersection between performativity and queerness and permits an important intervention into current assumptions about textual politics. Sedgwick identifies the critical deadlock that follows from what she calls the "premature domestication" of Foucault's critique of the "repression hypothesis," which bottoms out much engagé criticism in the predictable conclusion, "kinda subversive, kinda hegemonic" (Sedgwick 1993a, 15).

Perhaps some of the best examples of this interpretive deadlock occur in the literary criticism devoted to autobiographical writing by women and minorities that has sprung up in the wake of the feminist assimilation of the poststructuralist critique of the subject. A new nomenclature, in which "lifewriting" replaces the term "autobiographies," registers the impact of postcolonial and queer theories; the shift in terminology would acknowledge the performative nature of such writing practices and their potential political overtones and effects.[5]

"Life-writing" would seem to be a congenial term for texts such as *Dirty Plotte* and "How Did I Get So Anal?" both of which exploit the autobiographical confession, a cliché in Underground Comix since Robert Crumb. Crumb, a seminal figure in the development of Underground Comix, now perhaps more familiar because of the eponymous movie about him (1994, dir. Zwigoff), often features an autobiographical figure in his work who rants about his sexual obsessions and feelings of sexual inadequacy.[6] Like Underground Comix, 'zines have their origins in the accessibility of a new printing technology (offset litho printing for comix and the xerox machine for 'zines), and as self-produced, self-distributed publications, both share a tendency to obsess about personal matters. However, the frequency with which Underground Comix become autobiographical often seems to reflect the relations among various artists, whereas 'zines, as the logical extension of readers' columns that transformed into freestanding publications devoted to fandom, could be considered generically autobiographical. Perhaps these differences are magnified by the irony that the only pre-1990s analytical history of fanzines is by Fredric Wertham (1973), the man whose attack on comic books (Wertham 1953) resulted in the notoriously censorious Comics Code of 1954, a crucial enabling condition for the production of Underground Comix.[7]

But terminological congeniality aside, poststructuralist feminist criticism of autobiography tends to regard the autobiographical text as the site of a discursively produced subject whose struggle into legibility reveals the mutual constitution of margin and center, even as it expresses the particularities and localities of difference. The autobiographical text is thus routinely described as either complicit in, or in opposition to, colonizing forces, and its textuality is erased or subordinated to the demand that the text be representation. For Sedgwick, by contrast, 'zines are a site for articulating the connection between performativity and queerness, because they exemplify "the performative identity vernaculars that seem most recognizably 'flushed' . . . with [the] shame-consciousness and shame-creativity" she sees as key to the relations between performativity and queerness (Sedgwick 1993a, 13).

If 'zines illustrate the connections between performativity and queerness, their hyperpersonal nature suggests that they do so because of the ways they produce shame and are themselves produced out of it. Despite the fact that neither *Dirty Plotte* nor "How Did I Get So Anal?" self-identifies as queer, they both queer sexualities. Doucet's *Dirty Plotte* explores and exploits the ways nationality and sexuality are both constituted in shame. When read in conjunction with "How Did I Get So Anal?" which concentrates on the constitution of sexuality in shame, both texts illustrate the Foucauldian understanding of the discursive production of sexuality *and* resist the ways criticism has too often domesticated this paradigm. As I show in the readings that follow, they also mark the political limits of the deconstruction of the distinction between the sexual and the political.

Dirty Plotte no. 6 is almost wholly devoted to questioning the kinds of identities the sex/gender system confers. The title page of issue no. 6 features

Figure 2

a picture of "Julie" in western garb, toting two pistols, and asking Jimi Hendrix's famous question, "Are you experienced?" Three page-long strips called "If I Was a Man" are interspersed with three longer narratives, one featuring a male character named Ralf, the remaining two of which are "Julie's" dreams.

The first episode of "If I Was a Man" plays with the assumption that women are less aggressive than men. "Julie" tells us, "If I was a man . . . I would have a girlfriend with *big* tits . . . because I gotta huge penis." The accompanying pictures show "Julie," whose chest and shoulders have become muscular, grabbing a miniskirted woman, pushing her up against a car, rubbing her penis between the said big tits, cumming in her face, and finally zipping up her pants. "Haa the great mysteries of nature!" proclaims "Julie," as she peeps up the skirt of her victim, who, in the last frame, is depicted lying on the hood of the car. We see the woman's hand dripping with semen, and though her head is not represented, her speech balloon reads, "Goddammit!" (fig. 2).

The strip would seem to equate masculinity with sexual aggression. The next strip, "Regret, a Dream," speaks directly to "Julie's" usurpation of male prerogative and its violent consequences. The dream features "Julie" waking up in a hospital bed after a sex-change operation. At a party, she is propositioned by a girl, and then by her old boyfriend, who says, "I know about your operation . . . two men together, it's possible you know." "Julie's" initial excitement fades; gesturing toward her genitals, she worries, "But . . . what if I don't like it with this?" The strip ends, "Ooh what if . . . I . . . I miss my vagina?" (fig. 3).

Taken together, these two comics would seem to propose a genital determination of gender. Predatory male violence would seem to be testosterone driven; a woman might enjoy the privileges if she had a penis. And when "Julie" regrets her sex-change, she wonders if she will miss her vagina. But in "If I Was a Man," "Julie's" pleasure remains ambiguously gendered since she retains some recognizably feminine characteristics, even telling us in the first panel, "It's me, Julie." Moreover, genital organization does not determine sexual object-choice; in "Regret," "Julie" is presented with potential partners of both sexes. If missing her vagina is a response to only being able to penetrate anally with her male partner, the question of missing it, along with whether she will like sex with a penis, open up a gap between genitals and pleasure. These questions separate the Phallus from the penis, as "Julie's" sex-change gives her the power that goes with the former, even while she recognizes (through her past experience of the vagina) the inferior sexual pleasure of the latter. The surgical transplantation of organs, in Doucet's treatment, reveals that the genital determination of sex makes power the determinant of pleasure.

The next installment of "If I Was a Man" follows up the analysis of genital determination of sex by calling into question the genital determination of gender. The strip depicts the joys of shaving: a hirsute "Julie" proclaims, "I love to shave. It's one of the best parts of being a man, for me." Those who shave may enjoy the ritual, but Doucet's treatment invites us to ask: in what relation is this pleasure to masculinity? The sheer delight "Julie" takes in shaving pressures the idea that behavior simply follows from primary sexual characteristics (fig. 4).

A strip entitled, "Are You Plotteless?" interrupts parts two and three of the "If I Was a Man" trilogy. Here, Ralf decides to work on his female self, expanding the discrepancies between gender and genital sex that are introduced in part two of "If I Was a Man." After meeting a muscle-bound hunk at the health club who reveals that he has female rather than male genitalia, Ralf goes to a clinic to have a plotte put into his forehead. When his friends are not impressed because "the plotte thing is real popular," Ralf vows to show them that "this is not a common plotte." He teaches it to talk using ventriloquism. "Now I'm the most popular guy in town," Ralf announces, "Yes indeed, a plotte can

Figure 3

Figure 4

change your life! Try it!" Although this last frame has "end" written in the bottom right corner, an additional panel at the bottom of the page finishes — and also literally underwrites — the strip. The two-frame coda features "Julie" at her desk. "A few words from the artist" are promised, but "Julie" looks confused and embarrassed: "But . . . but I have nothing to say! I'm sorry." The artist's textual representative disavows ventriloquizing plottes, leaving it up to Ralf to advertize its wonders. Disavowing the ventriloquized plotte renders her speechless because she can't comment on the image of what, in some sense, she is accused of being (by misogynist consumer culture). Unable to celebrate genital womanhood, or the feminine gender that Ralf wants to develop, both of which she represents as ventriloquism (these celebrations are expressed by Ralf, her character, through his plotte), the artist reserves for herself other ways to explore sex/gender possibilities.

In the final "If I Was a Man," "Julie" describes her "useful penis" (fig. 5). Her penis's uses range from romance — the penis sprouts a flower to offer to "Julie's" date — to humor — the penis is represented as a horse named "Mustang." Most interesting, though, is the representation of "Julie's" giant hollow penis as a container for a "toothbrush, pens, underwear, condoms . . . [porno] magazines." Foregoing the logic of reversal and retribution that could describe the relations between male and female to this point, whether gendered behavior is represented as following from or reacting against genital sex, Doucet presents a visual pun in which the penis is unscrewed. Significantly, unscrewing the penis results from a full exploration of its uses. By suggesting that the penis can be a penetrator and a container, among other things, Doucet goes beyond the critique of phallocratic patriarchy, which opposes the penetrability of the (male) anus against the insistence on the impenetrability of the masculine. Representing alternative uses for the penis, Doucet sidesteps the foundation of the sex/gender system in the sexed body and avoids the need to affirm or deny that the anus is a "void." Unscrewing the penis queries, and thus queers, the possibilities for what counts as bodily sexual identity.

In the space freed from the constraints of rigid genital-identificatory alignments, Doucet places the premium on pleasure. "The Double" begins when "Julie" comes home from a boring party to a distorting mirror. Becoming afraid, she wonders whether she is dreaming, but instead of awakening, she exhorts herself to continue dreaming. Looking at herself in the mirror, "Julie" points, stating, "I say in this dream I'm a man!" However, she does not exactly

Figure 5

Figure 6

become a man; her reflection in the mirror remains female. The male "Julie" brings "his" female reflection over to "his" side of the mirror (by this point, it has become difficult to determine which side of the mirror is "real"), and we watch the two "Julies" begin to make love (fig. 6).

The "end" inscribed in the bottom right-hand corner of the last frame has a question mark. Is this freedom from the constraints of a single genital identity and the alternatives of gender identity (and their implied object-choices) trapped between a utopian hermaphrodism and an oppressive and hegemonic heterosexism? Or, is there a way to read the deferred ending of the strip, which insists on pleasure, as a way of capitalizing on having un-screwed the penis? Before deciding that Doucet's work is "kinda subversive, kinda hegemonic," I'd like to turn to Rick Trembles's 'zine text, "How Did I Get So Anal?" which may provoke other interpretive alternatives.

Since 1993, Trembles has been performing the comic strip as a slide show, entitled, perhaps more decorously, "Goopy Spasms," in which he appears on-stage in a dress with his electric guitar and a broom to accompany the slides with some aural and more visual punctuation. The comic begins in reminis-cence: "first time I stuck my finger slightly up my ass was in my snug parents' suburban home, late '70s . . . I was stumbling through William Burroughs' 'Naked Lunch' . . . Simply bored of jerking off regularly, sometimes I would spurt with my finger firmly poked up my innards. What I found most interest-ing about it, was how my anal insides uncontrollably clenched up as I ejacu-

Figure 7

Figure 8

lated. Little spasmodic twitches sucking my digit inwards, synchronized with each spurt of cum" (fig. 7).

No simple romance, "How Did I Get So Anal?" tells the story of the decline and failure of a heterosexual love affair, at the same time as it pursues an analysis of the narrator's erotic obsessions with his own asshole, shit, pimples, hair, and masturbatory practices (fig. 8). Associative rather than narrative logic propels the strip, and the juxtapositions that would seem to digress instead enrich its unfolding. Over the course of the strip, it becomes clear that the unifying subject of "How Did I Get So Anal?" is the relation between auto- and allo-eroticism.

In the early panels, the hero's gynophobia seems generated by the differences between a woman's body and his own. He finds the substances his own body produces to be soothing, though mysterious—he likes rolling extract from pimples around in his fingers and smelling them—but can't "bring [himself] to taste all that internal dew." But as Trembles explores the erotics of such gender underdetermined organs as the tongue and the asshole,[8] the

Figure 9

strip undergoes a transformation from what can seem to be a misogynist exploration of female sexuality to a productive confusion of auto- and allo-
eroticism that calls into question the gendering of organs of pleasure, the
boundaries of sexuality and the identity categories with which they supposedly line up. By the end, his erotic and autoerotic experiments and his relent-
less self-examination have overcome any easy opposition of male to female
bodies. Like Doucet's "The Double," though in a more poignant register,
"How Did I Get So Anal?" proposes the potential hermaphrodism of erotic
life, but in place of the self-sufficiency suggested by Doucet, Trembles registers
the need for companionship.

It is the narrator's asshole and how he understands his "anality" that facili-
tate this transition. The narrative of the hero's initiation into cunnilingus is
interspersed with his ruminations about his own anus. When one partner
offers him her asshole, he declines, asking, "Isn't that supposed to hurt you?"
The narrator continues to think about the size of assholes, but shifts from hers
to his own: "Poking my teeny-weeny finger around is hard enough to insert,
so how's the size of my hardened cock supposed to fit? But then again, I've
produced some monster turds and wondered how all that fit inside of me. I
guess the difference is that shit is soft and gooey. Once, I aimed a mirror at
my hole to witness just how wide the excrement would stretch it open."

The theory of successful cunnilingus, "The goal therefore, is for maximum
goo . . . to almost drown yourself and go into automatic pilot," leads to his fantasy of eating shit; eating her shit is presented as the equivalent of her desire
for a penis, and even though this ruse disguises his fantasy as hers, it also enables the transumption of the opposition between male and female bodies:

Figure 10

". . . After eating a hearty meal that I planned on making her . . . I hoped to connect my throat to her intestines via a long solid turd and then wash it down with her urine. I even wrote my desires in a letter to her, justifying the act as a fulfillment of *her* fantasy to have a penis. She told me she always wondered what it would be like to have an erect cock and fuck someone. I told her this turd could be her big brown dick, and I would be sucking it" (original emphasis) (fig. 10). Trembles's fantasy, in which eating shit transforms heterosex into homosex, thus destabilizes any alignments between genital sex, gender, sexual object-choice, and identity.

"How Did I Get So Anal?" ends with the lonely narrator, "adjusting" to bachelorhood by "loung[ing] around in women's clothing . . . shov[ing] things up [his] ass for a few days always fantasizing women's assholes." The last frame of "How Did I Get So Anal?" represents the narrator embarking on a new technique: in his "desperat[ion] to know how normal people live, [he] buy[s himself] a telescope to spy on the surrounding residents." Underneath the last panel is a question to the reader: "Multiple choice: should I be put out of my misery? __ Yes . . . __ No . . ." Trembles throws the responsibility of judging onto the reader, and thus interrupts the interpretive dead-ending of Doucet's "The Double" in endlessly deferred, possibly pleasurable ambivalence.

Being invited to choose whether or not to "put" the narrator "out of [his] misery," we are forced to accept that he is miserable. There is no question of understanding him to be in a happier state. We are thus forced into an awareness of what such a judgment about what to do with him might entail: we either condemn him to death or we tolerate him — in either case, we are cast into a normalizing liberal position. The irony of calling the binary options, yes or no, "multiple choice," keeps open the space of misalignment.

For Butler, the self-nomination "queer," as a performative interpellation that both repeats and exceeds its shaming and injurious uses, exemplifies a critical "ambivalence" that, like Doucet's "The Double," promises a political critique of the sex/gender system at the same time as it contains its potential validation. This ambivalence is a necessary feature of politics; furthermore, it invites the genealogical critique of the queer subject that will ensure the continuing democratization of queer politics (Butler 1993, 227–29). But for Berlant and Freeman, appropriation and subversion, the gestures that define the political field for Butler, and epitomize the political strategies of Queer Nation, stand in need of a supplementary critique that queer 'zines can provide. "Bitch nation" extends Queer Nation's critique of "nation" because it exposes the negativity of national life for non-white and non-male queers. For Berlant and Freeman, 'zines can supply the necessary supplement, in part, because of their class politics, that is, their explicit refusal of a property relation to information and art (Berlant and Freeman 1993, 220), and in part, because they aggressively name and negate their own audience (221). However, while 'zines are self-made and not-for-profit, to the extent that many of these publications sprung up around collecting, Berlant and Freeman's characterization of 'zines' politics itself requires modification.

The two 'zine texts discussed here suggest that at least some 'zines work through their refusal to speak on anyone's behalf. Both texts directly address their audience: "How Did I Get So Anal?" gives its readers an impossible and murderous pop quiz, and Doucet regularly solicits specific readers' contributions. At the end of *Dirty Plotte* no. 2, "Julie" announces, "Hey listen men, I need a model for some little drawings," and subsequent issues feature some men's submissions. One of the resulting comic strips plays out the seduction

Figure 11

of the male reader to the most macabre conclusions. "Le striptease du lecteur" (*Dirty Plotte* no. 3), begins with a photo of Steve, who is already naked. The photo's inscription, "Mon corps t'appartient" (My body belongs to you), initiates the next phase in this striptease in which "Julie" bludgeons Steve to death and cuts his skin. Toward the end of the strip, she castrates him and in the final frame, she writes "Fin" (end), with the bloody end of his chopped-off cock (fig. 11). The specification of an individual reader in "Le striptease du lecteur" is what permits this strip to be read at all—otherwise it would be a pure assault.

In place of naming and negating, or appropriating interpellations for subversive purposes, the critiques of the implied alignments of sex/gender/sexuality and identity that are offered by *Dirty Plotte* and "How Did I Get So Anal?" are facilitated by their replacement of an implied audience with one that is explicitly addressed, one that is invited, if not forced to reply. In contrast to interpellation and naming, processes in which "you" are either sutured into a social position (i.e., criminality in Althusser's formulation of being hailed by the police), or subsumed into a category represented by the abstract noun ("queer," "frog," "plotte," etc.), the specifications of the interlocutary "you" are open. Whereas interpellation or naming fixes "you" in at least one respect from one instance to the next, the "you" that is directly addressed can differ in any respect from one instance to the next. Entering into interlocution with Doucet or Trembles may be frightening and/or abjecting, but these consequences follow from being their reader rather than from any aspect of identity.

Notes

Dirty Plotte is published by Drawn and Quarterly, Montreal. Trembles distributes his own work. Those interested can send S.A.S.E. to Rick Trembles, Box 693, Tour de la Bourse, Montreal, Quebec, Canada, H4Z 1J9. I would like to acknowledge the help of Rick Trembles, who put his wonderful collection of comix and 'zines at my disposal, Cindy Patton, whose editorial savvy much improved this piece, and Robbie Schwartzwald, whose expertise on Quebecois culture enriched these readings.

1   See Butler 1993, 226–27, on "queer" as a shaming interpellation and the potential problems with reappropriating the term.
2   See Butler 1993, chapters 4 and 8, on the strengths and weaknesses of the strategies of appropriation and subversion.
3   Moreover, "queer" invites consideration of the ways "that race, ethnicity, post-colonial nationality criss-cross with these *and other* identity-constituting, identity-fracturing discourses" (Sedgwick 1993b, 9; original emphasis).
4   Shame, thus, interests Sedgwick politically, "because it generates and legitimates the place of identity—the *question* of identity—at the origin of the impulse to the performative, but it does so without giving that identity-space the standing of an essence" (Sedgwick 1993a, 14; original emphasis).
5   See, for example, Smith and Watson 1992.
6   *Zap Comix* (1967), Crumb's brain child, began as a self-published venture that was sold on street corners in San Francisco, and soon became the first widely available Underground Comix. According to Roger Sabin, *Zap* was the catalyst in the explosion of comix in the late 1960s, which was fueled by the accessibility of offset litho printing (Sabin 1993, 37).
7   Wertham (1973, 38–39) celebrates fanzines, describing their characteristics and speculating on their origins.
8   On the gender underdetermination of the asshole, see "A Poem Is Being Written" (Sedgwick 1993b, 177–214), for a provocative consideration of female anal eroticism.

Queer in Israel

I arrived in Jerusalem in the spring of 1991, a few days after my graduation from college, on a fellowship from the Dorot Foundation. Amir was, at the time, an overworked editor at a Haifa newspaper, still reacclimating to civilian life after three years in the army. We were "set up" by mutual friends, we hit it off, and our romantic partnership lasted through the summer of 1993 — my application to grad school in the United States had been accepted, and I was to leave Israel in September. The creation of a collection of personal narratives by Israeli gay men was an opportunity for us to spend time together, to teach one another, to argue, and to construct a permanent memorial to our fleeting relationship. Amir conceived of and asked most of the questions during our interviews, which were conducted in Hebrew; I did most of the translating, transcribing, and redacting afterward; we reviewed the resultant text together.

Arab citizens of Israel — "Israeli Arabs" — form a group that is often forgotten by the world. Most headlines are grabbed by a different group, the one and a half million Palestinian Arabs of Gaza and the West Bank, who lived without the rights of citizenship under Israeli military control from 1967 to 1996. But few coom to realize that, of the more than six million people resident within Israel's internationally recognized borders, over one million — 18 percent of the population — are also Arab. Most of them are Muslim, although a significant minority

*are Christian or Druze. They are Israeli citizens, carry Israeli passports, and—
officially—have civil rights equal to those of Jewish Israelis, although most of
them are not drafted into the Israeli army. Of course, one may well wonder what
it can mean to be a non-Jewish-yet-equal citizen of the "Jewish state."*

*In spite of Amir's rather right-wing take on Zionism, he was fully in agree-
ment with me that an interview with an Israeli Arab would form a necessary
component of our book if we were to make any pretense of providing a comprehensive picture of the experience of being Israeli and gay. A friend of ours—
an avowed computer junkie—told us that he had met someone "on line" who
seemed just right: "Walid" was an Israeli Arab who lived with his parents in
Haifa, where he was a college student. We made contact with him, and he was
willing to talk to us. Seeing Walid on the street, you would be unlikely to identify
his jeans-and-sweatshirt style of dress, his dark, slightly pudgy features, or his
slight build as distinctively Arab in any way. There was no denying that Walid's
Hebrew was accented: his r's tripped delicately off his tongue, instead of falling
harshly into his throat, as with most native speakers. Yet Israel is a nation of immigrants, and in comparison with the cacophony of contortions to which the language is daily subjected by Jews, Walid's language was but subtly distinguished.*
—J.P.

∗   ∗   ∗

I had a nice, normal childhood, just like other kids my age in Haifa. My parents didn't fight, and we all got along. I went to a Catholic school. It was run
by nuns. I was there up through eighth grade, and afterwards, I went to an
Eastern Orthodox Christian school. My parents aren't religious, but the good
Arab schools in Haifa are all private schools, and who runs private schools
besides religious institutions?

Both of my parents work in education. They weren't born in Haifa, but
they have lived here for a very long time. They are both from the Galilee area.
Both of the villages, my father's and my mother's, after 1948, ceased to exist.
What do you want—it was a war, the villages were destroyed. If you wanted
to put it in political terms, you could say that they were refugees in their
own country. They went from place to place until they settled down in Haifa,
twenty-six years ago.

Growing up in Haifa, I was never conscious of being a minority. It depends,
from the start, what there is for you to compare yourself with. And I don't

know, I never, in my childhood, compared myself to Jewish kids my age. I never felt different or something, because I never went to a Jewish school, I didn't go to a Jewish school. So, because your environment is basically homogeneously Arab, you don't feel different.

My neighborhood was once the symbol of coexistence. It has changed, in a slow process that began about ten years ago. All of the Jewish young people moved away, and only the old people are left, and they are getting fewer with the years, until now I figure that the population is about 95 percent Arab and 5 percent Jewish. It may be that the Russian immigration has changed that a little, but not a lot.

This kind of difference is a thing you don't talk about at home. A kid lives it, he, like, grows up with it. Someone who is growing up in an all-Arab village in the countryside would have a very different experience. Because, in spite of everything, I did have some contact with Jews, there is cooperation, on the bus, in the street, in the market, in life in general, and you see them. And you always meet Jews, some your own age, and even some of your parents' friends are part of that "other people," if you want to put it that way. So you live it, but you don't talk about it. Things that you live, and you feel all the time, you don't need to talk about. It is a matter for all sorts of psychologists who come from the outside and begin talking about it. But you live it, you don't feel it.

It is difficult for me to reconstruct the first time I felt that I am, basically, gay. But I don't think it was at a very young age. It may be that as a boy I felt something and I didn't know how to explain it, that is also possible. But I wouldn't say that I felt different from all the others in this respect. I never remember having any problems socially. When they talked about girls, I can't say that I found it particularly interesting, but I didn't suffer either. There were pornographic magazines that made their way around school, of course. They weren't gay magazines, they were regular ones, with women and men. I would look at them too. It wasn't a matter of playing along, you can't say that at all. It just wasn't an issue. I wasn't aware of anything.

Later on, I remember that I would look for items in the newspaper. I always remember myself reading the newspaper on Fridays, even at sixteen, and I remember that I would read the articles on the subject. I am talking about the Hebrew newspapers. I have yet to see news items on the subject in Arabic.

Let me tell you about the first time I told someone that I am, like, gay. I was almost seventeen. It was after reading an article in the newspaper. I remember that it was in 1986. There was a story in the Friday supplement of *Yedi'ot Aha-ronot*, a very long article, four pages, about an American guy who was found guilty of the manslaughter of his brother's friend.[1] Do you know the story? His father was a lawyer, the family was of high socioeconomic standing. He was "like that," but his parents didn't know about him, of course. He was gradu-ating high school and wanted to throw a party for guys he had met through computer talk-lines. So he had the party in his parents' summer house, while they were in another city altogether. Anyway, his brother and his brother's friend wanted to play a practical joke on him — so they eavesdropped on his conversations when he was inviting his friends, and that is when they found out that he was "like that." And in the middle of the party they came and sur-prised him, and afterwards, they went to this guy's parents, and told them that they, like, caught him with his pants down with someone, or something — I don't know what exactly. Afterwards, this guy asked them to go back to his parents and tell them that it was all a lie. They didn't exactly agree, so he stole his mother's credit card, ran away from home, and bought a gun. And he waited for his brother's friend in a parking lot somewhere, drove up behind him, closed him into his parking space, they argued, and then he took out his gun, fired a round of bullets into him, and ran away. He was a fugitive for two months, and then he turned himself in.

Reading this story was the first time I identified with someone "like that" in a very strong way. Really, I think I read it, like, three or four times. It really got to me. It was a very radical story. I really identified with that guy. It was written so beautifully, I don't know. I was very moved. So I brought the sub-ject up in conversation with someone who was then a good friend of mine. It was in the middle of twelfth grade, if I remember correctly. It wasn't like I had made a decision to tell him. It just came naturally in the course of the conver-sation. I told this friend of mine the story, and I said that I wouldn't want that to happen to me, and then I took the opportunity to say that I am "like that." He was very surprised. At first he didn't really believe me, but afterwards he did. And after a few days he got used to it. We are still friends. It wasn't a sud-den, dramatic thing for me. It was a process, and this was in some way, like, the culmination.

The whole thing was something that developed together with me, and only afterwards did I find a name for it. But I did finally define myself as gay before I had any sexual experience. I was certain about my definition without having to "check" it. My first sexual contact was more than a year after I talked to this friend.

I never tried to change myself. I never felt like this was something forbidden, terrible, and awful. I still don't feel that way. I never felt like this was going to make a mess out of my life or something. I don't know, I just didn't think. I knew that this is what I am, and that's it. You deal with it. Suddenly, as a seventeen-year-old kid, am I supposed to think about what will happen to me when I am sixty-five, old, and without children or something? Everyone has his own way of dealing with things, and it may be that I deliberately avoided thinking about it, but I don't remember myself in, like, week-long crying fits of depression, or anything like that. Not even close.

During this time I was always on the lookout for information on the subject. I read a lot of books. Really, a lot. I felt that I needed to learn a lot more, so that if there was an argument I would win. And that's it. I began to think about it a lot more, also. I remember myself reading the chapter about homosexuality in every book on the subject of sex I could find. They all said basically the same thing. I don't remember a lot of differences between them.

The books were all in Hebrew, except for one in Arabic, a very old Egyptian book. It said ridiculous things, but I didn't let that bother me. It said things so far removed from what I knew, I could just laugh at it. Things like that don't get to me—I know that it is the others who are wrong, and not me. That was always my approach. If I read something that said that homosexuality is a perversion and a terrible act, then it was the book that was wrong, and not me.

In Arabic, the word you use is "homo," like in Hebrew. It is basically a derogatory word. I have yet to find a word for it in Arabic with a positive connotation. I don't know. The pseudoscientific term for it in Arabic is "sexual perversion"—when you talk about "the sexual perversion," you are talking about homosexuality. That is the most common literary term. "The sexual perversion." Some people also use the word "Luti," which comes from the story of Lot in the Bible. But on the street, the word people use is "homo." It may be that there is slang in other Arab countries. I assume that there is Egyptian slang, for instance, but it doesn't reach us, because this is a different society.

It may be that someone who comes from the outside might, like, imagine that Arab boys have sexual relationships among themselves. I can see that. Because you often see friends holding hands in the street, which Jews don't do, for instance. But it doesn't mean anything. It is just natural, it just means they are good friends. I never held hands with my friends or anything like that, but I saw that others did. It is not unusual to see men walking along holding hands or embracing. But it is difficult for me to believe that it reaches a sexual stage beyond that. I remember that once I read somewhere a description of the Arab *debqah* folk dance as a basically homosexual dance. It was very funny, because I see it as a very masculine, macho thing. But the fact is that, in this dance, the men are all embracing one another. But Arab culture is a different culture. You can't look at it with Western eyes, that is what I am trying to say. I don't think that there is any sexual element in it when Arab men embrace.

You are not unusual if you don't date girls in high school. It is not out of the ordinary to hear a mother saying, "I am so proud of my son—he doesn't go out with girls." You can hear that sentence. Sure, among the other boys, you can get known as a kind of nerd, if you are not interested in girls, but nothing awful. Nothing more than that. That was me. A good student, good grades, obedient, a nice boy. I think that there are people who were in my class who still think of me that way. The ones that don't know about me.

I didn't feel any pressure or tension or problems from the people around me. It may be that it was just that I told the right people. They had no choice but to be with me, and they wanted to stay on good terms with me—they needed help in physics and chemistry! When I think about it now, they really needed me, a lot of them. So I told them, and it was a relief.

At this point, I began to look around. This is the point where I had come to terms with myself, and I could step out and begin looking for what I wanted. The first thing I did was to buy a pornographic video. Beginning in tenth grade, I worked on the weekends in a mini-market, and I had money from that. At that time, there was only one store in Haifa where you could buy such videos. I went in, asked for a video "like that," and he gave me one. It was French. I still remember it—it was a good movie. I wasn't disappointed. I had total privacy at home. There was no problem with that. And since then, I have always had one movie or another in my drawer, and no one has ever found it.

After the video stage, I began to feel that I really had to find someone. That I needed to meet people, flesh-and-blood people. It was clear to me from the very start that I was not going to try to meet Arabs. It is something that I never really thought about, really, looking for someone Arab. I don't know why. It wasn't that I wasn't attracted to other Arabs. But this was a case of a part of my life that I lived in Hebrew.

We speak Arabic at home, of course, but Arab schools begin to teach Hebrew in third grade. Today, I can think in both Arabic and Hebrew. It depends on the subject. I can't think about engineering in Arabic—I am not used to living with the Arabic technical vocabulary. Likewise, homosexuality is something I live in Hebrew, and not in Arabic. So it was clear that I would meet Jewish men. Even in the face of the difference between Jews and Arabs, I think it is much easier to meet Jews, to be the boyfriend of a Jewish guy than an Arab. Arab gay men are much more difficult to find.

I knew what was going on in the park, but I never went in there, because, I don't know, it frightened me.[2] Everyone knows about the park, even in Arab society. It is known that the park is a meeting place for gays. I always knew, but I never went there at night. It was, I don't know, a fear. I still don't think it is a very pleasant place. Not that I have got something against it, but it is not for me—so dark, you can't see anything, the whole atmosphere is as if you are doing something wrong. And that really bothers me. That is what keeps me from going there, that is all. You just can't go in there with the feeling that you are doing something good. It is just unpleasant to wander around in the dark. I have heard that some Arabs come from the territories [i.e., Gaza and the West Bank] to the park, but I have never met them.

At some point, I began to see the personal ads in the local paper, in *Qol Heifah.* I remember that I began to read them, the gay ads. I never answered any of them, but I would always buy the paper, because I knew that there were ads there. When I try to reconstruct events, I can't remember where my first ad was, but in the end I decided to put my own ad in. I think I put it in *Magaʻim.*[3]

The wording I chose was extraordinarily inappropriate—very, like, mature, very unsexy, intellectual, intimidating. A caricature really. I wrote, "college student"—I knew at this point that I had been accepted to the Technion, so it wasn't a lie—"college student, Arab, good-looking, humanist, likeable, looking for refined and intelligent young man for long-term, lasting relationship."[4] That's what it was. Really frightening, right? I remember that the only one who answered it the first time was a thirty-five-year-old man. I ended our meeting as quickly as I could.

I put "Arab" in because I didn't want any surprises on the first time. I have seen a lot of ads by now, and you rarely see someone saying that they are Arab, so, I don't know, most other Arabs either don't say they are Arab or don't publish personal ads. I have answered a lot of ads, and I have never answered the ad of someone who didn't say anything and turned out to be Arab. I have no idea what other Arab gays do. I really don't know.

I kept running the ad, and I met a few people, but they were awful. Now I understand that the ad was inappropriate, that it didn't even describe what I wanted. I mean, how many eighteen-year-old kids are looking for a "long-term, lasting relationship"? No one under twenty-five is going to answer such an ad, what with my being Arab on top of it all. That was the problem.

I published a post office box number in the ad, and people wrote me, I wrote them back, they wrote me back, and so on, until we got to the point of giving a telephone number. That was back when we would write six or seven letters back and forth until we got to the telephone number. We would meet, it would be clear that this was not it, and then I would leave. This scene repeated itself a number of times. I usually made sure that it was in a public place, but there were a few times when I went to people's houses. It was very difficult for me to tell people that I wasn't interested. If I got to a meeting, and immediately saw that I wasn't interested, I would just try to get it over with as quickly as possible and then cut off all contact. You don't have to answer letters you get in your post office box. It is a little unpleasant, threatening, even frightening, but there's nothing you can do.

I met, like, about twenty people through this ad, before I finally had my first time. It was very discouraging. That is a lot of letters, and lot of meetings. It was terrible. But I kept on meeting with people — you always have hope. As time went on I learned how to make a better process of elimination before meeting someone. These are things you just develop a sense for.

So I got to someone around the twentieth — maybe he was the eighteenth, maybe the twenty-third, I don't know. I was eighteen and a half years old at the time, I think. We met in his apartment. He had written that he was nineteen, good-looking, and so on. And it was there that I had my first sexual contact. We had sat and talked for about an hour. He was in the army, not that I get my kicks from soldiers. No, really, I have met soldiers of every kind, and they don't do anything for me. Besides, he wasn't a combat soldier, just a clerk. But seriously . . .

We sat across from each other the whole time, and after about an hour, maybe an hour and a half, he came and sat next to me, and then he asked me if it really was my first time, and I said yes. And he asked if I really wanted to give it a try, and I said yes. And it was already, like, happening. He wasn't looking for a "long-term, lasting relationship," that's for sure. But it was good sex. Afterwards, he didn't believe that it was my first time. I knew what to do—it was just like the movies.

Of course, I felt wonderful afterward. It was like a dream come true. Would you like me to be dramatic about this? Can I be? It really was something beautiful, something different from everything else. And I even told him that. This was a mistake, but that is a different story—it gave him a lot of power.

Anyway, I told him how I felt, at our first meeting, even. I felt that this guy, he was the one I really wanted. And time passed, and we met again, and again, and it kept on that way. But it was very spread out. There were a lot of telephone conversations—our schedules didn't exactly fit, and the conversations were basically about setting dates. You couldn't really say that we had a relationship. We met about once every two months over the course of a year and a half. It was basically, like, sexual. No—it was exclusively sexual.

The period when all this began was also the beginning of the intifadah. I was very strongly aware of the political implications of everything. Yes, I did feel the connection between sex, politics, the army—as the expression goes, "fuck the Arabs"—but then again, I was usually a top. No, no, that's just a joke, just a joke. But seriously, I think I just managed to keep everything separate. I don't know.

You are looking for something dramatic, I understand, so OK. I mean, none of this is really important—it is all just things that you live. But since you want drama, I will give you a drama. I remember once, it was 1988 I think, yes, the intifadah was at its peak, of course. And I went to a political demonstration in the morning, at eight in the morning at the gate of the Technion. I stood there for one very long hour, and I spent the whole time, like, thinking about how I had come home only five hours earlier, at three in the morning, after having had sex with a soldier. And there I was, standing and demonstrating against the occupation. And I just thought about how it didn't make any sense, it didn't fit together. But I don't know, I managed to keep things separate, it is something that is part of life. It is just life.

I always mentioned in my ads that I was Arab. I even felt that it was a matter of misrepresentation if I didn't say it. I felt that I had to say it, so I did. I never tried to hide it . . . well actually . . . this is going to be published in English, right? I hope it won't get translated. No, I'm kidding. But if you are looking for turning points for me, I think this is actually an important question.

At some point I really got discouraged—it doesn't happen to me easily, but it happens. I debated the question a lot, if I should say that I am Arab or not. From a marketing perspective, it was in my interest not to say it, that was clear. Maybe a lot of blacks and whites in the U.S. are attracted to each other, I don't know, but it isn't the same here. We are at war. And I knew that this fact wasn't helping me.

But I was unsure what I could do. So I made a few experiments—postponing the point where I say that I am Arab, to see how far I could go. Statistical exercises. But there was one incident that made me decide that I was through with experiments.

When I think back on it, it was pretty scary. I was twenty then, he was nineteen and a half, in the army. I think I answered his ad, and then he answered my letter, and I wrote him back, and finally there was a telephone call and we talked. And I didn't tell him I was Arab—he was part of the experimental group. We made a date to meet. He was on an army base somewhere, and he suggested that I come to meet him on the base! He was doing guard duty, and I think he, like, wanted to have sex right there. Of course, I refused that offer. There is a limit, after all. I said no, I can't, we are much better off doing it sometime later. So, to make a long story short, we met later on, in a public place, downtown.

We met, we passed each other's final inspection. He was coming back from the base to his parents' house, in the suburbs of Haifa. His parents weren't at home, and he invited me to go back to his house. Now, I had just come from the Technion, and I didn't have a backpack, only a sort of folder, which had a sticker on it saying, "Abort Abortion Restrictions," right? And he apparently was searching for subjects to talk about, so he said, "What, is that all you do in the Technion all day, throw slogans around?" He wanted to talk about abortion, whether you have got the right to do it or not, and pro and con, and so on. And from there, it was a very short distance to politics. And this is on the way to his house, right—everything was happening very fast.

So we got to politics, and then it turned out that he was very, very, very right wing. I mean very, very. OK—he didn't hide the fact that he was in

Kach's youth movement, Kahane's political party.[5] OK. So then I said to myself, OK, it's a good thing that I didn't say anything to him when we first met. And I was debating with myself during the whole trip, whether I should, like, say anything, get out of the car somehow, stop things or continue things. I didn't know. I was scared to death. In any case, it was clear to me that if I was going to go ahead with this then I would really have to hide it.

So we got to his house and we went into his room and, what do you know, there was the yellow flag of the Kach party there, on the wall of his bedroom. I remember that. I remember it as a horrible, horrible thing. Now I can laugh about it, but it was not a simple situation. I was afraid to try to leave once we got there. And he began to tell me about all the demonstrations he had been at. It was actually really interesting to hear his side of things, because I myself had been at some of these demonstrations too. It was very surprising to hear the other side's version. There was even something nice about it. He didn't hide the fact that he would sometimes go out to beat up Arabs, and he told me how he and his friends instigated violence at those demonstrations. It was very interesting. But it did, like, raise my blood pressure at the time.

And then he asked me about myself, where my family was from, what kind of an accent it was that I had. And I said that I was born in South America. And he also asked me who I vote for, and I said that I voted with the Left — I said that because my parents had been persecuted where we came from, I thought that it was wrong to persecute others — something like that. And I tossed in everything I know about South American history. Let's face it — this guy was an idiot. I have never lied so much in my life. I think he could have figured things out very easily.

I was very afraid to have sex with him. Very, very much. For one thing, he would be able to see that I wasn't Jewish. But when it got to that, I made something else up — I said that my mother was Jewish and my father wasn't, and he insisted, I don't know what I said — something totally unbelievable, in any case. But, what can you do, he was very stupid. I just wanted to get it over with.

When it was done, he offered me a ride back, and I said no, no, no, that's all right. He asked for my telephone number, which I had never given him before, and I wrote six totally random numbers on a sheet of paper, and gave it to him. And I remember that I left the house, walked calmly to the corner, and then, like, broke out into a sprint. I ran to the nearest bus stop and caught the first bus that came, just to get as far away from that place as I could. I didn't even care where it was going.

That was the first time I slept with someone who didn't know I was Arab, and I will never do that again. The lesson is that it isn't worth trying to hide it—you should just write it in the ad, and that's that. Since then, actually, I have answered very few ads, and published none.

Recently, in the last year, really, I have become more involved in gay social life. I actually tried to, like, get some sort of gay social life going in the Technion, but failed. It's a long story. What happened was that the student paper published a letter from a student who had been to a meeting of the gay and lesbian student group in Jerusalem. And he wrote asking, in a very ironic tone, why, in the macho Technion, the brotherhood of engineers, builders of Israel, or something like that, there were no meetings like this, why was this topic taboo? He had come to the conclusion that it was a result of the difficulties of exposing oneself in this masculine atmosphere, the difficulty of being first. I wrote a letter in response, basically saying I was taking the initiative, and that gays, lesbians, and bisexual students who were interested in evening meetings should write to my post office box. And I got fifteen letters—all of them from frightened Technion students who didn't want to meet anyone else, and didn't want to come to any public meetings! I don't know why they answered. I don't know what they wanted. A lot of them gave me their post office box addresses, and I wrote to them. And I met with every one of them separately, but no one wanted to meet anyone else, because they were afraid that they might be in the same calculus class some day. There's no figuring Technion students. It was a total failure.

Gay life interests me in general. I went to one meeting of the Haifa branch of the Agudah, about a month ago.[6] But if I go back, it certainly won't be every week. It was pretty disappointing. It isn't what I am looking for. Every week, to talk about the same thing with the same people, who you don't really have anything in common with, can be pretty boring. It might be that a group in the Technion, which would be a little more homogeneous, where there would be some more things to talk about, would be more successful. It may be that there will be another attempt, I don't know.

I am interested in gay rights, but it is not an obsession. I think the Agudah is doing very good work, but I don't really feel very much a part of it. I don't know. Maybe it is just because it is in Tel Aviv. It is a little far. I am not going to go to Tel Aviv twice a week or anything—for instance, I wouldn't take a special trip to Tel Aviv to participate in a march, if they had one. If I lived in the area, it might be that I would, like, stop by.

I have met a lot of people through the Internet, on the computer. I have always had a computer account, but I didn't know this existed until a friend showed me. He left me in front of the menu, and I, totally by chance, went into the "gblf" conversation—"gays, bisexuals, lesbians, and friends." Since then I have been hooked on it. Maybe a little too much, I don't know.

It is basically a party line on the computer. Everybody can type whatever they want into their own computer, and it appears on everybody's screen. The subjects are very diverse—it depends on who is there. If you tend to come on-line at regular hours, you meet the same people over and over, and you already have a kind of social life. They are people who you, theoretically, can talk to every day. People from universities all over the world, all sorts of countries. It is amazing. Any time that you are in front of the computer, any time you feel the impulse, you are going to find at least ten other people who are interested in talking about a subject that interests you. And it is not always homosexuality—it can be all sorts of crazy things. There are people who come on-line in the morning, and there are people who come on-line at night, but it works out that, like, you have a group of regulars that changes every few hours. People from Europe are usually on during the same hours I am—England, Holland, France, Italy, Poland. The United States, of course, is always on—there is always someone who comes to talk on the computer at four in the morning. But people are generally free during the same hours, so you always meet the same people. That is what makes it social.

I correspond with some people privately now, through electronic mail, and some even by conventional mail, exchanging pictures of ourselves and so on. Then there is even more of a relationship. And if you find someone who is close by, it may happen that it will develop into, like, an actual meeting. I never fell in love with anyone from the computer, but I did have some one-time meetings, sometimes two or three times. Not really love, because it was never the right person,

When you are on-line, sometimes you just make conversation, sometimes you tease one another, because you get to know people very well, after a time, so there are running jokes. They are just like regular friends. There is also computer sex—just like erotic stories, but much stronger, because it is a conversation, it is being written directly to you.

Of course, you are exposing yourself in a very serious way when you participate in these conversations, much more than, like, going to the park or something, because your name and even your identity card number are there, and anyone who is on-line can see. Anyone in the Technion who is a little curious can find me logged on there. But it doesn't bother me. I know for a fact that there are a lot of people in Israel who talk regularly on other channels who know who I am. But whenever I am working on the computer I also leave a window open and log on. You could say that I am addicted—when something interesting is going on in that window, I can leave everything that I am doing very quickly. It takes priority in my attention in certain ways.

I am twenty-three now. In the last two or three years I haven't really been in any serious relationships. I haven't been looking for that. There was one other guy who I was with for seven months. It was an exclusive relationship, at least on my part. I would like to find someone who I can be with for more than seven months and still find interesting and attractive. Maybe I would be able to move in with him at some stage. But that's a dream, right? I always try to be practical.

One positive thing that came out of that Technion story was a very close friendship with someone who is also a student. He has a steady boyfriend, of course. But through him, you could say that I have found a certain crowd in Haifa that he and his boyfriend are part of. I meet people through them, not that they try to set me up or anything. But they hang out with a group of people that it is really nice to be with.

Most of them are over thirty. There is one other Arab. The first gay Arab I have met. We have never had a private conversation, even though I knew him beforehand, from other contexts. He is also from Haifa, and he is a member of the same church as we are. I never knew he was gay. Now, if we were to meet in the street, I would talk to him. But I don't know how things will develop—it doesn't depend only on me. He has a Jewish boyfriend at the moment.

Everyone chooses his own surroundings. If your surroundings are not suitable to you, you find new ones. You don't have to accept everything you are born into. It is a decision that is totally under your control. You can't force yourself into membership someplace where you have no place. I have no problem leaving behind an environment that makes problems for me — what logical reason would there be to stay in it? For instance, I am not going to join the Islamic movement in order to change it, so that it will be more enlightened. There is nothing for me there, so I am not going to become a member. From the very start I choose for myself a different environment. Right now, I think that Jewish society is more enlightened than Arab society when it comes to homosexuality. So that is where I go, more and more.

It is clear that a lot of things would be easier for me abroad. Absolutely. It is a fact. I have thought about it seriously in the past, and I still think about it. But I have no specific plans. I want to go on for my master's degree — I will either study in Tel Aviv or in the U.S. There are pros and cons, and I still haven't made a final decision. If I can find a job here then I won't emigrate, at least not at this point. But I am thinking about this subject very seriously. It may be that I will leave in the end.

I don't feel any ideological need to stay. I will live wherever I feel comfortable, wherever I feel that I can live best. It's just life. I don't feel any special connection with Haifa. I could just as easily live in Denmark or the U.S. or any other place. You create your own social life, and you can find that in all sorts of places. That is not a problem.

I don't think my life is any different from lots of Jewish guys who live at home and whose parents don't know about them. I think my life is pretty similar. I can't say if my being gay has influenced how I feel about Arab culture as compared to Jewish culture — the whole thing is very hypothetical. It might be that if I hadn't been gay I would be different. I will never like gefilteh fish, though.[7]

I don't see myself as a victim. If I were to wake up one morning and there would not be any discrimination, I would think I was in a different place. I am not sure I would know what to do. It is part of my life. You find ways of coping, you deal with it, you live with it, and you even begin to, like, enjoy it. It isn't something so sad. OK, if, for example, you read something, that is written with the intention of upsetting you, you can laugh about it, you can't take everything to heart. It isn't healthy to take things seriously. Why get involved thinking about things that you know from the very start will only make problems? Why even get involved with it? Why think? Live the way you want, and that's it. Life is for living, not for thinking about all the time.

I define myself as Israeli. If I had to think up some sort of definition of what I am now, I would say I am a Palestinian-Israeli—an Israeli of Palestinian background. I think this defines me pretty well. I am reluctant to ever use the word "Arab" to describe myself, but there is no choice, you have got to use it. I dislike it, because it suggests connectedness with all sorts of places and people who I don't feel connected with at all. That is why I try to limit it.

I don't feel negatively about Zionism, which I define as the national liberation movement of the Jewish people. But I am not part of the Zionist project—I am part of the State of Israel. You are the ones who need to learn to differentiate between the two things, and you don't know how to do that. I can do that. With the creation of the state, I think that Zionism lost its meaning—at some point, it should have been replaced by "Israelism." But for all sorts of reasons, it wasn't replaced. And it stayed the way it was, and people still define themselves as Zionists or not. But that has nothing to do with me. It is your problem. I have no problem at all in defining myself as Israeli.

People need to think about the future, and not go backward all the time. Why should I waste my time researching the land where they are building a new Jewish settlement today, to find out to which tiny Arab village, which no longer exists, it belonged? For instance, I know that there has been an army base on the site of my father's village for many years now. OK—the fact is, after '48, there was no one there anymore. It doesn't really bother me, because I feel no connection to that place. I don't know, I barely feel a part of Haifa.

My feelings are for people—much more than for places, for earth. I get emotional over people—living, breathing, changing things, that you can touch—and not chunks of earth which could just as easily be in France or in Jordan or in Israel. It's pathetic, the way people look for a sense of attachment to a place, of belonging. I don't know why. They look for roots in a particular place, historical roots, but I don't feel any need for that. Old historical sites and tourist attractions are not for me. I live my life here and now, and I think about the future more than the past. I have no problem with that. And if I decide tomorrow that I want to be a Buddhist, then nothing is going to keep me from doing that, so long as it interests me. Afterward, I can change it, if I want. I chose my connectedness, and I can change it tomorrow if I want to. I belong to the groups that I choose for myself, and not to any homeland.

Notes

This chapter is excerpted from one of the twelve monologues that comprise Independence Park: The Lives of Gay Men in Israel *(Stanford University Press, 1999), by Amir Sumaka'i Fink and Jacob Press. Used with the permission of the publishers, © 1999 by the Board of Trustees of the Leland Stanford Junior University.*

1 *Yedi'ot Aharonot:* Israel's most widely read mass circulation daily tabloid newspaper.

2 There are two public parks that are meeting places for gay men in Haifa: Gan Hazikaron (Memorial Park) and Gan Binyamin (Benjamin Park).

3 *Maga'im:* Literally, "Contacts" or "Touches"; magazine for gay men printing personal advertisements, black-and-white pornographic photography, and news and feature articles; published with varying frequency from 1987 to 1995.

4 Technion: Israel Institute of Technology, located in Haifa; oldest institution of higher learning in Israel; leading university of the applied sciences.

5 Kach: Political movement founded by Rabbi Meyer Kahane, advocating Jewish theocracy and Israeli territorial expansion, as well as the elimination of all Arabs from Israeli-held territory. Banned by Israeli authorities as a terrorist organization in 1994. Kach is identified with the graffito slogan, "Death to the Arabs."

6 Agudah: Literally, "Society" or "Association"; the commonly used name for Israel's first — and for many years its only — gay social and political organization. The Agudah was founded in Tel Aviv in 1975, as the "Society for the Protection of Personal Rights." After Israel's dormant antisodomy law was repealed, in 1988, the Agudah added the phrase "for Gay Men, Lesbians, and Bisexuals in Israel" to its name. The organization opened a community center in downtown Tel Aviv in 1993. The Agudah voted to change its name to the "Association of Gay Men, Lesbians, and Bisexuals in Israel" in 1995, and in 1999 it added "Transgendered People" as well. On procedural grounds, the government agency responsible for the registration of nonprofit institutions has refused to acknowledge the above name-changes.

7 gefilteh fish: A Jewish delicacy; boiled chopped fish, usually carp.

WORKS CITED

Acevedo, Ramón L. 1976. *Augusto D'Halmar, Novelista: Estudio de "Pasión y Muerte del Cura Deusto."* Puerto Rico: Editorial Universitaria.

Allison, Anne. 1996. Permitted and *Prohibited Desires: Mothers, Comics, and Censorship in Japan.* Boulder: Westview Press.

Almaguer, Tomás. 1991. "Chicano Men: A Cartography of Homosexual Identity and Behavior." *differences* 3 (2): 75–100.

Alonso, Ana María, and Teresa Koreck. 1989. "Silences: 'Hispanics,' AIDS, and Sexual Practices." *differences* 1 (1): 101–24.

Alonso, Carlos. 1990. *The Spanish American Regional Novel: Modernity and Autochtony.* Cambridge University Press.

Anderson, Benedict. 1983. *Imagined Communities.* London: Verso.

Anzieu, Didier. 1986. *Freud's Self-Analysis.* Translated by Peter Graham. Preface by M. Masud R. Khan. Madison, Conn.: International Universities Press.

Appadurai, Arjun. 1991. "Global Ethnoscapes: Notes and Queries for a Transnational Anthropology." In *Recapturing Anthropology,* edited by R. Fox, 191–210. Santa Fe: School of American Research Press.

———. 1993. "Patriotism and Its Futures." *Public Culture* 5 (3): 411–29.

Apter, Emily. 1992. "Female Trouble in the Colonial Harem." *differences* 4 (1): 205–24.

Arenas, Reinaldo. 1967. *Celestino antes del alba.* La Habana: UNEAC.

———. 1968. *Le monde hallucinant.* Translated by Didier Coste. Paris: Editions du Seuil.

———. 1969. *El mundo alucinante.* Mexico: Editorial Diógenes.

———. 1971. *Hallucinations.* Translated by Gordon Brotherston. New York: Harper and Row.

———. 1972. *Con los ojos cerrados.* Montevideo: Editorial Arca.

———. 1975. *Le palais des très blanches mouffettes.* Translated by Didier Coste. Paris: Editions du Seuil.

———. 1977. *Der Palast der blütenweissen Stinktiere.* Translated by Monika López. Darmstadt: Luchterhand Verlag.

———. 1980a. *Celestino antes del alba.* Caracas: Monte Avila.

———. 1980b. *El palacio de las blaquísimas mofetas.* Caracas: Monte Avila.

———. 1981. *El central.* Barcelona: Seix Barral.

———. 1982. *Otra vez el mar.* Barcelona: Argos Vergara.

———. 1986a. *Farewell to the Sea.* Translated by Andrew Hurley. New York: Viking.

———. 1986b. *Necesidad de libertad: Mariel: testimonios de un intelectual disidente.* Mexico: Kosmos-Editorial.

———. 1987a. *Graveyard of the Angels.* Translated by Alfred J. MacAdam. New York: Avon.

———. 1987b. *La loma del ángel.* Miami: Mariel Press.

———. 1987c. "Al resplandor del infierno." Prologue to *Desertores del paraíso,* by Lázaro Gómez Carriles. Madrid: Playor.

———. 1987d. *Singing from the Well.* Translated by Andrew Hurley. Translation of *Celestino antes del alba.* New York: Viking.

———. 1991. *Final de un cuento.* Huelva: Diputación Provincial.

———. 1992. *Antes que anochezca: Autobiografía.* Barcelona: Tusquets.

———. 1993. *Before Night Falls: A Memoir.* Translated by Dolores Koch. New York: Viking.

Arenas, Reinaldo, and Jesús J. Barquet. 1991. "Conversando con Reinaldo Arenas sobre el suicidio." *Hispania* 74:934–36.

Art Forum. 1991. 30 (2): 23.

Art Forum. 1992. 30 (9): 125.

Asagawa Kiyo. 1921. "Joyū to onnayakusha (Actresses and women's role players)." *Josei Nihonjin* 4:112–113.

Asahi Shinbun. 1934a. Tokyo evening ed., 14 June, 2.

Asahi Shinbun. 1934b. Tokyo morning ed., 24 June, 3.

Aschheim, Steven E. 1982. *Brothers and Strangers: The East European Jew in German and German Jewish Consciousness, 1800–1923.* Madison: University of Wisconsin Press.

Asquerino, Eduardo. 1857. "Nuestro pensamiento." *La América* (Madrid), 24–25 March.

Bannon, Ann. 1962. *Beebo Brinker.* Greenwich, Conn.: Gold Medal/Fawcett.

Barale, Michèle Aina. 1993. "When Jack Blinks: Si(gh)ting Gay Desire in Ann Bannon's *Beebo Brinker.*" In *The Lesbian and Gay Studies Reader,* edited by Henry

Abelove, Michèle Aina Barale, and David Halperin, 604–15. New York and London: Routledge.

Ben-Ari E. 1990. "A Bureaucrat in Every Japanese Kitchen: On Cultural Assumptions and Co-Production." *Administration and Society* 21 (4): 472–92.

Benedict, Ruth. [1936] 1974. *The Chrysanthemum and the Sword.* New York: Meridian.

Benjamin, Walter. 1969a. "Theses on the Philosophy of History." In *Illuminations,* edited by Hannah Arendt, translated by Harry Zohn, 253–64. New York: Shocken Books.

———. 1969b. "The Work of Art in the Age of Mechanical Reproduction." In *Illuminations,* edited by Hannah Arendt, translated by Harry Zohn, 217–52. New York: Shocken Books.

———. 1978. "Critique of Violence." In *Reflections: Essays, Aphorisms, Autobiographical Writings,* edited by Peter Demetz, translated by Edmund Jephcott, 277–300. New York: Harcourt.

Beritela, Gerard F. 1993. "The Wish that Dares Not Speak Its Name: Homoerotic Longing in Freud's 'Myops' Dream." Unpublished paper.

Bernstein, G. 1991. *Recreating Japanese Woman 1600–1945.* Berkeley: University of California Press.

Berry, Chris. 1994. *A Bit on the Side: East-West Topographies of Desire.* Sydney: E. M. Press.

Bessatsu Takarajima. 1987. Special issue. *Onna o aisuru onnatachi no monogatari* (A tale of women who love women). No. 64.

Bhabha, Homi K. 1984. "Of Mimicry and Man: The Ambivalence of Colonial Discourse." *October* 28:125–33.

———. 1985. "Signs Taken For Wonders: Questions of Ambivalence and Authority Under a Tree Outside Delhi, May 1817." *Critical Inquiry* 12 (1): 163–84.

———. 1994. *The Location of Culture.* London: Routledge.

Boone, Joseph A. 1995. "Vacation Cruises; or, The Homoerotics of Orientalism." *PMLA* 110 (1): 89–107.

Bottomley, Gillian. 1992. *From Another Place: Migration and the Politics of Culture.* Melbourne: Cambridge University Press.

Bouvier, L. F., and A. J. Agresta. 1987. "The Future Asian Population of the United States." In *Pacific Bridges: The New Immigrants from Asia and the Pacific Islands,* edited by J. T. Fawcett and B. V. Cariño, 285–301. Staten Island, N.Y.: Center for Migration Studies.

Boyarin, Daniel. 1990. "The Eye in the Torah: Ocular Desire in Midrashic Hermeneutic." *Critical Inquiry* 16 (spring): 532–50.

———. 1994a. "Freud's Baby, Fliess's Maybe: Homophobia, Anti-Semitism, and the Invention of Oedipus." *GLQ* 2 (1–2): 115–47.

————. 1994b. A Radical Jew: Paul and the Politics of Identity. Berkeley and Los Angeles: University of California Press.

————. 1997. "The Colonial Drag: Zionism, Gender, and Mimicry." In *Unheroic Conduct: The Rise of Heterosexuality and the Invention of the Jewish Man.* Berkeley and
Los Angeles: University of California Press.

Boyarin, Daniel, and Jonathan Boyarin. 1993. "Diaspora: Generation and the Ground
of Jewish Identity." *Critical Inquiry* 19 (summer): 693–725.

————. 1995. "Self-Exposure as Theory: The Double Mark of the Male Jew." In *Rheto-
rics of Self-Making,* edited by Debbora Battaglia, 16–42. Berkeley and Los Angeles:
University of California Press.

Boyarin, Jonathan. 1992. *Storm from Paradise: The Politics of Jewish Memory.* Minneapolis: University of Minnesota Press.

Brenkman, John. 1993. *Straight Male Modern: A Cultural Critique of Psychoanalysis.*
New York: Routledge.

Briggs, Sheila. 1985. "Images of Women and Jews in Nineteenth- and Twentieth-
Century German Theology." In *Immaculate and Powerful: The Female in Sacred
Image and Reality,* edited by Clarissa W. Atkinson, Constance H. Buchanan, and
Margaret R. Miles, 226–59. Boston: Beacon Press.

Bruner, Edward M. 1986. "Experience and Its Expressions." In *The Anthropology of Experience,* edited by Victor W. Turner and Edward Bruner, 3–32. Urbana: University
of Illinois Press.

Bruss, Elizabeth W. 1976. *Autobiographical Acts: The Changing Situation of a Literary
Genre.* New York: Johns Hopkins University Press.

Buckley, Sandra. 1993. "Altered States." In *Postwar Japan as History,* edited by A. Gordon, 347–72. Berkeley: University of California Press.

Buckley, Sandra, ed. 1997. *Broken Silence: Voices of Japanese Feminism.* Berkeley: University of California Press.

Buckley, Sandra, and V. Mackie. 1985. "Women in the New Japanese State." In *Democracy in Contemporary Japan,* edited by G. McCormack and Y. Sugimoto, 173–85.
New York: M. E. Sharpe.

Buhrich, Neil, and Carlson Loke. 1988. "Homosexuality, Suicide, and Parasuicide in
Australia." *Journal of Homosexuality* 15 (1–2): 113–129.

Burroughs, William. 1987. *Queer.* New York: Penguin.

Butler, Judith. 1993. *Bodies That Matter: On the Discursive Limits of "Sex."* New York:
Routledge.

Cabrera Infante, Guillermo. 1983. "Entre la historia y la nada: Notas sobre una ideolo-
gía del suicidio." *Vuelta* 74:11–22.

Cannell, Fenella. 1991. "Catholicism, Spirit Mediums and the Ideal of Beauty in a Bico-
lano Community, Philippines." Ph.D. diss., London School of Economics.

Cariño, Benjamin. 1987. "The Philippines and Southeast Asia: Historical Roots and Contemporary Linkages." In *Pacific Bridges: The New Immigrants from Asia and the Pacific Islands,* edited by James W. Fawcett and Benjamin Cariño, 305–25. Staten Island, N.Y.: Center for Migration Studies.

Carrier, Joseph M. 1976. "Cultural Factors Affecting Urban Mexican Male Homosexual Behavior." *Archives of Sexual Behavior* 5 (2): 103–24.

Certeau, Michel de. 1988. *The Practice of Everyday Life.* Translated by Steven Rendall. Berkeley: University of California Press.

Chen, Xiaomei. 1992. "Occidentalism as Counterdiscourse: 'He Shang' in Post-Mao China." *Critical Inquiry* 18 (4): 686–712.

Cheyette, Bryan. 1995. "Neither Black Nor White: The Figure of 'the Jew' in Imperial British Literature." In *The Jew in the Text: Modernity and the Politics of Identity,* edited by Linda Nochin and Tamar Garb, 31–41. London: Thames and Hudson.

Chow, Rey. 1993. *Writing Diaspora: Tactics of Intervention in Contemporary Cultural Studies.* Bloomington: University of Indiana Press.

Clifford, James. 1990. "Documents: A Decomposition." In *Anxious Visions: Surrealist Art,* edited by Sidra Stick. New York: Abbeville.

Cooper, Wayne F. 1987. *Claude McKay: Rebel Sojourner in the Harlem Renaissance.* Baton Rouge: Louisiana State University Press.

Craft, Christopher. 1995. *Another Kind of Love: Male Homosexual Desire in English Discourse, 1850–1920.* Berkeley and Los Angeles: University of California Press.

Crimp, Douglas. 1987a. "AIDS: Cultural Analysis/Cultural Activism." *October* 43:3–16.

———. 1987b. "How to Have Promiscuity in an Epidemic." *October* 43:237–50.

———. 1990. "Mourning and Militancy." In *Out There: Marginalization and Contemporary Cultures,* edited by Russell Ferguson, Martha Gever, and Trinh T. Minh-Ha, 233–46. New York: New Museum of Contemporary Art and MIT Press.

D'Halmar, Augusto. 1969. *La pasión y muerte del cura Deusto.* 1924. Reprint, Santiago: Nascimento.

———. 1929. "Joaquín Edwards Bello y su novela española." *Atenea* 11 (July): 497–500.

———. 1934. *La Mancha de Don Quijote.* Santiago: Ercilla.

———. 1935. *Los alucinados.* Santiago: Ercilla.

———. 1963. *Antología de Augusto d'Halmar. El hermano errante.* Selección y Prólogo de Enrique Espinoza. Santiago: Zig-Zag.

———. 1970a. *Gatita.* In *Obras escogidas.* Santiago: Editorial Andrés Bello.

———. 1970b. *La sombra del humo en el espejo.* In *Obras escogidas.* Santiago: Editorial Andréo Bello.

———. n.d. *Nirvana. Viajes al Extremo-Oriente.* Barcelona: Editorial Maucci.

"Dansō no reijin (Cross-dressed beauty)." 1935. *Asahi Shinbun,* Osaka morning ed., 28 January, 11.

"Dansō no reijō no kashutsu jiken (The cross-dressed beauty's escape from her home)." 1935. *Fujō Shinbun,* 3 February, 3.

Davidson, Arnold I. 1987. "Sex and the Emergence of Sexuality." *Critical Inquiry* 14 (1): 16–48.

———. 1992. "Sex and the Emergence of Sexuality." In Forms of Desire: Sexual Orientation and the Social Constructionist Controversy, edited by Edward Stein, 89–132. New York: Routledge.

Deleuze, Gilles, and Félix Guattari. 1987. "Treatise on Nomadology." In *A Thousand Plateaus,* translated by Brian Massumi. Minneapolis: University of Minnesota Press.

de Man, Paul. 1979. "Autobiography as Self-Defacement." *Modern Language Notes* 94: 919–30.

Derrida, Jacques. 1972. "Structure, Sign and Play in the Social Sciences." In *The Structuralist Controversy,* edited by R. Macksey and E. Donato. Baltimore: Johns Hopkins Press, 1972.

———. 1973. "Différance." In *Speech and Phenomena and Other Essays on Husserl's Theory of Signs,* translated by David B. Allison, 129–60. Evanston: Northwestern University Press.

———. 1991. "Interpretations at War: Kant, the Jew, the German." *New Literary History* 22 (winter): 39–96.

De Vos, George. 1973. *Socialization for Achievement: Essays on the Cultural Psychology of the Japanese.* Berkeley: University of California Press.

Díaz Arrieta, Hernán. 1963. *Los cuatro grandes de la literatura Chilena del siglo XX.* Santiago: Zig-Zag.

Dibble, Sandra and Elinor Barkett. 1990. "Para Reinaldo Arenas, era tiempo de morir." *El nuevo Herald,* 11 December, 4c.

Dictionary of American Slang. 1975. 2d supplemented edition. Edited by Harold Wentworth and Stuart Flexner. New York: Thomas Y. Crowell.

Diedrich, Maria. 1972. *Kommunismus im afroamerikanische Roman: Das Verhältnis afroamerikanischer Schriftsteller zur Kommunistischen Partei der USA zwischen den Weltkriegen.* Stuttgart: Peter Lang.

Dijkstra, Bram. 1986. *Idols of Perversity: Fantasies of Feminine Evil in Fin-de-siècle Culture.* New York: Oxford University Press.

Djbilou, Abdellah, ed. 1986. *Diwan modernista: Una visión del Oriente.* Madrid: Taurus.

Dollimore, Jonathan. 1991. *Sexual Dissidence: Augustine to Wilde, Freud to Foucault.* Oxford: Clarendon Press.

Donoso, José. 1966. *El lugar sin límites.* Mexico: Joaquín Mortiz.

———. 1972. *Hell Has No Limits.* In *Triple Cross.* New York: Dutton.

"Dōseiai no onna san'nin shinjū (The suicide of three lesbians)." 1934. *Asahi Shinbun,* Tokyo evening ed., 13 June, 2.

"Dōseiai no seisan (Settlement of differences among lesbians)." 1934. *Asahi Shinbun,* Tokyo morning ed., 13 June, 11.

Doucet, Julie. 1990–94. *Dirty Plotte.* Nos. 1–6. Montreal, Quebec: Drawn and Quarterly.

Douglas, Ann. 1995. *Terrible Honesty: Mongrel Manhattan in the 1920s.* New York: Farrar Straus.

Du Bois, W. E. B. 1928. "The Browsing Reader." *The Crisis* 35:202.

Edwards Bello, Joaquín. 1966. *Recuerdos de un cuarto de siglo.* Santiago de Chile: Zig-Zag.

Efron, John. 1994. *Defenders of the Race: Jewish Doctors and Race Science in Fin-de-siècle Europe.* New Haven: Yale University Press.

Eilberg-Schwartz, Howard. 1990. *The Savage in Judaism: An Anthropology of Israelite Religion and Ancient Judaism.* Bloomington: Indiana University Press.

Ellenson, David. 1994. "German Orthodoxy, Jewish Law, and the Uses of Kant." In *Between Traditional and Culture: The Dialectics of Modern Jewish Religion and Identity,* 15–26. Atlanta: Scholars Press.

Espinoza, Enrique. 1963. Prologue to *Antología de Augusto d'Halmar. El hermano errante.* Santiago: Zig-Zag.

Ette, Ottmar. 1992. "La obra de Reinaldo Arenas: una visión de conjunto." In *La escritura de la memoria. Reinaldo Arenas: Textos, estudios y documentación,* edited by Ottmar Ette, 95–138. Frankfurt am Main: Vervuert Verlag.

Fernández, James. 1994. "The Bonds of Patrimony: Cervantes and the New World." *PMLA* 109 (5): 969–81.

Fernández-Robaina, Tomás. 1992–93. "Carta acerca de *Antes que anochezca,* autobiografía de Reinaldo Arenas." *Journal of Hispanic Research* 1:152–56.

Foucault, Michel. 1971. *The Order of Things.* New York: Pantheon Books.

———. 1973. *The Order of Things.* New York: Vintage.

———. 1978. *The History of Sexuality: An Introduction.* Translated by Robert Hurley. New York: Pantheon.

———. 1983. Preface to *Anti-Oedipus,* by Gilles Deleuze and Félix Guattari, translated by Robert Hurley, Mark Seem, and Helen R. Lane. London: Athlone Press.

———. 1985. *The Use of Pleasure.* Vol. 2, *The History of Sexuality.* New York: Pantheon.

Fout, John C. 1992. "Sexual Politics in Wilhelmine German: The Male Gender Crisis, Moral Purity, and Homophobia." *Journal of the History of Sexuality* 2 (3): 388–421.

Freud, Sigmund. [1955] 1984. *Beyond the Pleasure Principle.* 1920. Vol. 11, *Pelican Freud Library,* translated by James Strachey, 275–338. Harmondsworth, England: Penguin.

———. 1955a. Civilization and Its Discontents. 1930. Vol. 21, *The Standard Edition of the Complete Psychological Works of Sigmund Freud,* edited and translated by James Strachey and Anna Freud, 59–145. London: The Hogarth Press.

———. 1955b. " 'Civilized' Sexual Morality and Modern Nervous Illness." 1908. Vol. 9, *The Standard Edition of the Complete Psychological Works of Sigmund Freud,* edited and translated by James Strachey and Anna Freud, 179–204. London: The Hogarth Press.

———. 1955c. *From the History of an Infantile Neurosis.* 1918. Vol. 17, *The Standard Edition of the Complete Psychological Works of Sigmund Freud,* edited and translated by James Strachey and Anna Freud, 3–123. London: The Hogarth Press.

———. 1955d. *The Interpretation of Dreams (First Part).* 1900. Vol. 4, *The Standard Edition of the Complete Psychological Works of Sigmund Freud,* edited and translated by James Strachey and Anna Freud, 1–338. London: The Hogarth Press.

———. 1955e. *The Interpretation of Dreams (Second Part).* 1900–1901. Vol. 5, *The Standard Edition of the Complete Psychological Works of Sigmund Freud,* edited and translated by James Strachey and Anna Freud, 339–627. London: The Hogarth Press.

———. 1955f. *Moses and Monotheism: Three Essays.* 1939. Vol. 23, *The Standard Edition of the Complete Psychological Works of Sigmund Freud,* edited and translated by James Strachey and Anna Freud, 3–137. London: The Hogarth Press.

———. 1955g. *The Moses of Michelangelo.* 1914. Vol. 13, *The Standard Edition of the Complete Psychological Works of Sigmund Freud,* edited and translated by James Strachey and Anna Freud, 211–36. London: The Hogarth Press.

———. 1955h. *Psycho-analytic Notes on an Autobiographical Account of a Case of Paranoia (Dementia Paranoides).* 1911. Vol. 12, *The Standard Edition of the Complete Psychological Works of Sigmund Freud,* edited and translated by James Strachey and Anna Freud, 3–79. London: The Hogarth Press.

———. 1955i. *Totem and Taboo.* 1913. Vol. 13, *The Standard Edition of the Complete Psychological Works of Sigmund Freud,* edited and translated by James Strachey and Anna Freud, 3–149. London: The Hogarth Press.

———. 1960. *Letters of Sigmund Freud.* Edited and selected by Ernst L. Freud. Translated by Tania Stern and James Stern. Introduction by Steven Marcus. New York: Basic.

Frieden, Ken. 1989. *Freud's Dream of Interpretation.* Foreword by Harold Bloom. Albany: SUNY Press.

Frühstück, Sabine. 1996. "Die Politik der Sexualwissenschaft: Zur Produktion und Popularisierung sexologischen Wissens in Japan 1900–1941 (The politics of sexology: the creation and popularization of the science of sexuality in Japan 1900–1941)." Ph.D. diss., Institute for Japanese Studies, University of Vienna, Austria.

———. 1998. "Then Science Took Over: Sex, Leisure and Medicine at the Beginning of the Twentieth Century." In *The Culture of Japan as Seen Through Its Leisure,* edited by Sepp Linhart and Sabine Frühstück. Albany: SUNY Press.

Fukushima Shirō. [1935] 1984. *Fujinkai sanjūgonen* (Thirty-five years of Women's World). Tokyo: Fuji Shuppansha.

Furukawa, Makoto. 1994. "The Changing Nature of Sexuality: The Three Codes Framing Homosexuality in Modern Japan." Translated by Alice Lockyer. *U.S.-Japan Women's Journal* (English supplement) 7:98–127.

Gálvez, Manuel. 1986. "Las Sombras de Taric." In *Diwan modernista: Una visión del Oriente,* edited by Abdellah Djbilou, 248–58. Madrid: Taurus.

Garber, Eric. 1990. "The Lesbian and Gay Subculture of Jazz Age Harlem." In *Hidden From History: Reclaiming the Gay and Lesbian Past,* edited by Martin Duberman, Martha Vicinus, and George Chauncey Jr. New York: Meridian.

Garber, Marjorie. 1992. *Vested Interests: Cross-Dressing and Cultural Anxiety.* New York: Routledge.

Gay, Peter. 1986. *The Tender Passion.* Vol. 2, *The Bourgeois Experience: Victoria to Freud.* New York: Oxford University Press.

Geertz, Clifford. 1986. "Making Experience, Authoring Selves." In *The Anthropology of Experience,* edited by Victor W. Turner and Edward Bruner, 373–80. Urbana: University of Illinois Press.

Geller, Jay. 1992. "(G)nos(e)ology: The Cultural Construction of the Other." In *People of the Body: Jews and Judaism from an Embodied Perspective,* edited by Howard Eilberg-Schwartz, 243–82. Albany: SUNY Press.

———. 1993. "A Paleontological View of Freud's Study of Religion: Unearthing the Leitfossil Circumcision." *Modern Judaism* 13:49–70.

Genet, Jean. [1944] 1988. *Our Lady of the Flowers.* Translated by Bernard Frechtman. London: Paladin.

George, Rosemary Marangoly. 1992. "Traveling Light: Of Immigration, Invisible Suitcases, and Gunny Sacks." *differences* 4 (2): 72–99.

Giles, James R. 1976. *Claude McKay.* Boston: G. K. Hall.

Gilman, Sander L. 1986. *Jewish Self-Hatred: Anti-Semitism and the Hidden Language of the Jews.* Baltimore: Johns Hopkins University Press.

———. 1991a. *The Jew's Body.* London: Routledge.

———. 1991b. "Karl Kraus's Oscar Wilde: Race, Sex, and Difference." In *Inscribing the Other,* 173–90. Lincoln: University of Nebraska Press.

——— 1993a. *The Case of Sigmund Freud: Medicine and Identity at the Fin de Siècle.* Baltimore: Johns Hopkins University Press.

———. 1993b. *Freud, Race, and Gender.* Princeton: Princeton University Press.

———. 1994. "Dangerous Liaisons." *Transitions* 64:41–52.

———. 1995. "Otto Weininger and Sigmund Freud: Race and Gender in the Shaping of Psychoanalysis." In *Jews and Gender: Responses to Otto Weininger,* edited by Nancy A. Harrowitz and Barbara Hyams, 103–20. Philadelphia: Temple University Press.

Gilroy, Paul. 1993. *The Black Atlantic: Modernity and Double Consciousness.* Cambridge, Mass.: Harvard University Press.

Glick Schiller, Nina, Linda Basch, and Cristina Blanc-Szanton. 1992. "Transnationalism: A New Analytic Framework for Understanding Migration." In *Towards a Transnational Perspective on Migration. Annals of the New York Academy of Science* 645:ix–xiv.

Global Programme on AIDS. 1989. "Broadcasters' Questions and Answers on AIDS." Geneva: World Health Organization.

———. 1993. *World AIDS Update.* Winter. Geneva: World Health Organization.

Goldstein, Bluma. 1992. *Reinscribing Moses: Heine, Kafka, Freud, and Schoenberg in a European Wilderness.* Cambridge: Harvard University Press.

Gómez Carrillo, Enrique. 1919. "Marta y Hortensia." In *Almas y Cerebros,* 73–80. Paris: Garnier.

Gott, Ted. 1993. "Lips of Coral: Sex and Violence in Surrealism." In *Surrealism, Revolution By Night,* 126–55. Canberra: National Gallery of Australia.

Goux, Jean-Joseph. 1990. *Symbolic Economies: After Marx and Freud.* Translated by Jennifer Curtis Cage. Ithaca: Cornell University Press.

Grinstein, Alexander. 1980. *Sigmund Freud's Dreams.* New York: International Universities Press.

Hagiwara Hiroyoshi. 1954. *Takarazuka kageki 40nenshi* (Forty-year history of the Takarazuka Revue). Takarazuka: Takarazuka Kagekidan Shuppanbu.

Hall, Stuart. 1990. "Cultural Identity and Diaspora." In *Identity: Community, Culture, Difference,* edited by J. Rutherford, 222–37. London: Lawrence and Wishart.

Halperin, David. 1990. "The Democratic Body: Prostitution and Citizenship in Classical Athens." *differences* 2 (1): 1–28.

Harpham, Geoffrey Galt. 1994. "So . . . What Is Enlightenment? An Inquisition into Modernity." *Critical Inquiry* 20 (spring): 524–56.

Hayashi Misao. 1926. "Danjo to shiyū (Man and woman, male and female)." *Nihon Hyōron* 3:319–25.

Heller, Peter. 1981. "Quarrel over Bisexuality." In *The Turn of the Century: German Literature and Art, 1890–1915,* edited by Gerald Chapple and Hans H. Schulte, 87–116. Bonn: Bouvier.

Henríquez Ureña, Max. 1918. *Rodó y Rubén Darío.* La Habana: Sociedad Editorial Cuba Contemporánea.

Hernández Catá, Alfonso. 1929. *El ángel de Sodoma*. Prólogo del Dr. Gregorio Marañón. Epílogo del Dr. Giménez de Azúa. Valparaíso: El Callao.

Hernández-Miyares, Julio, and Perla Rosencvaig, eds. 1990. *Reinaldo Arenas: Alucinaciones, fantasías y realidad*. Glenview, Ill.: Scott, Foresman/Montesinos.

Herzl, Theodor. 1955. "The New Ghetto: A Play in Four Acts." Abridged. In *Theodor Herzl: A Portrait for This Age*, edited by Ludwig Lewisohn, 152–93. Cleveland: World Publishing.

Hirschfeld, Magnus. 1935. *Women East and West: Impressions of a Sex Expert*. London: William Heinemann (Medical Books).

Hoberman, John. 1994. "German-Jewish Ideas about Courage at the Fin de Siècle." Paper presented at the annual convention of the Modern Language Association. San Diego.

"Hogosha wa kokoro seyo—byōteki na fuan buri (Guardians, beware of pathological fandom)." 1935. *Asahi Shinbun*, Tokyo morning ed., 31 January, 8.

Hyam, Ronald. 1976. *Britain's Imperial Century, 1815–1914: A Study of Empire and Expansion*. London: Barnes and Noble.

Hyman, Paula E. 1995. *Gender and Assimilation in Modern Jewish History: The Roles and Representation of Women*. Seattle: University of Washington Press.

Imago. 1991. *Tokushū: rezubian* (Special issue: Lesbian). 2 (8).

Ivy, Millie. 1993. "Formations of Mass Culture." In *Postwar Japan as History*, edited by A. Gordon, 239–58. Berkeley: University of California Press.

Jacob, Mary Jane. 1993. "The Continuing Tradition: The Impact of Surrealism on Contemporary Art." In *Surrealism, Revolution by Night*, 196–203. Canberra: National Gallery of Australia.

Jekyll, Walter. 1904. *The Bible Untrustworthy*. London: Rationalist Press Association.

Jones, Ernest. 1951. "The Madonna's Conception Through the Ear." In *Essays in Applied Psychoanalysis*, 266–357. Vol. 2. London: Hogarth Press.

———. 1953. "The Young Freud." In *The Life and Work of Sigmund Freud*. New York: Basic Books.

Kazanjian, David. 1993. "Notarizing Knowledge: Paranoia and Civility in Freud and Lacan." *Qui Parle: Literature, Philosophy, Visual Arts, History* 7 (fall/winter): 102–39.

Keene, Donald. 1976. *World Within Walls: Japanese Literature of the Pre-Modern Era 1600–1867*. New York: Grove Press.

Klein, Dennis B. 1985. *Jewish Origins of the Psychoanalytic Movement*. Chicago: University of Chicago Press.

Koestenbaum, Wayne. 1989. *Double Talk: The Erotics of Male Literary Collaboration*. New York and London: Routledge.

Komine Shigeyuki. 1985. *Dōseiai to dōseiai shinjū no kenkyū* (A study of homosexuality and homosexual double suicide). Tokyo: Komine Kenkyūjo.

Kondo, D. 1990. *Crafting Selves: Power, Gender and Discourse of Identity in a Japanese Workplace.* Chicago: University of Chicago Press.

"Kore mo jidaisō ka (Is this, too, the shape of the times?)." 1935. *Asahi Shinbun,* Tokyo morning ed., 30 January, 7.

Kornberg, Jacques. 1993. *Theodor Herzl: From Assimilation to Zionism, Jewish Literature and Culture.* Bloomington: Indiana University Press.

Lacan, Jacques. 1985. "The Meaning of the Phallus." In *Feminine Sexuality: Jacques Lacan and the école Freudienne,* edited by Juliet Mitchell and Jacqueline Rose, translated by Jacqueline Rose, 74–85. New York: Norton.

Lamming, George. 1953. *In the Castle of My Skin.* London: Michael Joseph.

Lancaster, Roger. 1988. "Subject Honor and Object Shame: The Construction of Male Homosexuality and Stigma in Nicaragua." *Ethnology* 27 (2): 111–25.

Laplanche, J., and J. B. Pontalis. 1973. *The Language of Psycho-analysis.* Translated by Donald Nicholson-Smith. Introduction by Daniel Lagache. New York: Norton.

Latour, Bruno. 1988. *The Pasteurization of France.* Cambridge, Mass.: Harvard University Press.

Lebra, Takie. 1976. *Japanese Patterns of Behavior.* Honolulu: University of Hawaii Press.

Lee, Chun-Jean. 1989. "Address." *Human Retroviruses and AIDS.* Proceedings of the symposium. 11–13 November 1988.

Lee, Ho-Chin, et al. 1989. "Update: AIDS and HIV-I Infection in Taiwan, 1985–1988." *Human Retroviruses and AIDS.* Proceedings of the symposium, 11–13 November 1988.

Le Rider, Jacques. 1993. *Modernity and Crises of Identity: Culture and Society in Fin-de-siècle Vienna.* Translated by Rosemary Morris. New York: Continuum.

Leupp, Gary. 1995. *Male Colors: The Construction of Homosexuality in Tokugawa Japan (1603–1868).* Berkeley: University of California Press.

Levine, Martin. 1990. "Gay Macho: Ethnography of the Homosexual Clone." Ph.D. diss., New York University.

Lewis, David L. 1979. *When Harlem Was in Vogue.* New York: Knopf.

Lewis, Rupert, and Maureen Lewis. 1977. "Claude McKay's Jamaica." *Caribbean Quarterly* 23 (2–3): 38–53.

Lloyd, Genevieve. 1993. *The Man of Reason: "Male" and "Female" in Western Philosophy.* 2d ed. Minneapolis: University of Minnesota Press.

Locke, Alain. 1976. "Spiritual Truancy." In *Voices From the Harlem Renaissance,* edited by Nathan Huggins. New York: Oxford University Press.

Loewenberg, Peter. 1970. "A Hidden Zionist Theme in Freud's My Son the Myops Dream." *Journal of the History of Ideas* 31 (Jan.–March): 29–32.

Logue, Cal M. 1975. "Rhetorical Ridicule of Reconstruction Blacks." *Quarterly Journal of Speech* 62:400–409.

Lugo-Ortiz, Agnes. 1995. "Community at Its Limits: Orality, Law, Silence and the Homosexual Body in Luis Rafael Sánchez's '¡Jum!' " In *¿Entiendes?*, edited by Bergmann and Smith, 115–36. Durham: Duke University Press.

Luxon, Thomas J. 1995. Letter to the author (Daniel Boyarin).

Maalki, Lisa. 1992. "National Geographic: The Rooting of People and the Territorialization of National Identity Among Scholars and Refugees." *Cultural Anthropology* 7 (1): 24–49.

Manalansan, Martin F. 1994. "Searching for Community: Filipino Gay Men in New York City." *Amerasia* 20 (1): 59–73.

Martí, José. 1977. "Political Prison in Cuba." In *Our America*. New York: Monthly Review Press.

———. 1982. *Ismaelillo. Versos Libres. Versos Sencillos.* Edited by Ivan A. Schulman. Madrid: Cátedra.

———. 1992. "El presidio político en Cuba." In *Obras escogidas,* 1:25–52. Havana: Editorial de Ciencias Sociales.

Martin, Adrian. 1993. "The Artificial Night: Surrealism and Cinema." In *Surrealism, Revolution by Night,* 190–95. Canberra: National Gallery of Australia.

Masson, Jeffrey Moussaieff, ed. and trans. 1985. *The Complete Letters of Sigmund Freud to Wilhelm Fliess, 1887–1904.* Cambridge: Harvard University Press.

McGrath, William J. 1986. *Freud's Discovery of Psychoanalysis: The Politics of Hysteria.* Ithaca: Cornell University Press.

McKay, Claude. 1912a. *Constab Ballads.* New York: Books for Libraries.

———. 1912b. *Songs of Jamaica.* New York: Books for Libraries.

———. 1920. *Spring in New Hampshire and Other Poems.* London: Richards.

———. 1928. *Banjo: A Story Without a Plot.* New York: Harper.

———. 1929. *Home to Harlem.* New York: Harper.

———. 1961. *Banana Bottom.* 1933. Reprint, New York: Harcourt, Brace and Jovanovich.

———. 1970. *A Long Way from Home: An Autobiography.* Introduction by St. Clair Drake. New York: Harcourt, Brace and World.

———. 1979. *My Green Hills of Jamaica and Five Jamaican Stories.* Edited with an introduction by Mervyn Morris. Kingston: Heinemann Educational Books.

Mercer, Kobena. 1988. "Diaspora Culture and the Dialogic Imagination." In *Blackframes: Critical Perspectives on Black Independent Cinema,* edited by M. Cham and C. Watkins. London: MIT Press.

Michaels, Eric. 1990. *Unbecoming: An AIDS Diary.* Rose Bay, New South Wales: Empress.

Mizukawa Yōko. 1987. "Tachi: Kono kodokuna ikimono (Butch: This lonely creature)." *Bessatsu Takarajima* 64:18–23.

Mochizuki, Mamor[u]. 1959. "Cultural Aspects of Japanese Girl's Opera." In *Japanese Popular Culture*, edited by Hidetoshi Kato, 165–74. Tokyo: Charles E. Tuttle.

"Modan otona tōsei manga yose (The latest variety comics for modern adults)." 1935. *Asahi Shinbun*, Osaka evening ed., 17 February. 4.

Moeller, Robert G. 1994. "The Homosexual Man Is a 'Man,' the Homosexual Woman Is a 'Woman': Sex, Society, and the Law in Postwar West Germany." *Journal of the History of Sexuality* 4 (January): 395–429.

Montenegro, Ernesto. 1934. Prologue to *Capitanes sin barco*, by Augusto d'Halmar. Santiago: Ediciones Ercilla.

Morris, Megan. 1997. "L'Affaire Sagawa." In *Broken Silence: Voices of Japanese Feminism*, edited by Sandra Buckley. Berkeley: University of California Press.

Morris, Mervyn. 1975. "Contending Values: The Prose Fiction of Claude McKay." *Jamaica Journal* 9 (2–3): 36–42, 52.

Muñoz, Jose Esteban. 1995. "*Choteo*/Camp Style Politics: Carmelita Tropicana's Performance of Self-Enactment." *Women and Performance* 7 (2)/8 (1): 38–51.

Naficy, Hamid. 1991. "The Poetics and Practice of Iranian Nostalgia in Exile." *Diaspora* 1 (3): 285–302.

Nakajima, Takehiro, dir. 1992. *Okoge* (film). Japan.

Nakano Eitarō. 1935. "Dansō no reijin to Saijō Eriko: dōseiaishi misui no ikisatsu (The cross-dressed beauty and Saijō Eriko: the circumstances of their double suicide attempt)." *Fujin Kōron* 3:161–67.

Neuda, Fanny. 1862. *Stunden der Andacht: Ein Gebet und Erbauungsbuch für Israels Frauen und Jungfrauen*. Prague: Verlag von Wolf Pascheles.

New Dictionary of American Slang. 1986. Edited by Robert Chapman. New York: Harper Row.

Nogami Toshio. 1920. "Gendai seikatsu to danjo ryōsei no sekkin (The association of modern life and androgyny)." *Kaizō* 2 (4): 185–204.

Nolte, Sharon, and Sally Hastings. 1991. "The Meiji State's Policy Towards Women, 1890–1910." In *Recreating Japanese Women, 1600–1945*, edited by Gail Bernstein, 151–74. Berkeley: University of California Press.

Ōhara, Kenshirō. 1963. *Isho no kenkyū* (A study of wills and suicide notes). Tokyo: Nihon Bungeisha.

———. 1965. *Nihon no jisatsu: kodoku to fuan no kaimei* (Suicide in Japan: An interpretation of loneliness and anxiety). Tokyo: Seishin Shobō.

———. 1973. *Shinjūkō: ai to shi no byōri* (A treatise on double suicide: The pathology of love and death). Tokyo: Rogosu Sensho.

Ohnuki-Tierney, Emiko. 1993. *Rice as Self: Japanese Identities through Time.* Princeton: Princeton University Press.

Okamura, Jonathan. 1993. "The Filipino American Diaspora: Sites of Space, Time and Ethnicity." Paper presented at the 1993 Association for Asian American Studies, Cornell University, Ithaca, N.Y.

Olender, Maurice. 1992. *The Languages of Paradise: Race, Religion, and Philology in the Nineteenth Century.* Translated by Arthur Goldhammer. Cambridge: Harvard University Press.

Ozaki Hirotsugi. 1986. "San'nin no joyū o chūshin ni (Focusing on three actresses)." In *Meiji no joyūten* (Exhibition of Meiji-period actresses), edited by Hakubutsukan Meiji-mura, 10–16. Nagoya: Nagoya Tetsudō.

Ōzumi Narumitsu. 1931. "Hentai seiyoku (Deviant sexual desire)." *Hanzai Kagaku* 4:75–83.

Panos Institute. 1989. AIDS *in the Third World.* Philadelphia: New Society Publishers.

Parmar, Pratibha. 1993. "That Moment of Emergence." In *Queer Looks,* edited by M. Gever, J. Greyson, and P. Parmar, 3–11. New York: Routledge.

Patton, Cindy. 1991. "From Nation to Family: Containing African AIDS." In *Nationalisms and Sexualities,* edited by Andrew Parker, Mary Russo, Doris Sommer, and Patricia Yaeger. New York: Routledge.

———. 1996. *Fatal Advice.* Durham: Duke University Press.

Pellegrini, Ann. Forthcoming. "Without You I'm Nothing: Performing Race, Gender, and Jewish Bodies." In *Jews and Other Differences: The New Jewish Cultural Studies,* edited by Jonathan Boyarin and Daniel Boyarin. Minneapolis: University of Minnesota Press.

Pinguet, Maurice. [1984] 1993. *Voluntary Death in Japan.* Translated by Rosemary Morris. Cambridge, England: Polity Press.

Plummer, Ken. 1992. "Speaking Its Name: Inventing a Gay and Lesbian Studies." In *Modern Homosexualities: Fragments of Lesbian and Gay Experience,* edited by Ken Plummer, 3–28. London: Routledge.

Proust, Marcel. 1993. *Sodom and Gomorrah.* Translated by C. K. Scott Moncrieff and Terence Kilmartin. Revised by D. J. Enright. *In Search of Lost Time.* New York: Modern Library.

Rank, Otto. 1985. "The Essence of Judaism (1905)." In *Jewish Origins of the Psychoanalytic Movement,* edited by Dennis B. Klein. Chicago: University of Chicago Press.

Redcam, Tom. 1912. "An All-Jamalcan Entertainment." *Jamaica Times* 11.

Reyles, Carlos. [1922] 1980. *El embrujo de Sevilla.* Montevideo: Editorial Kapelusz.

Rich, B. Ruby. 1983. "Maedchen in Uniform: From Repressive Tolerance to Erotic Liberation." *Jump Cut* 24/25:44–50.

Robertson, Jennifer. 1989. "Gender-Bending in Paradise: Doing 'Female' and 'Male' in Japan." *Genders* 5:48–69.

———. 1992. "The Politics of Androgyny in Japan: Sexuality and Subversion in the Theater and Beyond." *American Ethnologist* 19 (3): 419–42.

———. 1995. "Mon Japan: Theater as a Technology of Japanese Imperialism." *American Ethnologist* 22 (4): 970–96.

———. 1998a. "It Takes a Village: Internationalization and Nostalgia in Postwar Japan." In *Mirror of Modernity: Invented Traditions in Modern Japan,* edited by Stephen Vlastos, 209–39. Berkeley: University of California Press.

———. 1998b. *Takarazuka: Sexual Politics and Popular Culture in Modern Japan.* Berkeley: University of California Press.

Roden, Donald. 1990. "Taishō Culture and the Problem of Gender Ambivalence." In *Culture and Identity: Japanese Intellectuals during the Interwar Years,* edited by J. Thomas Rimer, 37–55. Princeton: Princeton University Press.

Rodríguez Mallarini, Adolfo. 1980. Prologue to *El embrujo de Sevilla,* by Carlos Reyles. 1922. Reprint, Montevideo: Editorial Kapelusz.

Rodríguez-Monegal, Emir. 1990. "El mundo laberíntico de Reinaldo Arenas." In *Reinaldo Arenas: Alucinaciones, fantasías y realidad,* edited by Julio Hernández-Miyares and Perla Rosencvaig, 5–13. Glenview, Ill.: Scott, Foresman/Montesinos.

Rogin, Michael. 1992. "Blackface, White Noise: The Jewish Jazz Singer Finds His Voice." *Critical Inquiry* 18:417–53.

Sabin, Roger. 1993. *Adult Comics: An Introduction.* London: Routledge.

Said, Edward. [1978] 1979. *Orientalism.* New York: Vintage.

Saijō Eriko. 1935. "Dansō no reijin Masuda Fumiko no shi o erabu made (Up until Masuda Fumiko, the cross-dressed beauty, chose death)." *Fujin Kōron* 3:168–78.

Sakabe Kengi. 1924. *Fujin no shinri to futoku no kiso* (The foundation of women's psychology and morality). Tokyo: Hokubunkan.

Sakuma Hideka. 1934. "Jōshi o ketsui suru made (Until [we] resolved to commit love suicide)." *Fujin Gahō* 8:82–83.

Sánchez-Eppler, Karen. 1993. *Touching Liberty: Abolition, Feminism and the Politics of the Body.* Berkeley: University of California Press.

Santí, Enrico Mario. 1990. "Vida y milagros de Reinaldo Arenas." In *Reinaldo Arenas: Alucinaciones, fantasías y realidad,* edited by Julio Hernández-Miyares and Perla Rosencvaig, 29–37. Glenview, Ill.: Scott, Foresman/Montesinos.

Santiván, Fernando. 1965. *Memorias de un Tolstoyano.* In *Obras Completas.* Santiago: Zig-Zag.

Santner, Eric. 1996. *My Own Private Germany: Daniel Paul Schreber's Secret History of Modernity.* Princeton: Princeton University Press.

Sarduy, Severo. 1987. "Escritura/travestismo." In *Ensayos Generales Sobre el Barroco,* 258–63. Mexico-Buenos Aires: Fondo de Cultura Económica.

Sassy. 1993. January, 36.

Scarry, Elaine. 1985. *The Body in Pain: The Making and Unmaking of the World.* Oxford: Oxford University Press.

Schalow, P. G., trans. 1990. *Great Mirror of Male Love,* by Ihara Saikaku. Stanford: Stanford University Press.

Scheman, Naomi. 1993. *Engenderings: Constructions of Knowledge, Authority, and Privilege.* New York: Routledge.

Scruggs, Charles. 1984. *The Sage in Harlem: H. L. Mencken and the Black Writers of the 1920s.* Baltimore: Johns Hopkins University Press.

Sebreli, Juan José. 1983. "Historia Secreta de Los Homosexuales Porteños." *Perfil* (Buenos Aires) 2 (27): 6–13.

Sedgwick, Eve Kosofsky. 1985. *Between Men: English Literature and Male Homosocial Desire.* New York: Columbia University Press.

———. 1993a. *Tendencies.* Durham: Duke University Press.

———. 1993b. "Queer Performativity: Henry James's *The Art of the Novel.*" *GLQ* 1 (1): 1–16.

Seeberg, Reinhold. 1923. "Antisemitismus, Judentum und Kirche." In *Zum Verstandnis der Gegenwartigen Krisis in der Europaischen Geisteskultur,* 115–50. Leipzig: A. Deichert.

Seidensticker, Edward. 1990. *Tokyo Rising: The City Since the Great Earthquake.* New York: Knopf.

Seshadri-Crooks, Kalpana. 1994. "The Primitive as Analyst." *Cultural Critique* 28 (fall): 175–218.

Seward, Jack. 1968. *Hara-Kiri: Japanese Ritual Suicide.* Rutland, Vt.: Charles E. Tuttle.

"Shōjo no hi no sei mondai: Haru no mezame (Girls' day and the problem of sex: Spring awakening)." 1934. *Asahi Shinbun,* Tokyo morning ed., 18 June, 9.

Sifuentes-Jáuregui, Benigno. Forthcoming. "Gender without Limits: Transvestism and Subjectivity in *El lugar sin límites.*" In *Rethinking Gender and Sexuality in Latin American Studies,* edited by Daniel Balderston and Donna Guy, 44–61. New York: New York University Press.

Sievers, Sharon. 1983. *Flowers in Salt: The Beginnings of Feminist Consciousness in Modern Japan.* Stanford: Stanford University Press.

Silverberg, Miriam. 1991. "The Modern Girl as Militant." In *Recreating Japanese Women, 1600–1945,* edited by Gail Bernstein, 239–66. Berkeley: University of California Press.

———. 1992. "Constructing the Japanese Ethnography of Modernity." *Journal of Asian Studies* 51 (1): 30–54.

———. 1993. "Constructing a New Cultural History of Prewar Japan." In *Japan in the World,* edited by Masao Miyoshi and H. D. Harootunian, 115–43. Durham: Duke University Press.

Singer, Linda. 1993. *Erotic Welfare: Sexual Theory and Politics in the Age of Epidemic.* New York: Routledge.

Smith, Sidonie, and Julia Watson, eds. 1992. *Decolonizing the Subject: The Politics of Gender in Women's Autobiography.* Minneapolis: University of Minnesota Press.

Smith-Rosenberg, Caroll. 1985. *Disorderly Conduct: Visions of Gender in Victorian America.* New York and Oxford: Oxford University Press.

Sprengnether, Madelon. 1990. *The Spectral Mother: Freud, Feminism, and Psychoanalysis.* Ithaca: Cornell University Press.

Stewart, Kathleen. 1992. "Nostalgia: A Polemic." In *Rereading Cultural Anthropology,* edited by George E. Marcus, 252–66. Durham: Duke University Press.

Stieg, Gerald. 1995. "Kafka and Weininger." Translated by Barbara Hyams. In *Jews and Gender: Responses to Otto Weininger,* edited by Nancy A. Harrowitz and Barbara Hyams, 195–206. Philadelphia: Temple University Press.

Stoff, Michael B. 1972. "Claude McKay and the Cult of Primitivism." *In The Harlem Renaissance Remembered,* edited by Arna Bontemps. New York: Dodd, Mead.

Suárez, José León. 1929. *Mitre y España. A Propósito de la Exposición Iberoamericana de Sevilla.* Madrid: Maestre.

Sugahara Tsūzai. 1971. *Dōseiai* (Homosexuality). Tokyo: San'aku Tsuihō Kyōkai.

Sugita Naoki. 1929. "Seihonnō ni hisomu sangyakusei (Sado-masochistic qualities latent within sexual instinct)." *Kaizō* 4:70–80.

———. 1935. "Shōjo kageki netsu no shinden (All-female revue; a sanctuary for feverish infatuation)." *Fujin Kōron* 4:274–78.

Tachibana Kyō. 1890. "Fūzoku hōtan (Forsaking custom)." *Fūzoku Gahō* 14:15–16.

Tadai Yoshinosuke and Katō Masa'aki. 1974. *Nihon no jisatsu o kangaeru* (A consideration of suicide in Japan). Tokyo: Igaku Shoin.

Tamura Toshiko. 1913. "Dōseiai no koi (Same-sex love)." *Chūō Kōron* 1:165–68.

Tani Kazue. 1935. " 'Dansō no reijin' no jogakusei jidai o kataru (On the girls' school years of the 'cross-dressed beauty')." *Hanashi* 4:250–56.

Tanizaki Junichirō. 1995. *Quicksand.* Translated by Howard Hibbett. New York: Vintage Books. (Originally published in Japanese as *Manji,* first as a serialized novel, 1928–30, and as a book in 1947.)

Taussig, Michael. 1993. *Mimesis and Alterity.* New York: Routledge.

Tillery, Tyrone. 1992. *Claude McKay: A Black Poet's Struggle for Identity.* Amherst: University of Massachusetts Press.

Tomioka Masakata. 1938. "Dansei josō to josei dansō (Males in women's clothing, females in men's clothing)." *Kaizō* 10:98–105.

Torgovnick, Marianna. 1990. *Gone Primitive: Savage Intellects, Modern Lives.* Chicago: University of Chicago Press.

Trembles, Rick. 1992. *Sugar Diet.* No. 2. Montreal, Quebec: Self-published.

Unamuno, Miguel de. 1925. "Recuerdo de su última Estada en París." *Nosotros* 19 (199): 429–32.

Ushijima Yoshitomo. 1943. *Joshi no shinri* (Female psychology). Tokyo: Ganshodō.

Vaid, Urvashi. 1993. "Alien Nation." *Advocate,* September, 80.

Van Herik, Judith. 1982. *Freud on Femininity and Faith.* Berkeley and Los Angeles: University of California Press.

Vasconcelos, José. 1982. *Ulises Criollo, Memorias.* Vol. 1. Mexico: Fondo de Cultura Económica.

Vicinus, Martha. 1989. "Distance and Desire: English Boarding School Friendships, 1870–1920." In *Hidden from History: Reclaiming the Gay and Lesbian Past,* edited by Martin Duberman, Martha Vicinus, and George Chauncey, 212–29. New York: New American Library.

Watanabe Tsuneo. 1990. "Serufu rabu: otoko to iu yokuatsu kara nogareru tame ni (Self love: In order to escape the oppression of maleness)." *Bessatsu Takarajima* 107:80–90.

Watanabe Tsuneo, and Jun'ichi Iwata. 1989. *The Love of the Samurai: A Thousand Years of Japanese Homosexuality.* Translated by D. R. Roberts. London: GMP.

"Watashi wa koi no shorisha (I am a survivor of love)." 1934. *Asahi Shinbun,* Tokyo morning ed., 14 June, 11.

Weeks, Jeffrey. 1981. *Sex, Politics and Society: The Regulation of Sexuality Since 1800.* London: Longman.

Weininger, Otto. 1975. *Sex and Character.* 1906. Reprint, New York: AMS.

Wertham, Frederic. 1953. *Seduction of the Innocent.* New York: Rinehart.

———. 1973. *The World of Fanzines: A Special Form of Communication.* Carbondale: Southern Illinois University Press.

Wolfe, Alan. 1990. *Suicidal Narrative in Modern Japan.* Princeton: Princeton University Press.

Yamana Shōtarō. 1931. *Nihon jisatsu jōshiki* (A history of suicide and love suicide in Japan). Tokyo: Ōdōkan Shoten.

Yasuda Tokutarō. 1935. "Dōseiai no rekishikan (Historical perspectives on homosexuality)." *Chūō Kōron* 3:146–52.

Yoshimoto, Banana. 1988. *Kitchen.* Tokyo: Fukutake Shoten.

Yoshimoto, Mitsuhiro. 1989. "The Postmodern and Mass Images in Japan." *Public Culture* 1 (2): 8–25.

Yoshitake Teruko. 1986. *Nyonin Yoshiya Nobuko* (The woman Yoshiya Nobuko). Tokyo: Bunshun Bunkō.

INDEX

CONTRIBUTORS

MICHÈLE AINA BARALE is Associate Professor of English and of Women's and Gender Studies at Amherst College. She is an editor of the *Lesbian and Gay Studies Reader* and author of the forthcoming *Below the Belt: Essays in Queer Reading* (Duke).

DANIEL BOYARIN is Taubman Professor of Talmudic Culture at the University of California, Berkeley. His books include *Intertextuality and the Reading of Midrash, Carnal Israel: Reading Sex in Talmudic Culture, A Radical Jew: Paul and the Politics of Identity, Unheroic Conduct: The Rise of Heterosexuality and the Invention of the Jewish Man,* and the forthcoming *Dying for God: Martyrdom and the Making of Christianity and Judaism.*

SANDRA BUCKLEY is Director of the Center for the Arts and Humanities at the State University of New York, Albany. She is editor of *Broken Silence: Voices of Japanese Feminism.*

RHONDA COBHAM is Professor of English and of Black Studies at Amherst College. She is coeditor of *Watchers and Seekings: Writing by Black Women in Britain,* and her essays have appeared in *Callaloo, Transition,* and *Research in African Literatures.*

AMIR SUMAKA'I FINK is a graduate student in the Department of Near Eastern Languages and Civilizations at the University of Chicago. He has published in Hebrew on the subject of contemporary gay politics, and is coauthor of *Independence Park: The Lives of Gay Men in Israel.*

MARCIE FRANK is Associate Professor of English at Concordia University in Montréal. She is currently finishing a book-length study of the emergence of literary criticism in the writings of John Dryden and his female heirs, Aphra Behn, Catherine Trotter and Delarivier Manley, as well as working on a project about Gore Vidal's status as a public intellectual.

MARTIN F. MANALANSAN IV is Assistant Professor of Anthropology at the University of Illinois, Urbana–Champaign. His book on Filipino gay men in the diaspora, entitled *Diasporic Deviants, Global Divas* is forthcoming (Duke).

SYLVIA MOLLOY is Albert Schweitzer Professor of Humanities at New York University. Her publications include *La Diffusion de la litterature hispano-americaine en France au Xxe siecle, Signs of Borges* (Duke), *At Face Value: Autobiographical Writing in Latin America,* and a novel, *En breve carcel* (1981) translated into English as *Certificate of Absence* (1989). She is also co-editor of *Women's Writing in Latin America* (1991) and *Hispanisms and Homosexualities* (Duke).

CINDY PATTON is Associate Professor of Interdisciplinary Studies in the Graduate Institute of the Liberal Arts and is a Distinguished Researcher at Emory University. Her most recent works are *Fatal Advice* (Duke) and *Global AIDS/Local Contexts.*

JACOB PRESS is an advanced graduate student in the Department of English at Duke University. His essays have appeared in *Novel Gazing* (Duke), and in *Queer Theory and the Jewish Question.* He is coauthor of *Independence Park: The Lives of Gay Men in Israel.*

JENNIFER ROBERTSON is Professor of Anthropology at the University of Michigan. She is author of *Native and Newcomer: Making and Remaking a Japanese City,* and *Takarazuka: Sexual Politics and Popular Culture in Modern Japan.*

BENIGNO SÁNCHEZ-EPPLER's work has appeared in *Differences, American Literary History,* and *Romantic Review.* He has taught Latin American literature and cultural studies at Amherst College, Brandeis University, and Brown University. He now teaches at the Pioneer Valley Performing Arts High School.

Library of Congress Cataloging-in-Publication Data

Queer Diasporas / edited by Cindy Patton and Benigno Sánchez-Eppler.

p.   cm. — (Series Q)

Includes bibliographical references and index.

ISBN 0-8223-2387-7 (cloth : alk. paper). — ISBN 0-8223-2422-9 (paper : alk. paper)

1. Homosexuality.   2. Lesbianism.   3. Gays—Identity.   4. Lesbians— Identity.   5. Gay and lesbian studies   I. Patton, Cindy, 1956–   .

II. Sánchez-Eppler, Benigno.   III. Series.

HQ76.25.S4994   2000

306.76′6—dc21   99-29367   CIP